Grails in Action

Grails in Action

GLEN SMITH
PETER LEDBROOK

MANNING
Greenwich
(74° w. long.)

For online information and ordering of this and other Manning books, please visit
www.manning.com. The publisher offers discounts on this book when ordered in quantity.
For more information, please contact

  Special Sales Department
  Manning Publications Co.
  Sound View Court 3B   fax: (609) 877-8256
  Greenwich, CT 06830   email: orders@manning.com

Manning Publications Co.   Development editor: Cynthia Kane
Sound View Court 3B   Copyeditor: Andy Carroll
Greenwich, CT 06830   Typesetter: Dottie Marsico
                                     Cover designer: Leslie Haimes

ISBN 978-1-933988-93-1
Printed in the United States of America
1 2 3 4 5 6 7 8 9 10 – MAL – 14 13 12 11 10 09

To Kylie, who sacrifices daily to let me chase such crazy dreams.
Love you so much, matie!
                                                            —G.S.

To my parents, for always being there.
                                                            —P.L.

brief contents

contents

ix

foreword

Grails in Action is a book for practitioners from practitioners. Glen's "20-hour challenge," in which he implemented the www.groovyblogs.org service in Grails, has become legendary. That site is still my one-and-only resource for staying up to date with Groovy and Grails. Not only has he been one of the frontrunners of Grails, he made his achievements publicly available, both by sharing his code and by sharing his insights through blogging and public speaking. I have long wished that he would capture his wisdom in a book, and I can hardly believe that I can now hold it in my hands.

Glen's "from the trenches" experience is ideally complemented by Peter's insider knowledge, which he has shown thousands of times when answering questions on the Grails user mailing list. If anybody on this planet knows what people ask about Grails, he does.

Writing a good book on Grails is a challenge. As an author, you are tempted to present the full cornucopia of features, but you would like to also get across the simplicity that Grails brings to Java web application development.

Glen and Peter have found an excellent balance between providing a low-barrier entry into the Grails world and covering the issues that you are likely to encounter when using Grails in more demanding scenarios.

Grails in Action takes a practical stance. It leads you through the process of creating a Grails application and explains the sights along the way. This applies to the various pieces of technology: models, tests, views, controllers, services, and the like, but also— and maybe even more importantly—to the sequence of when and how you go from one to the next.

For creating your first Grails application, I can only advise you to follow their path. When you later want to deviate, you will find inspiration by looking at the later chapters.

Reading this book is a bit like talking to Glen. One can almost hear his "Aussie" voice, and when reading the encouraging, conversational, humorous style I cannot help but thinking, "flying koala."

The linkage between Grails and the style of this book is no coincidence. It's all about rock-solid solutions delivered with ease.

Enjoy!

DIERK KÖNIG
Author, *Groovy in Action*

preface

Both of us came to Grails a few years ago while looking for a better, easier way to build web applications on the Java platform. Although there were lots of interesting Java frameworks available, the ones we tried seemed clunky and required too much setup. Around that time, the buzz surrounding Ruby on Rails was at a high. Its promise of quick and easy web development was too alluring to ignore, but it meant ditching the Java platform.

That's when Grails arrived. This was a framework that you could use with just a simple text editor and still be tremendously productive. It was a breath of fresh air for longtime Java developers like us. Even at version 0.1 we could knock out useful applications with a minimum of effort, and since then Grails has grown into a major player that can be used for lots of projects, big and small. I was busy porting my unfinished home SpringMVC projects over to Grails and actually getting them live! My first SMS Gateway application went public on Grails 0.2 beta. At the same time, Peter was surreptitiously introducing Grails into his company–guerilla-style.

Like many good things in our lives, this book started over a hot coffee. I was hanging out with Dierk Koenig (a Groovy legend) for breakfast in Washington during the Groovy/Grails Experience (2GX) conference. After quizzing him on the process of writing *Groovy in Action* for Manning (which remains one of our all-time favorite programming books), we started to discuss writing an "in the trenches" Grails book that would cover the stuff that developers *really* need to know, rather than every possible corner case. Dierk said, "Glen, if you write that book, I will buy your first copy." The strength of that encouragement set the scene for the rest of the project. At the same time, Peter was putting in long hours on Grails support and gathering an internal fact sheet on the topics that developers were really struggling with.

Within a month or two, Manning had made contact, wondering if anyone was interested in writing a book. The timing could not have been better, and we jumped at the chance. Despite a boom in Grails' popularity, for a long time there was only one book dedicated to Grails, so everything was coming together for a *Grails in Action* book. The Grails community is an unbelievably supportive one, and when I showed Graeme Rocher a copy of the first draft Table of Contents, he suggested Peter Ledbrook and Jeff Brown as potential collaborators. As it turns out, Jeff ended up working on Graeme's book, and Peter came on board for *Grails in Action*. That kind of collaboration is indicative of the friendly spirit in the Grails ecosystem.

Despite the fact that we are antipodean (Peter is from London and I'm from Canberra, Australia), we worked out a way to meet and develop the book through weekly Skype conference calls (at very odd hours). Peter is a core committer for Grails and has done more Grails support work than anyone on the planet. His input really shaped the ideas around "what do working Grails developers really need to know?" He's also written a lot of the core parts of Grails (including the testing subsystem, the JSecurity plugin, and a lot of the plugin subsystem). His "deep dive" knowledge on Grails added a new dimension to the topics we covered in *Grails in Action*, making the book a one-stop-shop for learning the key parts of the framework. Peter's sense of humor and encouraging nature made him an ideal coauthor. The collaboration worked perfectly!

From the start, we wanted not only to teach the reader how to use Grails, but also to distill as much of our practical Grails experience as possible into the book. We wanted it to become an invaluable aid to professional developers. In truth, we could have added even more information, but we hope that we have struck a good balance between useful content and weight. We also hope that you enjoy the book and that it helps you unleash the full potential of Grails.

GLEN SMITH

acknowledgments

As with any new undertaking, you never know what you're getting yourself into when you write a book for the first time. Fortunately, we had a great team at Manning to guide us through the process and help us create something we can be proud of. We would like to thank everyone involved in the production of this book. Particular thanks go to our development editor, Cynthia Kane, who put up with late-night telephone conferences and kept our motivation high. Our copy editor, Andy Carroll, did a marvelous job of tightening up our prose, and he picked up a number of ambiguities and inconsistencies.

We hope that everything in this book is 100 percent accurate, but that would have been difficult to achieve without Burt Beckwith's eagle eyes. He kept us honest, picking up technical errors and ambiguities. We'd also like to thank our reviewers for taking the time to send detailed feedback on the manuscript at various stages in its development: Josh Reed, Paul Stusiak, Bill Fly, Kenneth DeLong, Lester Lobo, Peter Johnson, Robert O'Connor, Joe McTee, Jonas Bandi, Tim Moore, Carol McDonald, Dave Klein, Doug Warren, Gordon Dickens, John Guthrie, John G. Ledo, Kenrick Chien, Lee Butts, Mark Eagle, Paul King, Robert Fletcher, and Zan Thrash.

The early MEAP subscribers also did a sterling job of pointing out typos, grammatical errors, confusing explanations, and other issues. Possibly more important to us was all the positive feedback we received from them, which helped keep our spirits up.

Thanks also to Dierk König for his encouragement and for agreeing to write the foreword to our book. And last, but not least, we would like to thank Graeme Rocher for producing such a wonderful framework that has made software development fun again.

GLEN SMITH

When I was a kid, one of my mentors, Paul Le Lievre, said to me, "Glen, there's no such thing as a free lunch. It's only free because someone else pays." That's good advice. Someone always pays. And the main person who paid for this book to happen was my amazing and long-suffering wife, Kylie. For over 12 months, she lived the life of a "book widow"—basically single-parenting my beautiful children and putting up with my grumpy and stressed manner as *Grails in Action* was born. Matie, you are the best! Consider this book a voucher for unlimited childcare-free weekends redeemable at your leisure. Bubble bath will be supplied.

My beautiful children, Isaac and Zoe, also paid a hefty price for this tome. Love you guys so much. Daddy is home, and months of extended bike rides and endless cuddles await!

Both my parents, Alby and Jan Smith, and parents-in-law, Steve and Joy Salter, have been a great encouragement for this project and a great help with childcare. Thanks for your support!

Jo Giddings, my line manager, made the way for this book to happen, generously allowing reduced work hours to let this vision run. Dean Macaulay has been covering me at work while constantly encouraging me to get this project done. You guys are awesome!

Sven Haiges, my co-host on the Grails podcast (grailspodcast.com), has been a great promoter of this project and continued to put up with my terrible mixing skills and crazy time-zone compromises in the final stages of this book. Bring on the next 100 shows, buddy!

A lot of these chapters were drafted during lunch hours at my local cafe, The Tea Caddy, which let me take up table space for very extended periods (and which makes the best BLTs in Canberra). Thanks guys!

Finally, Peter Ledbrook, my coauthor, was a calm voice of encouragement when I was drowning in an ever-growing to-do list. He's a very humble and low-profile guy who is always willing to help without any kind of bravado or drama. He knows more about Grails than any non-Graeme person and has written all the technically challenging stuff in this book. He's become a real friend over the course of this project, and it's much better for his partnership.

PETER LEDBROOK

First and foremost, I would like to thank my coauthor, Glen Smith, whose energy and enthusiasm know no bounds. Writing this book was a tough endeavor, and without his optimism and encouragement, it would have been even tougher.

My friend Linda Jordan deserves special mention for her invaluable advice on how to write, for providing an ear when I needed one, and for telling me to just get on with it. Thanks also to my parents for feeding and looking after me whenever I needed a time out.

I would like to thank the folks at G2One/SpringSource for allowing me the time to work on the book and for providing a job that meant I could work with Grails full time. May the Groovy and Grails juggernaut continue to roll!

about this book

Grails in Action is a comprehensive introduction to the Grails framework covering the nuts and bolts of all core Grails components: controllers, views, services, webflows, taglibs, Ajax, and plugins. But much more than an introduction, *Grails in Action* is jam-packed with skills, techniques, and insights from the trenches: solving the challenges you're likely to face developing your next killer web app.

Roadmap

Grails in Action gives you a fast-paced and accessible introduction to the world of agile web development.

The book is divided into four parts:

- Part 1: Introducing Grails
- Part 2: Core Grails
- Part 3: Everyday Grails
- Part 4: Advanced Grails

Part 1 will introduce you to Grails by taking you through building your first Grails application—a simple Quote of the Day application. You'll get a taste for all the parts of the Grails ecosystem and for how all the parts hang together to create a complete application. But in order to make any sophisticated use of Grails, you'll need an appreciation for Groovy—the dynamic language that forms the foundation of your Grails coding. So we'll spend some time training you on all the basics.

Part 2 begins our deeper exploration of the core Grails artifacts. You'll learn how models, views, and controllers interact, and you'll gain a deep understanding of all the core features that make up the heart of Grails applications. We'll introduce you to Hubbub, our sample social-networking application, and implement all the features that you'll commonly find in Grails applications: domain modeling, querying, skins and layout, form handling, and more. By the end of part 2, you'll be confidently developing your own basic applications.

Because real-world web applications involve a lot more than just forms and databases, part 3 will tackle the skills you'll need to take your application to the world. We'll explore testing strategies to ensure your code is implemented correctly, and we'll show how to give your application that Web 2.0 feel through time-saving third-party plugins. No application is very useful without some kind of security model, so we'll explore the security implications of taking your Grails application online. Finally, we'll look at remoting strategies for designing RESTful APIs and conclude with a survey of the asynchronous technologies that are becoming increasingly popular in developing scalable applications.

In part 4, we conclude our tour of Grails with the most advanced features of the framework. We'll look at how you can tune your data access for maximum performance and integrate with legacy databases, and we'll look deep inside Grails' underlying technologies, Spring and Hibernate. We'll also show you how to integrate Grails with your existing build processes. Finally, we'll end with a deep discussion of writing and publishing your own Grails plugins.

Who should read this book

Whether you're a seasoned Java developer ready to dip your toes in the waters of dynamic web frameworks, or a hardcore web developer making the switch to the latest Convention over Configuration paradigm, *Grails in Action* will give you the tools to get productive quickly and the deep knowledge to handle the corner cases when you get stuck.

Some experience with web development (in particular CSS, HTML, and JavaScript) is assumed, along with a basic knowledge of programming. Previous experience with Java web development is an advantage, but we take the time to explain core Java web concepts in sidebars where applicable. If you're coming from another language background (such as Ruby, Perl, or PHP), you should find the move to Grails quite natural.

Code conventions

This book provides copious examples that show how you can make use of each of the topics covered. Source code in listings or in text appears in a `fixed-width font like this` to separate it from ordinary text. In addition, class and method names, object properties, and other code-related terms and content in text are presented using the same `fixed-width font`.

Code and command-line input can be verbose. In many cases, the original source code (available online) has been reformatted; we've added line breaks and reworked indentation to accommodate the page space available in the book. In rare cases, when even this was not enough, line-continuation markers were added to show where longer lines had to be broken.

Code annotations accompany many of the listings, highlighting important concepts. In some cases, numbered cueballs link to additional explanations that follow the listing.

Getting the source code

You can access the source code for all of the examples in the book from the publisher's website at www.manning.com/GrailsinAction. All source code for the project is hosted at GitHub (github.com)—a commercial Git hosting firm. We will maintain the current URL via the publisher's website. The source is maintained by chapter, so, for example, you can download /source-code/ch06 and you will have a full copy of the source up to that point in the book.

Keeping up to date

The Grails world moves very quickly. There have been substantial changes in Grails in the year it took us to develop *Grails in Action*. Moving from Grails 1.0 to 1.1 caused numerous new sections to be written, and existing sections to be rewritten to take advantage of new features!

Although we developed the book targeting Grails 1.1, a subsequent Grails version may well have been released by the time you read this. New Grails versions bring new functionality, but Grails rarely introduces serious breaking changes, so all the knowledge you learn here will put you in great stead for future releases.

If there are portions of source code needing modification for a future release, you'll be able to find information on the *Grails in Action* Author Online forum (www.manning.com/GrailsinAction).

Author Online

Purchase of *Grails in Action* includes free access to a private web forum run by Manning Publications where you can make comments about the book, ask technical questions, and receive help from the authors and from other users. To access the forum and subscribe to it, point your web browser to www.manning.com/GrailsinAction. This page provides information on how to get on the forum once you are registered, what kind of help is available, and the rules of conduct on the forum. It also provides links to the source code for the examples in the book, errata, and other downloads.

Manning's commitment to our readers is to provide a venue where a meaningful dialog between individual readers and between readers and the authors can take place. It is not a commitment to any specific amount of participation on the part of the authors, whose contribution to the Author Online remains voluntary (and unpaid). We suggest you try asking the authors some challenging questions lest their interest stray!

The Author Online forum and the archives of previous discussions will be accessible from the publisher's website as long as the book is in print.

about the authors

GLEN SMITH started "stunt programming" the day his school took delivery of its first set of Hitachi Peach computers (in the early '80s) and has been doing it ever since. He's worked as a Unix/C systems programmer, Perl hacker, and even Visual Basic dude (but he tells everyone it was just a phase). When Java came along, he lost interest in everything else. These days, he spends most of his time consulting in Java EE technologies to the Australian government.

He has been involved in the Grails community since Grails 0.1 and launched the first public-facing Grails app (an SMS gateway) on Grails 0.2. He is a regular on the Groovy and Grails speaking circuit, the cohost of the Grails podcast (http://grailspodcast.com), and the man behind groovyblogs.org.

Glen lives in Canberra, Australia, with his wife, two children, three chickens, and one dachshund. He blogs at http://blogs.bytecode.com.au/glen and twitters at http://twitter.com/glen_a_smith.

PETER LEDBROOK started his software development career as a teenager learning to program in the comfort of his bedroom. After surviving the trials and tribulations of C and C++, he switched to Java during his first job and has stayed with it ever since.

An avid fan of open source software since those early days, he has always looked to that community for innovative and useful solutions. He discovered Grails while investigating Ruby on Rails and was astonished at how easy it was to write web applications using the framework. The love affair began.

He wrote several popular plugins (Remoting, JSecurity, and GWT) and then became a core Grails committer when he joined G2One as a consultant at the end of 2007. He also has plenty of battle scars from actively working on several public-facing applications and helping teams make the most of Grails.

about the technical editor

BURT BECKWITH is an enterprise Java and Grails developer with over 10 years of experience in a variety of industries including biotech, travel, e-learning, social networking, and financial services. He worked briefly with Groovy when it was first released, but it wasn't until he discovered Grails that the combination clicked for him, and he has no intention of looking back. He has a blog at http://burtbeckwith.com/blog/, and you can follow him on Twitter at http://twitter.com/burtbeckwith.

about the title

By combining introductions, overviews, and how-to examples, Manning's *In Action* books are designed to help learning and remembering. According to research in cognitive science, the things people remember are things they discover during self-motivated exploration.

Although no one at Manning is a cognitive scientist, we are convinced that for learning to become permanent, it must pass through stages of exploration, play, and, interestingly, retelling of what is being learned. People understand and remember new things, which is to say they master them, only after actively exploring them. Humans learn in action. An essential part of an *In Action* guide is that it is example-driven. It encourages the reader to try things out, play with new code, and explore new ideas.

There is another, more mundane, reason for the title of this book: our readers are busy. They use books to do a job or solve a problem. They need books that allow them to jump in and jump out easily and learn just what they want, just when they want it. They need books that aid them *in action*. The books in this series are designed for such readers.

about the cover illustration

The figure on the cover of *Grails in Action* is a "Jeune Fille de Plouneour-Trez," or a young woman from a town in the province of Bretagne in northern France. The illustration is taken from a French book of dress customs, *Encyclopedie des Voyages* by J. G. St. Saveur, published in 1796. Travel for pleasure was a relatively new phenomenon at the time and illustrated guides such as this one were popular, introducing both the tourist as well as the armchair traveler to the inhabitants of other countries of the world, as well as to the regional costumes of France.

The diversity of the drawings in the *Encyclopedie des Voyages* speaks vividly of the uniqueness and individuality of the world's towns and regions just 200 years ago. This was a time when the dress codes of two regions separated by a few dozen miles identified people uniquely as belonging to one or the other, and when members of a social class or trade or profession could be easily distinguished by what they were wearing.

Dress codes have changed since then and the diversity by region, so rich at the time, has faded away. It is now often hard to tell the inhabitant of one continent from another. Perhaps, trying to view it optimistically, we have traded a world of cultural and visual diversity for a more varied personal life…or a more varied and interesting intellectual and technical life.

At a time when it is hard to tell one computer book from another, Manning celebrates the inventiveness and initiative—and the fun—of the computer business with book covers based on the rich diversity of regional life of two centuries ago, brought back to life by the pictures from this collection.

Part 1

Introducing Grails

Great strides have been made in the field of Java-based web application frameworks, but creating a new application with them still seems like a lot of work. Grails' core strength is developing web applications quickly, so we'll jump into writing our first application right away.

In chapter 1, we'll expose you to the core parts of Grails by developing a simple Quote of the Day application from scratch. You'll store and query the database, develop business logic, write tests, and even add some AJAX functionality. By the end of it, you'll have a good feel for all the basic parts of Grails.

In order to develop serious Grails applications, you'll need a firm grasp of Groovy—the underlying dynamic language that makes Grails tick. In chapter 2, we'll take you on a whirlwind tour of core Groovy concepts and introduce you to all the basic syntax.

By the end of part 1, you'll have a real feel for the power of Groovy and Grails and be ready to take on the world. Feel free to do so—Grails encourages experimentation. But you might want to stick around for part 2, where we take you deeper into the core parts of Grails.

Grails in a hurry...

1

This chapter covers

- What is Grails?
- Core Grails philosophy
- Installing Grails
- The key components of a Grails application
- Developing and deploying your first Grails application

"Help, I've lost my Mojo!" That statement is probably the most concise summary of what developers feel when working with one of the plethora of Java web frameworks. So much time editing configuration files, customizing web.xml files, writing injection definitions, tweaking build scripts, modifying page layouts, restarting apps on each change, aaaahhhh! "Where has all the fun gone? Why has everything become so tedious? I just wanted to whip up a quick app to track our customer signups! There's got to be a better way..." We hear you.

Grails is a "next-generation" Java web development framework that draws on best-of-breed web development tooling, techniques, and technologies from existing Java frameworks, and combines them with the power and innovation of dynamic language development. The result is a framework that offers the stability of technologies you know and love, but shields you from the noisy configuration, design complexity, and boilerplate code that make existing Java web development so tedious. Grails allows you to spend your time implementing features, not editing XML.

But Grails isn't the first player to make such claims. You're probably thinking, "please don't let this be YAJWF (Yet Another Java Web Framework)!" Because if there's one thing that the Java development world is famous for, it's for having an unbelievably large number of web frameworks available. Struts, WebWork, JSF, Spring MVC, Seam, Wicket, Tapestry, Stripes, GWT, and the list goes on and on—all with their own config files, idioms, templating languages, and gotchas. And now we're introducing a new one?

The good news is that this ain't your Grandma's web framework—we're about to take you on a journey to a whole new level of getting stuff done—and getting it done painlessly. We're so excited about Grails because we think it's time that Java web app development was fun again! It's time you were able to sit down for an afternoon and crank out something you'd be happy demoing to your boss, client, or the rest of the internet. Grails is that good.

In this chapter, we're going to take you through developing your first Grails app. Not a toy, either. Something you could deploy and show your friends. An app that's data-driven and Ajax-powered, and that has full CRUD (create, read, update, delete) implementation, a template-driven layout, and even unit tests. In half an hour, with less than 100 lines of code. Seriously.

But before we get our hands dirty writing code, you may need a little more convincing as to why Grails should be on your radar. Before you fire up your IDE, let's quickly review the history to learn why Grails is such a game-changer.

1.1   Why Grails?

Grails is a next-generation Java web development framework that generates great developer productivity gains through the confluence of a dynamic language, a Convention over Configuration philosophy, powerfully pragmatic supporting tools, and an agile perspective drawn from the best emerging web development paradigms.

1.1.1   First there was Rails...

Some have incorrectly labeled Grails a port of Ruby on Rails to the Java platform, but this fails to recognize several points about Grails:

- The amazing innovations that Grails, itself, has brought to the enterprise development sector with its own secret sauces
- The broad range of platforms that have influenced Grails (which include Ruby, Python, PHP, and Java frameworks)
- The many features that Grails brings to the table that aren't presently available in Rails—features drawn from the JVMs long history of use in enterprise settings

Nevertheless, Grails does embrace many of the innovative philosophies that Rails brought to web development. When Ruby on Rails hit the web development landscape (in 2004), and started gaining real industry traction and critical acclaim (during 2006), a whole new set of ideas about web development started to germinate.

None of the ideas were particularly new, but the execution was truly stunning. Things like Convention over Configuration, scaffolding, code templates, and easy database integration made bootstrapping an application lightning fast. The killer demo was when David Heinemeier Hansson (the Rails founder) developed a database-driven blog application from scratch in 15 minutes. Everyone's jaw dropped.

The real power of these ideas was brought to the fore in Rails by using a dynamic language (Ruby) to perform amazing metaclass magic. For those of us in enterprise Java-land, there wasn't a compelling Java equivalent. We were stuck with a statically typed language that didn't give us the same agility to do the metaclass work that made it all work so elegantly.

1.1.2 Why Grails changed the game

Then, in 2006, along came Grails. Taking full advantage of Groovy as the underlying dynamic language, Grails made it possible to create a `Book` object and query it with dynamic methods like `Book.findByTitle("Grails in Action")` or `Book.findAllByDatePublishedGreaterThanAndTitleLike(myDate, "Grails")`, even though none of those methods really existed on the `Book` object.

Even better, you could also access any Java code or libraries you were already using, and the language syntax was similar enough to Java to make the learning curve painless. But best of all, at the end of the day, you had a WAR file to deploy to your existing Java app server—no special infrastructure required, and no management awareness needed.

The icing on the cake was that Grails was built on Spring, Hibernate, and other libraries already popular in enterprise Java—the stuff developers were already building applications on. It was like turbo-charging existing development practices without sacrificing reliability or proven technologies.

Grails' popularity exploded. Finally Java web developers had a way to take all the cool ideas that Rails had brought to the table and apply them to robust enterprise-strength web application development, without leaving any of their existing skills, libraries, or infrastructure behind.

That's probably enough history about how Grails ended up being such a popular Java web framework. But if you (or your manager) need further convincing about why Grails is an outstanding option for your next big web app project, the following subsections discuss seven of the big ideas (shown in figure 1.1) that have driven Grails to such a dominant place in the emerging next-gen Java web frameworks market.

Figure 1.1   The Grails ecosystem is a powerful confluence of people, ideas, and technology.

1.1.3   *Big idea #1: Convention over Configuration*

One of the things you'll notice about developing with Grails is how few configuration files there are. Grails makes most of its decisions based on sensible defaults drawn from your source code:

- Add a controller class called Shop with an action called order, and Grails will expose it as a URL of /yourapp/shop/order.
- Place your view files in a directory called /views/shop/order, and Grails will look after linking everything up for you without a single line of configuration.
- Create a new domain class called Customer, and Grails will automatically create a table called customer in your database.
- Add some fields to your Customer object, and Grails will automatically create the necessary fields in your customer table on the fly (including the right data types based on the validation constraints you place on them). No SQL required.

But as Jason Rudolph is quick to point out, Grails is about Convention *over* Configuration, not Convention *instead of* Configuration. If you need to tweak the defaults, all the power is there for you to do so. Grails makes overriding the defaults easy, and you still won't need any XML. But if you want to use your existing Hibernate configuration XML files in all their complex glory, Grails won't stand in your way.

1.1.4   *Big idea #2: agile philosophy*

Grails makes a big deal about being an agile web framework, and by the time you finish this chapter, you'll understand why. By making use of a dynamic language (Groovy), Grails makes things that were once a real pain in Java a complete joy. Whether it's processing form posts, implementing tag libraries, or writing test cases, there's a conciseness and expressiveness to the framework that makes these operations both easier and more maintainable at the same time.

The Grails infrastructure adds to the pleasure by keeping you iterating without getting in the way. Imagine starting up a local copy of your application and adding controllers, views, and taglib features while it's running—without having to restart it! Then imagine testing those features, making tweaks, and clicking refresh in your browser to view the updates. It's a joy.

Grails brings a whole new level of agility to Java web application development, and once you've developed your first complete application, which you'll do over the next 30 minutes or so, you'll start to appreciate some of the unique power Grails provides.

1.1.5 *Big idea #3: rock-solid foundations*

Even though Grails itself is full of innovation and cutting-edge ideas, the core is built on rock-solid proven technologies: Spring and Hibernate. These are the technologies that many existing Java shops are using today, and for good reason: they're reliable and battle tested.

Building on Spring and Hibernate also means that there's very little magic going on under the hood. If you need to tweak things in the configuration (by customizing a Hibernate configuration class) or at runtime (by getting a handle to a Spring `ApplicationContext`), there's no new magic to learn. None of your learning time on Spring and Hibernate has been wasted.

If you're new to Grails and don't have a background in Spring and Hibernate, it doesn't matter. There are few Grails development cases where you need to fall back to that level anyway, but you can feel good knowing it's there if you need it.

This same philosophy of using best-of-breed components has translated to other areas of the Grails ecosystem—particularly third-party plugins. The scheduling plugin is built on Quartz, the search plugin is built on Lucene and Compass, and the layout engine is built on SiteMesh. Wherever you go in the ecosystem, you'll see popular Java libraries wrapped in an easy-to-use instantly productive plugin. Peace of mind plus amazing productivity!

Another important part of the foundation for enterprise developers is having the formal backing of a professional services, training, and support organization. When SpringSource acquired G2One in November 2008, Groovy and Grails inherited the backing of a large company with deep expertise in the whole Groovy and Grails stack. This also introduced a range of support options to the platform useful to those organizations looking for 24/7 Groovy and Grails support backup.

1.1.6 *Big idea #4: scaffolding and templating*

If you've ever tried bootstrapping a Spring MVC application by hand, you'll know that it isn't pretty. You'll need a directory of JAR files, a bunch of bean definition files, a set of web.xml customizations, a bunch of annotated POJOs, a few Hibernate configuration files, a database-creation script, and then a build system to turn it all into a running application. It's hard work, and you'll probably burn a day in the process.

By contrast, building a running Grails application is a one liner: `grails create-app myapp`, and you can follow it up with `grails run-app` to see it running in your browser. All of the same stuff is happening behind the scenes, but based on conventions and sensible defaults rather than on hand-coding and configuration.

If you need a new controller class, `grails create-controller` will generate a shell for you (along with a shell test case). The same goes for views, services, domain classes, and all of the other artifacts in your application. This template-driven approach bootstraps you into a fantastic level of productivity, where you spend your time solving problems, not writing boilerplate code.

Grails also offers an amazing feature called "scaffolding." Based on the fields in your database model classes, Grails can generate a set of views and controllers on the fly to handle all your basic CRUD operations—creating, reading, updating, and deleting—without a single line of code.

1.1.7   *Big idea #5: Java integration*

One of the unique aspects of the Groovy and Grails community is that, unlike some of the other JVM languages, we love Java! We appreciate that there are problems and design solutions that are much better implemented in a statically typed language, so we have no problem writing our web form processing classes in Groovy, and our high-performance payroll calculations in Java. It's all about using the right tool for the job.

We're also in love with the Java ecosystem. That means we don't want to leave behind the amazing selection of Java libraries we know and love. Whether that's in-house DTO JARs for the payroll system, or a great new Java library for interfacing with Facebook, moving to Grails means you don't have to leave anything behind—except a lot of verbose XML configuration files. But as we've already said, you can reuse your Hibernate mappings and Spring resource files if you're so inclined!

1.1.8   *Big idea #6: incredible wetware*

One of the most compelling parts of the Grails ecosystem is the fantastic and helpful user community. The Groovy and Grails mailing list is a hive of activity where both die-hard veterans and new users are equally welcome. The Grails.org site hosts a Grails-powered wiki full of Grails-related information and documentation.

A wealth of third-party community websites have also sprung up around Grails. For example, groovyblogs.org aggregates what's happening in the Groovy and Grails blogosphere and is full of interesting articles. And sites like grailscrowd.com, Facebook, and LinkedIn host Grails social networking options. There's even a Grails podcast (grailspodcast.com) that runs every two weeks to keep you up to date with news, interviews, and discussions in the Grails world.

But one of the coolest parts of the community is the amazing ever-growing list of third-party plugins for Grails. Whether it's a plugin to implement full-text search, Ajax widgets, reporting, instant messaging, or RSS feeds, or to manage log files, profile performance, or integrate with Twitter, there's something for everyone. There are literally hundreds of time-saving plugins available (and in chapter 8, we'll introduce you to a bunch of the most popular ones).

1.1.9 *Big idea #7: productivity ethos*

Grails isn't just about building web applications—it's about executing your vision quickly so you can get on with doing other "life stuff" that's more important. For us, productivity is the new black, and developing in Grails is about getting your life back, one feature at a time. When you realize that you can deliver work in one day that used to take you two weeks, you start to feel good about going home early. Working with such a productive framework even makes your hobby time more fun. It means you can complete all those Web 2.0 startup website ideas you've dreamed about, but which ended up as half-written Struts or Spring MVC apps.

Developing your applications quickly and robustly gives you more time to do other, more important stuff: hanging out with your family, walking your dog, learning rock guitar, or getting your veggie patch growing really big zucchinis. Web apps come and go; zucchinis are forever. Grails productivity gives you that sort of sage-like perspective. Through the course of this chapter, we'll give you a taste of the kind of productivity you can expect when moving to Grails.

Most programmers we know are the impatient type, so in this chapter we'll take 30 minutes to develop a data-driven, Ajax-powered, unit-tested, deployable Web 2.0 website. Along the way, you'll get a taste of the core parts of a Grails application: models, views, controllers, taglibs, and services. Buckle up—it's time to hack.

1.2 *Getting set up*

In order to get Grails up and running, you'll need to walk through the installation process shown in figure 1.2.

First, you'll need to have a JDK installed (version 1.5 or later—run `javac-version` from your command prompt to check which version you have). Most PCs come with Java preinstalled these days, so you may be able to skip this step.

Once you're happy that your JDK is installed, download the latest Grails distro from www.grails.org and unzip it to your favorite installation area.

You'll then need to set the `GRAILS_HOME` environment variable, which points to your Grails installation directory, and add GRAILS_HOME/bin to your path. On Mac OS X and Linux, this is normally done by editing the ~/.profile script to contain lines like these:

```
export GRAILS_HOME=/opt/grails
export PATH=$PATH:$GRAILS_HOME/bin
```

On Windows, you'll need to go into System Properties to define `GRAILS_HOME` and update your `PATH` setting.

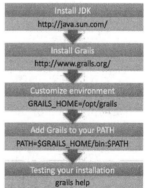

Figure 1.2 The Grails installation process

You can verify that Grails is installed correctly by running `grails help` from the command line. This will give you a handy list of Grails commands, and it'll confirm that everything is running as expected and that your GRAILS_HOME is set to a sensible location:

```
grails help
```

```
Welcome to Grails 1.1 - http://grails.org/
Licensed under Apache Standard License 2.0
Grails home is set to: /opt/grails
```

Looks like everything is in good working order.

When you develop more sophisticated Grails applications, you'll probably want to take advantage of some of the fantastic Grails IDE support out there. There's now Grails plugin support for IntelliJ, NetBeans, and Eclipse—whichever your preferred IDE, there will be a plugin to get you going. We won't be developing too much code in this chapter, so a basic text editor will be all you need. Fire up your favorite editor, and we'll talk about our sample application.

1.3   *Our sample program: a Web 2.0 QOTD*

If we're going to the trouble of writing a small application, we might as well have some fun. Our example is a quote-of-the-day (QOTD) web application where we'll capture and display famous programming quotes from development rock stars throughout time. We'll let the user add, edit, and cycle through programming quotes, and we'll even add some Ajax sizzle to give it a Web 2.0 feel. We'll want a nice short URL for our application, so let's make "qotd" our application's working title.

NOTE   You can download the sample apps for this book, including CSS and associated graphics, from the book's site at manning.com.

It's time to get started world-changing Web 2.0 quotation app, and all Grails projects begin the same way. First, find a directory to work in. Then create the application:

```
grails create-app qotd
cd qotd
```

Well done. You've created your first Grails application. You'll see that Grails created a qotd subdirectory to hold our application files. Change to that directory now, and we'll stay there for the rest of the chapter.

Because we've done all the hard work of building the application, it'd be a shame not to enjoy the fruit of our labor. Let's give it a run:

```
grails run-app
```

Grails ships with a copy of Jetty (an embeddable Java web server—there is talk that a future version will switch to Tomcat), which Grails uses to host your application during the development and testing lifecycle. When you run the `grails run-app` command, Grails will compile and start your web application. When everything is ready to go, you'll see a message like this on the console:

```
Server running. Browse to http://localhost:8080/qotd
```

This means it's time to fire up your favorite browser and take your application for a spin: http://localhost:8080/qotd/. Figure 1.3 below shows our QOTD application up and running in a browser.

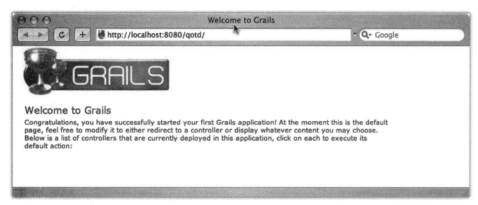

Figure 1.3 Our first app is up and running.

Once you've taken in the home page, you can stop the application by pressing Ctrl-C. Or you can leave it running and issue Grails commands from a separate console window in your operating system.

Running on a custom port (not 8080)

If port 8080 is just not for you (because perhaps you have another process running there, like Tomcat), you can customize the port that the Grails embedded application server runs on using the -Dserver.port command-line argument. If you want to run Grails on port 9090, for instance, you could run your application like this:

```
grails -Dserver.port=9090 run-app
```

If you decide to always run a particular application on a custom port, you can create a custom /grails-app/conf/BuildConfig.groovy file with an entry for grails.server. port.http=9090 to make your custom port the default. Or make a system-wide change by editing the global $HOME/.grails/settings.groovy file. You'll find out more about these files in chapter 15.

1.3.1 Writing your first controller

We have our application built and deployed, but we're a little short on an engaging user experience. Before we go too much further, now's a good time to learn a little about how Grails handles interaction with user—that's via a *controller*.

Controllers are at the heart of every Grails application. They take input from your user's web browser, interact with your business logic and data model, and route the user to the correct page to display. Without controllers, your web app would be a bunch of static pages.

Like most parts of a Grails application, you can let Grails generate a skeleton controller by using the Grails command line. Let's create a simple controller for handling quotes:

```
grails create-controller quote
```

Grails will create this skeleton controller in /grails-app/controllers/QuoteController.groovy. You'll notice that Grails sorted out the capitalization for you. The basic skeleton is shown in listing 1.1.

Listing 1.1   Our first quote controller

```
class QuoteController {
    def index = { }
}
```

Not so exciting, is it? The index entry in listing 1.1 is a Grails *action*, which we'll return to in a moment. For now, let's add a home action that sends some text back to the browser—it's shown in listing 1.2.

Listing 1.2   Adding some output

```
class QuoteController {
    def index = { }

    def home = {
        render "<h1>Real Programmers do not eat Quiche</h1>"
    }
}
```

Grails provides the `render()` method to send content directly back to the browser. This will become more important when we dip our toes into Ajax waters, but for now let's use it to deliver our "Real Programmers" heading.

How do we invoke our action in a browser? If this were a Java web application, the URL to get to it would be declared in a configuration file, but not in Grails. This is where we need to introduce you to the Convention over Configuration pattern.

Ruby on Rails introduced the idea that tons of XML configuration (or configuration of any sort) can be avoided if the framework makes some opinionated choices for you about how things will fit together. Grails embraces the same philosophy. Because our controller is called `QuoteController`, Grails will expose its actions over the URL /qotd/quote/youraction. The following gives a visual breakdown of how URLs translate to Grails objects.

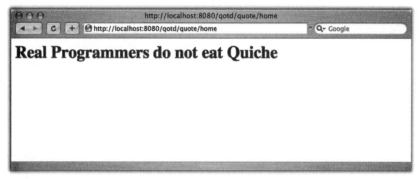

Figure 1.4   Adding our first bit of functionality

In the case of our `hello` action, we'll need to navigate to this URL:

`http://localhost:8080/qotd/quote/home`

Figure 1.4 shows our brand new application up and running, without a single line of XML.

If you were wondering about that `index()` routine in listing 1.1, that's the method that's called when the user omits the action name. If we decide that all references to /qotd/quote/ should end up at /qotd/quote/home, we need to tell Grails about that with an index action, like the one in listing 1.3.

Listing 1.3   Handling redirects

```
class QuoteController {

    def index = {
        redirect(action: home)
    }

    def home = {
        render "<h1>Real Programmers do not each quiche!</h1>"
    }
}
```

It's looking pretty good so far, but it's pretty nasty to have that HTML embedded in our source. Now that we've learned a little about controllers, it's time to get acquainted with views.

1.3.2   *Writing stuff out: the view*

Embedding HTML inside your code is always a bad idea. Not only is it difficult to read and maintain, but your graphic designer will need access to your source code in order to design the pages. The solution is to move your display logic out to a separate file, which is known as the *view*, and Grails makes it simple.

If you've done any work with Java web applications, you'll be familiar with JavaServer Pages (JSP). JSPs render HTML to the user of your web application. Grails applications, conversely, make use of Groovy Server Pages (GSP). The concepts are quite similar.

We've already discussed the Convention over Configuration pattern, and views take advantage of the same stylistic mindset. If we create our view files in the right place, everything will hook up without a single line of configuration.

First, in listing 1.4, we implement our random action. Then we'll worry about the view.

Listing 1.4   A random quote action

```
def random = {
    def staticAuthor = "Anonymous"
    def staticContent = "Real Programmers don't eat much quiche"
    [ author: staticAuthor, content: staticContent]
}
```

What's all that square bracket-ness? That's how the controller action passes information to the view. If you're an old-school servlet programmer, you might think of it as request-scoped data. The [:] operator in Groovy creates a Map, so we're passing a series of key/value pairs through to our view.

Where does our view fit into this, and where will we put our GSP file so that Grails knows where to find it? We'll use the naming conventions we used for the controller, coupled with the name of our action, and we'll place our GSP in /grails-app/views/quote/random.gsp. If we follow that pattern, there's no configuration required.

Let's create a GSP file and see how we can reference our Map data, as shown in listing 1.5.

Listing 1.5   Implementing our first view

```
<html>
<head>
    <title>Random Quote</title>
</head>

<body>

    <q>${content}</q>
    <p>${author}</p>

</body>

</html>
```

The ${content} and ${author} format is known as the GSP Expression Language, and if you've ever done any work with JSPs, it will probably be old news to you. If you haven't worked with JSPs before, you can think of those ${} tags as a way of displaying the contents of a variable. Let's fire up the browser and give it a whirl. Figure 1.5 shows our new markup in action.

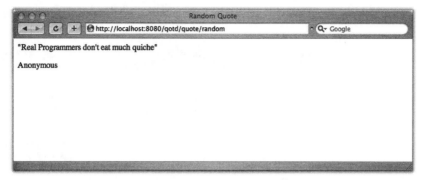

Figure 1.5 Our first view in action

1.3.3 *Adding some style with Grails layouts*

We now have our first piece of backend functionality written. But the output isn't engaging—there are no gradients, no giant text, no rounded corners. Everything looks pretty mid-90s.

You're probably thinking it's time for some CSS action, but let's plan ahead a little. If we mark up random.gsp with CSS, we're going to have to add those links to the header of every page in the app. There's a better way: Grails layouts.

Layouts give you a way of specifying layout templates for certain parts of your application. For example, we might want all of the quote pages (random, by author, by date) to be styled with a common masthead and navigation links; only the body content should change. To do this, let's first mark up our target page with some IDs that we can use for our CSS. This is shown in listing 1.6.

Listing 1.6 Updating the view

```
<html>
<head>
   <title>Random Quote</title>
</head>

<body>

   <div id="quote">
      <q>${content}</q>
      <p>${author}</p>
   </div>

</body>

</html>
```

Now, how can we apply those layout templates (masthead and navigation) we were discussing earlier? Like everything else in Grails, layouts follow a Convention over Configuration style. To have all our `QuoteController` actions share the same layout, we'll create a file called /grails-app/views/layouts/quote.gsp. There are no Grails shortcuts for layout creation, so we've got to roll this one by hand. Listing 1.7 shows our first attempt at writing a layout.

Listing 1.7   Adding a layout

```
<html>
  <head>
    <title>QOTD &raquo; <g:layoutTitle/></title>          ①  Merges title from
                                                              our target page
    <link rel="stylesheet" href="
          <g:createLinkTo dir='css' file='snazzy.css' />    ②  Creates relative
    " />                                                         link to CSS file
    <g:layoutHead />          ③  Merges head elements
  </head>                         from target page
  <body>
    <div id="header">
      <img src="
        <g:createLinkTo dir='images' file='logo.png'/>
      " alt="logo"/>
    </div>
    <g:layoutBody />          ④  Merges body elements
  </body>                         from target page
</html>
```

That's a lot of angle brackets—let's break it down. The key thing to remember is that this is a template page, so the contents of our target page (random.gsp) will be merged with this template before we send any content back to the browser. Under the hood, Grails is using SiteMesh, the popular Java layout engine, to do all of that merging for you. The general process for how SiteMesh does the merge is shown in figure 1.6.

In order for our layout template in listing 1.7 to work, it needs a way of accessing elements of the target page (when we merge the title of the target page with the template, for example). That access is achieved through Grails' template taglibs, so it's probably time to introduce you to the notion of taglibs in general.

If you've never seen a tag library (taglib) before, think of them as groups of custom HTML tags that can execute code. In listing 1.7, we took advantage of the `g:create-LinkTo`, `g:layoutHead`, and `g:layoutBody` tags. When the client's browser requests the page, Grails replaces all of those tag calls with real HTML, and the contents of the

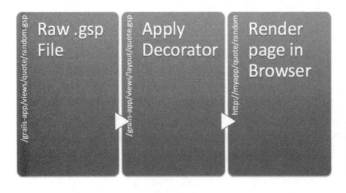

Figure 1.6 SiteMesh decorates a raw GSP file with a standard set of titles and sidebars.

HTML will depend on what the individual tag generates. For instance, that first createLinkTo tag ❷ will end up generating a link fragment like /qotd/css/snazzy.css.

In the title block of the page, we include our QOTD title and then follow it with some chevrons (>>) represented by the HTML character code », and then add the title of the target page itself ❶.

After the rest of the head tags, we use a layoutHead call to merge the contents of the HEAD section of any target page ❸. This can be important for search engine optimization (SEO) techniques, where individual target pages might contain their own META tags to increase their Google-ability.

Finally, we get to the body of the page. We output our common masthead div to get our Web 2.0 gradient and cute icons, and then we call <g:layoutBody> to render the BODY section of the target page ❹.

Let's refresh our browser to see how we're doing. Figure 1.7 shows our styled page.

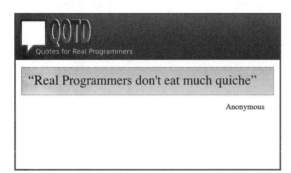

Figure 1.7 QOTD with some funky CSS skinning

Our app is looking good. Notice how we've made no changes to our relatively bland random.gsp file. Keeping view pages free of cosmetic markup reduces your maintenance overhead significantly. And if you need to change your masthead, add some more JavaScript includes, or incorporate a few additional CSS files. You do it all in one place: the template.

Fantastic. We're up and running with a controller, view, and template. But things are still pretty static in the data department. We're probably a little overdue to learn how Grails handles stuff in the database. Once we have that under our belt, we can circle back and implement a real random action.

1.4 *Creating the domain model*

We've begun our application, and we can deploy it to our testing web container. But let's not overstate our progress—Google isn't about to buy us just yet. Our app lacks a certain pizzazz. It's time to add some interactivity so that our users can add new quotations to the database. To store those quotations, we're going to need to learn how Grails handles the data model.

Grails uses the term "domain class" to describe those objects that can be persisted to the database. In our QOTD app, we're going to need a few domain classes, but let's start with the absolute minimum: a domain class to hold our quotations.

Let's create a `Quote` domain class:

```
grails create-domain-class quote
```

In your Grails application, domain classes always end up under /grails-app/domain. Take a look at the skeleton class Grails has created in /grails-app/domain/Quote. groovy:

```
class Quote {

  static constraints = {
  }

}
```

That's pretty uninspiring. We're going to need some fields in our data model to hold the various elements for each quote. Let's beef up our class to hold the content of the quote, the name of the author, and the date the entry was added, as shown in listing 1.8.

Listing 1.8 Our first domain class with teeth

```
class Quote {

    String content
    String author
    Date created = new Date()

    static constraints = {
    }
}
```

Now that we've got our data model, we need to go off and create our database schema, right? Wrong. Grails does all that hard work for you behind the scenes. Based on the definitions of the types in listing 1.8, and by applying some simple conventions, Grails creates a quote table, with `varchar` fields for the strings, and `Date` fields for the date. The next time we run `grails run-app`, our data model will be created on the fly.

But how will it know which database to create the tables in? It's time to configure a data source.

1.4.1 Configuring the data source

Grails ships with an in-memory database out of the box, so if you do nothing, your data will be safe and sound in volatile RAM. The idea of that makes most programmers a little nervous, so let's look at how we can set up a database that's a little more persistent.

In your /grails-app/conf/ directory, you'll find a file named DataSource.groovy. This is where you define the data source (database) that your application will use— you can define different databases for your development, test, and production environments. When you run `grails run-app` to start the local web server, it uses your development data source. Listing 1.9 shows an extract from the standard DataSource file, which shows the default data source.

Listing 1.9   Data source definition—in memory

```
development {
    dataSource {
        dbCreate = "create-drop"          Recreates database
        url = "jdbc:hsqldb:mem:devDB"     on every run
    }                                     Specifies an in-memory
}                                         database
```

We have two issues here. The first is that the `dbCreate` strategy tells Grails to drop and re-create your database on each run. This is probably not what you want, so let's change that to `update`, so Grails knows to leave our database table contents alone between runs (but we give it permission to add columns if it needs to).

The second issue relates to the URL—it's using an HSQLDB in-memory database. That's fine for test scripts, but not so good for product development. Let's change it to a file-based version of HSQLDB so we have some real persistence.

Our updated file is shown in listing 1.10.

Listing 1.10   Data source definition—persistent

```
development {
    dataSource {
        dbCreate = "update"                        Preserves tables
        url = "jdbc:hsqldb:file:devDB;shutdown=true"  between runs
    }                                              Specifies file-based
}                                                  database
```

Now we have a database that's persisting our data, so let's look at how we can populate it with some sample data.

1.4.2   *Exploring database operations*

We haven't done any work on our user interface yet, but it would be great to be able to save and query entries in our quotes table. To do this for now, we'll use the Grails console—a small GUI application that will start your application outside of a web server and give you a console to issue Groovy commands.

You can use the `grails console` command to tinker with your data model before your app is ready to roll. When we issue this command, our QOTD Grails application is bootstrapped, and the console GUI appears, waiting for us to enter some code. Figure 1.8 shows saving a new quote to the database via the console.

For our first exploration of the data model, it would be nice to create and save some of those `Quote` objects. Type the following into the console window, and then click the Run button (at the far right of the toolbar):

```
new Quote(author: 'Larry Wall',
    content: 'There is more than one method to our madness.').save()
```

The bottom half of the console will let you know you're on track:

```
Result: Quote : 1
```

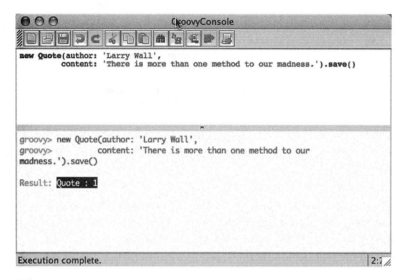

Figure 1.8   The Grails console lets your run commands from a GUI.

Where did that `save()` routine come from? Grails automatically endows domains with certain methods. Let's add a few more entries, and we'll get a taste of querying:

```
new Quote(author: 'Chuck Norris Facts', content: 'Chuck Norris always uses his
       own design patterns, and his favorite is the Roundhouse Kick').save()
new Quote(author: 'Eric Raymond', content: 'Being a social outcast helps you
       stay concentrated on the really important things, like thinking and
       hacking.').save()
```

Let's use another one of those dynamic methods (`count()`) to make sure that our data is being saved to the database correctly:

```
println Quote.count()
3
```

Looks good so far. It's time to roll up our sleeves and do some querying on our Quote database. To simplify database searches, Grails introduces special query methods on your domain class called *dynamic finders*. These special methods utilize the names of fields in your domain model to make querying as simple as this:

```
def quote = Quote.findByAuthor("Larry Wall")
println quote.content
There is more than one method to our madness.
```

Now that we know how to save and query, it's time to start getting our web application up and running. Exit the Grails console, and we'll learn a little about getting those quotes onto the web.

1.5   *Adding UI actions*

Let's get something on the web. First, we'll need an action on our `QuoteController` to return a random quote from our database. We'll work out the random selection later—for now, let's cut some corners and fudge our sample data, as shown in listing 1.11.

```
def random = {
    def staticQuote = new Quote(author: "Anonymous",
        content: "Real Programmers Don't eat quiche")
    [ quote : staticQuote]
}
```

We'll also need to update our /grails-app/views/quote/random.gsp file to use our new `Quote` object:

```
<q>${quote.content}</q>
<p>${quote.author}</p>
```

There's nothing new here, just a nicer data model. This would be a good time to refresh your browser and see our static quote being passed through to the view. Give it a try to convince yourself it's all working.

Now that you have a feel for passing model objects to the view, and now that we know enough querying to be dangerous, let's rework our action in listing 1.12 to implement a real random database query.

```
def random = {
    def allQuotes = Quote.list()        ❶ Obtains list of
    def randomQuote                         quotes
    if (allQuotes.size() > 0) {         ❷ Selects
        def randomIdx = new Random().nextInt(allQuotes.size())    random
        randomQuote = allQuotes[randomIdx]                        quote
    } else {                            ❸ Generates
        randomQuote = new Quote(author: "Anonymous",    default quote
            content: "Real Programmers Don't eat Quiche")
    }
    [ quote : randomQuote]              ❹ Passes quote to
}                                          the view
```

With our reworked `random` action, we're starting to take advantage of some real database data. The `list()` method ❶ will return the complete set of `Quote` objects from the quote table in the database and populate our `allQuotes` collection. If there are any entries in the collection, we select a random one ❷ based on an index into the collection; otherwise, we use a static quote ❸. With all the heavy lifting done, we return a `randomQuote` object to the view in a variable called `quote` ❹, which we can access in the GSP file.

Now that we've got our random feature implemented, let's head back to http://localhost:8080/qotd/quote/random to see it in action. Figure 1.9 shows our random feature in action.

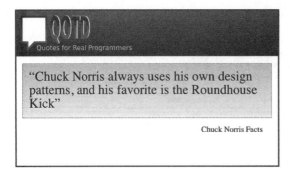

Figure 1.9   Our random quote feature in action

1.5.1   *Scaffolding: just add rocket fuel*

We've done all the hard work of creating our data model. Now we need to enhance our controller to handle all the CRUD actions to let users put their own quotes in the database.

That's if we want to do a slick job of it. But if we want to get up and running quickly, Grails offers us a fantastic shortcut called *scaffolding*. Scaffolds dynamically implement basic controller actions and views for the common things you'll want to do when CRUDing your data model.

How do we scaffold our screens for adding and updating quote-related data? It's a one-liner for the `QuoteController`, as shown in listing 1.13.

Listing 1.13   Enabling scaffolding

```
class QuoteController {
   def scaffold = true
   // our other stuff here...
}
```

That's it. When Grails sees a controller marked as `scaffold = true`, it goes off and creates some basic controller actions and GSP views on the fly. If you'd like to see it in action, head over to http://localhost:8080/qotd/quote/list and you'll find something like the edit page shown in figure 1.10.

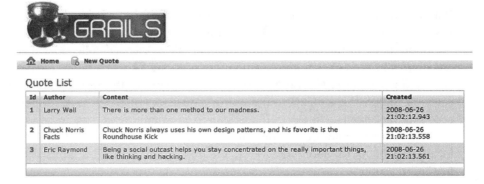

Figure 1.10   The `list()` scaffold in action

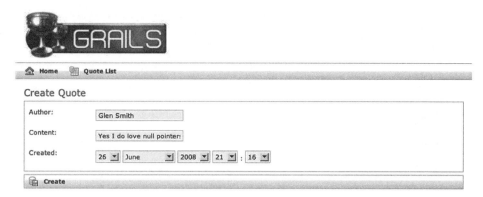

Figure 1.11   Adding a quote has never been easier.

Click on the New Quote button, and you'll be up and running. You can add your new quote as shown in figure 1.11.

That's a lot of power to get for free. The generated scaffolds are probably not tidy enough for your public-facing sites, but they're absolutely fantastic for your admin screens and perfect for tinkering with your database during development (where you don't want the overhead of mocking together a bunch of CRUD screens).

1.5.2   Surviving the worst case scenario

Our model is looking good and our scaffolds are great, but we're still missing some pieces to make things a little more robust. We don't want users putting dodgy stuff in our database, so let's explore some validation.

Validation is declared in our `Quote` object, so we just need to populate the constraints closure with all the rules we'd like to apply. For starters, let's make sure that users always provide a value for the author and content fields, as shown in listing 1.14.

Listing 1.14   Adding basic validation

```
class Quote {

    String content
    String author
    Date created = new Date()

    static constraints = {
        author(blank:false)                        Enforces data
        content(maxSize:1000, blank:false)         validation
    }

}
```

These constraints tell Grails that neither `author` nor `content` can be blank (neither `null` nor 0 length). If we don't specify a size for `String` fields, they'll end up being defined `VARCHAR(255)` in our database. That's probably fine for `author` fields, but our content may expand on that a little. That's why we've added a `maxSize` constraint.

Entries in the `constraints` closure also affect the generated scaffolds. For example, the ordering of entries in the `constraints` closure also affects the order of the fields in generated pages. Fields with constraint sizes greater than 255 characters are rendered as `HTML TEXTAREA`s rather than `TEXT` fields. Figure 1.12 shows how error messages display when constraints are violated.

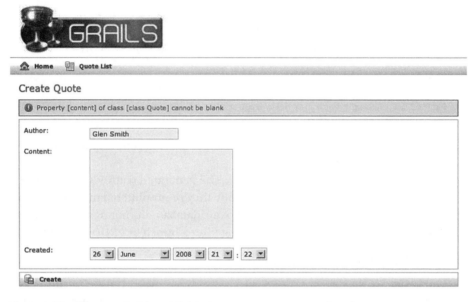

Figure 1.12   When constraints are violated, error messages appear in red.

1.6   *Improving the architecture*

Spreading logic across our controller actions is all well and good. It's pretty easy to track down what goes where in our small app, and maintenance isn't a concern right now. But as our quotation app grows, we'll find that things get a little more complex. We'll want to reuse logic in different controller actions, and even across controllers. It's time to tidy up our business logic, and the best way to do that in Grails is via a service.

Let's create our service and learn by doing:

```
grails create-service quote
```

This command creates a skeleton quote service in /grails-app/services/Quote-Service.groovy:

```
class QuoteService {

    boolean transactional = true

    def serviceMethod() {

    }
}
```

You'll notice that services can be marked transactional—more on that later. For now, let's move our random quote business logic into its own method in the service, as shown in listing 1.15.

Listing 1.15 Beefing up our service

```
class QuoteService {

   boolean transactional = false

   def getStaticQuote() {
      return new Quote(author: "Anonymous",
         content: "Real Programmers Don't eat quiche")
   }

   def getRandomQuote() {

      def allQuotes = Quote.list()
      def randomQuote = null
      if (allQuotes.size() > 0) {
         def randomIdx = new Random().nextInt(allQuotes.size())
         randomQuote = allQuotes[randomIdx]
      } else {
         randomQuote = getStaticQuote()
      }
      return randomQuote

   }
}
```

Now our service is implemented. How do we use it in our controller? Again, conventions come into play. We just add a new field to our controller called quote-Service, and Grails will inject the service into the controller. Listing 1.16 shows the updated code.

Listing 1.16 Invoking our service

```
class QuoteController {

   def scaffold = true

   def quoteService

   def random = {
      def randomQuote = quoteService.getRandomQuote()
      [ quote : randomQuote ]
   }

}
```

Doesn't that feel much tidier? Our QuoteService looks after all the business logic related to quotes, and our QuoteController helps itself to the methods it needs. If you have experience with Inversion of Control (IoC) containers, such as Spring or Google Guice, you will recognize this pattern of application design as Dependency Injection (DI). Grails takes DI to a whole new level by using the convention of variable names to determine what gets injected. But we have yet to write a test for our business logic, so now's the time to explore Grails' support for testing.

1.6.1   *Your first Grails test case*

Testing is a core part of today's agile approach to development, and Grails' support for testing is wired right into the framework. Grails is so insistent about testing that when we created our `QuoteService`, Grails automatically created a shell unit-test case in /grails-app/test/unit/QuoteServiceTests.groovy to encourage us to do the right thing. But unit tests (which we'll explore in chapter 7) require a bit of mock trickery to simulate database calls. For now, we want an integration test (which gives us a "real" in-memory database to test against). We create one of those with this command:

```
grails create-integration-test QuoteServiceIntegration
```

This will tell Grails to create a shell /grails-app/test/integration/QuoteService-IntegrationTests.groovy file. We've given the test an "IntegrationTests" suffix to make sure its class name doesn't clash with our existing unit test in /test/unit/Quote-ServiceTests.groovy. Listing 1.17 shows what the initial integration test looks like.

Listing 1.17   Our first test case

```
import grails.test.*

class QuoteServiceTests extends GrailsUnitTestCase {

    protected void setUp() {
        super.setUp()
    }

    protected void tearDown() {
        super.tearDown()
    }

    void testSomething() {

    }
}
```

It's not much, but it's enough to get us started. The same Convention over Configuration rules apply to tests, so let's beef up our `QuoteServiceIntegrationTests` case to inject the service that's under test, as shown in listing 1.18.

Listing 1.18   Adding real tests

```
class QuoteServiceTests extends GrailsUnitTestCase {

    def quoteService

    void testStaticQuote() {
        def staticQuote = quoteService.getStaticQuote()
        assertEquals("Anonymous", staticQuote.author)
        assertEquals("Real Programmers Don't eat Quiche", staticQuote.content)
    }
}
```

There's not too much that can go wrong with the `getStaticQuote()` routine, but let's give it a workout for completeness. To run your tests, execute `grails test-app`. You should see something like the results in listing 1.19.

Listing 1.19 Test output

```
-------------------------------------------------------
Running 1 Integration Tests...
Running test QuoteServiceIntegrationTests...
            testStaticQuote...SUCCESS
Integration Tests Completed in 284ms
-------------------------------------------------------
```

Listing 1.19 shows us that our tests are running fine. Grails also generates an HTML version of our test results, which you can view by opening /grails-app/test/reports/html/index.html in a web browser. From there you can browse the whole project's test results visually and drill down into individual tests to see what failed and why, as shown in figure 1.13.

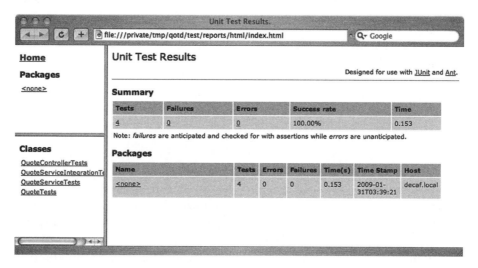

Figure 1.13 HTML reports from the integration test run

We'll learn how to amp up our test-coverage in chapter 7, but for now we have a test up and running, and we know how to view the output.

1.6.2 *Going Web 2.0: Ajax-ing the view*

Our sample application wouldn't be complete without adding a little Ajax (Asynchronous JavaScript and XML) secret sauce to spice things up. If you haven't heard much about Ajax, it's a way of updating portions of a web page using JavaScript. By using a little Ajax, we can make our web application a lot more responsive by updating the quote without having to reload the masthead banners and all our other page content. It also gives us a chance to look at Grails tag libraries.

Let's Ajax-ify our random.gsp view. First, we have to add the Ajax library to our <head> element (we'll use Prototype, but Grails also lets you use YUI, Dojo, or others). An updated portion of random.gsp is shown in listing 1.20.

Listing 1.20   Adding a JavaScript library for Ajax

```
<head>
   <title>Random Quote</title>
   <g:javascript library="prototype" />
</head>
```

Then, in the page body of random.gsp, we'll add a menu section that allows the user to display a new quote or head off to the admin screens. We'll use Grails' taglibs to create both our Ajax link for refreshing quotes and our standard link for the admin interface. Listing 1.21 shows our new menu HTML. We'll add this snippet before the <div> tag that hosts the body of the page.

Listing 1.21   Invoking Ajax functionality

```
<ul id="menu">
   <li>
      <g:remoteLink action="ajaxRandom" update="quote">
         Next Quote
      </g:remoteLink>
   </li>
   <li>
      <g:link action="list">
         Admin
      </g:link>
   </li>
</ul>
```

You've seen these sorts of tag library calls earlier in the chapter (in section 1.3.3), where we used them to generate a standardized layout for our application. In this example, we introduce a g:remoteLink, Grails' name for an Ajax hyperlink, and g:link, which is the tag for generating a standard hyperlink.

When you click on this link, Grails will call the ajaxRandom action on the controller that sent it here—in our case, the QuoteController—and will place the returned HTML inside the div that has an ID of quote. But we haven't written our ajaxRandom action, so let's get to work. Listing 1.22 shows the updated fragment of Quote-Controller.groovy with the new action.

Listing 1.22   The server side of Ajax

```
def ajaxRandom = {
   def randomQuote = quoteService.getRandomQuote()
   render "<q>${randomQuote.content}</q>" +
               "<p>${randomQuote.author}</p>"
}
```

We'd already done the heavy lifting in our quote service, so we can reuse that here. Because we don't want our Grails template to decorate our output, we're going to write our response directly to the browser (we'll talk about more elegant ways of doing this in later chapters). Let's take our new Ajax app for a spin, as shown in figure 1.14.

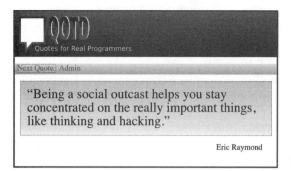

Figure 1.14 Our Ajax view in action

To convince yourself that all the Ajax snazziness is in play, click on the Next Quote menu item a few times. Notice how there's no annoying repaint of the page? You're living the Web 2.0 dream.

1.6.3 *Bundling the final product: creating a WAR file*

Look how much we've achieved in half an hour! But it's no good running the app on your laptop—you need to set it free and deploy it to a real server out there in the cloud. For that, you'll need a WAR file, and Grails makes creating one a one-liner:

```
grails war
```

Watch the output, and you'll see Grails bundling up all the JARs it needs, along with your Grails application files, and creating the WAR file in your project's root directory:

```
Done creating WAR /Users/glen/qotd/qotd-0.1.war
```

Now you're ready to deploy.

1.6.4 *And 55 lines of code later*

We've learned a lot. And we've coded a fair bit too. But don't take my word for it; let's let Grails crunch the numbers for us with a `grails stats` command. Listing 1.23 shows the `grails stats` command in action.

Listing 1.23 Crunching numbers: the `grails stats` command in action

```
grails stats

    +----------------------+-------+-------+
    | Name                 | Files | LOC   |
    +----------------------+-------+-------+
    | Controllers          |    1  |   13  |
    | Domain Classes       |    1  |    9  |
    | Services             |    1  |   17  |
    | Integration Tests    |    3  |   16  |
    +----------------------+-------+-------+
    | Totals               |    6  |   55  |
    +----------------------+-------+-------+
```

Only 55 lines of code (LOC)! Maybe we haven't coded as much as we thought. Still, you'd have to say that 55 lines isn't too shabby for an Ajax-powered, user-editable, random quote web application.

That was quite an introduction to Grails. We've had a taste of models, views, controllers, services, taglibs, layouts, and unit tests. And there's much more to explore. But before we go any further, it might be good to explore a little Groovy.

1.7   *Summary and best practices*

Congratulations, you've written and deployed your first Grails app, and now you have a feel for working from scratch to completed project. The productivity rush can be quite addictive.

Here are a few key tips you should take away from this chapter:

- *Rapid iterations are key.* The most important take-away for this chapter is that Grails fosters rapid iterations to get your application up and running in record time, and you'll have a lot of fun along the way.
- *Noise reduction fosters maintenance and increases velocity.* By embracing Convention over Configuration, Grails gets rid of tons of XML configuration that used to kill Java web frameworks.
- *Bootstrapping saves time.* For the few cases where you do need scaffolding code (for example, in UI design), Grails generates all the shell boilerplate code to get you up and running. This is another way Grails saves you time.
- *Testing is inherent.* Grails makes writing test cases easy. It even creates shell artifacts for your test cases. Take the time to learn Grails' testing philosophy (which we'll look at in depth in chapter 7) and practice it in your daily development.

There's certainly a lot more to learn. We'll spend the rest of the book taking you through all the nuts and bolts of developing full-featured, robust, and maintainable web apps using Grails, and we'll point out the tips, tricks, and pitfalls along the way.

The Groovy essentials 2

This chapter covers
- Introducing Groovy
- Differences between Java and Groovy
- Groovy's dynamic features

Grails is a great framework that removes much of the drudgery from the development of web applications. You have already seen how easy it is to get a usable application up and running from scratch. A large part of that productivity gain comes from using Groovy as the main language for Grails development.

This chapter aims to be a primer for Java developers, covering basics that will be useful for following the rest of the book. The pace is fast, but you don't have to understand everything in one go. In fact, we encourage you to refer back to this chapter as your experience grows and you need to dig a bit deeper into Groovy. If you're already familiar with the language, you may still want to browse through the chapter—we talk about some subtleties and pitfalls that you may not be aware of.

We begin by covering the many small differences between Groovy and Java, most of which amount to simple variations in the syntax. We then highlight the Java features that are missing from Groovy (there are only a few), before moving on to closures and the dynamic nature of the language. Even after a quick read through, you'll know enough to follow the examples in the book and write your own code. Beyond that, there is enough information in this chapter for you to become a competent Groovy (and Grails!) developer.

2.1   An introduction

We could go straight into explaining how Groovy and Java differ, but there is nothing like getting your hands dirty to get a real feel for a language. With that in mind, we'll introduce you to a couple of Grails commands that allow you to experiment with Groovy easily and safely. We'll follow that up by explaining a few minor but nonetheless important differences between the two languages that will enable you to follow the rest of the examples in the chapter.

2.1.1   Let's play with Groovy!

You have Grails installed, and now you want to try out this outrageously named programming language called Groovy with a minimum of fuss. What can you do? Well, you saw in the first chapter how you can use the `create-app` command to create a Grails project. There are also two commands that provide interactive environments for running Groovy code. They can be used to interactively play with your Grails application.

> **Grails and Groovy versions**
>
> This book targets Grails version 1.1, which comes with its own copy of Groovy 1.6, so that's the version of Groovy that this chapter is based on. Most of the information is also applicable to Groovy 1.5, but some code may not work with that version.

The first command is `shell`. This starts an interactive shell or command prompt in which you can type Groovy expressions and see the results. Figure 2.1 shows an example session. As you can see, to exit the shell, simply type `quit` on its own.

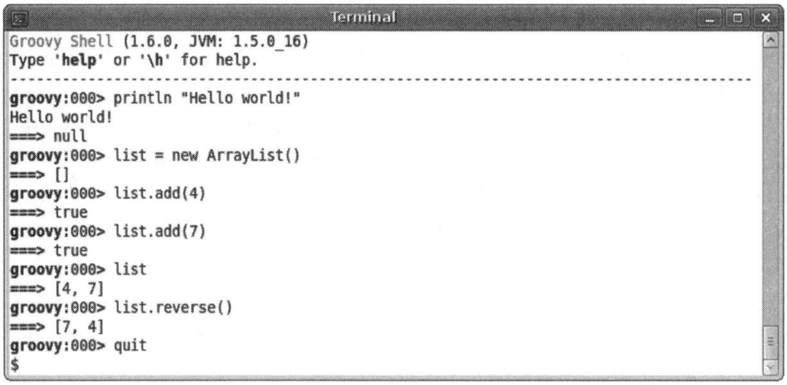

```
Groovy Shell (1.6.0, JVM: 1.5.0_16)
Type 'help' or '\h' for help.
---------------------------------------------------------------------
groovy:000> println "Hello world!"
Hello world!
===> null
groovy:000> list = new ArrayList()
===> []
groovy:000> list.add(4)
===> true
groovy:000> list.add(7)
===> true
groovy:000> list
===> [4, 7]
groovy:000> list.reverse()
===> [7, 4]
groovy:000> quit
$
```

Figure 2.1   An example session with the Grails shell, started with the `shell` command

The shell is great for evaluating expressions and checking the results of method calls, and it's even powerful enough that you can define new classes from within it. But it isn't possible to edit code that you have already written, so it's somewhat limited.

The Grails console, started with the `console` command, is a Swing application that makes it easy to write simple scripts and run them—it even gives you syntax highlighting! The console consists of two panes: the upper one contains your Groovy code, and the one below shows the output from running the script. The console's biggest advantage over the shell is that you can change a script and immediately run it with those changes. You can also save the script and load it back in at a later date. Figure 2.2 shows the console application in action.

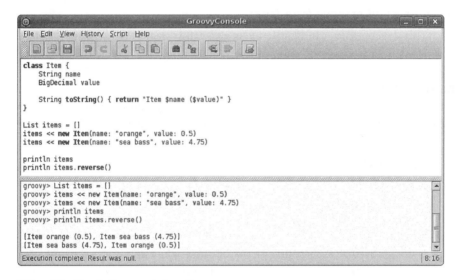

Figure 2.2   The Grails console in action

NOTE   You can only start the `shell` and `console` commands from within a Grails project. It's also worth pointing out that the two commands use the standard Groovy shell and console, respectively, which explains the references to "Groovy Shell" and "GroovyConsole" in the interfaces. However, Grails adds some magic that allows you to interact with your Grails project in ways that you can't with the standard Groovy shell and console.

The script in figure 2.2 highlights a few of the differences between Groovy and Java that we're about to cover, but first we should explain what scripts are.

WHAT'S THIS SCRIPT BUSINESS, THEN?

In order to run Java code directly, you must create a class and define a static `main()` method. This doesn't sound particularly onerous, but it's a surprisingly effective disincentive to writing simple applications. To remove this hurdle, Groovy supports scripts: collections of statements in text files that are executed in order. You can think of them as the body of a `main()` method, but without the class and method definitions. As you can see in figure 2.2, you can even include class definitions.

Try this simple script in the Grails console:

```
println "Hello world!"
```

Either use the Script > Run menu item or the Ctrl-R keyboard shortcut to execute the script. And that's it! You have now written and executed a simple Groovy script.

Now that you know how to use the console, you're ready to test the examples as we go. Let's take a look at some of the basic language features that you need to be aware of.

2.1.2 *Some basic differences from Java*

With a few exceptions, valid Java code is also valid Groovy. But writing *idiomatic* Groovy means taking advantage of some of its extra features. We start with some familiar Java concepts that vary slightly in Groovy.

FEWER IMPORTS

As you know, all classes in the `java.lang` package are automatically imported by Java. Groovy extends this behavior to include the following packages:

- `java.io`
- `java.math`
- `java.net`
- `java.util`
- `groovy.lang`
- `groovy.util`

This is convenient when writing scripts because you often end up using classes from these core packages extensively, and it gets pretty tedious running a script only to find that you missed one of those imports.

ASSERTIONS

Many of the examples in this chapter make use of the `assert` keyword:

```
assert 1 == 1
assert 'c' != 'z'
```

All `assert` does is throw a `java.lang.AssertionError` if the corresponding expression evaluates to `false` (according to Groovy Truth, which we look at next). You should be familiar with `assert` from Java, but be aware that although it has similar semantics to the Java version, it can't be switched on and off via the `-ea` argument to the JVM.

THE TRUTH ...

You might expect "Groovy Truth" to hold the answer to life, the universe, and everything. Sadly, you'll have to find that elsewhere. Its actual meaning is far more prosaic and relates to what Groovy views as `true` or `false`.

In Java, conditions only work with Boolean values, which often makes for verbose code:

```
if (mySet == null || mySet.isEmpty()) {
   ...
}
```

Groovy helps to reduce this verbosity and improve readability by coercing other objects to Booleans. For example, a `null` reference and an empty collection will both evaluate to `false`, so the equivalent Groovy code would look like this:

```
if (!mySet) {
   ...
}
```

Table 2.1 lists the coercions used by Groovy Truth. Note that the `null` object reference coercion applies to all the object types listed, so both a `null` map and an empty map will evaluate to `false`.

Table 2.1 Groovy Truth evaluations

Type	Evaluates to `false`
`Boolean`	`false`, `Boolean.FALSE`
Object reference	`null`
`Number`	`0`
`String`, `GString`	Zero-length string
`Collection`	Empty `Collection`
`Map`	Empty `Map`
`Iterator`	`hasNext()` returns `false`
`Enumeration`	`hasMoreElements()` returns `false`
`java.util.regex.Matcher`	`find()` returns `false`

Be careful when using Groovy Truth—are you checking the behavior you really want? Ask yourself whether you should be checking for `null` or for some other value instead. For example, if you know you're testing a collection and you want to treat a `null` reference the same as an empty collection, using Groovy Truth is appropriate. However, if you want to treat an empty collection and `null` differently, make the check explicit, with code like `obj == null`. This makes the intent clear to anyone reading your code.

PUBLIC IS THE DEFAULT SCOPE

As you know, Java has four scopes: `private`, `protected`, `public`, and the default (package) scope. The designers of Groovy decided that the last of these is redundant, so it only supports the other three. This, in turn, led to the decision to make `public` the default scope, because it's the most commonly used. If a class, field, or method has no explicit scope declared, it's automatically `public` rather than Java's default package scope.

CHECKED EXCEPTIONS DON'T HAVE TO BE CAUGHT

Error-handling is nearly the same in Groovy as it is in Java. Syntactically, exceptions are treated identically using `try...catch...finally` blocks. The difference is that you don't have to catch checked exceptions in Groovy. This means that checked exceptions are, for all intents and purposes, the same as runtime exceptions.

On the whole, this results in less boilerplate code, because you only catch the exceptions you know what to do with. But there are occasions when it's important not to forget that you're dealing with checked exceptions. For example, Spring's default transaction behavior only works with runtime exceptions (as you'll see in chapter 14). If that doesn't mean anything to you at the moment, don't worry—just remember that checked exceptions are still checked exceptions, even if you don't have to catch them!

That wasn't so bad, was it? We now have the foundations to move on to the more substantial differences, all of which are geared toward making your life easier.

2.1.3 *Some new operators*

You're undoubtedly familiar with operators such as these: + - . and so on. Groovy supports all of the same operators as Java, but it also introduces a few new ones that will make your life easier and your code easier to read.

?. (NULL-SAFE OBJECT NAVIGATION)

Have you ever been annoyed at having to check whether a reference is `null` before calling a method on it? The Groovy developers have, so they added a null-safe dot (`.`) operator to the language.

Consider this common idiom from Java, which checks whether an object or one of its properties is `null`:

```
if (obj != null && obj.value != null) {
    ...
}
```

In Groovy, you can write this as

```
if (obj?.value != null) {
    ...
}
```

In this example, the field `value` is only accessed if `obj` isn't `null`. Otherwise the entire expression, `obj?.value`, evaluates to null—no more `NullPointerException`! You can chain the operator too, and in fact you should. Otherwise, you'll see that dreaded exception. So do this:

```
user.company?.address?.state?.name
```

rather than this:

```
user.company?.address.state.name
```

Once you use `?.` in a chain, you should use it in the rest of the chain too.

?: (ELVIS!)

Both Java and Groovy have what is known as the *ternary operator*, which is a concise form of the `if...then...else` structure:

```
<condition> ? <expr1> : <expr2>
```

So, if the condition is `true`, `expr1` is evaluated; otherwise you get `expr2`.

Here is an example of a common idiom using this operator:

```
String name = (person.getName() != null) ? person.getName() : "<unknown>"
```

In words, if the person's name is set, we use that. Otherwise we use a default value.

This is so commonly used (and verbose) that Groovy introduces a shorthand form:

```
String name = person.getName() ?: "<unknown>"
```

This is the Elvis operator, and it returns the value of the left expression if it evaluates to `true` (according to Groovy Truth), but the value of the right expression otherwise.

Why "Elvis"? Rotate the operator 90° clockwise and you'll see!

*. (THE SPREAD-DOT OPERATOR)

No operator is better disguised by its name than "spread-dot." What does it do? Surprisingly, something useful: it calls a method on every item in a collection, and it creates a new list containing the results of those methods.

For example, imagine you have a list of objects that all have a `getName()` method; the following code will create a new list containing the names of the original items:

```
List names = people*.getName()
```

The resulting list has the same order as the original, so in the preceding example the names will be in the same order as the people. The operator can also be used on other types of collections, but the result is always a list and its items are always in the iteration order of the original collection.

We could also use property notation, which is described in a later section:

```
List names = people*.name
```

This is probably the most common use of the operator you'll see in both examples and real code.

<=> (COMPARISONS WITH A SPACESHIP)

Java has plenty of operators for comparing two values, so why should we want another one? If you have ever implemented the `Comparable.compareTo()` or `Comparator.compare()` methods, you'll know why.

Here is a naive implementation of a comparator for integers:

```
public int compare(int i1, int i2) {
    if (i1 == i2) return 0;
    else if (i1 < i2) return -1;
    else return 1;
}
```

You can reduce this to a one-liner for numbers, but it's not so easy for other types. So what would the method look like if we had an operator with identical behavior to the `compare()` method? Let's see:

```
public int compare(int i1, int i2) {
    return i1 <=> i2;
}
```

That's the Groovy "spaceship" operator, which can be used on any types that implement `Comparable`. It's particularly useful for custom comparators and, in combination with some other features of Groovy that we'll see later, for sorting lists. It returns a negative number if the left side is less than the right side, zero if the operands are equal, and a positive number otherwise. There are no guarantees as to the absolute value of nonzero results—only the sign is significant.

== (EQUALS())

When you use == in Groovy, the generated code uses the `equals()` method. It's also null-safe, which means that it will work if either or both of the operands are `null`.

The following example demonstrates the behavior using assertions and strings:

```
String str = null
assert str == null
assert str != "test"

str = "test"
assert str != null
assert str == "test"

str += " string"
assert str == "test string"
```

This example doesn't tell the whole story, and there is an exception to this rule: if the object on the left side implements `java.lang.Comparable`, then == uses the `compareTo()` method rather than `equals()`. In this case, the result is `true` if the `compareTo()` method returns 0, or `false` otherwise.

In case you're wondering why Groovy does this, remember that 0.3 and 0.30 are *not* equivalent according to the `BigDecimal.equals()` method, whereas they are with the `compareTo()` method. Again, the principle of least surprise suggests that the expression `0.3 == 0.30` should evaluate to `true`, which is exactly what happens in Groovy.

Lastly, how do you get the Java behavior for ==? Use the `is()` method:

```
BigDecimal x = 0.234
BigDecimal y = x

assert y.is(x)
assert !y.is(0.234)
assert y == 0.234
```

As you can see, it will only return `true` if two objects are the same instance.

Although these operators may be unfamiliar now, it won't be long before you're confidently using them in your own code. So with that gentle introduction out of the way, it's time to look at the Groovy type system.

2.2   *Exploring types*

As with most things in Groovy, if you start from the assumption that its type system is the same as Java's, you won't go far wrong. Nonetheless, there are some key differences between the two languages when it comes to types and their handling, which you need to know to unlock the full potential of the language.

2.2.1 *Looking at basic types*

All the types you expect from Java are there in both primitive and object form: `boolean`, `int`, `double`, `String`, and so on. This makes both the transition to the language and integration with Java relatively easy. But the type systems aren't identical. Take primitive types: even if you declare a variable as a primitive, you can still treat it as an object by calling methods on it. This is most obvious in the handling of numbers.

NUMBERS

Not only can primitive variables be treated as objects, but this behavior also extends to numeric literals. So `1` is an instance of `Integer` and `546L` is an instance of `Long`. Here is how you can call a method on an integer literal:

```
assert (-12345).abs() == 12345
```

A subtle but notable feature in Groovy is that floating-point arithmetic is based on `BigDecimal` rather than `double` or `float`. At first this may seem strange, but Groovy aims for the principle of least surprise, and one of the most surprising things in Java is that `0.1D * 3` is `0.300...04` rather than `0.3` exactly. Because Groovy isn't targeted at high-performance floating-point calculations, it prefers to use `BigDecimal` so that `0.1 * 3` is `0.3`.

You may be worried about having to use the `BigDecimal` API, but fear not! Groovy helpfully makes the normal arithmetic operators work transparently with the class. Here's a quick example:

```
assert 0.25 instanceof BigDecimal
assert 0.1 * 3 == 0.3
assert 1.1 + 0.1 == 1.2
assert 1 / 0.25 == 4
```

Anyone who has tried to perform `BigDecimal` division in Java will truly appreciate the simplicity in Groovy.

GROOVY STRINGS

You have seen that Java string literals also work in Groovy, but there are some significant differences.

To begin with, Groovy has no character literal like Java. Single quotes (`' '`) delimit string, not character, literals. So what is the difference between single quotes and double quotes? The latter allow you to embed Groovy expressions in the string. This means that rather than manually concatenating strings as in Java, you can use code like this:

```
String name = "Ben"
String greeting = "Good morning, ${name}"
assert greeting == 'Good morning, Ben'

String output = "The result of 2 + 2 is: ${2 + 2}"
assert output == "The result of 2 + 2 is: 4"
```

Anything inside the `${}` will be evaluated, converted to a string via the `toString()` method, and inserted into that position. If your string contains dollar symbols, you can either use the single-quote form or escape them using a backslash (`"\$"`). This type of string is known as a GString.

Both forms of string literal have corresponding *multiline* versions. These allow you to easily create string literals that include line breaks. If you have ever tried to build these strings in Java, you'll understand how big a deal this is. Take, for example, a simple method that returns the body of an email given a person's name. In Groovy, the code would be as follows:

```
String getEmailBody(String name) {
    return """Dear ${name},

Thank you for your recent inquiry. One of our team members
will process it shortly and get back to you. Some time in
the next decade. Probably.

Warmest and best regards,

Customer Services
"""
}
```

See how we have embedded the `name` variable inside the string? Simple and elegant. One word of warning, though: any whitespace that appears between the triple quotes will be included in the string. Make sure that each line starts in column one of the file unless you *want* the text indented in the resulting string.

You can also use the slash (`/`) character to delimit string literals, although this approach doesn't have a multiline version. You may find this option a bit strange, but you'll see later that it comes into its own with regular expressions.

That's it for string literals, but you must be asking yourself how you can declare a `char` literal. There are two options: either assign a single-character string to a `char` variable, or use the `as` keyword. Here are examples of both:

```
char ch = 'D'
assert ch instanceof Character

String str = "Good morning Ben"
str = str.replace(' ' as char, '+' as char)
assert str == "Good+morning+Ben"
```

Although we use single quotes for our character literals in the preceding example, you can use double quotes. It comes down to user preference, but there is an advantage to our method—the preceding example is almost valid Java. Remove the two `as char` elements and you have pure Java code! The other advantage of using single quotes for character literals and double quotes for string literals is that plain Java developers will be more comfortable with the code—a benefit not to be sneezed at.

Speaking of Java developers, that `as` keyword will be new to them. What does it do?

YOUR FLEXIBLE FRIEND: AS

In Java, you can cast an object to a type as long as the object is actually an instance of that type. Groovy supports the Java cast, but as you'll find out, it's redundant in a dynamically typed language. Something that *would* be useful is a means of easily converting between types.

Imagine you have the string "12345". It looks like a number, but as far as Java and Groovy are concerned, it's a string. To convert it to a number in Java, you have to use Integer.parseInt() or a similar method. That's all well and good, but what if you want to convert an array to a list? For that you can use Arrays.asList(). You can similarly perform other conversions in Java, but you have to find the appropriate method—something that's not always trivial.

Like a knight in shining armor, Groovy comes to the rescue with its as operator. This allows you to perform conversions like string to number or array to list using a consistent syntax. As an added bonus, your code will tend to be easier to read because as is implemented as an operator. Here are some examples of its syntax:

```
assert 543667 as String == "543667"

assert 1234.compareTo("34749397" as int) < 0
```

Groovy supports several conversions by default, a subset of which are listed in table 2.2. You may not understand all of them at this stage, but we'll come across many of them later in the book.

You can also add custom conversions to a class by implementing the asType(Class) method. This is how Grails adds its own conversions, such as those involving the XML and JSON converters described in chapter 11 on REST.

That's pretty much it, as far as the basic types go. Hopefully you'll find GStrings and type coercion as useful as we do. Certainly they're more elegant alternatives to string concatenation and casting. Yet these improvements are minor compared to Groovy's collection and map support.

Table 2.2 Conversions supported by as

Source type	Target type	Description
String	Number (int, double, Long, BigDecimal, and so on)	Parses a string as if it were a number
List	Array	Converts a list to an array; for example, myList as String[] (Groovy doesn't support Java's array literals)
List or array	Set	Converts a List or array to a Set
Anything	boolean	Uses Groovy Truth to convert a value to either true or false
Collection	List	Creates a list that's a copy of the original collection; the items in the list are in the iteration order of the original collection
String	List	Treats a string as a sequence of characters and turns it into a list

2.2.2 *Syntax sugar for lists, maps, and ranges*

Lists, maps, and ranges are so common that some other languages have them built into their type systems. Yet Java only has limited support for them—it's almost as if they were tacked on as an afterthought. Groovy goes some way toward rectifying this situation by effectively treating them as first class citizens at the language level.

LIST AND MAP LITERALS

If you have ever tried to build up a list or map of reference data in Java, you know how painful the experience is. You first have to create an instance of the collection, and then add each item explicitly. Groovy makes life much easier in this respect, with its list and map literals. A list literal is a comma-separated sequence of items between square brackets, and a map literal is the same, but each "item" is a key and value separated by a colon. Listing 2.1 compares the Groovy and Java syntaxes for creating lists and maps, while at the same time showing the list and map literals in action.

Listing 2.1   Initializing lists and maps in Groovy

```
List myList = new ArrayList()
myList.add("apple")
myList.add("orange")
myList.add("lemon")                  Creates lists and
                                     maps the Java way
Map myMap = new HashMap()
myMap.put(3, "three")
myMap.put(6, "six")
myMap.put(2, "two")

List myList = [ "apple", "orange", "lemon" ]     Creates lists and
Map myMap = [ 3: "three", 6: "six", 2: "two" ]   maps the Groovy way

List l = []        Creates empty list and map
Map m = [:]
```

These literals are instances of `java.util.List` and `java.util.Map`, so they have all the methods and properties you would expect. For example,

```
assert 3 == [ 5, 6, 7 ].size()
```

uses `List`'s standard `size()` method to determine the number of elements in the list literal.

ARRAY-STYLE NOTATION FOR LISTS AND MAPS

Java has a rather clunky syntax for accessing items in lists and maps because it relies on methods. Groovy improves the situation dramatically by extending Java's array notation to both lists and maps. This is best understood by example—listing 2.2 demonstrates getting and setting values with both types.

Listing 2.2   Accessing list and map elements

```
List numbers = [ 5, 10, 15, 20, 25 ]
assert numbers[0] == 5       Gets item from list
assert numbers[3] == 20
```

```
assert numbers[-1] == 25        ① Indexes from
assert numbers[-3] == 15           end of list

numbers[2] = 3                  ← Replaces item in list
assert numbers[2] == 3

numbers << 30                   ←② Adds item to list
assert numbers[5] == 30

Map items = [ "one":   "apple",
              "two":   "orange",
              "three": "pear",
              "four":  "cherry" ]
assert items["two"] == "orange"    Gets item from map
assert items["four"] == "cherry"

items["one"] = "banana"         ← Replaces item in map
assert items["one"] == "banana"

items["five"] = "grape"         ← Adds item to map
assert items["five"] == "grape"
```

As you can see, Groovy makes using lists and maps pleasant and intuitive. Worthy of particular note is the ability to index lists (and arrays!) from the end rather than the beginning, as demonstrated by ① (a value of -1 refers to the last item). Listing 2.2 also shows the left-shift operator in action ②. This is the standard way of appending items to a list in Groovy (or anything else that implements `Collection`).

A NEW TYPE: RANGE

Somewhat related to lists is Groovy's *range* type. In fact, all range objects implement the `java.util.List` interface. A full account of the capabilities of this type is outside the scope of this book, but you'll need to recognize integer range literals and understand some of their uses. You can find out more on the Groovy website: http://groovy.codehaus.org/Collections.

In essence, a range is the combination of a lower and an upper bound, which in the case of an integer range represents all numbers between the two bounds. The lower bound is always inclusive, but you can specify ranges with either an inclusive or exclusive upper bound.

Listing 2.3 shows code that iterates over a list of strings, printing each item in the list to the console, and then printing a subset of the items.

Listing 2.3 Ranges

```
List fruit = [
   "apple",
   "pear",
   "lemon",
   "orange",
   "cherry" ]
                                          ① Iterates through an
for (int i in 0..<fruit.size()) {    ←      exclusive range
   println "Fruit number $i is '${fruit[i]}'"
}
                                     ② Extracts a list slice
List subList = fruit[1..3]    ←
```

```
for (int i in 0..<subList.size()) {
   println "Sub list item $i is '${subList[i]}'"
}
```

The listing demonstrates the two most common uses for ranges: as something to iterate over ❶, and as an argument to the array accessor ❷.

You may not be familiar with the `for` loop shown at ❶, but don't worry. The code is simply iterating over the integers from 0 to 4 inclusive (there are 5 items in the list), and assigning the current integer to the variable `i`. In this case, the exclusive upper bound notation is being used: `lower..<upper`. Also note that you can use variables and expressions as range bounds.

❷ shows how you can get a slice of a list, or in Java terms a sublist. Here we used the inclusive upper bound notation to extract items 2 through 4 from the list of fruit. Note that any changes to the original list will be reflected in the slice. If you were to change the third fruit from "lemon" to "lime", the second item of the slice would also be "lime".

If all that hasn't got you excited, then either you're coming from a language that already has rich support for collections and maps, or nothing will! Those of you coming from Java will wonder how you managed without these features.

And so we end our coverage of the type system. Next we'll look at some features that are difficult to pigeonhole.

2.3   Time-saving features

Before we move on to the most significant features of Groovy, let's take a look at some of the quiet helpers. We start with the seemingly innocuous semicolons at the end of statements.

2.3.1   Who needs semicolons?

One of the most obvious differences between Java and Groovy is that the latter doesn't require semicolons at the end of lines, or, to put it more accurately, at the end of statements. If you want to put more than one statement on a single line in Groovy, you must still separate them with semicolons, as in Java.

This flexibility comes at a cost. You must be careful how you break statements across multiple lines, because some code arrangements will cause compiler errors. Listing 2.4 shows some examples of invalid and valid line breaks.

Listing 2.4   Valid and invalid line breaks

```
private void invalidMethod          ◁— Invalid line break in method
      (String name) {
   String fruit = "orange, apple, pear, "      ◁┐ Invalid line break
      + "banana, cherry, nectarine"             │ in concatenation
}                                   ┌─ Valid line break
private int validMethod(       ◁─┘ in method
      String name) {                              ┐ Valid break in
   String furniture = "table, chair, sofa, bed, " +  ◁─┘ concatenation
```

```
        "cupboard, wardrobe, desk"
    String fruit = "orange, apple, pear, " \          ①  Valid line continuation
        + "banana, cherry, nectarine"
                                                    Valid multiple
    int i = 0; i++; return i;                       statements
}
```

You can get around these limitations by using a line continuation ① that effectively says "this line hasn't ended yet." You may be tempted to insert semicolons to achieve the same result, but that won't work. For multiline statements, Groovy parses the end of lines before it ever sees the relevant statement terminator, so it will still throw an error.

At this stage, you're probably wondering about the underlying rules that determine whether a given format is valid. If a single line is a valid statement, then Groovy treats it as such, and the next line should be the start of a new statement. Otherwise Groovy combines the first line with the following one and treats them as a single statement. In general, if you run into a compilation error because of this problem, use a line continuation.

AND WHO NEEDS PARENTHESES?

You'll soon notice that method calls don't seem to need parentheses. The classic example is the `println()` method provided by the Groovy JDK (which we'll get to in section 2.4.3):

```
println "Hello, world!"
```

Method calls that take a closure as a single argument (see section 2.4.1) also usually lack parentheses due to the improved readability. However, you *must* use parentheses for zero-argument method calls or if the first argument is a list or map literal:

```
println()
println([1, 2, 3, 4])
```

There are probably other instances where parentheses are required by Groovy, so we recommend that you use them in most cases, leaving them out only in a small set of common cases (such as `println()` and with closures). Doing this also makes your code easier for Java developers to read.

YOU DON'T NEED RETURN STATEMENTS EITHER?

It may seem strange, but the `return` statement is unnecessary in Groovy. If no `return` is present, a nonvoid method will return the result of the last expression evaluated.

For example, the following method returns the result of `value + 1`:

```
int addOne(int value) { value + 1 }
```

You may be wondering why this feature exists. Simple: conciseness. It's particularly useful when inlining closures, which you'll see later in section 2.4.1. But this doesn't prevent you from using `return` if you wish, and sometimes including it is more readable for Java-attuned eyes.

Optional elements like these need to be discussed, but they're hardly satisfying. You need something to really sink your teeth into, and we have just the thing.

2.3.2 *Native regular expressions*

Regular expression support was introduced into the core Java API with version 1.4. Groovy builds on this and provides support for regular expressions at the language level. It provides new literals, new operators for regular expression matching, and a nice syntax for extracting groups, all of which make working with regular expressions a more productive experience.

LITERALS

Let's start with the new form of string literal that uses slashes (/). Why do we need or even want another type of string literal?

Regular expressions use the backslash (\) as an escape character; for example, \b represents a word boundary. Unfortunately, Java's string literals also use the backslash as an escape character, so regular expressions in Java can quickly enter backslash hell. As an example, take this regular expression that matches a backslash followed by any word character: "\\\\\\w".

The slash-based strings introduced by Groovy are a solution to this problem. They don't use the backslash as an escape character (except when you need a literal slash), making regular expressions much easier to write. With / as a delimiter, the previous expression becomes /\\\w/. We have halved the number of backslashes!

You should also be aware that these string literals are GStrings, so you can embed Groovy expressions. For example, /${name}: \w+/.

If you prefer to deal explicitly with java.util.regex.Pattern instances, you can create them by prefixing any string literal with a ~:

```
assert ~"London" instanceof java.util.regex.Pattern
assert ~/\w+/ instanceof java.util.regex.Pattern
```

This technique is useful if you want to reuse a pattern, but it's not common.

MATCHING

Literal patterns aren't the only language-level support Groovy provides for regular expressions. It also introduces two new operators for matching that should be familiar to Perl and Ruby developers.

The first of these is =~, which matches if the pattern on the right side can be found in the string on the left side. For example,

```
assert "Speaking plain English" =~ /plain/
```

will pass because the string we're testing contains "plain". On the other hand, we get different behavior with the ==~ operator:

```
assert !("Speaking plain English" ==~ /plain/)
```

This is because the test string doesn't match the pattern *exactly*—only part of the test string matches, not the whole of it. Adding a couple of wildcards to the pattern results in an exact match:

```
assert "Speaking plain English" ==~ /.*plain.*/
```

Behind the scenes, there is a more fundamental difference between the two operators. The =~ operator returns an instance of `java.util.regex.Matcher`, whereas ==~ returns a Boolean.

So why can we use =~ directly in an assertion? Because Groovy automatically coerces `Matcher` to a Boolean when required. Under the hood, Groovy calls `find()` on the matcher and returns the result.

GROUPS

Some regular expressions include capturing groups and you can access them via array notation.

The example in listing 2.5 extracts all words that contain "ain", printing out the prefix and suffix of each match. When run, you'll see this printed to the console:

```
Found: 'rain' – prefix: 'r', suffix: ''
Found: 'Spain' – prefix: 'Sp', suffix: ''
Found: 'mainly' – prefix: 'm', suffix: 'ly'
Found: 'plain' – prefix: 'pl', suffix: ''
```

Listing 2.5 Regular expression capture groups

```
import java.util.regex.Matcher

String str = "The rain in Spain falls mainly on the plain"
Matcher m = str =~ /\b(\w*)ain(\w*)\b/          ◁──  Matches with two
                                                      capture groups
if (m) {
    for (int i in 0..<m.count) {
        println "Found: '${m[i][0]}' – " +     ❶  Access whole match
            "prefix: '${m[i][1]}'" +                and sub-groups
            ", suffix: '${m[i][2]}'"
    }
}
```

You can see how the slash-literals, match operator, and groups come together to make using regular expressions far more concise than in Java. The only tricky part is understanding the array notation ❶.

In listing 2.5, the test string has four bits that match the pattern: "rain", "Spain", "mainly", and "plain". The first array index allows us to pick one of these, so an index value of 1 refers to the match "Spain". The second index allows us to access specific groups within that match. An index value of 0 refers to the whole of the match (for example, "Spain"), but index values of 1 and upwards refer to the groups. So in our example, a second index value of 1 gets us the prefix, whereas 2 refers to the suffix ❶.

That's it for the regular expression support. We recommend that you take full advantage of it in your own code if you can, but remember that you can always fall back to using the Java classes and methods if you aren't comfortable with the Groovy feature.

We only have one more minor feature left to discuss, but it's an important one because almost all Groovy code uses it. OK, maybe that's an exaggeration, but not much of one.

2.3.3   *Property notation*

The JavaBeans specification introduced the concept of an *object property* but left us with an unwieldy syntax: getter and setter methods. Groovy rectifies this problem by letting us use field access notation for JavaBeans properties.

Take the `java.util.Date` class. It has the methods `long getTime()` and `void setTime(long milliseconds)`, which conform to the JavaBeans specification and represent a `long` property named `time`. In Groovy you can access this property as if it were a field:

```
Date now = new Date()
println "Current time in milliseconds: ${ now.time }"

now.time = 103467843L
assert now.time == 103467843L
```

Once you start using this syntax, you won't look back. It's far more natural than calling the methods, requires less typing, and is more readable. What more can we say?

Using properties is all well and good, but you still have to define those getter and setter methods, don't you?

DEFINING PROPERTIES

Writing getter and setter methods is so laborious that IDEs will autogenerate the code for you. Even so, your class still ends up polluted with boilerplate methods that don't contain any real logic. Thankfully, Groovy provides a shortcut.

If you declare a field without any scope, Groovy will automatically make the field private and generate the getter and setter methods behind the scenes. You can even override those methods if you wish. All of the fields in the following example are properties, except for the last one:

```
class MyProperties {
    static String classVar

    final String constant = "constant"
    String name

    public String publicField
    private String privateField
}
```

That's it—nothing could be easier. Note that for Boolean properties, Groovy will even generate an `is...()` method. And for non-Java programmers, the `final` qualifier means that the variable can't be modified once it has been initialized (which can be done in a constructor or as part of the declaration, as in the example).

All that's left now is a trick for instantiating and initializing beans.

INSTANTIATING BEANS

When you define a bean, it must have a default constructor, and Groovy uses that requirement to provide a shortcut for initializing instances of such classes. All you need is to provide a list of *named arguments* matching the properties you wish to set.

This example creates a new instance of `java.text.SimpleDateFormat` using this approach:

```
DateFormat format = new SimpleDateFormat(
    lenient: false,
    numberFormat: NumberFormat.getIntegerInstance(),
    timeZone: TimeZone.getTimeZone("EST"))
```

The named arguments look like a map without the square brackets, in which the key is the name of a property on the class. In fact, behind the scenes, Groovy uses an instance of LinkedHashMap. You can even pass your own map instance to the constructor. This is a common idiom when creating domain classes from web request parameters, as you'll see later in chapter 5.

Speaking of maps, Groovy allows you to get and set map entries using property notation. Here's an example:

```
Map values = [ fred: 1, peter: 5, glen: 42 ]
assert values.fred == 1
values.peter = 10
assert values.peter == 10
```

This syntax is widespread, and it's particularly useful when combined with duck typing, which you'll see in the next section. You can effectively treat maps as objects!

NOTE Groovy treats map keys as strings unless they are numeric or inside parentheses. In the previous example, fred is the string "fred", not a variable. The quotes are optional unless the key contains a space, a dash, or some other character that is invalid in Groovy identifiers. If fred were a variable and you wished to use its value as the map key, you would put it in parentheses: [(fred): 1].

So, you've now heard a lot about what features Groovy provides over and above Java, but what about the other way round?

2.3.4 *Anything in Java that's not in Groovy?*

As we have already stated, most Java code is also valid Groovy. A few constructs are missing though, so it's important to be aware of them.

CHARACTER LITERALS

We showed in the previous section that single quotes are used as string delimiters, so Groovy has no character literal. But you can coerce single character strings to chars using the as keyword.

JAVA "FOR" LOOP

Groovy has limited support for the standard Java for loop in that you can't use the comma (,) operator. This works:

```
for (int i = 0; i < 10; i++) { ... }
```

But this doesn't:

```
for (int i = 0, j = 0; i < 10; i++, j++) { ... }
```

DO...WHILE

There is no do...while loop, but we doubt that anyone will mourn its passing. We have rarely, if ever, seen it in the wild, and you can always use while and for loops to get the same effect.

INNER AND ANONYMOUS CLASSES

You can't declare inner or anonymous classes. Support for these is coming, but, on the whole, both closures and the ability to declare more than one class in a Groovy file mean that this is only a real issue with libraries and frameworks that heavily depend on them.

2.4   *Expert Groovy*

You should now be fairly confident in your ability to understand and write Groovy code. So far, most differences between Groovy and Java have fallen under the heading of "syntactic sugar." We now move on to two important concepts that separate Groovy from Java on a more fundamental level: closures and Groovy's dynamic nature.

2.4.1   *Discovering closures*

You're probably familiar with the sort() method in java.util.Collections for sorting a list using a given comparator. This simple fragment of Java code will sort a list of strings, ignoring case, and print them to the console:

```
List<String> fruit = Arrays.asList(
    "apple", "Orange", "Avocado",
    "pear", "cherry");

Collections.sort(fruit, new Comparator<String>() {
    public int compare(String str1, String str2) {
        return str1.compareToIgnoreCase(str2);
    }
});

System.out.println("Sorted fruit: " + fruit);
```

The result is this output:

```
Sorted fruit: apple, Avocado, cherry, Orange, pear
```

Notice how the comparator is a single method implementation? All we want to do is pass a two-argument function to the sort() method, but this isn't possible in Java, so you need an interface to host the function and an object to implement it. Fortunately for us, the JDK provides the java.util.Comparator interface and anonymous classes. But what if you wrote an algorithm that traverses a tree and performs a function on each leaf node? You'd have to write an interface to host the function and pass an object that implements that interface to the algorithm.

This seems like more work than it should be, and even anonymous classes leave one aching for a more elegant alternative. As usual, Groovy offers a solution: closures. You can think of these as anonymous functions that can be assigned to variables, passed to methods, or even returned from methods. Or, you can think of them as single-method anonymous classes.

The syntax can be difficult at first, so we'll introduce it by example. This code does the same thing as the Java code you just saw, but it uses a `sort()` method that compares items using a closure:

```
List fruit = [ "apple", "Orange", "Avocado", "pear", "cherry" ]

fruit.sort { String a, String b -> a.compareToIgnoreCase(b) }

println "Sorted fruit: ${fruit}"
```

You may be wondering where this strange `sort()` method comes from—don't worry, Groovy adds it to `List` implementations via the Groovy JDK, which we introduce shortly, in section 2.4.3.

In this example, we have not only declared a closure but also passed it as an argument to the `sort()` method. See how the closure looks like a method body without a name? The major difference is that the arguments are declared *within* the curly braces.

Before we move on, we should point out two things in the preceding example. The first is that the `sort()` method is called without parentheses. This is common when a method only has a single argument and that argument is a closure. The second point is that the closure uses an implicit return value to help keep the code compact.

The standard syntax for a closure is

```
{ <arguments> -> <body> }
```

where <arguments> is the list of typed or untyped parameters to the closure, and <body> is the equivalent of a regular method body. A zero-argument closure can be expressed with no argument declarations before the arrow: `{-> ... }`. There is also a special case that you need to be aware of, which is demonstrated by this example:

```
[ "apple", "pear", "cherry" ].each { println it }
```

When a closure definition has no `->`, it's created with a single implicit argument that you can access via the special variable `it`. So in the preceding example, `each()` calls the closure for each item in the list, passing the current item in as an argument. Therefore, `it` contains the current list item (the name of a fruit), and the code prints out each item in the list to the console.

You have seen closures declared at the point of use—as method arguments—but we also mentioned that you could assign them to variables and pass them around, sort of like a function pointer. Listing 2.6 modifies the previous Groovy sorting example so that you can see how a reference to a closure can be used.

Listing 2.6 Closure assigned to a variable

```
Closure comparator = { String a, String b ->          ◁─┐  Assigns closure
    a.compareToIgnoreCase(b)                             │  to variable
}

List fruit = [ "apple", "Orange", "Avocado", "pear", "cherry" ]

fruit.sort(comparator)                    ◁─┐
                                            │  Uses closure reference
println "Sorted fruit: ${fruit}"          ❶  as argument

assert comparator("banana", "Lemon") < 0     ◁─❷  Calls closure directly
```

Passing a closure to a method via a reference looks just like a regular method call ❶. We have also included an example of how you can call a closure directly, as if it were a method ❷. This notation isn't particularly surprising when you consider that closures are effectively anonymous functions. When you assign a closure to a variable, you bind it to a name, so it effectively becomes a named function.

What's in a name?

The term *closure* has a specific meaning in computer science, and there have been various arguments in the past over whether Groovy's closures should be named as such. The key point is that they aren't simply blocks of code; they capture references to variables and methods *outside* of the closure definition. Try this simple example in the console:

```
def n = 14
def msg = "'n' is ${->n}"
println msg
n = 10
println msg
```

The second `println` will display the message with a value of 10 for n, because the closure embedded in the string captures the variable reference, not just its value. Anonymous classes can do something similar, but they can only access variables that are declared `final`.

We have now covered enough ground that you'll be able to follow the many examples in this book where closures are used. But to become truly comfortable with them in the context of Grails, you need to know a few more things.

First, single-argument closures are unique: they can be called with or without an argument; for example, `myClosure(1)` or `myClosure()`. In the latter case, the closure is passed a value of `null`.

Second, there is a simple restriction on the special syntax used in the early examples of this section. Take the following example, which sums the items in a list. Don't worry, you don't have to understand how it works—we're only interested in the syntax at the moment.

```
List list = [ 1, 3, 5, 6 ]
assert 15 == list.inject(0) { runningTotal, value -> runningTotal + value }
```

The closure is declared *after* the method's closing parenthesis, and yet it is passed to the `inject()` method as the second argument. This is one of those syntactic tricks that Groovy provides to make code easier to read. That method call could equally be written like this,

```
list.inject(0, { runningTotal, value -> runningTotal + value })
```

but this form doesn't work well with larger, multiline closures. So what is the restriction we mentioned? You can only use the former syntax if the closure is the last argument to the method, whereas the latter form will work irrespective of the argument position.

The final point is possibly the most important: closures aren't methods! The way in which they're used means that they often look like methods, but they're still objects, whereas proper methods in Groovy compile to regular Java methods. In many cases, the distinction is unimportant, but you should understand that the standard rules for overriding methods don't apply. For example, if you're extending a class like this,

```
Class SuperClass {
   Closure action = {
      ...
   }
}
```

we recommend that you don't declare an `action` property in your subclass. If you want polymorphic behavior, use methods. Inheritance isn't the only area where using closures can cause problems. You may not be aware of or familiar with aspect-oriented programming (AOP), but it has been growing in popularity in the last few years. Many AOP libraries and tools work with methods, so if you start using closures everywhere, you'll lose easy AOP integration.

Hopefully you'll take these as words of caution rather than as a reason never to use closures. They're powerful and will make it easier to formulate solutions to certain problems. But as with any new toy, there is a danger of using them to the exclusion of other techniques.

2.4.2 *Programming dynamically*

Dynamic languages sound exciting, don't they? It's built into their name: "dynamic." But what do we mean by that term?

Throughout this chapter, we have assumed that you already know Java. In Java, all variables, properties, method arguments, and method returns must have declared types. This allows the compiler to perform type-checking, eliminating a potential source of bugs before the application is ever run.

Now imagine that we have a `Person` class with the properties `givenName`, `family-Name`, `age`, and `country`. In Java, we can easily sort a list of `Person` objects by one of these properties, like so:

```
public void sortPeopleByGivenName(List<Person> personList) {
   Collections.sort(personList, new Comparator<Person>() {
      public int compare(Person p1, Person p2) {
         return p1.getFamilyName().compareTo(p2.getFamilyName());
      }
   });
}
```

But what if you don't know which property to sort on until runtime? This might happen if a user can select which property to sort by in a user interface. Life suddenly becomes much trickier in Java. You either write a sort method like the preceding one for each of the properties and link them to the user interface somehow, or you use reflection in the comparator. The first option means duplication of the comparator code, which is both tedious and error prone. The second option would involve some pretty nasty code, so we'll save you the pain of looking at it.

Instead, let's look at how we would do it in Groovy using untyped variables and *dynamic dispatch*. As required, this method sorts a list of people by a given property:

```
def sortPeople(people, property) {
   people.sort { p1, p2 -> p1."${property}" <=> p2."${property}" }
}
```

We've thrown you into the deep end with this example, but trust us—you'll be swimming in no time! Let's break the example down into bits, starting with the method signature. It looks like any other method signature, apart from the `def` keyword and the lack of types on the method arguments. The `def` keyword defines both untyped variables and methods, which means a variable declared using `def` can be assigned any value. You can even assign it a string on one line and then an integer on the next. When used on methods, it means that the method can return any type of value or be void. Effectively, `def` is like using `java.lang.Object`.

Untyped method and closure arguments don't even need the `def` keyword. Leave out the type and they will be treated as untyped variables. Although Groovy is almost (if not quite) unique in dynamic languages by supporting declared types, most developers tend to quickly move to using untyped variables, arguments, and methods because the code is more concise and easier on the eye.

In the closure passed to the `sort()` method, you'll see some strange notation involving a `GString`. The first thing to understand is that Groovy will accept strings as property and method names. To see what we mean, here is an example in which the two lines do exactly the same thing:

```
peopleList.sort()
peopleList."sort"()
```

The string notation can be particularly useful with Groovy builders, such as the XML markup builder we introduce in section 2.4.4, but in this case it's the ability to specify a property or method at runtime that's important. So if the `property` argument contains the string age, the closure body in our example `sortPeople()` method becomes

```
p1."age" <=> p2."age"
```

so the method sorts on the age property. The exact same code can be used to sort on any of `Person`'s properties. In fact, you'll notice that the method has no dependency at all on `Person`, which means that the method can sort any list of objects so long as they have the given property!

You have just seen how powerful a combination of untyped variables and dynamic dispatch can be. This pattern has a name.

DUCK TYPING

No discussion of a dynamic language is complete without a mention of *duck typing*. The term comes from the saying, "if it walks like a duck and talks like a duck, it's probably a duck." Applied to dynamic languages, it means that if an object has a particular property or method signature, then it doesn't matter what type the object is, you can still call that method or access that property.

This is only possible in dynamic languages because properties and methods are resolved at *runtime*. This behavior also allows you to add methods and properties to classes without modifying the class itself. This is how Groovy itself extends some of the JDK classes—see section 2.4.3 on the Groovy JDK to see some of the extra methods and properties it provides.

So, whenever you see references to methods or properties that have no declaration, chances are that Grails has injected them into the class. Don't worry, we'll mention when this happens in our examples, and now you know where they'll be coming from!

THE DANGERS

> *Remember, with great power comes great responsibility.*

> —Uncle Ben,
> *Spiderman*, 2002

Using Groovy for the first time can often feel like a straitjacket has been removed. It gives you great freedom in your coding and makes it easier to express your ideas and designs in code. But with this power come pitfalls that you need to be aware of.

First, the compiler can't pick up type violations or missing properties and methods, because these are all resolved at runtime. You're likely to become quite familiar with MissingPropertyException and its relative MissingMethodException early on in your Groovy experience. You'll be surprised how rarely they appear later on, but you should get into the habit of writing tests for your code at an early stage, and we cover this in chapter 7.

Second, Groovy applications are more difficult to debug, particularly with dynamically injected properties and methods. Using the "step into" feature of a debugger is likely to cause plenty of pain. Instead, make judicious use of breakpoints and the "run to cursor" feature.

Finally, overusing dynamic injection and even untyped variables can make it difficult to understand code. In both cases, it's important to use descriptive names, and in the case of dynamic injection, you should document what methods and properties you are adding and what they do. Also consider using declared types for method and closure arguments: not only will people find it easier to use those methods, but IDEs can highlight potential type errors in the calling code.

Used judiciously, dynamically injected properties and methods can improve your productivity by enhancing classes in a non-invasive way. Probably the best example of this is the Groovy JDK, which is a set of enhancements to the core JDK classes.

2.4.3 *The Groovy JDK*

Have you ever bemoaned the lack of a method in the JDK or wondered why you have to use helper classes like java.util.Collections? Groovy tries to fill in any gaps it sees in the JDK and make code more uniformly object oriented than Java through the Groovy JDK, a set of enhancements to some of the more commonly used JDK classes.

We can't cover all the extra properties and methods because there are too many, but we'll look at some of the more useful ones. For a full rundown, see the Groovy JDK reference online: http://groovy.codehaus.org/groovy-jdk/.

Probably the most useful additions relate to collections. Most of these also apply to arrays and strings, the latter of which are generally treated as lists of characters. There are also some nice enhancements to `java.io.File`. We round off with some miscellaneous improvements.

COLLECTION/ARRAY/STRING.SIZE()

In the interest of consistency, Groovy provides the `size()` method for both arrays and strings. Its behavior matches the `length` property for arrays, and the `length()` method on `String`. No longer do you have to remember which property or method to use for a particular type!

COLLECTION/ARRAY/STRING.EACH(CLOSURE)

You've already seen the `each()` method in action in some of the examples earlier in the chapter. It iterates over all elements of a collection, applying the given closure to each one in turn. Remember, a string is treated as a sequence of characters, so this code,

```
"Test".each { println it }
```

will print this to the console:

```
T
e
s
t
```

COLLECTION/ARRAY/STRING.FIND(CLOSURE)

Once you begin to use `find()` (and its sibling, `findAll()`), you'll wonder how you ever managed to live without it. It does exactly what it says on the tin: finds an element within a sequence. More specifically, it returns the first element for which the given closure returns `true`. If there is no such element, the method returns `null`. The closure effectively acts as the criteria.

In this example, we retrieve the first object in a list for which the `firstName` property is "Glen":

```
def glen = personList.find { it.firstName == "Glen" }
```

Whereas `find()` returns the first element that matches the criteria, `findAll()` will return all matching elements as a list. If there are no matching elements, it will return an empty list rather than `null`.

COLLECTION/ARRAY/STRING.COLLECT(CLOSURE)

`collect()` is one of those methods that takes some getting used to but becomes invaluable once you do. In some other languages, it's called the "map" function, and it iterates through the collection, applying the given closure to each element and adding the return value to a new list.

For example, say we have a list of strings and we want the lengths of those strings as a list. We can do that like so:

```
def names = [ "Glen", "Peter", "Alice", "Graham", "Fiona" ]
assert [ 4, 5, 5, 6, 5 ] == names.collect { it.size() }
```

Note that the new list has the same size and order as the original.

COLLECTION/ARRAY.SORT(CLOSURE)

The `sort()` method sorts a collection using the given closure as a comparator. The closure can either take a single argument, in which case it should return a value that's itself comparable, such as a string, or it can take two arguments (like the `compareTo()` method) and return an integer representing the relative order of the two values.

To demonstrate what this means in practice, we'll sort a list of names based on their lengths using both approaches. First, here's a single-argument closure:

```
def names = [ "Glen", "Peter", "Ann", "Graham", "Veronica" ]
def sortedNames = names.sort { it.size() }
assert [ "Ann", "Glen", "Peter", "Graham", "Veronica" ] == sortedNames
```

Next we use a two-argument closure:

```
def names = [ "Glen", "Peter", "Ann", "Graham", "Veronica" ]
def sortedNames = names.sort { name1, name2 ->
    name1.size() <=> name2.size()
}

assert [ "Ann", "Glen", "Peter", "Graham", "Veronica" ] == sortedNames
```

The effect is the same in both cases, so the first form is preferable. More complicated comparisons may require the second form.

COLLECTION/ARRAY.JOIN(STRING)

The `join()` method creates a string by concatenating the elements of the collection together in order, using the given string as a separator. If the elements aren't strings themselves, `toString()` is called before performing the concatenation.

One of the most common uses for this method is to convert a real list of strings to a comma-separated "list" like so:

```
def names = [ "Glen", "Peter", "Alice", "Fiona" ]
assert "Glen, Peter, Alice, Fiona" == names.join(", ")
```

The effect can be reversed by using the standard `String.split(String)` method of the JDK.

FILE.TEXT

The `text` property reads the given file and returns its content as a string.

FILE.SIZE()

`File.size()` returns the size of the file in bytes. It corresponds to the `File.length()` method.

FILE.WITHWRITER(CLOSURE)

There are various `with...()` methods for streams and files, but we'll only cover this one here. See the Groovy JDK reference for the others.

The `File.withWriter()` method conveniently creates a `java.io.Writer` from the file and passes it to the closure. Once the closure executes, the underlying output stream is closed automatically and safely (it doesn't throw any exceptions). No more try...catch blocks just to write to a file!

MATCHER.COUNT

The count property returns the number of matches found by the given Matcher. This is unrelated to the number of groups in the corresponding pattern.

NUMBER.ABS()

Finally! You can now call the abs() method directly on numbers.

NUMBER.TIMES(CLOSURE)

The times() method calls the given closure *n* number of times, where *n* is the number the method is called on. Note that this only makes sense with integers. The closure is passed the current iteration number, which starts from 0.

We have only shown a fraction of the available properties and methods in the Groovy JDK, but these are some of the most common, and they're used extensively throughout this book. As you become more experienced with Groovy, you should get into the habit of checking the Groovy JDK for any other useful properties or methods on the classes you're working with. You never know what gems might be hidden in there!

There are two more features we'd like to introduce before wrapping up this chapter. They pop up all over the place in Grails, so it's important to understand what they do and how they work. They also happen to make XML fun to work with!

2.4.4   *Creating and parsing XML the easy way*

The Java universe is full of XML: libraries for generating it, libraries for parsing it, and XML configuration files everywhere! Because Grails lives in that universe, it's great news that Groovy makes both creating and parsing XML simple. Its support comes in the shape of a "markup builder" for generating XML and an "XML slurper" for parsing it.

Listing 2.7 demonstrates both features in a single example. It first writes this XML to a file using the markup builder:

```
<root>
  <item qty="10">
    <name>Orange</name>
    <type>Fruit</type>
  </item>
  <item qty="6">
    <name>Apple</name>
    <type>Fruit</type>
  </item>
  <item qty="2">
    <name>Chair</name>
    <type>Furniture</type>
  </item>
</root>
```

Then it parses that file using the slurper. Finally, it extracts different pieces of information from the XML and prints them to the console.

Listing 2.7 Playing with XML the Groovy way

```groovy
import groovy.xml.MarkupBuilder
import groovy.util.XmlSlurper

def file = new File("test.xml")
def objs = [
   [ quantity: 10, name: "Orange", type: "Fruit" ],
   [ quantity: 6, name: "Apple", type: "Fruit" ],
   [ quantity: 2, name: "Chair", type: "Furniture" ] ]
def b = new MarkupBuilder(new FileWriter(file))      ⟵  Starts the XML
b.root {                                                 document
   objs.each { o ->
      item(qty: o.quantity) {
         name(o.name)         ❶ Generates XML
         type(o.type)            elements
      }
   }
}

def xml = new XmlSlurper().parse(file)
assert xml.item.size() == 3
assert xml.item[0].name == "Orange"         ❷ Navigates
assert xml.item[0].@qty == "10"                in-memory XML
println "Fruits: ${xml.item.findAll {it.type == 'Fruit'}*.name }"
println "Total: ${xml.item.@qty.list().sum {it.toInteger()} }"
```

Have you ever seen so little code for generating XML and extracting information from it? Let's start with the code that creates the XML. All we're doing is creating a new instance of MarkupBuilder and calling a method on it (root()). The builder doesn't have a method called "root" itself, so rather than throw an exception, it treats the method as the start of a new XML element. As you can guess, the name of the XML element comes from the name of the method.

A story of two markup builders

Interestingly, MarkupBuilder isn't the only builder you can use to create XML. Groovy also comes with StreamingMarkupBuilder. This is superficially similar to the builder we have been using, but its internals are different.

From the user's perspective, the streaming builder has more features but it does no indenting at all (the XML is created as a single line). Check out the online Groovy documentation for more info.

Nested elements are then implemented via closures ❶, where the closure is the last argument of the corresponding method. In listing 2.7, item(), name(), and type() are unknown methods, so they become XML elements. Attributes are declared as named arguments of the method, whereas simple text content is passed as an unnamed string argument. Those are the technical aspects, but you'll get the general idea by looking at the example code.

It's also worth noting that you can intermingle regular code with the markup, as we have done with the each loop. This allows for succinct code that can generate large quantities of XML. Once you get used to this form of markup, you'll find XML itself verbose and annoying. You have been warned!

The next stage involves parsing the generated XML using the XmlSlurper class. When using this approach, you end up with an in-memory representation of the XML that you can navigate using property notation ❷. When the slurper parses XML, it returns an object representing the root element of the document. In fact, it's an instance of the GPathResult class, but that doesn't matter. We're more interested in how it behaves.

As you can see in listing 2.7, you access the elements of the XML by referring to properties of the same name. You navigate nested elements through multiple levels of property access, or multiple dots (.), if you will. So, to get hold of the name elements, we have to go through the item property:

```
def names = xml.item.name
```

This little example raises the question: what do the item and name properties return?

Based on listing 2.7, you could be forgiven for thinking that the properties return lists. That's almost correct, because they do behave like lists in many ways, but they don't implement the List interface. This is an important point to understand. You can call the size() and findAll() methods on the result, but you only get a real list if you call the special list() method.

One last thing: getting the values of attributes is simply a case of prepending the property name with an @ character.

That's it for now—the whistle-stop tour of Groovy and XML is now complete. Although we have mainly included coverage because Grails uses both extensively, we think you'll be inspired to start using Groovy XML processing in non-Grails projects too!

Hopefully, this discussion of Groovy and XML has highlighted how closures and dynamic methods can come together to provide novel, easy-to-use solutions for common problems. Even if you have found some of the concepts tough going, don't worry about it. You don't need an in-depth understanding at this stage, and you'll see plenty more examples in the coming chapters that will help you understand the features better.

2.5　*Summary and best practices*

We have covered Groovy at a rather rapid pace, so let's stop and take stock. From the early sections and examples in this chapter, you should be feeling pretty confident and hopefully excited about programming in Groovy. Even if you feel overwhelmed at this stage, don't worry. This chapter includes more information than you need to get started. As you progress through the rest of the book, flip back here whenever you see something in an example you don't quite understand.

At first, you'll just need to recognize some of the syntax and constructs that are unique to Groovy. Later on, a firm grasp of the dynamic nature of Groovy will help your confidence level and help you avoid common pitfalls. We expect that you'll soon enjoy Groovy's expressivity and power. Just don't blame us if you no longer want to program in plain Java!

Here are a few simple guidelines to smooth your way:

- *Use idiomatic Groovy.* The syntax sugar in Groovy is there to make your life easier and your code clearer, so make use of it. You'll also find it easier to follow example Groovy code if you are used to using the various idioms that differentiate Groovy from Java. After this chapter, all example Groovy code is idiomatic rather than Java-style.
- *Experiment.* The Grails shell and console allow you to easily experiment with Groovy code. This is a great way to learn the language and find out just what you can do.
- *Use methods where appropriate.* Although closures are powerful, don't forget that methods are too. You may not be able to pass methods as arguments or treat them as objects, but they integrate well with Java, and the rules for inheritance are well understood.
- *Use explicit types in method signatures.* It's tempting to use untyped variables and arguments everywhere, but consider using explicit types for method arguments and return types. Not only do they document what the method expects and returns, but they can also be used by IDEs to detect incorrect usage. And if you call a method with incorrect types, the code will fail quickly with an error that makes it clear what went wrong.

   That said, when there is a clear benefit to a method supporting duck typing, or if a method can work with multiple types for a particular argument, it makes sense to use one or more untyped arguments. Just make sure that you clearly document in the javadoc what the method expects from untyped arguments.

Before we move on to the Grails fundamentals, remember that Groovy isn't just a language for Grails. It can be used for a variety of purposes: writing scripts, scripting a Java application, rapid prototyping, and more! For a more comprehensive look at the language itself, check out *Groovy in Action*, by Dierk Koenig with Andrew Glover, Paul King, Guillaume Laforge, and Jon Skeet.

You have seen how quickly an application can be built from scratch. You should be able to understand and write Groovy without fear. It's now time to introduce you to the fundamental concepts of a Grails application, starting with domain classes.

Part 2

Core Grails

In part 1, we gave you a whirlwind introduction to both the core parts of Grails and the underlying Groovy language that powers it. In part 2, we'll start a more thorough exploration of the three core parts of the Grails ecosystem: models, controllers, and views.

In chapter 3, we'll look at domain modeling—the heart of any Grails application. You'll learn about saving and updating domain classes, explore the many faces of validation, and cover all basic relationships for domain classes (1:1, 1:m, m:n).

Chapter 4 will put your modeling skills to work by taking you through the numerous query mechanisms that Grails offers for searching your domain model. We'll also investigate Grails' fantastic scaffolding features, which allow you to build a functional UI in record time.

By the time we reach chapter 5, you'll be ready to explore some of the web-oriented features of Grails. In particular, how you can route a user around the different features in your application using Grails controllers. We'll also cover binding data from web forms, write a request filter, and even create some custom URL mappings to add user-friendly permalinks to your application.

In chapter 6, we'll turn our attention to the user interface components of a Grails application, exploring Grails tags for UI construction. We'll show you how to quickly add a consistent and sophisticated look and feel to your applications, and even how to build custom skins for your application. Finally, we'll introduce Grails' AJAX support, and show you how to add some slick animations to your applications.

In chapter 7, we'll teach you how to build robust tests for your newly developed code, so you can make sure everything works properly before your code is deployed. We'll start with unit tests for all the basic Grails artifacts you've developed so far. We'll then build on those fine-grained testing skills with the broader ideas of integration and functional testing. By the end of chapter 7, testing will be your middle name.

Once you've finished this part of the book, you'll have a comprehensive understanding of all the basics of Grails and be well on your way to becoming a productive Grails developer. In part 3, we'll introduce you to more sophisticated Grails features that will really make your application ready for production.

Modeling the domain

This chapter covers

- What GORM is and how it works
- Defining domain model classes
- How domain classes are saved and updated
- Techniques for validating and constraining fields
- Domain class relationships (1:1, 1:m, m:n)

In this chapter, we'll explore Grails' support for the data model portion of your applications, and if you're worried we'll be digging deep into outer joins, you'll be pleasantly surprised. We won't be writing a line of SQL, and you won't find any Hibernate XML mappings here either. We'll be taking full advantage of the Convention over Configuration paradigm, which means less time configuring and more time getting work done.

We'll be spending most of our time exploring the basics of how Grails persists domain model classes using GORM—the Grails object relational mapping implementation. You'll also learn how GORM models various relationships (one to many, many to many, and so on).

But we're practitioners, not theorists, so we'll discuss these topics while building the heart of the sample application we'll use throughout this book: Hubbub. We won't be spending much time on the user interface (UI) in this chapter, but the concepts we'll cover are fundamental for building the rock-solid data models that back our applications.

Without further ado, let's look at our sample application.

3.1 Hubbub: starting our example application

Our goal in this book is to take you to the stage where you could work as a productive Grails developer. We'll give you a thorough mentoring in all the skills you need to produce world-class applications in record time. And we'll do it by getting you involved in developing a real application.

The example we'll be using for the rest of the book is Hubbub, a simple microblogging application in the style of Twitter. You might think of it as a system that lets you write one-line blog posts about what you're hacking on right now. Friends can follow your posts to see what you're geeking out on and get motivated to check out some things for themselves. You can follow your friends' posts, too. Figure 3.1 shows a complete version of Hubbub in action.

TIP   If you haven't used Twitter yet, it's time to head on over to twitter.com and see what all the fuss is about. If you need some friends to follow, check out @glen_a_smith and @pledbrook. We have pretty geeky tweets, but we're mostly harmless.

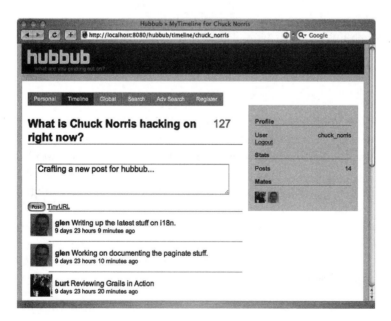

Figure 3.1   The Hubbub we're heading towards

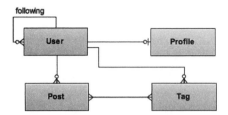

Figure 3.2 The basic Hubbub data model demonstrates all the basic relationship types.

The basic domain model for Hubbub is simple. Figure 3.2 shows the Hubbub Entity Relationship (ER) model in all its glory.

The User class holds the user's authentication details (user ID and password). But all good social networking applications let you associate lots of info with each user (email, blog, time zone, and favorite rock star, for example), so we'll model that in a Profile class (which is a 1:1 relationship—each User has one Profile, and each Profile relates to one, and only one, User).

The point of Hubbub is to let users create posts—one-line blog entries that describe what they're hacking on right now. A user will write many posts, and each Post has a single author, so that is a classic 1:m relationship.

But what's a Web 2.0 application without tags? Every time a user creates a Post, they can apply various tags to it—a given Post can have many tags. But that means the reverse is also true. Each Tag can also relate to many Posts. We have an m:n (many-to-many) relationship. We're also going to link the Tag back to the User object (because it would be handy to see all the tags that a user has available without searching all their posts.

We've saved the trickiest part until last: the User object has some self-references. A User can follow many other Users (which we're calling a "following" relationship). That sounds like it would be exhausting to implement, but it turns out to be straightforward.

Don't worry about getting it all perfectly straight in your head yet. We'll be spending plenty of time with these classes over the next few chapters, and all will become clear. Just get a feel for the function of the main objects, and we'll be on our way.

3.1.1 *Domain-driven design*

If you're as impatient as we are, you're probably wondering why we're starting with all this domain model design stuff here. Why not something a little more sexy, like an autocompleting Ajax-powered search gizmo? Don't worry, we'll certainly get to that.

Grails is designed to be an interactive agile development framework. That means you can start anywhere you like, refactor, make changes, and still end up with a fantastic app. You can start with the UI, domain modeling, service classes, or even the test cases if you like.

But when we're working on Grails apps, the first thing we usually do is scratch out some screen designs on graph paper, as shown in figure 3.3. This gives us a good feel

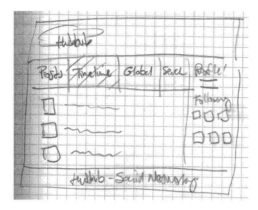

Figure 3.3   Early screen designs for the Hubbub UI

for how the user will interact with the system, and some sense of how the finished product might end up looking. This gets us in the headspace of the application and gives us some ideas about the user experience.

But the UI is only part of the story. Once we have our UI sketches mocked up, we move on and define the domain model: how all of the persistent data in the system fits together. This gives us a good feel for how the core parts of the system will collaborate, and it helps us flesh out our thinking. Grails makes domain modeling so easy that we usually do this bit directly in code without any real data model on paper. That's the reason this chapter is our first in-depth one: domain modeling is a great place to start your Grails application development journey.

After we define our data model, we use Grails to generate a quick-and-dirty scaffold UI (we introduced you to these autogenerated UI gems in chapter 1, and we'll look more closely at them later in this chapter). With our autogenerated UI, we feel like we've made some progress—we have a basic app running and persisting to a database—so we're motivated to move on to the next level of functionality in our app and start implementing our graph paper scratchings as a real UI.

You might be more disciplined and might not need the carrot of seeing things up and running, but you're stuck with us for this chapter, so let's get Hubbub to the point where you can see it running in a browser.

3.1.2   *Hubbub kick-start: from 0 to first hit*

We have the rough version of our screens on paper, and we have a "napkin-level" data model to work from, so it's time to start generating our application. Let's create the app:

```
grails create-app hubbub
```

We always find it's good encouragement to do a `cd hubbub` followed by an initial `grails run-app` to start our newly created application. Point your browser at http://localhost:8080/hubbub/ to see things up and running, as shown in figure 3.4.

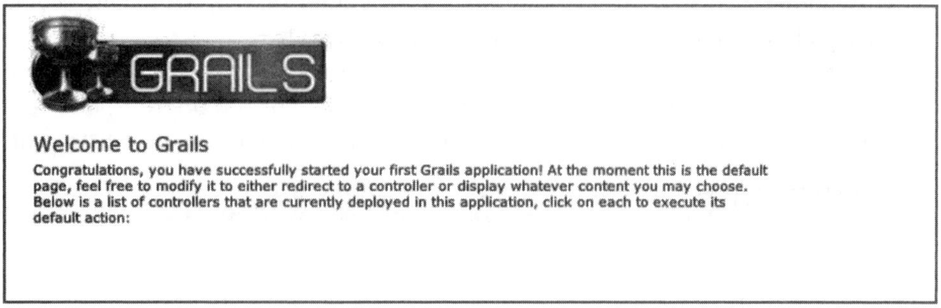

Welcome to Grails

Congratulations, you have successfully started your first Grails application! At the moment this is the default page, feel free to modify it to either redirect to a controller or display whatever content you may choose. Below is a list of controllers that are currently deployed in this application, click on each to execute its default action:

Figure 3.4 The newly created Hubbub application

With the shell of Hubbub created, it's time to put some meat on the bones. Let's generate our first domain class.

3.1.3 *Introducing GORM (Grails object relational mapping)*

Before we generate our first domain class, let's take a quick look at GORM, the Grails object relational mapping implementation.

Object-relational mapping (ORM) is the process of getting objects into and out of a relational database. It means you can (mostly) be oblivious to the SQL that's happening behind the scenes and get on with the coding. For example, if you call `user.firstName = "Glen"`, the ORM manages the SQL UPDATE statement to ensure that the object is persisted in your database. In Java applications, that role is usually handled by an ORM like Hibernate or JPA; in Grails, it's done by GORM, which takes full advantage of Groovy's dynamic typing to make data access simple.

If you've used Hibernate, TopLink, or another Java ORM library, you'll know that a lot of configuration is required. Often there's a bunch of XML mapping files to write or annotations to add. GORM, like most of Grails, uses Convention over Configuration to get you up and running without a single line of XML.

Now that you know a bit about GORM, it's time to define our first domain model object and see things in action.

3.2 *Your first domain class object*

We outlined the preliminary model at the beginning of this section, and we have our application shell in place, so it's time to define our data model classes. One of the first things we'll need to define is a `User` object, so that our users can sign up and start using the system.

The first step is to ask Grails to create a skeleton of our domain class for us:

```
grails create-domain-class com.grailsinaction.User
```

This creates a new class file in /grails-app/domain/com/grailsinaction/User.groovy (and a corresponding unit test in /test/unit/com/grailsinaction/UserTests.groovy).

It's good practice to store classes in packages rather than in the default scope, so we'll keep all of our source in a package called com.grailsinaction.

Now it's time to start thinking about some of the fields we'll want to define for new User accounts. We don't want the signup process to be too onerous, but we'll need at least a few basics from our users. Listing 3.1 introduces our first basic User object.

Listing 3.1   Our first basic User object

```
package com.grailsinaction

class User {

    String userId
    String password
    String homepage
    Date dateCreated

}
```

> **Types that can be used in domain classes**
>
> We've used Strings and Dates in our User object so far, but you can use an extensive range of Java types: Integer, Long, Float, Boolean (and their corresponding primitive types), Date, Calendar, URL, and byte[] are all in the list of supported types. Grails will also make sensible choices about an appropriate database type to map what you're storing. See the Hibernate documentation for a full set of supported types.
>
> Grails provides special support for date fields named dateCreated and lastUpdated. If you have fields with such names, Grails will automatically set the current timestamp value on first save to dateCreated or on every save to lastUpdated. We'll take advantage of dateCreated to preserve the user's registration time.

We can now store a user's details. We don't have a UI to enter anything yet, but we do have the shell of a test case, which Grails created for us. It's supposed to make you feel guilty right from the start, so let's ease our conscience.

3.2.1   *Saving and retrieving users via tests*

We first introduced you to the idea of automated testing in chapter 1, when we created tests for our QuoteService. But tests are useful across your application. So useful, in fact, that we'll spend chapter 7 on testing strategies for all of the phases of the development lifecycle.

For now, though, tests will give us a chance to show you how GORM saves your objects to the database, and how to get them back. Tests provide a great way for you to tinker with some of these ideas right from the start. Let's write our first integration test case.

As we discussed, Grails creates a unit test case shell in /test/unit/com/grailsinaction/UserTest.groovy. But we want an integration test, because we want to be able to

Unit versus integration tests?

When you create any artifact from the command line, Grails automatically generates a corresponding unit test in /grails-app/test/unit/YourArtifactTest.groovy. Unit tests run in isolation and rely on mocking techniques (which you'll learn about in chapter 7), which means its up to you to simulate the database and any other infrastructure you need.

In this chapter, we'll be working with integration tests. For integration tests, Grails bootstraps the database and wires up all components as it would for a running application. That means we can simulate what happens when we create, save, and delete domain objects, and we don't have to mess with any tricky mocking features yet. Integration tests are a little slower to run, but they're fantastic for the learning and experimenting we'll be doing in this chapter.

run against our database. You'll recall from chapter 1 that we create integration tests with this command:

```
grails create-integration-test com.grailsinaction.UserIntegration
```

This generates /test/integration/com/grailsinaction/UserIntegrationTests.groovy.

We'll first create and save a `User` object in the database (for the user joe). Then we'll see if we can query the database to find the user based on the user ID. Listing 3.2 introduces our first saving test.

Listing 3.2 Saving and retrieving a domain object from the database

```
package com.grailsinaction

import grails.test.*

class UserIntegrationTests extends GrailsUnitTestCase {

    void testFirstSaveEver() {

        def user = new User(userId: 'joe', password: 'secret',
            homepage: 'http://www.grailsinaction.com')
        assertNotNull user.save()                       ①  Checks save() succeeded
        assertNotNull user.id                           ②  Checks save() set the id

        def foundUser = User.get(user.id)
        assertEquals 'joe', foundUser.userId            ③  Retrieves User
    }                                                       object by ID

}
```

The process of creating a new instance of a domain object normally consists of constructing the object, and then invoking the `save()` method ①. When we invoke `save()`, GORM generates the SQL to insert our `User` object into the database. GORM will return the saved `User` object (or `null` if `save()` fails, which we'll talk about later). Once the `User` has been saved to the database, it will be assigned an `id` field in the database ❷. We can then use this id with the get() method ❸ to query for the object (you can also use the read() method if you want a read-only copy of the object).

There are much snazzier ways to query for objects than get() and read(), and we'll cover them when we get to *dynamic finders* in the next chapter, but get() will serve us well for now.

It's time to confirm that our test case works, so let's ask Grails to execute our test case:

```
grails test-app -integration
```

You can use grails test-app if you want to run both unit and integration tests, but we're only interested in integration tests for now. You'll get lots of output in the console, but somewhere in the middle you'll see the good news we've been looking for:

```
--------------------------------------------------------
Running 1 Integration Test...
Running test com.grailsinaction.UserIntegrationTests...
                testFirstSaveEver...SUCCESS
Integration Tests Completed in 1772ms
--------------------------------------------------------
```

And we're all green (that's what people say when tests pass, because most IDEs display passing tests a with green bar). That "SUCCESS" is telling us that all of our assert calls are passing, as we expected.

What does save() do behind the scenes?

Behind the scenes, save() uses the Hibernate session that Spring puts on the current thread, then adds our User object to that session. In Hibernate lingo, this means the User object moves from being a transient to persistent object.

The flush to the database (the real SQL inserts) from the Hibernate session occurs at the end of the thread's lifetime, but if you want to force your object to be persisted immediately, you can do an explicit user.save(flush: true). But we're getting ahead of ourselves.

We'll cover this in more detail in chapter 13.

3.2.2 *Updating user properties*

We've completed our first save, so let's try implementing an update routine. Update is a special case of saving, so let's try our hand at updating joe's password programmatically.

NOTE We have to create our "joe" user every time we run a test cycle because integration tests always return the database to the way they found it. Our changes execute in a transaction that's rolled back at the end of each test to ensure that the database is clean for each test.

We'll start with our usual save() and get(), as in our previous test, and then we'll modify some user fields and repeat the save() and get() to make sure the update has worked. Listing 3.3 takes us through the save-and-update test cycle.

Listing 3.3   Updating users by changing field values and calling `save()`

```
void testSaveAndUpdate() {

    def user = new User(userId: 'joe', password: 'secret',
        homepage: 'http://www.grailsinaction.com')
    assertNotNull user.save()

    def foundUser = User.get(user.id)          ❶ Modifies retrieved
    foundUser.password = 'sesame'                  User object directly
    foundUser.save()                            ❷ Calls save() to
                                                   update database
    def editedUser = User.get(user.id)
    assertEquals 'sesame', editedUser.password  ❸ Checks that password
                                                   has been persisted
}
```

You'll be used to the save() and get() cycle from our previous test. But notice how executing an update is just a matter of changing property values ❶ and invoking save() ❷ to persist the change to the database. We then requery the database to confirm that the password change has actually been applied ❸.

Let's confirm that our change is working as we expected by invoking another grails test-app -integration:

```
--------------------------------------------------------
Running 2 Integration Tests...
Running test com.grailsinaction.UserIntegrationTests...
               testFirstSaveEver...SUCCESS
               testSaveAndUpdate...SUCCESS
Integration Tests Completed in 1939ms
--------------------------------------------------------
```

3.2.3   Deleting users

We now have a good feel for loading and saving. But those pesky bots will soon be filling our database with dodgy user registrations, so we'll need to delete User objects too.

It's time for our third and final test case. Listing 3.4 shows how to use the delete() method to remove an object from the database.

Listing 3.4   Deleting objects from the database is a one-liner

```
void testSaveThenDelete() {

    def user = new User(userId: 'joe', password: 'secret',
        homepage: 'http://www.grailsinaction.com')
    assertNotNull user.save()

    def foundUser = User.get(user.id)          ❶ Removes the user
    foundUser.delete()                             immediately

    assertFalse User.exists(foundUser.id)      ❷ Checks for object
                                                   ID in database
}
```

Deleting gives us a chance to introduce two new domain class methods: `delete()` and `exists()`. You can call `delete()` on any domain class that you've fetched from the database ❶. Even though the object is removed from the database, your instance handle won't be nullified, which is why we can reference `foundUser.id` in the later `exists()` call, even after `foundUser` has been deleted from the database.

You can check for the existence of any domain instance with the `exists()` method ❷. As you would expect, `exists()` returns `true` if that ID exists in the database.

We now have a good handle on saving, updating, and deleting our `User` objects. But although we've tested that our `save()` calls work correctly, we haven't encountered any reason for a `save()` call to fail. The main reason for such failure is a domain class field constraint-validation failure, and it's time to introduce you to the features Grails offers for validation.

3.3   *Validation: stopping garbage in and out*

We've created our new `User` object and successfully tested saving it to the database, but you might already be thinking a little defensively: "What keeps clients from putting all sorts of junk (including nulls and blanks) into our domain object and saving them?" The answer is, nothing yet. That's our cue to talk about validation.

Grails goes out of its way to make all the common validations easy, and when things don't quite match your validation needs, it's not hard to customize them. Say we want to make sure that all passwords have at least six characters but not more than eight. We can apply this sort of constraint through a special `constraints` closure that uses a comprehensive DSL to specify constraints. There are validators available to limit the size of fields, enforce non-nullability, check (via patterns) whether a field contains a URL, email address, or credit card number, and so on.

Let's add some basic constraints to our `User` object. We'll make sure the `userId` and `password` fields have size limits and that the `homepage` contains a valid URL. Listing 3.5 shows our updated domain class with the new constraints.

Listing 3.5   Grails makes adding constraints straightforward

```
package com.grailsinaction

class User {

    String userId
    String password
    String homepage
    Date dateCreated

    static constraints = {
        userId(size:3..20, unique: true)      ❶  Specifies min and
        password(size: 6..8)                      max field lengths
        homepage(url: true, nullable: true)   ❷  Checks against a URL
    }                                             pattern which may be null

}
```

The size constraint ❶ makes sure the userId field is between 3 and 20 characters. When applied to a String field, size checks the length of the string. But if you apply it to a numeric field, it will ensure that the number entered is within the range. For example, an Integer field called quantity could be constrained to ensure the user doesn't order more than 10 items with quantity (size: 0..10). We've also specified a unique constraint on the User to ensure that two users don't have the same userId.

You don't have to list all fields in your constraints block—only those you want to supply specific validations for. One thing to note, though, is that fields aren't nullable by default, so if you want a field to be optional, you have to specify the nullable constraint explicitly. We allow our homepage field ❷ to be optional (nullable), but if it's supplied, we force it to match a URL pattern. This kind of combination gives you a lot of power for specifying validations concisely, yet expressively.

What happens if the user tries to save an object that doesn't satisfy the constraints on an object? Let's write a test case and see. It's time to introduce you to the validate() method that's available on every domain class. When you call validate(), Grails checks to see if the constraints have been satisfied and provides an errors object that you can interrogate to see which fields failed.

Listing 3.6 augments our UserIntegrationTests.groovy file with a new test that attempts to save an instance that doesn't satisfy the constraints.

Listing 3.6 Interrogating the results of a failed validation

```
void testEvilSave() {
    def user = new User(userId: 'chuck_norris',
        password: 'tiny', homepage: 'not-a-url')

    assertFalse user.validate()              ◁──❶ Returns false
    assertTrue user.hasErrors()              ❷ errors holds list of
                                               failing values
    def errors = user.errors             ◁─┘

    assertEquals "size.toosmall",            ❸ errors contains codes
        errors.getFieldError("password").code  ◁─┘ describing failure
    assertEquals "tiny",
        errors.getFieldError("password").rejectedValue    ◁─┐
                                                       errors holds
    assertEquals "url.invalid",                        ❹ failing value
        errors.getFieldError("homepage").code
    assertEquals "not-a-url",                          ❺ Checks valid fields
        errors.getFieldError("homepage").rejectedValue    are not in errors
                                                            collection
    assertNull errors.getFieldError("userId")    ◁─┘

}
```

As we mentioned, the validate() method ❶ checks whether all of the constraints on the domain class have been satisfied, and it returns true or false to let you know. As a result, this is a common idiom you'll see in Grails controllers:

```
if (user.validate()) {
    user.save()
} else {
```

```
    // go and give them another crack at it... or
    user.discard()
}
```

After you have checked for validation, you can access the domain object's `errors` property to see what went wrong ❷. The returned `errors` object holds a collection of `fieldError` objects, each representing a different field in your domain object. Each `fieldError` object has a code ❸ that describes the type of validation that failed and a `rejectedValue` ❹ that contains the data the user entered. If the field has no errors, its `fieldError` object will be `null`, which is the case for our `userId` ❺.

In case you're wondering about those error codes, we'll give you a full set of them in the next section (in table 3.1). But for now, just know that you can find out exactly what is failing the validators. In chapter 7, we'll show you how to do all of these checks in a unit test, which makes things a lot more concise.

Now that we know how to cause an error to occur (by violating a constraint), let's write a test case that repairs the damage after a bad save attempt. This isn't something you'd typically be able to do when processing a web request, but it will help demonstrate how these validations work. Listing 3.7 shows a test case that first attempts a `save()` with invalid data and then repairs the damage and performs a valid `save()`.

Listing 3.7   Recovering from a failed validation

```
void testEvilSaveCorrected() {
    def user = new User(userId: 'chuck_norris',         ❶ Uses invalid URL
        password: 'tiny', homepage: 'not-a-url')   ⟵┘     and password
    assertFalse(user.validate())
    assertTrue(user.hasErrors())      ⟵──❷ Returns true
    assertNull user.save()

    user.password = "fistfist"
    user.homepage = "http://www.chucknorrisfacts.com"
    assertTrue(user.validate())
    assertFalse(user.hasErrors())     ⟵──❸ Removes errors
    assertNotNull user.save()

}
```

Our original `User` object had an invalid URL and password ❶, which caused the object to fail validation ❷. After correcting the troublesome fields, `validate()` is happy again and the `errors` object is reset ❸.

We've now exercised our constraints and have some confidence that our database fields will be persisted consistently. So far, we've only exposed you to size and URL constraints, but there are several Grails validators available, which we'll explore next.

3.3.1   *Standard validators*

Now that you know how the basic constraint mechanism works, you may be wondering what Grails validators are available out of the box. There are plenty, and table 3.1 lists the most common ones.

Table 3.1   Grails gives you lots of validators out of the box.

Name	Description	Example	Error properties
`blank`	Ensures string isn't blank (or `null`)	`password(blank:false)`	blank
`email`	Ensures field is a well-formed email address	`userEmail(email:true)`	`email.invalid`
`inList`	Ensures value appears in supplied range or collection	`country(inList:['Australia', 'England')`	`not.inList`
`matches`	Ensures field matches the supplied regular expression	`userId(matches: '[0-9]{7} [A-Za-z]')`	`matches.invalid`
`maxSize`	Ensures size of field in database doesn't exceed supplied value	`orderQuantity(maxSize:100)`	`maxSize.exceeded`
`minSize`	Ensures size of field in database always exceeds supplied value	`orderQuantity(minSize:10)`	`minSize.notmet`
`nullable`	Specifies whether the property is allowed to be `null`	`password(nullable: false)`	`nullable`
`size`	Specifies a range for min and max length of a `string` or size of an `int` or collection	`userId(size:3..20)`	`size.toosmall` or `size.toobig`
`unique`	Specifies whether the property must be unique or not	`userId(unique:true)`	`unique`
`url`	Ensures that the field contains a valid URL	`homepage(url:true)`	`url.invalid`
`validator`	Allows custom validation by supplying a closure	*See section 3.3.3*	`validator.error`

You can find a complete set of validators in the Grails reference documentation at http://grails.org/doc/1.1/.

Blank isn't null?

You may have noticed in table 3.1 that there are separate validators for nullable and blank. This is important, because when you submit HTML forms with empty fields, they're presented to Grails as "blank" fields that would pass a `nullable:true` validation. The rule of thumb is that if you always want the user to supply a value, use `blank:false`. If you don't mind if a user provides a value or not, use `nullable:true`.

3.3.2 *Custom validation with regular expressions*

Of course, your validation rules are different. You'll need to customize your validations.

If your validation is a variation on a regular expression pattern, the `matches` constraint will probably do. Say you're writing a student system for your local university, and all student IDs are seven numbers followed by a letter. You might implement that with a straight regular expression:

```
static constraints = {
    userId(matches: '[0-9]{7}[A-Za-z]')
}
```

Regular expressions unlock a whole lot of power. But there are still situations when they aren't powerful enough.

3.3.3 *Cross-field validation tricks*

Regular expressions can take you a certain distance, but there are situations when you need to do cross-field validations. For example, take the business rule that a user's `password` must not match their `userId`. For these sorts of situations, you'll need the `validator` closure constraint. It's a little trickier to understand, but it gives you the power to do anything!

When you specify the `validator` constraint, you supply a closure with one or two parameters. The first is the value that the user tried to place in the field, and the second, if you supply one, references the instance of the domain class itself. The closure should return `true` if the data entered is valid for that field.

In our case, we need the two-argument version because we want to confirm that what the user typed in their `password` field doesn't match their `userId`:

```
static constraints = {
    password(size: 6..8,
        validator: { passwd, user ->
            return passwd != user.userId
        })
    homepage(url: true, nullable: true)
}
```

Things are getting quite tricky. When the domain class is saved, the password validators now ensure that the password is between 6 and 8 characters inclusive, and that the supplied password doesn't match the user's `userId`. You can get as creative as you like with custom validators because they give you the power to programmatically check just about anything.

TIP   Several of the constraints (such as `size`, `maxSize`, and `nullable`) have a direct impact on how Grails generates the fields in your database. For example, if you specify a `maxSize` of 8, Grails will generate a database field with a column size of 8. Check out the reference guide for specific advice on how certain constraints affect database generation.

3.4 *Defining the data model—1:1, 1:m, m:n*

We now know how CRUD operations work, how we can apply validations to our domain class fields, and even how to generate a quick and dirty UI. But Hubbub is going to need a lot more than a User class to get work done, so it's time to learn about modeling relationships in the data model.

Just because you're using an ORM, it doesn't mean you should have to compromise on how you model your domain classes. Grails gives you the flexibility to use whatever relationships make sense for you: one-to-one (1:1), one-to-many (1:m), or many-to-many (m:n). Even better, GORM looks after creating the appropriate table structures, using sensible naming conventions.

3.4.1 *One-to-one relationships*

We'll first model a one-to-one relationship. This is probably the easiest relationship to understand.

In our Hubbub example, it's time to refactor out the user's authentication fields (user ID, password, last login) and profile information (homepage, email, photo, and whatever else comes along). We're moving toward our original Hubbub data model (shown in figure 3.2), which includes a Profile object. The relevant section of the data model is shown in figure 3.5.

Figure 3.5 Each User object has an optional Profile object.

We'll start by creating a Profile domain class:

```
grails create-domain-class com.grailsinaction.Profile
```

Next, we'll update our newly created object to handle the Profile-related features of the existing User class. We'll pull out the homepage field, and add new entries for email and even a photo. Listing 3.8 shows the refactored Profile object.

Listing 3.8 Refactored Profile object with a 1:1 relationship with the User object

```
package com.grailsinaction

class Profile {                          ❶ Declares Profile is
    static belongsTo = User                owned by a User object

    byte[] photo                    ❷ Models binary
    String fullName                   data in a byte[ ]
    String bio
    String homepage
    String email
    String timezone
    String country
    String jabberAddress
```

```
static constraints = {
   fullName(nullable: true)
   bio(nullable: true, maxSize: 1000)
   homepage(url: true, nullable: true)
   email(email: true, nullable: true)
   photo(nullable: true)
   country(nullable: true)
   timezone(nullable: true)
   jabberAddress(email: true, nullable: true)
}

}
```

The most obvious new feature in this domain class is the belongsTo field ❶. This field tells GORM that this object has a relationship to User. It also tells GORM how to cascade updates and deletes (as discussed in the sidebar).

In listing 3.8, belongsTo is assigned the owning class, which means the relationship is unidirectional. You can get to a Profile via a User, but there's no link back from a Profile to a User. There's also a form of belongsTo that lets us make a bidirectional mapping, which we'll explore in section 3.4.2 on 1:m relationships.

We've introduced several new fields and constraints on the Profile object. We've added placeholders for full name, bio, country, and time zone. We've added optional fields for home page and email and used the built-in validators to make sure they're conformant. Because they're optional, we've marked them nullable right from the get-go. Jabber addresses have the same form as email addresses, so we can apply a validator to that field too.

We also want to store the user's photo with their profile as a BLOB (binary large object). In this case, marking the field as a byte array (byte[]) tells GORM to store it as a BLOB ❷.

> **BelongsTo and cascading**
>
> GORM only cascades to objects marked with belongsTo. In listing 3.8, Profile belongsTo User, so if any User is deleted, the matching Profile object will also be deleted. Without a belongsTo, the matching profile would not be deleted. This becomes increasingly important in 1:m relationships, where you want to ensure you tidy up.
>
> belongsTo also has a special meaning in m:n relationships, where addTo*() methods can only be persisted from the owning side. But more on that later.

Now that we have the Profile class set up, it's time to link it up from our User object. In listing 3.9, we create a field of type Profile in our User class and specify some constraints about how the relationship works.

Listing 3.9   Adding a 1:1 relationship from `User` to `Profile`

```
package com.grailsinaction

class User {

    String userId
    String password

    Date dateCreated                    ❶ Declares Profile
    Profile profile        ⊲┘              part of User

    static constraints = {
        userId(size:3..20, unique: true)
        password(size: 6..8, validator: { passwd, user ->
            passwd != user.userId
        })
        dateCreated()                    ❷ Marks Profile
        profile(nullable: true)  ⊲┘        as optional
    }

    static mapping = {                   ❸ Tells Grails to load
        profile lazy:false   ⊲┘            Profile with User
    }

}
```

We've introduced a few new features to our `User` class in the 1:1 refactoring. First, we've added a `Profile` field to our `User` so Grails knows the link is 1:1 ❶. (It would need to be a set (or list) of `Profile`s to be 1:m.)

We've also added a constraint to make the profile `nullable` ❷. If you don't specify this, Grails will force you to create a `Profile` instance every time you create a `User` object, which is overhead we can avoid for now.

Finally, we've added a new mapping closure to our `User`. The mapping block lets you customize all kind of advanced database interactions, including caching, table and field names, and loading strategies. Here we've set the `Profile` object to load eagerly ❸, which means every time Grails loads a `User` it will phrase the query in a way that `Profile` is always returned in the same `ResultSet`.

You don't always need to make the profile `nullable` and set it to load eagerly. In many cases you won't need either, which makes a 1:1 association as simple as declaring an instance of the child object against the parent.

Eager and lazy fetching strategies

By default, GORM uses a lazy fetching strategy to retrieve attached collections as they're accessed. Most of the time, that's exactly what you want. But in the case of 1:1 mapping, if your access strategy involves accessing the linked object immediately (as we do with our `Profile` object), it makes sense to have Hibernate retrieve the `Profile` at the same time as the related `User`. This is an *eager fetching* strategy, and in these scenarios it improves performance.

> **Eager and lazy fetching strategies** *(continued)*
>
> If you're using a 1:1 relationship with eager fetching, it might make sense to use Grails' composition feature. This allows you to embed the `Profile` object into the same table as the `User` object (but still use different object references to talk to each). We'll talk more about this in chapter 13 on advanced GORM use.

Now that we have some experience with 1:1 mappings, it's time to turn to the more common one-to-many (1:m) modeling scenario.

3.4.2 *One-to-many relationships*

In our Hubbub example, each user will be capable of making many *posts* or *entries*, and each post will belong to one (and only one) user, as shown in figure 3.6. That's a classic one-to-many (1:m) relationship.

Figure 3.6   Each `User` can have zero to many `Post` objects.

We'll first create the relationship, and then we'll look at how you can apply some sorting to the many side of the relationship.

CREATING THE ONE-TO-MANY RELATIONSHIP

We'll need a new domain class for `Post`, so let's create it:

```
grails create-domain-class com.grailsinaction.Post
```

Grails introduces two domain class property types to model the relationship: `hasMany` (on the "one" side of the relationship) and `belongsTo` (on the "many" side of the relationship). Let's implement the `Post` object first, because it just needs a content field and the date it was created. Listing 3.10 shows the class.

Listing 3.10 The Post object models all the posts for a given User

```
package com.grailsinaction

class Post {

    String content
    Date dateCreated

    static constraints = {
        content(blank: false)
    }
                                        ❶ Points to the
    static belongsTo = [ user : User ]       owning object

}
```

We saw the `belongsTo` field ❶ in our 1:1 relationship (listing 3.8) and learned how it affects cascading operations. In particular, when the `User` is deleted, all their matching `Post` objects will be deleted too.

> ## The two forms of belongsTo
>
> We saw `belongsTo` in our `Profile` class (listing 3.8), where it referenced the owning class directly `belongsTo = User`. This creates a unidirectional relationship; you can get to a `Profile` via a `User` but the reverse isn't true.
>
> In listing 3.10, we use the *map style* of `belongsTo`, where we create a bidirectional link between `User` and `Post` classes. This creates a new field on `Post` called `user` that is the bidirectional mapping back to the owning `User`. This lets us move backwards to `post.user.userId`, for example. This will be handy later, when we query for posts and want to show the associated user's ID.

We've told Grails that `Post` belongs to a `User`, so now we need a way of telling it that our `User` object should link to many `Post` objects. That's done with a `hasMany` closure:

```
class User {

    // existing code here

    static hasMany = [ posts : Post ]

}
```

With `hasMany` and `belongsTo` in place, we have all the basics of the one-to-many relationship. But how do we tell Grails about adding new `Posts` for a given `User`? With some more GORM magic.

Once you have a one-to-many relationship between User and Post, Grails automatically adds two new methods to your `User` class: `User.addToPosts()` and `User.removeFromPosts()`. We'll create a new integration test for `Post` so we can exercise these new capabilities. We start with the usual process:

```
grails create-integration-test com.grailsinaction.PostIntegration
```

With the shell of our test case in place, let's write some code to create a user and add a bunch of new posts to their account. In listing 3.11, we'll take full advantage of the new `addToPosts()` method to make our `User` a little more prolific.

Listing 3.11 The `User.addToPosts()` method makes 1:m relationships easy

```
package com.grailsinaction
import grails.test.*

class PostIntegrationTests extends GrailsUnitTestCase {

    void testFirstPost() {

        def user = new User(userId: 'joe',
                    password: 'secret').save()        ❶ Creates User to
                                                         hold Posts
        def post1 = new Post(content: "First post... W00t!")
        user.addToPosts(post1)                         ❷ Persists Post by
        def post2 = new Post(content: "Second post...")   adding to a User
        user.addToPosts(post2)
        def post3 = new Post(content: "Third post...")
```

```
        user.addToPosts(post3)
        assertEquals 3, User.get(user.id).posts.size()

    }
}
```

Notice that we have to call `save()` on the `User` object to persist it in the database ❶. Once the `User` is attached to the database, though, any additions we make to its object graph (like adding new `Post` objects via `addToPosts()` ❷) are automatically persisted. For this reason, we don't need to call `save()` on each `Post` we create. If you're feeling skeptical, rerun your test cases to make sure everything works as you expect:

```
grails test-app -integration
```

By taking advantage of some of GORM's magic dynamic properties, we've added our user and a few posts. But how do we retrieve those posts when we want to do some work? A typical approach is to get a handle to the `User` object, and iterate through their posts. Listing 3.12 shows a test case that accesses all posts for a given user.

Listing 3.12   Accessing a User's posts by walking the object graph

```
void testAccessingPosts() {
    def user = new User(userId: 'joe', password: 'secret').save()
    user.addToPosts(new Post(content: "First"))
    user.addToPosts(new Post(content: "Second"))     Adds posts to User
    user.addToPosts(new Post(content: "Third"))
                                                    ❶ Loads User via id
    def foundUser = User.get(user.id)
    def postNames =                                  ❷ Iterates through
        foundUser.posts.collect { it.content }          User's posts
    assertEquals(['First', 'Second', 'Third'],       ❸ Sorts posts
        postNames.sort())                               alphabetically

}
```

In this example, we load the user via id ❶, and then we use the Groovy `collect()` method ❷ to iterate through each post, retrieving the content. `collect()` returns a `List` of `Post` content entries that we compare to ensure they match ❸. By default, you won't know the ordering of 1:m collections (because they're mapped as `Sets`), so for our test case we sort them alphabetically to make the comparison meaningful ❸.

To present the user's posting history, you'll typically want to sort their posts by descending creation date, but sorting by hand every time is going to get old pretty quickly. In the next section, we'll look at a way to return posts already sorted.

KEEPING THE MANY SIDE SORTED

When using one-to-many relationships, you often won't care about the ordering on the many side, such as for items on an invoice. For these situations, it makes sense to use the default Grails ordering. When you do need to apply some ordering, you can take advantage of Grails' more sophisticated search options (like the Criteria API, which we cover later in chapter 4) to do the ordering at the time.

But sometimes you'll want to access the many side of a relationship in a prescribed order. For example, in a blog application you'll likely want to keep entries in descending date order (so your front page will display the most recent entries). For these situations, Grails lets you specify your own ordering mechanism using the mapping closure (which we used earlier in our Profile example in listing 3.9).

In order to implement this type of sorting, we need to let Grails know that our Posts need to be returned in a sorted order based on the date they were created. This is achieved by adding a new mapping block to our Post domain class, as shown in listing 3.13.

Listing 3.13 Sorting Posts by creation date

```
package com.grailsinaction

class Post {

    String content
    Date dateCreated

    static constraints = {
        content(blank: false)
    }

    static belongsTo = [ user : User ]

    static mapping = {                    ⟵┐ Specifies sort order
        sort dateCreated:"desc"                Post collections
    }

}
```

You can specify the sort order as either ascending or descending. In this example, all queries to the Post object will return in a descending order.

But what if you only want the posts to be sorted when accessing them via the User object (such as when iterating over user.posts.each)? For those scenarios, Grails lets you specify the sort on the relationship itself, rather than on the Post object. We could update our User class (instead of the Post class) with a mapping block like this:

```
static mapping = {
    profile lazy:false
    posts sort:'dateCreated'
}
```

This form of the mapping tells Grails that we only want to sort by dateCreated when accessing the posts collection via a user. This feature is presently problematic in Grails 1.1 for certain scenarios (see issue GRAILS-4089 in the Grails JIRA) but it is likely to be fixed by the time you read this.

Now that we've looked at sorting, it's time to move on to the trickiest relationship of them all: many-to-many.

3.4.3   *Many-to-many relationships*

Where would our Web 2.0 social networking application be without tags? Tags give users the chance to group and cluster their posts, browse posts associated with particular tags, and generally categorize their posts. Let's make some provision in our domain model for tagging.

It's also time to consider how we might want to use tags. Let's imagine these are our requirements:

- Generate a tag cloud for the user on their home page
- Provide an RSS feed for all posts with a given tag
- See all tags for a given post

To include those requirements in our domain model, we'll need to model two relationships:

- A User creates many Tags, so each Tag relates to one User (1:m)
- A Post has many Tags, and each Tag may relate to many Posts (m:n)

That's quite a mouthful, but the model in figure 3.7 might make things a little clearer.

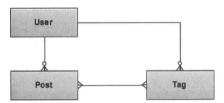

Figure 3.7   A tricky many-to-many scenario between Users, Posts, and Tags

The good news about many-to-many relationships is that there's little new syntax to learn. If two objects are in a many-to-many relationship, they will both have a hasMany clause pointing to the other object. Listing 3.14 updates our Post class to add the new hasMany relationship with our Tag class.

Listing 3.14   Modeling a Post that can have many Tags

```
class Post {

    String content
    Date dateCreated

    static constraints = {
        content(blank: false)
    }

    static belongsTo = [ user : User ]

    static mapping = {
        sort dateCreated:"desc"
    }                                   │  Models a Post
                                        ◁─┘  with many Tags
    static hasMany = [ tags : Tag ]

}
```

We've seen `hasMany` before in one-to-many scenarios, and this is the same beast. The [tags : Tag] map tells us that a `Post` relates to many `Tag` objects, and that the relationship is stored in an attribute named `tags`.

Let's introduce our `Tag` domain model, which we can link back to our `Post` object. In listing 3.15, we specify that a `Tag hasMany Posts`.

Listing 3.15   The `Tag` object models relationships to both `Post` and `User`

```
class Tag {

    String name
    User user

    static constraints = {
       name(blank: false)
    }

    static hasMany = [ posts : Post ]                    Affects which side objects
                                                         can be added from
    static belongsTo = [ User, Post ]        ◁┘

}
```

We can see the `hasMany` relationship in listing 3.15, this time linking back to the `Post` object. The other important difference in this class is that the `Tag belongsTo` both `User` and `Post`. This `belongsTo` relationship is important in the many-to-many context: it affects how `addTo*()` methods work (see the sidebar for more info).

How belongsTo affects many-to-many relationships

The `belongsTo` field controls where the dynamic `addTo*()` methods can be used from. In listing 3.15, we're able to call `User.addToTags()` because `Tag belongsTo User`. We're also able to call `Post.addToTags()` because `Tag belongsTo Post`. But `Post` doesn't `belongTo Tag`, so we can't call `Tag.addToPosts()`.

The last change that we need to make relates to the `User` object, which now needs to be updated to reference the Post and Tag classes. Listing 3.16 updates the hasMany clause.

Listing 3.16   `User` now hasMany `Posts` and `Tags`

```
package com.grailsinaction

class User {

    // .. existing code                                 Specifies User has
                                                         many Posts and Tags
    static hasMany = [ posts : Post, tags : Tag ]    ◁┘

}
```

We've now referenced both `Post` and `Tag` in the `User` class's `hasMany` clause. With all the pieces of the many-to-many relationship in place, let's write a test case to make sure that our assumptions still hold true. Listing 3.17 presents a basic test case for a post with one or more tags.

Listing 3.17 A complex many-to-many scenario for posts and tags

```
void testPostWithTags() {

    def user = new User(userId: 'joe', password: 'secret').save()

    def tagGroovy = new Tag(name: 'groovy')
    def tagGrails = new Tag(name: 'grails')         Sets up tags, adds
    user.addToTags(tagGroovy)                       them to user
    user.addToTags(tagGrails)

    def tagNames = user.tags*.name
    assertEquals([ 'grails', 'groovy'] , tagNames.sort())

    def groovyPost = new Post(content: "A groovy post")    ❶ Adds post to
    user.addToPosts(groovyPost)                               user, tag to post
    groovyPost.addToTags(tagGroovy)
    assertEquals 1, groovyPost.tags.size()

    def bothPost = new Post(content: "A groovy and grails post")
    user.addToPosts(bothPost)
    bothPost.addToTags(tagGroovy)                  Adds multiple
    bothPost.addToTags(tagGrails)                  tags to post ❷
    assertEquals 2, bothPost.tags.size()

}
```

Because our `Tag` class is 1:m to `User` and m:n to `Post`, we have to add the tag to the user, and the tag to the post. Behind the scenes, Grails manages both the `User` and `Post` fields on the newly added `Tag` object, ensuring that all the relationships are kept bidirectional.

In listing 3.17, we have a `groovyPost` ❶ with one tag ("groovy") and a `bothPost` ❷ with two tags ("groovy" and "grails"). By making numerous calls to `post.addToTags()`, you can add as many tags to each post as the user wants.

As you can see, many-to-many relationships are the trickiest of the standard relationships, so it's worth making sure you've got a good handle on how the `addTo*()` methods work. Listing 3.17 will get you started, but we encourage you to experiment with your own use cases.

Cascading: the rules for deletes and updates

GORM does a lot of work behind the scenes to make all those 1:m and m:n relationships work smoothly. We've explored the `addTo*()` methods already, but we haven't looked into how GORM handles the cascading.

The rules around 1:m relationships are pretty straightforward. In our Hubbub example, if you delete a `User`, all of the associated `Post` objects will also be deleted by GORM automatically.

> **Cascading: the rules for deletes and updates** *(continued)*
>
> But let's take the trickier situation of Tags. A Post may have many Tags, and each Tag may relate to more than one Post. In this case, GORM settles things by looking at the belongsTo clause. If there's no belongsTo clause defined on the object, no cascades will happen in either direction, and we're on our own.

3.4.4   *Self-referencing relationships*

The final part of the Hubbub data model models the "follows" process—how a User can follow other Users. The data model includes it as a self-referencing relationship, as shown in figure 3.8.

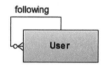

following

There's nothing special about the self-referencing part. It's a specialized version of the one-to-many relationship you've already seen. We'll update the User class's hasMany reference to model the relationship, as shown in listing 3.18.

Figure 3.8   Modeling the "follows" relationship

Listing 3.18   Modeling a User following other Users

```
class User {

   //... other code omitted

   static hasMany = [ posts : Post, tags : Tag, following : User ]
}
```

As usual, we'll write a test case to make sure we have a feel for how things will work. Listing 3.19 adds people the user is following.

Listing 3.19   A simple test case for adding users

```
void testFollowing() {
     def glen = new User(userId: 'glen', password:'password').save()
     def peter = new User(userId: 'peter', password:'password').save()
     def sven = new User(userId: 'sven', password:'password').save()

     glen.addToFollowing(peter)                    │ addTo*() works on
     glen.addToFollowing(sven)                     │ self-references too
     assertEquals 2, glen.following.size()

     sven.addToFollowing(peter)
     assertEquals 1, sven.following.size()
   }
```

As you can see, addToFollowing() works the same way for self-references as in the previous one-to-many scenario.

We have now explored all the basic relationship types in Grails, and we have a full set of unit tests to prove it. Grails has also been busy generating the tables and fields

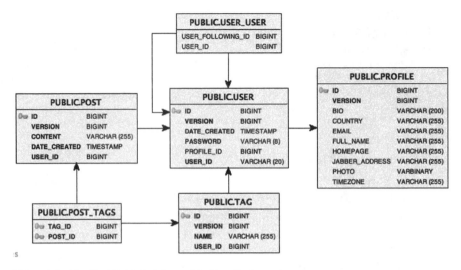

Figure 3.9   The final Hubbub data model after all of our changes

behind the scenes (including the foreign key relationships). If you look inside the Hubbub database, you'll see that it now consists of five tables that hold all the data and relationships in our application. Figure 3.9 shows the full layout of the database, which makes a lot of sense when you match it up with the domain model fields we've created to date.

3.5   *Summary and best practices*

We've covered an immense amount of material in this chapter. A lot of the concepts we've introduced are foundational and will be reinforced in the next few chapters where we cover controllers and views.

We've introduced the basic domain model class, including all of the common domain model relationships. We've also learned about validation and how to create custom constraints.

These are some of the best practices covered in this chapter:

- *Use domain-driven design.*   Create your basic domain model classes as the first step in your application, and use scaffolding to get them online. This will help you stay motivated and understand your domain better.
- *Learn the basic modeling options well.*   You'll spend a lot of time setting up Grails models in your future development work. Take the time to learn all the basic relationship types presented in this chapter. The test cases will give you valuable experimentation fodder.
- *Use tests to experiment.*   Domain model test cases provide a great way of experimenting with tricky save() scenarios and testing out your validations.

- *Don't trust users—validate.*   Make use of validators to keep your domain objects in order. Custom validators aren't hard to implement, so don't be afraid to roll your own if the situation demands. It's better to encapsulate the validation logic in your domain class than to use dodgy controller hacks.

Armed with those basics, we need to develop a little more UI kung fu and we'll be all set for our first fully functional version of Hubbub, which is only a few short chapters away.

Putting the model to work

4

> ## This chapter covers
> - Generating UIs instantly with scaffolding
> - Customizing scaffolds for your project
> - Using dynamic finders for easy querying
> - Advanced query techniques

We spent a lot of time last chapter on the basics of domain modeling. It wasn't easy defining all those relationships, but it did lay down the fundamentals you'll need to build on in each new Grails project. In this chapter, we'll take our new domain knowledge and build a simple UI for our Hubbub application.

You'll learn how scaffolds can make bootstrapping a UI lightning fast, and how they can be customized to generate a unique look and feel for your application. Then, once you have some experience building basic scaffolds for domain classes, we'll teach you some query skills to put that domain model to work. Along the way, we'll implement a basic search form for Hubbub. With this search form in place, we'll teach you some powerful grouping query skills and finish up writing a tag cloud.

First things first, though. Let's explore the amazing productivity gains available through Grails scaffolding.

4.1 Creating instant UIs with scaffolding

In chapter 3, we created a basic User object and explored CRUD operations and querying by hand. But we took you via the scenic route. We could have implemented our feature set in one line of code, without any HTML, by taking advantage of Grails' scaffolding.

We wanted you to know how to write basic CRUD operations by hand, but now that you do, it's time to show you how to get things up and running with a lot less code.

4.1.1 Scaffolding Hubbub's domain classes

In chapter 1, we introduced Grails' scaffolding. Scaffolding lets you automatically generate CRUD screens and matching controller actions for your domain classes on the fly with a single line of code. When you're starting work on an application, this is a fantastic way to get a feel for how your site might work, and scaffolds even prove useful later on for the basic admin screens that end users never see.

Let's create a scaffold for our User object. The first step is to create the controllers that would normally expose our CRUD logic to the web:

```
grails create-controller com.grailsinaction.User
grails create-controller com.grailsinaction.Profile
grails create-controller com.grailsinaction.Post
grails create-controller com.grailsinaction.Tag
```

With our controllers generated, it's time to edit each of the created classes to turn on scaffolding. For example, here's how you would edit the /grails-app/controllers/com /grailsinaction/UserController.groovy file:

```
package com.grailsinaction

class UserController {

    def scaffold = true

}
```

Repeat the process for the ProfileController, PostController, and TagController files, and then start the Grails application to see the scaffolding in action. Do a `grails run-app` and point your browser to http://localhost:8080/hubbub. Click on the UserController link that appears on the home page, and you'll be presented with an empty list of users. Click on the New User button to create a new user. Grails will display a basic editing screen so you can populate the user's details, as shown in figure 4.1.

The generated User scaffold includes options for assigning the related one-to-one Profile object we generated in the last chapter. Any validations that we've applied to fields are also honored in the generated form. For instance, the text box generated for the password field is limited to 8 characters based on the `size: 6..8` validation setting we generated for that field.

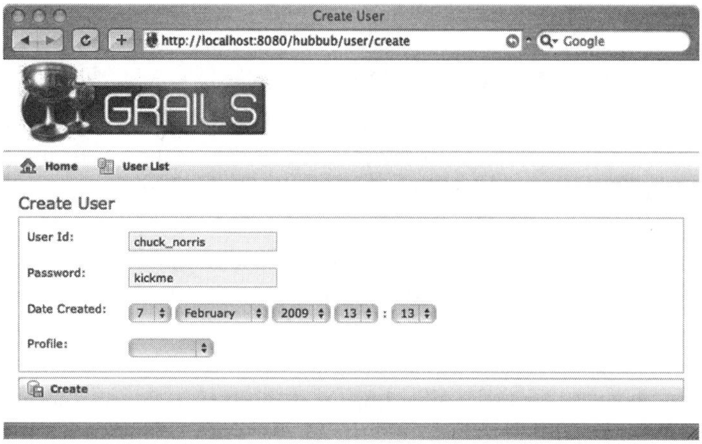

Figure 4.1   Scaffolding also includes relationships and validations.

Validation ordering dictates scaffolding ordering

The order of the fields in your generated scaffold follows the ordering of the constraints in your domain class. If you don't have any constraints, the field order is random (almost never what you want for a form). You'll recall from last chapter that our User object has the following constraints:

```
static constraints = {
    userId(size:3..20)
    password(size: 6..8, validator: { passwd, user ->
        passwd != user.userId
    })
    dateCreated()
    profile(nullable: true)
}
```

Compare the ordering of these constraints with the generated form in figure 4.1. Notice how the order matches?

In our constraints, we've included dateCreated() but applied no validators to it. This technique is useful when you need to influence scaffold ordering but don't want to apply any real constraints on the field.

Although our constraints permit a user to have no assigned profile, we're going to be doing some profile experiments in upcoming sections, so let's work through the process of assigning one. In order to assign a Profile object to the User, you'll first need to create a Profile object using the Profile scaffold, which is obviously not ideal. But let's create one to keep the scaffolds working. Point your browser to http://localhost:8080/hubbub/profile/create and create a new user profile.

4.1.2   *Scaffolding and validation*

While we're creating our new `Profile` object, we can explore how the scaffold handles failing validations. Let's review the `Profile` domain class, which is shown in listing 4.1.

Listing 4.1   The `Profile` class models the personal attributes of a user.

```
package com.grailsinaction

class Profile {

    static belongsTo = User

    byte[] photo

    String fullName
    String bio
    String homepage
    String email
    String timezone
    String country
    String jabberAddress

    static constraints = {                          ⟵⎤ Validates fields with a
        fullName(nullable: true)                        constraints block
        bio(nullable: true, maxSize: 1000)
        homepage(url: true, nullable: true)
        email(email: true, nullable: true)
        photo(nullable: true)
        country(nullable: true)
        timezone(nullable: true)
        jabberAddress(email: true, nullable: true)
    }

}
```

We have constraints on the home page (an optional URL) and the email address (an optional email), and we have a `byte[]` to handle the uploaded photo.

Figure 4.2 shows what happens if we try to create a profile with an invalid home page URL and email address.

Notice that the failing fields are highlighted, and appropriate error messages are displayed at the top of the screen. The descriptions might not be quite to your taste (we'll customize them shortly), but you have to be impressed with the amount of UI functionality we've been able to get for a few lines of code. There's even a file upload control for the photo.

Now it's time to customize those error messages.

Figure 4.2   Validation errors are handled for scaffolds, and so are file uploads and `textareas` for large fields.

4.1.3   *Customizing error messages*

Our validation is now in place, but the default error messages might not be to your taste. It's time to customize those messages. At the same time, we'll internationalize (i18n) things for our Hubbub global market.

Our exploration starts in the /grails-app/i18n/messages.properties file, which is Grails' default resource bundle:

```
default.invalid.url.message=Property [{0}] of class [{1}] with value [{2}]
is not a valid URL
default.invalid.creditCard.message=Property [{0}] of class [{1}] with value
[{2}] is not a valid credit card number
default.invalid.email.message=Property [{0}] of class [{1}] with value
[{2}] is not a valid e-mail address
default.invalid.size.message=Property [{0}] of class [{1}] with value [{2}]
does not fall within the valid size range from [{3}] to [{4}]
```

Here you'll find the standard Grails validation error messages. You'll recognize the URL and range messages from figure 4.2. These can be customized for your needs.

You can see that there are special placeholder fields:

- {0} for a property name
- {1} for a class name
- {2} for a value

There are also others for certain maximum and minimum values required by some constraints. Grails will inject these into your message at runtime if you wish to make use of them.

Default error messages are fine, but typically there's some context required to clearly communicate the problem. Consider our home page and email address fields. To make sure the user is given nice user feedback we can create an entry in messages.properties specifically for it, like so:

```
profile.homepage.url.invalid=You must provide a valid web address for your
➥homepage. [{2}] simply does not cut it
profile.email.email.invalid=You must provide a valid email address. [{2}]
➥is just not the business
```

The format for the entries is {className}.{field}.{errorCode}. These are the same error codes we introduced in the last chapter—if you need a refresher, take a look at section 3.3.1, "Standard validators."

You can change the resource file, messages.properties, while your application is running, and the next validation will pick up the changes. Figure 4.3 shows our new, and more casual, error messages in action.

Those error messages might still need some drafting, but you'll recognize the power of externalizing all your messages to a separate file. If you've done work on internationalizing applications, you might recognize that messages.properties looks like a resource bundle file—because it's a resource bundle! This means Grails makes it straightforward to internationalize your error messages (as discussed in the sidebar).

With our journey through error handling and customization finished, it's time to wire up our new `Profile` object to our `User`.

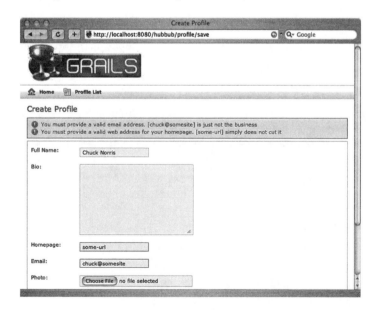

Figure 4.3   You can create your own error messages in resource bundle files.

Scaffolds and internationalization (i18n)

You may notice that the i18n directory contains error messages for several different languages (or *locales*, as they're known), each with a different filename suffix. Grails automatically determines the user's locale based on the `Accept-Language` header their browser sends, but for testing you can pass in a `?lang=fr` header to any of your controllers to simulate a French user. Grails will even remember your locale setting in a cookie for future requests. Here's a sample editing screen with French error messages:

But there's not much point internationalizing your error messages if the rest of your scaffold form is in English. For this reason, Marcel Overdijk developed an i18n Templates plugin that you can install into your Grails application. We cover the details of how plugins work in chapter 8, so skip ahead if you're super keen.

The i18n Templates plugin provides versions of the scaffolding templates that are entirely driven by message bundles, like the ones for the error messages. You can provide internationalized versions of button labels, headings, and user feedback messages for all your domain class elements. Check it out in the plugins section of the Grails website at http://grails.org/Plugins.

4.1.4 Managing relationships via scaffolds

Once we have created a valid `Profile` through the scaffold, we return to the Create User screen and attach the `Profile` to the `User`. Figure 4.4 shows the Create User screen with the new profile attached.

Figure 4.4   The User scaffold lets you select and attach a Profile.

If we'd created many profiles, it would be difficult to select one based on its database ID, but this presentation can be customized (as discussed in the sidebar).

TIP   Grails allows you to make source code changes whilst your application is running. This is a fantastic facility for improving your productivity, because you don't waste time stopping and starting your application to pick up any changes. If Grails detects any changes, it will automatically restart your application. Be warned, though. If your dataSource.groovy has a dbCreate property set to create-drop, your database will be recreated and all data lost.

Grails' scaffolding supports all of the common relationship types: 1:1, 1:m, and m:n. With a few lines of code, you can scaffold your entire application to the point where you can enter both data and relationships.

Customizing scaffolding combo boxes with toString()

Grails scaffolds use the toString() method of the object to populate the combo box, so let's customize the Profile class's toString() method to make it a little more selectable:

```
class Profile {

    // existing domain class code here

    String toString() {
        "Profile for ${fullName} (${id})"
    }

}
```

Customizing scaffolding combo boxes with toString() *(continued)*

If we try to create the user again, Grails will populate the Profile combo box using this new `toString()` routine, as shown here:

This does get pretty unmanageable when there are a lot of relationships going on, particularly in parent-child forms. For those situations, you're better off hand-coding your UI.

Should I use scaffolding in production applications?

Because Grails makes basic CRUD screens easy to generate, you might wonder whether you could use Grails scaffolding for your production applications. Although they probably don't have the cosmetics or ease-of-use that a public-facing site demands, they're fine for internal applications. They're perfect for admin screens that contain reference data, and for CRUD screens that don't need the sophistication of a custom UI. In the next section, we'll even show you how to skin them, so they can look like your other internal apps. And in chapter 10, we'll show you how to secure them so that only admin users can get to them.

4.1.5 *Tweaking scaffold layouts with CSS*

Although the default scaffolds are powerful, they can sometimes look a little "default." Sometimes all that's necessary is adding a skin, and the built-in templates are fine for production use (particularly for internal admin use).

If you want to change the CSS styling for elements in your scaffolds, you can edit the CSS file directly in /web-app/css/main.css. This file is included in all the standard Grails templates, so make your changes and refresh your browser. If your customization goes deeper, and you want to change the layout of the pages themselves (to add banners and footers, for example), you'll need to edit the standard Grails layout that's applied to your scaffolds.

In chapter 1, we introduced layout templates. We said then that Grails makes use of these templates (sometimes known as decorators) to add standard headers, footers, and sidebars to the pages of our applications. You'll learn more about the details of layouts in chapter 6, but for now it's enough to know that you can override the global layout for your site by editing /grails-app/views/layouts/main.gsp. Listing 4.2 updates this file with a new Hubbub skin.

Listing 4.2 Changing the standard layout decorator for Hubbub

```
<html>
   <head>
      <title>Hubbub &raquo; <g:layoutTitle default="Welcome" /></title>
      <link rel="stylesheet" href="
         <g:createLinkTo dir='css'
                  file='hubbub.css'/>"            Adds custom CSS layout
      />
      <g:layoutHead />
   </head>
   <body>
      <div>
         <div id="hd">
            <a href="<g:createLinkTo dir="/"/>">
               <img id="logo"
                  src="${createLinkTo(
                     dir: 'images',                Uses custom
                     file: 'headerlogo.png')}"      masthead image
                  alt="hubbub logo"/>
            </a>
         </div>
         <div id="bd"><!-- start body -->
            <g:layoutBody/>
         </div>  <!-- end body -->
         <div id="ft">
            <div id="footerText">
               Hubbub - Social Networking on Grails
            </div>
         </div>
      </div>
   </body>
</html>
```

This revision adds custom images and CSS files to our main Hubbub layout page. It changes the standard scaffolds so they look like figure 4.5.

Using this technique, you can quickly change the layout for your entire scaffolded site. Even better, once you learn more about how layouts work (in chapter 6), you'll be able to override the layouts on a per-controller basis (just for profiles, for example) or even per-action basis (just for profile edits).

Figure 4.5 You can change the skin for scaffolds to use your own layouts.

4.1.6 What can't you do with dynamic scaffolds?

Dynamic scaffolds give you an incredible amount of power out of the box, and we've shown you several techniques for customizing them, but there are situations where using them doesn't make sense:

- Complex cross-domain forms are tricky to implement with dynamic scaffolds (and you end up with a UI that only a mother could love).
- Dynamic scaffolds have no Ajax support (though you could get around this by customizing the scaffold templates themselves, which we'll talk about soon).
- Dynamic scaffolds have limited support for interaction customizations. (We've done tricky work with CSS and layout customization, but there's not much you can do to customize the generated UI without changing the generator itself, which we'll also do shortly.)

As you can see, dynamic scaffolds aren't the answer to every situation. Fortunately, dynamic scaffolds aren't the only scaffolds in town. Grails allows you to generate static scaffolds, which you can then edit by hand to add your own features. It's time to generate some static view files and take a look at what static scaffolding offers.

4.1.7 Static scaffolding: generating and customizing scaffold code

There are times when dynamic scaffolding is not a good fit for your project. Perhaps you've got some complex many-to-many or parent-child form interactions that need a craftsman's hands. Or maybe you want to use a completely different approach to handing the view.

For these sorts of situations, Grails can generate some basic static scaffolding to get you started. By handing you a dump of all the controller and view source files that it would normally generate dynamically, you can get up and running quickly.

To cater for specific situations, Grails offers two methods of generating static scaffolding files. The first generates all the controller and view files at once:

```
grails generate-all com.grailsinaction.User
```

The second generates only the view files, and leaves your controller class alone:

```
grails generate-views com.grailsinaction.User
```

If you have existing controller or view files, you will be prompted as to whether you want to overwrite them.

It's useful having separate Grails commands for each operation, because your controller code is likely to be fairly insensitive to changes in the domain classes. For example, controller code performs operations like `User.save(params)` or `User.get(params.id)` rather than accessing individual properties of the domain objects. Views, however, will need to display and edit each property on a domain class, so they are very sensitive to any changes made to the domain class. Views, in contrast, are dependent on model changes (adding new fields, renaming fields, and so on), so it can be handy to be able to regenerate just the view code on demand.

The standard controller code is not rocket science. You've written trickier stuff by hand in the previous few chapters. But it's worth knowing which methods are generated for you—they're shown in table 4.1.

A standard static scaffold generates only four GSP files (list, show, edit, and create) and the rest is done in controller logic.

Table 4.1 The basic scaffolding controller methods

Action name	Function	Rendered view
index	Redirects to `list()`.	N/A
list	Shows paginated list of domain class instances.	`list.gsp`
show	Shows a table of all properties for one instance of the domain class.	`show.gsp`
delete	Deletes a given ID, then redirects to `list()`.	N/A
edit	Displays an editing form for a domain instance, and then submits it to `update()`.	`edit.gsp`
update	Updates a given instance of a domain class with new values. Redirects to either `list()` or `edit()` depending on validation.	None
create	Shows a blank editing form for a new domain class instance, and then submits it to `save()`.	`create.gsp`
save	Saves new instances of domain classes. Redirects to either `list()` or `create()` depending on validation.	N/A

4.1.8   *Customizing scaffolding templates: building your own UI generator*

Working with the standard Grails templates is a big time saver, but they won't always provide the functionality you need for your particular project. It's easy enough to style the templates at runtime using CSS, but you might find that you want to customize the behavior, perhaps removing the Delete button for non-admin users. For these sorts of scenarios, you need to edit the templates that Grails uses to generate the scaffolds. You'll be pleased to know you can!

The first step is installing the templates into your application:

```
grails install-templates
```

This will create a bunch of template files in /src/tem- plates that you can customize. Figure 4.6 shows a full list of the files that will be generated.

The files we're concerned with are the entries under /templates/scaffolding. These represent the code that's generated dynamically during scaffolding. You can cus- tomize every aspect of the template process, from the controller code to the GSP files that are generated.

The entries in the artifacts directory are the shell classes that are generated when you execute Grails commands. For example, when you execute `grails generate-controller`, it's the /templates/artifacts/ Controller.groovy file that will be copied over. Hooking into this process can be useful if you want to generate standard license headers or some basic coding stan- dards for new classes.

We'll talk about customizing web.xml in chapter 15 a little later in the book. But keep in mind that Grails won't hold you back from tweaking UI templates in whatever ways make sense for your applications.

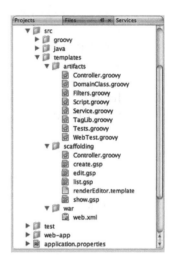

Figure 4.6   The generated template files you can install and modify for scaffolds

4.2   *Groovy querying with dynamic finders and Query by Example*

We've covered a lot of scaffolding territory and put our data model to work generating scaffolds to handle all the basic data-model operations (creating, editing, and delet- ing). But there's one glaring omission: querying.

The fastest way to query your data model in Grails is through a facility known as *dynamic finders*. They are a concise way of querying the data model using a natural- language type of syntax. In this section, we'll start exploring dynamic finders in real depth. We'll also look at Query By Example (QBE), which provides a useful way to query domain objects based on a partially populated template object. Then we'll take a look at some of the useful Grails query facilities for listing and counting objects.

4.2.1 Implementing a basic search form

One of the best ways to get familiar with dynamic finders is by implementing a basic search form for Hubbub. Suppose we want to search to see if any of our friends are already signed up with Hubbub. Let's enhance our `User` scaffold to allow this.

First, we'll create a search form in /grails-app/views/user/search.gsp, as shown in listing 4.3.

Listing 4.3 A basic search form for Hubbub

```html
<html>
<head>
    <title>Search Hubbub</title>
    <meta name="layout" content="main"/>
</head>
<body>

    <formset>
        <legend>Search for Friends</legend>          ❶ Submits form to
                                                       results action
    <g:form action="results">
        <label for="userId">User Id</label>
        <g:textField name="userId" />               ❷ Provides userId
                                                       input field
        <g:submitButton name="search" value="Search"/>
    </g:form>

    </formset>

</body>
</html>
```

There are a few special `<g:>` tags in listing 4.3 that you won't be familiar with. The `<g:form>` tag ❶ specifies that when the user clicks Submit, the form values should be sent to the `results` action on the current controller, which in this case is `User`. The `<g:textField>` tag ❷ names the text box `userId`, which means that it can be handled inside the `results` action as `params.userId`.

With this basic search form in place, we can point our browser to /hubbub/user /search and enter our search criteria. Figure 4.7 shows the search form in action. We've seen basic form code like this earlier in the chapter. What's new is how we can implement the search in the controller. Let's customize our UserController scaffold to handle the new form submission. Listing 4.4 shows the controller with two new actions: `search` and `results`.

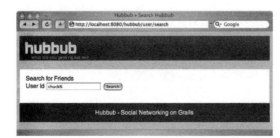

Figure 4.7 A basic Hubbub search form in action

Listing 4.4   Adding the search logic to the UserController.groovy file

```
class UserController {

    def scaffold = true                    ❶ Passes through
                                              to search.gsp
    def search = {
    }                                       ❷ Handles form
                                              submission
    def results = {
        def users = User.findAllByUserIdLike(params.userId)   ❸ Find user based on
        return [ users: users, term : params.userId ]            form parameter
    }                                                         ❹ Pass matching users and
}                                                               search term to view
```

Notice how we've kept our scaffolding on the `User` object, but augmented it with our new search operation. We've added a `search` action with no logic ❶. This is for when we want to display the search form. When the user navigates to /user/search, this action will fire, and Grails will pass the user through to /grails-app/views/user /search.gsp, which acts as a placeholder for the target form.

When the user clicks Search, the form tag submits the search form to the `results` action ❷, which executes a dynamic finder on the `User` object ❸ and places the search term and the matching user objects in the view ❹.

The `User` class doesn't have a `findByUserIdLike()` method, but Grails creates one dynamically using the Groovy `MetaClass`. By using Groovy's dynamic language features, Grails lets you create queries based on all of the available persistent properties in your class. You can even chain two criteria together using `And` and `Or`. A login action might do something like this:

```
def user = User.findByUserIdAndPassword(params.userId, params.password)
if (user) {
    // found them in the database..
}
```

In the next section, we'll explore the options for these dynamic finders, but for now, let's be content with our `findAllUserIdLike()` call. In figure 4.7 we make use of the SQL wildcard operator (`%`) to search for all users starting with "chuck". But it's impractical to force the user to enter those `%` characters for wildcards in their searches. Let's smarten up our controller code to do the magic for them:

```
def users = User.findAllByUserIdLike("%${params.userId}%")
```

This line adds wildcards to either end of the search term to simulate a full-text search.

With our search operations in place, we're going to need a basic results screen. Listing 4.5 implements a results.gsp page (in the same directory as search.gsp) so our controller can return the results to the user.

Listing 4.5   A basic results screen for the search

```
<html>
    <head>
        <title>Search Results</title>
```

```
        <meta name="layout" content="main"/>
    </head>
    <body>
                                                    Displays count of ❶
                                                     all User records
        <h1>Results</h1>
        <p>Searched ${com.grailsinaction.User.count()} records
        for items matching <em>${term}</em>.
        Found <strong>${users.size()}</strong> hits.
        </p>
        <ul>                                        ❷ Iterates over all
            <g:each var="user" in="${users}">         matched Users
                <li>${user.userId}</li>
            </g:each>
        </ul>

        <g:link action='search'>Search Again</g:link>

    </body>
</html>
```

The results page in listing 4.5 takes advantage of another dynamic routine, User.count(), to display a count of all User objects in the database ❶. It then uses another Grails tag, <g:each>, to iterate through all the matching User objects to print out their names ❷. Figure 4.8 shows our Search Results screen in action.

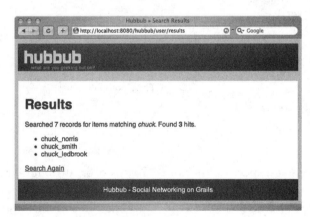

Figure 4.8 The Search Results screen displays several chucks.

We have a basic search function in place, but there's a lot more to learn about query operations. Let's explore some test cases to see what's achievable.

4.2.2 *The many faces of dynamic finders*

Dynamic finders can be used to compose almost all of the basic queries you're likely to want, and their natural-language domain-specific language (DSL) makes them easy to understand and maintain. Let's create a new integration test so we can write a few exploratory queries:

```
grails create-integration-test QueryIntegration
```

Listing 4.6 demonstrates a variety of ways you can use dynamic finders to search for particular values of any attributes on your domain class. In this test case, we'll search for a user by username, by username and password, and by date.

Listing 4.6   A variety of dynamic finders in action

```
import grails.test.*
import com.grailsinaction.Profile
import com.grailsinaction.User

class QueryIntegrationTests extends GrailsUnitTestCase {

   void testBasicDynamicFinders() {

       new User(userId: 'glen', password: 'secret',
          profile: new Profile(email: 'glen@glensmith.com')).save()
       new User(userId: 'peter', password: 'sesame',
          profile: new Profile(homepage: 'http://www.peter.com/')).save()

       def user = User.findByPassword('sesame')        ◁──┐  ❶ Searches on one
       assertEquals 'peter', user.userId                     attribute

       user = User.findByUserIdAndPassword('glen',    ┌── ❷ Searches on two
                               'secret')              │       attributes
       assertEquals 'glen', user.userId

       def now = new Date()
       def users =                                    ┌ ❸ Searches within
          User.findAllByDateCreatedBetween(now-1, now) │      a range
       assertEquals 2, users.size()

       def profiles =                                 │ Finds non-null values
          Profile.findAllByEmailIsNotNull()
       assertEquals 1, profiles.size()

   }

}
```

The findBy*() method lets you specify either one ❶ or two ❷ attribute names to query on and returns a single value (or null if no value is found). There's a corresponding findAllBy*() method ❸ that returns all matching values or an empty List if nothing matches.

Say we wanted to find all users created in the last day or two. We could make use of the findAllBySignupDateBetween() method and have a List of users returned as shown in the following code:

```
def now = new Date()
def users = User.findAllBySignupDateBetween(now-1, now)
assertEquals 2, users.size()
```

Dynamic finders are powerful, and they have a lot of options. Table 4.2 shows some of the basic dynamic finders that are available. You can join criteria with And, but you can only query on two fields.

Table 4.2   A selection of available dynamic finders

Search criteria	Example
LessThan	`User.findAllByDateCreatedLessThan(lastWeek)`
LessThanEquals	`User.findAllByDateCreatedLessThanEquals(lastWeek)`
GreaterThan	`User.findAllByDateCreatedGreaterThan(lastWeek)`
GreaterThanEquals	`User.findAllByDateCreatedGreaterThanEquals(lastWeek)`
Like	`User.findAllByPasswordLike("secret")`
Ilike	`User.findAllByPasswordIlike("Secret")`
NotEqual	`User.findAllByPasswordNotEqual("password")`
Between	`User.findAllByDateCreatedBetween(lastWeek, now)`
IsNotNull	`User.findAllByPasswordIsNotNull()`
IsNull	`User.findAllByPasswordIsNull()`
And	`User.findAllByDateCreatedGreaterThanAndUserIdLike(lastWeek, 'glen')`
Or	`User.findAllByPasswordIsNullOrPasswordLike("secret")`

Writing test cases is a great way to ensure that your code is working as you expect. But what about when you're starting to compose your domain queries and you're looking for a quick way to prototype a whole bunch of different query values? We find the fastest way is to take advantage of the Grails console. If you start your application with `grails console`, Grails launches a small Swing console with a full Grails environment where you can try out your queries and get instant feedback.

> ### How dynamic finders work
>
> After seeing dynamic finders in action, you're probably curious about how they work. Methods with those names don't exist, and it would be inefficient for Grails to generate methods for every possible query combination on each object, right?
>
> Dynamic finders use the Groovy `MetaClass` to intercept method calls on your domain object. By using Groovy's `methodMissing` feature, Grails catches the call to a nonexistent method and creates a Hibernate query from it. It also caches the method so future invocations are quicker. Make sure `MetaClass` exploration is on your to-do list for increasing your Groovy kung fu.

4.2.3   Tuning dynamic finders with eager and lazy fetching

When GORM executes a search like `findByUserId`, it queries for all the fields of the `User` domain class, but any nested collections (such as `Post`) are returned lazily by default. That means the first time you access the posts field of the User object, GORM goes off and retrieves all the matching Post objects related to that user (using a second query). This is called *lazy fetching*. GORM (Hibernate) works this way by default because it's a waste of time retrieving nested objects just in case the user wants to access them.

When you formulate your own queries, though, you often know whether you will access those nested collections right away. In those cases, it makes sense to bring back all the nested objects you want in one SQL query—this is called *eager fetching*. You can do this by telling Grails which collections you'd like to fetch eagerly in the query. We could create a user query that eagerly fetches their related posts, like this:

```
def user = User.findByUserId('glen', [fetch:[posts:'eager']])
```

If you're not sure how many queries you're issuing, you can set logSql=true in your DataSource.groovy configuration file. This will print every database query that Hibernate issues to the console, making it easier to spot places where eager fetching would make a big difference. If you always access the nested collection straight away, you can add a mapping entry to configure GORM to always eagerly fetch the collection. We cover data source tuning and fetch mapping options in chapter 13.

4.2.4 *When dynamic finders don't deliver*

Dynamic finders are powerful, but they have some limitations. The most important one is that you can only use dynamic finders on a maximum of two fields. If you need to query on more than two fields, you need to use criteria or Hibernate Query Language (HQL) queries.

The same applies if you need to do more complex relational queries based on attributes of a contained object. For those scenarios, we'll need to resort to HQL. But don't worry. We'll explore both those options in depth in section 4.3.

4.2.5 *Introducing Query by Example (QBE)*

Grails has several ways to query for objects, and we've started to look at dynamic finders. But there are many other search options in Grails, like Query by Example (QBE). With QBE, you create a domain object and populate it with properties that you wish to query for (anything that's null will be skipped). The search then looks for similar objects.

Let's add a new test case to QueryIntegrationTests (from listing 4.6) to see how QBE works. Our new test is shown in listing 4.7.

Listing 4.7 QBE works by populating a sample object and searching for similar objects

```
void testQueryByExample() {
    new User(userId: 'glen', password: 'password').save()
    new User(userId: 'peter', password: 'password').save()
    new User(userId: 'cynthia', password: 'sesame').save()
```

```
def userToFind = new User(userId: 'glen')
def u1 = User.find(userToFind)
assertEquals('password', u1.password)

userToFind = new User(userId: 'cynthia')
def u2 = User.find(userToFind)
assertEquals('cynthia', u2.userId)

userToFind = new User(password: 'password')
def u3 = User.findAll(userToFind)
assertEquals(['glen', 'peter'], u3*.userId)
```

1 Finds single user based on template user

2 Finds all users matching template user

```
}
```

In this test, we populate our sample User objects with the fields we wish to search on, and we pass them into either User.find() to find the first matching object **1** or User.findAll() to return all instances matching the criteria **2**. If User.find() matches more than one entry, you only get the first one back.

4.2.6 *Getting dynamic with list(), listOrderBy(), and countBy()*

We've had a good look at the Grails find()-based commands, but we haven't yet explored some of the other useful query routines that Grails adds to domain classes, such as list() and count(). User.list() gives you a List of all User objects from the database, and User.count() gives you an integer count of how many User objects there are, but things can be customized a whole lot more than that.

Let's start by exploring some more sophisticated uses of list(). First, there's a truckload of options available to the list() command that control sorting, ordering, and offsets, as shown in table 4.3.

Let's invoke the list() call with some of those options. Let's say we want to see the first five users ordered by ascending userId, and we also want to eagerly fetch the posts associated with those users to iterate them quickly. That's simple:

```
def users = User.list([sort: 'userId', order: 'asc',
              max: 5, fetch: [posts: 'eager']])
```

Table 4.3 Options for the list() method

Option	Description
max	Specifies the maximum number of rows to return
sort	Specifies the field to sort on in the returned list
order	Specifies the order of the sort: 'desc' or 'asc' (default is 'asc')
ignoreCase	Sets sorting to ignore case (true by default)
fetch	Specifies eager/lazy fetch strategy as a Map of options
offset	Specifies the number of elements into the ResultSet to start at when returning values (useful for pagination)

Now that you've seen some of the power of list(), it's time to introduce list-OrderBy*(). This method lets you pick a field to order by. For instance, if we want to sort by ascending userId, we could use this method:

```
def users = User.listOrderByUserId()
```

You can still pass in the max, order, and offset options if you need to control sort ordering or offsets for paginating your results.

Now it's time to see the corresponding countBy*() method in action. To find all users with dodgy passwords in our application, we might try something like this:

```
def dodgyCount = User.countByPassword("password")
```

This will return a count of all users with the password "password".

4.3   *More sophisticated query options*

Dynamic finders are concise and quite powerful. Being able to do something like User.findByUserId("joe") is a productive way to query, but there are situations where that's not enough. Grails won't leave you stranded: it's time to explore criteria queries and HQL.

This section takes advantage of some pretty advanced query skills in Grails, so don't get discouraged if some of this seems tricky the first few times. Once you start writing your own applications and can't implement the features you want with dynamic finders, you'll find yourself coming back here to review these advanced query features. Buckle up.

4.3.1   *With great power: criteria querying*

Dynamic finders are great for basic querying, but sometimes you want something more complex. Perhaps you're querying on more than two fields, or perhaps you require a sophisticated nested query. Or perhaps you're building a query dynamically from user input in a search form. It's time to experience the power of GORM criteria queries.

Let's look at a Hubbub example. Hubbub lets us tag posts with keywords, so suppose we wanted to find all of a user's posts created in the last day and tagged with "Grails". For this sort of scenario, criteria queries are what you want. Listing 4.8 demonstrates a basic criteria query.

Listing 4.8   Criteria queries give you astonishing power.

```
def user = User.findByUserId(params.user)          ❶ Creates
                                                        query object
def entries = Post.createCriteria().list {
    and {                                          ❷ Ensures all conditions are true
        eq('user', user)
        between('created', new Date()-1, new Date())
        tags {                      ❹ Queries across        ❸ Supplies
            eq('name', 'Grails')       relationships            query values
        }
    }
}
```

```
    maxResults(10)                    5  Constrains
    order("created", "desc")             ResultSet
}
```

That's a lot of parentheses. Let's take a closer look. After creating the `Criteria` object on the domain class that we wish to query ❶, we call the `list` method and pass in the criteria using the GORM Criteria DSL. In this case we're doing an and ❷ because we want all of the criteria nested within the and `{ }` block to match (we could also use `or` or `not` here, depending on how we want to join the data logically).

Next we add a few parameters, called "restrictions," to our query. In this case, we're using an `eq` restriction to require that the `Post`'s `User` matches our existing `User` object, and a `between` restriction ❸ to restrict the search to a date range. The final item is the subquery on tags to ensure that we only find those posts that are tagged with "Grails" ❹.

Having built the main query, we can add other restrictions. You'll recognize `maxResults()` and `order()` ❺, but here we can specify the order in one instruction, rather than having separate `orderBy` and `sort` fields.

> **Where can I get a full list of available restrictions?**
>
> The GORM Criteria DSL is a thin wrapper over the Hibernate `Restrictions` class. If you take a look at the Restrictions Javadocs, you'll find all of the options. Included are things like `ilike` (for case-insensitive matching), `ge` (greater equal), and `isNotEmpty` (for fields having a value).

There are a few more shortcuts available for criteria queries. First, because `list()` is the most common operation on a `Criteria` instance, you can omit it entirely (though we prefer keeping an explicit `list()` to make things more readable). Criteria queries also support a `count()` method for returning a count of the matching values, or a `get()` method to return a unique result.

Criteria queries are so handy that there's a special `withCriteria` closure that's available on all domain classes. This is often a concise way of expressing a criteria query inline with your controller code:

```
def entries = Post.withCriteria {
   and {
      eq('user', user)
      between('created', new Date()-1, new Date())
   }
}
```

The shorter `withCriteria()` form of the query has all of the same Criteria DSL goodness that we saw for the longer `.createCriteria().list()` version.

4.3.2 *Dynamic queries with criteria*

Criteria objects make complex queries simple, but they're also great for generating queries dynamically. Imagine that we want to generate a basic search form for Hubbub profiles. We'll provide the user with form fields to search on (maybe their full name, email, and homepage), and we'll give them AND, OR, and NOT options to join their criteria.

First, we'll generate a basic form with field names that match our `Profile` object, as shown in figure 4.9.

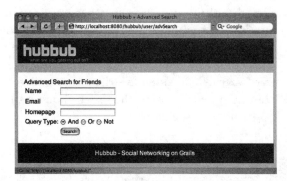

Figure 4.9 A more advanced search screen with Boolean operators

With our query fields in place, we can now write a generic search action that builds a `Criteria` object on the fly, based on the fields the user populates in the form. Because of the flexibility of the `Criteria` object, we can take advantage of Boolean operations (and, or, not) when constructing the search. Listing 4.9 shows what a dynamic criteria search might look like.

Listing 4.9 A dynamic search form

```
def advResults = {

    def profileProps =
        Profile.metaClass.properties*.name          ❶ Generates list of available
    def profiles = Profile.withCriteria {              Profile methods
        "${params.queryType}" {                      ❷ Applies Boolean operator

            params.each { field, value ->            ❸ Iterates incoming
                if (profileProps.grep(field)            parameters
                    && value) {
                    ilike(field, value)
                }                     Provides constraints for
            }                            supplied params ❹
        }
    }
    [ profiles : profiles ]
}
```

We've had to do a little work here. Because Grails populates the params object with its own values, not just those from our form fields, we have to extract from the params just those values related to our Profile object. To perform this filtering, we use the Groovy MetaClass to find all the properties in the Profile class ❶. We then construct a Criteria object, and set the join type to match the Boolean operation the user selects: and, or, or not ❷. Finally, we iterate through all the incoming params ❸, and, for those that correspond to a Profile property, we apply an ilike operator ❹.

This is a pretty advanced use case, so don't be worried if it sounds a bit complex. It will make more sense when you experiment with the source code. In figure 4.10 we give it a test by combining a few options with an Or constraint. We've even thrown in some wildcard operators for good measure (%).

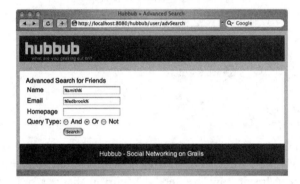

Figure 4.10   An advanced search screen with ANDing and ORing

We can see our results in figure 4.11, which uses a basic output form.

You can see that Criteria objects are fantastic for building up dynamic queries. But there are even more powerful Criteria features for creating report-style queries. It's time we explored groupBy functionality.

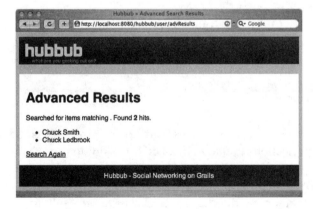

Figure 4.11   A basic results screen shows two profiles matching our criteria

4.3.3   *Creating a tag cloud using report-style query projections*

Criteria queries shine for complex and dynamic queries, but they can also do projections. Projections are aggregating, reporting, and filtering functions that can be applied after the query has finished.

A common use for projections is to summarize data in a query. For example, to build a tag cloud for a user, we need to find their tags and count how many posts are associated with each. This is a good use case for a count() projection, as shown in listing 4.10.

Listing 4.10   Using projections to group and count search results

```
def tagList = Post.withCriteria {        ◁——❶ Creates Criteria query

    createAlias("user", "u")         ❷ Defines aliases
    createAlias("tags", "t")            for later user        ❸ Ensures Post belongs
    eq("u.userId", "glen")              ◁                         to correct User

    projections {               ◁——— ❹ Applies projections
        groupProperty("t.name")              to ResultSet
        count("t.id")
    }
                          Specifies which
}                         projections to apply ❺
```

Projection queries are normal criteria queries, so we start by specifying what we're querying for—in this case, a collection of Post objects ❶. Because we're selecting and grouping on multiple object sets inside Post, we need to set up an alias tag for both our User and Tag fields ❷. This will let us reference these fields in later groupBy clauses.

With all the infrastructure in place, we start specifying our query. Our first restriction finds all posts related to user "glen" using the eq operator ❸. Once we have all posts related to glen, we can start grouping them by specifying the projections clause ❹. We specify the field we want to group by, t.name, along with the operation we want to perform on that grouping, count() ❺.

The result of the query is a List of key/value pairs containing the tag name and the number of posts with that tag. All we need now is to convert that list into a Map, with tagName as the key, and tagCount as the value. It's time to dust off those Groovy skills:

```
def tagcloudMap = tagList.inject([ : ]) { map, tag ->
    map[ tag[0] ] = tag[1]; map
}
```

This creates a map of tag name to tag count that's ready to be fed to a tag cloud taglib.

There are lots more projections available in GORM. In addition to count(), you can use max(), min(), avg(), sum(), and all sorts of other statistical methods. GORM projections are merely DSL enhancements to the standard Hibernate projections. Check out the Hibernate Javadocs on the Projections class to see a full list.

It's time to look at one final Grails query option: raw HQL. You won't need it often, but for the fringe cases, it's a real lifesaver.

When should I use criteria queries and when dynamic finders?

The choice between criteria queries and dynamic finders comes down to developer preference. We've found that dynamic finders are fantastic for most query needs, and they're probably your best first stop. You don't have to sacrifice fetching strategy, ordering, or offsets, and they give you a clear and maintainable way of expressing queries.

But if you need to query on more than two attributes, to take advantage of query caching, or to express a query based on subrelationships (for example, find all Users that have a Profile with an email of glen@glen.com), criteria querying is your best bet.

Criteria queries also shine when generating a set of query constraints dynamically based on an HTML form (such as when users specify which fields to include in the form, and what the constraints should be, and you generate the criteria on the fly). We showed an example of this scenario in section 4.3.2.

4.3.4   *Using HQL directly*

If you've come from a Hibernate background, you're probably used to expressing complex Hibernate queries using HQL—Hibernate's query language. If you need the power of HQL from Grails, you can take full advantage of HQL directly from find() and findAll(). You should only need HQL for the most complex queries, and you will sacrifice quite a bit of maintenance and readability by using it. But there are situations where this is demanded.

A basic HQL query looks like this:

```
println User.findAll("from User u where u.userId = ?", [ "joe" ])
```

You can insert a question mark (?) as a placeholder for any pieces of the query that you need to supply dynamically. The final argument to the call is a list of substitutions that should replace the question-mark placeholders (the number of items in the list should match the number of question marks). In the preceding example, we've supplied "joe" as a static substitution, but in a real application you'd be more likely to supply a dynamic value, such as params.userId.

Mitigating against SQL injection attacks

One of the most common web security vulnerabilities is the SQL injection attack. In this type of attack, the user passes in malicious query parameters to alter the queries sent to the database (for example, ...?userId=abc123;delete+from +users;). This is why you should never do your own concatenations of HQL query strings. If you use the property placeholder (?) form of HQL queries, you will always be protected from these sorts of attacks.

But those question marks aren't particularly readable. If you've ever used HQL, you may be familiar with *named criteria*. These let you replace those question marks with a more readable identifier prefixed with a colon (:). You can then provide a corresponding map of name/value pairs at the end of the parameter list to the call. Let's try it again with named queries:

```
User.findAll("from User u where u.userId = :uid", [ uid: "joe" ])
```

If you're in the middle of paginating, perhaps via the <g:paginate> tag, the usual max: and offset: fields can be used in addition to your named criteria:

```
User.findAll("from User u where u.userId like :uid",
        [ uid: "j%", max: params.max, offset: params.offset ] )
```

HQL gives you a lot of power, and in some circumstances you will need to take advantage of it. But there aren't many things that you can do in HQL that you can't already do with criteria queries, so HQL should probably not be your first choice.

That concludes our whirlwind journey through Grails query options. There's only one more aspect of domain models to explore—the bootstrapping of domain model reference data.

4.4   Bootstrapping reference data

Sometimes it's useful to populate reference data in your database as soon as it's created. For example, you might always want to create an admin user with a known password for system configuration. But if Grails is creating your database tables for you, how do you hook into the process?

The answer is found in /grails-app/conf/BootStrap.groovy. This file has two closures, init and destroy, which Grails invokes when the system starts and when it's shut down, respectively.

During the bootstrapping process, you typically have different behavior for different environments (for example, to create several standard dummy users in development, but not in production). Grails allows you to tailor your bootstrap file in a per-environment way.

In the Bootstrap.groovy file in listing 4.11, we create admin users for our development environment, but skip them in production.

Listing 4.11   Bootstrapping reference data based on the environment

```
import com.grailsinaction.*
import grails.util.Environment

class BootStrap {

    def init = { servletContext ->
        switch (Environment.current) {                ① Checks the
                                                         environment
            case Environment.DEVELOPMENT:             ② Invokes methods on
                createAdminUserIfRequired()              per-environment basis
                break;
```

① Checks the environment

② Invokes methods on per-environment basis

```
            case Environment.PRODUCTION:
                println "No special configuration required"
                break;

        }

    }

    def destroy = {
    }

    void createAdminUserIfRequired() {
        if (!User.findByUserId("admin")) {
            println "Fresh Database. Creating ADMIN user."
            def profile = new Profile(email: "admin@yourhost.com")
            def user = new User(userId: "admin",
                password: "secret", profile: profile).save()
        } else {
            println "Existing admin user, skipping creation"
        }
    }
}
```

❸ **Ensures admin user doesn't exist**

You'll notice that we check the current environment ❶ and only create our admin user if we're running in development (that is, if we're running via `grails run-app`) ❷. We also test to see if our admin user exists in the database before we create it ❸. Although the standard HSQLDB in-memory driver guarantees we'll have an empty database every time, that won't be the case if your target users switch to using a persistent database like MySQL. Always check before inserting sample data.

One final thing to note about bootstrapping is that there's no guarantee that `destroy()` will be called. If the server terminates or other bad things happen, this closure may never execute. You've been warned.

4.5 Summary and best practices

In this chapter, we've explored Grails scaffolding and seen how we can make use of scaffolds to create an instant UI for our application. We also saw how to skin the application with our own CSS and layouts, and customize error messages and templates. We even added our own custom search actions right in with the generated templates to demonstrate scaffold flexibility.

Applying our knowledge of scaffolds to querying, we demonstrated lots of techniques for querying in Grails. Dynamic finders are great for creating two-field queries and keeping things maintainable. But for the situations where dynamic finders don't cut it, we looked at advanced query techniques using criteria queries, projections, and even bare-metal HQL.

Let's revisit some of the key ideas from this chapter, which you can take away and apply to your own Grails apps:

- *Use scaffolds for instant gratification and to stay motivated.* Scaffolds give you a good feeling of progress and keep you focused on getting your app out the door. Also, don't be afraid of using scaffolding code for admin screens in production code.

- *Understand your customization options.*   You can do a lot to make scaffold screens integrate with custom pages. Take advantage of CSS and layouts to skin them in a way that harmonizes with the rest of your app.
- *Dynamic finders are fantastic for two-field queries.*   Dynamic finders are self-documenting and easy for other developers to understand. If you need to query on more fields, criteria queries make more sense.
- *Use the Grails console.*   The Grails console is ideal for prototyping tricky dynamic finder queries, and it lets you try out lots of options without recompiling.
- *Harness the power of criteria queries.*   Criteria queries give you a lot more query power than dynamic finders, but they come at the price of a little complexity. Use criteria projections for grouping and reporting queries.
- *Always use named params for HQL.*   Using named params avoids SQL injection risks. Never build HQL query strings dynamically (use criteria queries for that).
- *Use bootstraps conditionally.*   Grails lets you perform different bootstrap operations in each environment, so make use of that. Don't assume that your user's development database is an in-memory one, and always check whether your sample data exists before re-creating it.

In the next chapter, we'll take our domain modeling skills and apply them to working with forms and controllers in the UI layer. It'll be a refreshing break from writing unit tests.

5
Controlling application flow

This chapter covers

- How controllers, models, and views interact
- Implementing custom URLs and permalinks
- Writing filter code to reroute requests
- Using services for more maintainable architecture
- Data binding and error handling
- Using Command objects for tricky form validations
- Uploading and rendering images

In chapters 3 and 4, we spent plenty of time looking at how Grails handles domain objects. Along the way, we've used controllers and implemented a few GSP views to host our forms, but we've largely ignored how controllers work. It's time to set that right.

In this chapter, we'll focus on controllers. We'll learn more advanced binding techniques for passing variables between forms and controllers, get some insight into how redirects work, implement file uploads, open the lid on filters, and even render custom content types. Along the way, we'll beef up Hubbub to handle uploading and display profile photos, and we'll implement the core business of creating Users and Posts. By the end of the chapter, you'll be ready to implement the common controller use cases in your own applications, and quite a few of the edge cases.

We'll get the chapter underway by pulling together all you've learned so far about controllers, forms, and domain classes. We'll modify Hubbub to add and display user posts on a Twitter-style timeline.

5.1   Controller essentials

In our exploration of the Grails ecosystem so far, we've been more focused on the model (saving and querying domain objects) and passed over the gritty details of how controllers, views, and taglibs work together. Let's take a more detailed look at form-controller interactions with a focus on the controllers.

Imagine that we want to display a timeline of a user's recent posts. We'd need to implement a controller action (perhaps `timeline` in the `Post` controller) to retrieve the posts for a user, then pass them to a view (/views/post/timeline.gsp) to display them in the browser. As we discovered in chapter 1, Grails exposes controller actions as URLs using conventions. Here's how Grails translates controller action names into URLs :

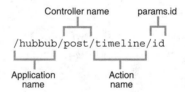

When the user points their browser at http://localhost:8080/hubbub/post/timeline/chuck_norris, for example, Grails will fire the `timeline` action on the `Post` controller, passing chuck_norris as the id. Typically, that action will retrieve some data from the database and pass it to the view to display. Under Grails conventions, the view name matches the action name (but with a .gsp extension), so the `timeline` action will retrieve the data and pass it to /views/post/timeline.gsp to be rendered. Figure 5.1 demonstrates this flow.

You saw this flow in action in chapter 1 and in the search form examples in chapter 4. Let's apply our knowledge of controllers to add a timeline to Hubbub.

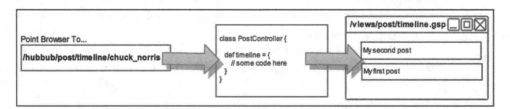

Figure 5.1   From URL to controller to view

5.1.1 *Implementing a timeline for Hubbub*

A timeline for a user should display a list of posts for the user mixed with posts by everyone they follow. But let's start small and implement the capability to display all the posts for one user.

We'll start by updating our `PostController` to implement a `timeline()` action. Listing 5.1 shows our first implementation of a user timeline:

Listing 5.1 Adding the timeline action to our `PostController`

```
package com.grailsinaction

class PostController {

    def scaffold = true

    def timeline = {
        def user = User.findByUserId(params.id)      ❶ Retrieves user based
        [ user : user ]                                  on id parameter
    }                          ❷ Passes matched
                                  user to view
}
```

As you've seen in earlier chapters, actions typically process form parameters and use them to interact with the data model. In this case, we're using the optional id parameter to hold the user's ID, and we use it to retrieve the entire `User` object from the database ❶. In a production application, you'd probably want to do some `null` checking there. We'll add some error handling later in the chapter.

Once you've retrieved the `User` object, the result of the action then gets placed into a map that is returned to the view ❷, which is typically a GSP file. The view can access any objects in the map to display them to the user. We could use an explicit `return` statement at the end of our action, but there's no need. Groovy always considers the last line of a closure or method as the return value, and it's common for Grails programmers to omit `return` in controller actions.

The optional id param

You may not have seen the id field in action yet. As illustrated at the beginning of section 5.1, the conventional URL-to-controller mapping is /controller/action/id, where the id portion is passed into the params.id field. Because the format of the field is free-form, it gives you some cool options for permalinks.

For example, /user/profile/chuck_norris would fire the profile() action on the User controller, passing in chuck_norris to the params.id. This was how people commonly did permalinking before Grails implemented custom URL mappings, which we'll get to in section 5.7 of this chapter.

Grails scaffolds use the id field to represent the database ID, so you'll often see URLs like /user/show/57 being used to display the user with id 57 from the database. It's practical, but it sure ain't pretty.

We can now retrieve the user from the database, so it makes sense to implement a view to display the information. Following Grails conventions, we'll implement our view in a file that has the same name as our controller and action. In this case, the view will be named /grails-app/views/post/timeline.gsp. Listing 5.2 shows our first effort at displaying the user's timeline.

Listing 5.2   Displaying a user's timeline

```
<html>
   <head>
      <title>
         Timeline for ${user.profile.fullName}
      </title>
      <meta name="layout" content="main"/>             ❶ Accesses nested
   </head>                                                 domain objects
   <body>
      <h1>Timeline for ${user.profile.fullName}</h1>
                                                        ❷ Iterates through
      <div class="allPosts">                               user's posts
         <g:each in="${user.posts}" var="post">
            <div class="postEntry">
               <div class="postText">
                  ${post.content}                      ❸ Displays
               </div>                                      each post
               <div class="postDate">
                  ${post.dateCreated}
               </div>
            </div>
         </g:each>
      </div>

   </body>
</html>
```

By making use of the User object that the controller placed into our request scope (which we'll discuss in section 5.1.3), we're able to read the User's fields and display the data in the browser. In this example, we access the User's Profile object, and display the full name ❶.

We can reference objects in request scope by enclosing their name in Groovy's interpolation syntax, ${}. If you pass complex objects to your view (for example, a domain object with relationships to other domain objects), you can access them as you would in any other setting. In listing 5.2, we render ${user.profile.fullName} ❶.

We also iterate over each of the User's Post objects ❷, displaying the content and dateCreated of each post ❸.

Figure 5.2 shows our new timeline view in action. With the timeline in place to show all the user's posts, we can now work on adding new posts to the timeline. This will give us a good chance to create and save domain objects.

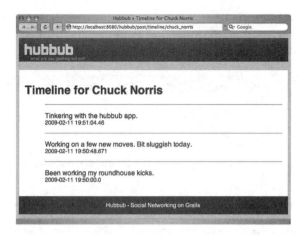

Figure 5.2   Our first timeline in action

Breaking view name conventions

If you don't want your view name to match your action name, you can use the `render()` method. For instance, if you want to use user_timeline.gsp to generate the output for your timeline action, you can use the view argument to `render()`:

```
render(view: "user_timeline", model: [ user: user ])
```

Notice that you omit the .gsp extension when referring to the view.

5.1.2   Adding new posts

In chapter 3, we learned how to create and save `Post` objects from a unit test. Now that we know a little about how controllers work, let's apply our knowledge to the UI.

First, let's enhance our view to give our user the ability to add new posts. We want to end up with the sort of capability shown in figure 5.3.

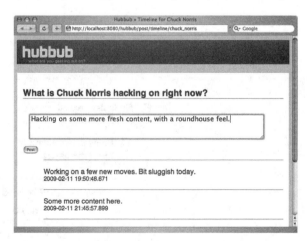

Figure 5.3   Adding posting capabilities to Hubbub

For this to work, we need to add a form to timeline.gsp to capture the new content for the post. We'll need a textArea component so the user can enter the body of the post. Listing 5.3 shows the div we'll add to our timeline.gsp file to handle the new input.

Listing 5.3   Adding a form for new posts

```
<div id="newPost">

    <h3>
        What is ${user.profile.fullName} hacking on right now?
    </h3>                                                         ❶ Retains id from
                                                                      current URL
    <p>
        <g:form action="addPost" id="${params.id}">   ◀
            <g:textArea id='postContent' name="content"    ❷ Provides textArea
                rows="3" cols="50"/><br/>                        to enter post
            <g:submitButton name="post" value="Post"/>
        </g:form>
    </p>
</div>
```

In listing 5.3 we've added a new form to the page using the `<g:form>` tag, with the target of the form being the addPost action ❶. We pass through the current id field to the form submission, so the addPost action knows which user ID it's being invoked for. For example, the form submission URL for the "chuck_norris" user ID would be /post /addPost/chuck_norris.

We've also added the `<g:textArea>` tag to let the user enter their post contents ❷. Because the control is named content, we can expect params.content to turn up in our controller logic somewhere.

Listing 5.4 shows our updated `PostController` code, which now handles adding new posts to the user's timeline.

Listing 5.4   The updated `PostController` handles new `Post` objects

```
package com.grailsinaction

class PostController {

    def scaffold = true

    def timeline = {
        def user = User.findByUserId(params.id)
        [ user : user ]                               ❶ Finds user based
    }                                                     on id param

    def addPost = {
        def user = User.findByUserId(params.id)   ◀   ❷ Binds params data to
        if (user) {                                       new Post object
            def post = new Post(params)           ◀   ❸ Links new post
            user.addToPosts(post)                 ◀       to existing user
            if (user.save()) {                    ◀
                                                          save() returns
                flash.message = "Successfully created Post"  ◀  false if Post
            } else {                                         ❹ validation fails
                                          Informs user of
                                          success or failure ❺
```

```
        user.discard()
        flash.message = "Invalid or empty post"
      }
    } else {
      flash.message = "Invalid User Id"
    }
    redirect(action: 'timeline', id: params.id)
  }

}
```

⑤ Informs user of success or failure

⑥ Returns user to timeline

When we were saving domain models in chapter 3, we wrote integration tests. Now we're doing it for real from the UI. Like our `timeline` action, `addPost` starts by retrieving the `User` object based on its ID **①**, but here we've added some basic error handling to test whether the user exists.

If the `User` exists in the database, we create a new `Post` object, passing in the `params` map **②**. As you learned in chapter 2, when you pass a map into a constructor, Groovy binds the properties of the map to fields on the object, skipping the ones that don't match. In this case, `params.content` will be mapped to the `Post`'s `content` field. Figure 5.4

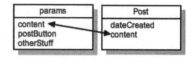

Figure 5.4   Binding a `params` map to a `Post` object

shows how the `content` field of the `params` object maps to the `Post` object. Grails refers to this process as *data binding*.

With the form data bound to our new `Post` object, the new `Post` is added to the `User` object **③**. Finally, we can attempt a `save()` to ensure that constraints on the `Post` object are satisfied **④**.

Whether things go well or fail dismally, we keep the user informed by providing feedback with `flash.message` **⑤**. We'll discuss flash scope in the next section, but in short it's a way to communicate information to the user. Later in the chapter, we'll show you a more robust way of handling validation errors, but `flash.message` will be fine for now.

When everything is done, we redirect the user back to the `timeline` action **⑥** which will rerender the timeline with the new post. Notice that the redirect includes the `id` param. This is important, because the timeline action relies on having the user's ID, and when we redirect programmatically (rather than typing in a browser URL), we need to explicitly provide the value.

We now need to update our timeline.gsp file to output those error or success messages to the user. The following code fragment shows the updated `div` for our flash message:

```
<g:if test="${flash.message}">
   <div class="flash">
     ${flash.message}
   </div>
</g:if>
```

We'll need to style the `div` with CSS so that it stands out as a warning message. If you download the source for the chapter you'll find the necessary CSS styling to match the screen shots that follow.

With our basic error handling in place, it's time to experiment with adding an invalid post. Figure 5.5 shows the result of attempting to add a blank post. Our validation is firing and we've implemented the capability to add new posts to Hubbub.

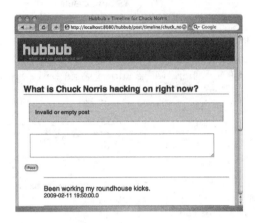

Figure 5.5   Adding a blank post generates an error.

You've now implemented a basic version of two of Hubbub's major features: displaying the user's timeline, and adding posts. You've also applied your knowledge of creating domain objects (from chapter 3) and using dynamic finders to query them (from chapter 4).

But there are still a few things unexplained. Where did all these `flash` objects come from, and what do they do? And why aren't we using the standard validation messages we saw in chapter 4? Fear not. By the end of the chapter, you'll understand all these essential controller issues.

We'll start with the `flash` object, which relates to how Grails handles scope.

5.1.3   *Exploring scopes*

You've seen how controller actions can return a map that gets passed through to the view, and you've seen the `flash` object also passing data from controller to view. This passing of information, and the lifetime of the variables that you pass, is known as variable *scope*.

Grails supports different scopes to store information in, and each of them lasts a different length of time. When you passed data in a map from a controller to a view, you were implicitly making use of *request scope*. But Grails lets you reference the different scopes explicitly so you can store data for as long as you need it. In particular, Grails offers you four special map-like storage scopes that you can reference by name in every controller action. They are listed in table 5.1.

NOTE   `request`, `flash`, `session`, and `servletContext` aren't really Java `Maps`. For example, request is a Java `HttpServletRequest` object. But the underlying objects have been enhanced via some advanced Grails `Meta-Class` operations to expose map-like storage, making things much easier for the programmer.

Table 5.1   Grails supports four storage contexts for passing content between controllers and forms

Scope variable	Survival time for entries in this scope
`request`	Survive until the target GSP finishes rendering
`flash`	Survive to the next page, and the one after that
`session`	Survive until the current user closes the browser
`servletContext`	Survive until the application is restarted (this map is shared by all users)

If you've done work with Java web applications before, you've probably seen request, session, and servlet-Context scopes. Flash scope is unique to Grails, and it's a real life saver. Figure 5.6 shows the relative lifespans of the different scopes. We'll look at each scope individually, next.

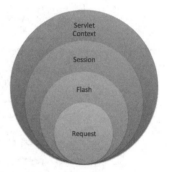

REQUEST SCOPE

Request scope is great when you want to store data that is shared only between your controller and the view (normally a GSP page). In this case, the server is said to "forward" the request to the page (meaning that the browser location doesn't change—it's all handled within the server itself). Even though you weren't aware of it, we've been using request scope every time we

Figure 5.6   Request scope is the shortest lived, and servletContext the longest.

returned a `Map` from our controller actions. Request scope is used to hold that data until the view has finished rendering it.

But what about our `addPost()` action? We do the heavy lifting of adding a post, but then we want to redirect the browser to the user's timeline to display a "Successfully added" message. That means the browser is involved, which means our request scope is gone.

For these scenarios, Grails offers *flash scope*.

FLASH SCOPE

Entries in the flash map survive one (and only one) redirect, after which they're removed. That's exactly what we need for our `addPost()` action. We can safely place a "Successfully added" message into our flash map and know that it will survive the redirect back to our `timeline` action.

Like all of these scope maps, `flash` is a general purpose map, but convention dictates that you put these kind of UI messages in an attribute called `flash.message`.

You'll commonly see flash scope referenced in GSP files wrapped in a conditional to keep things tidy, as in our earlier Post example. Here's a sample of the kind of code you'll commonly encounter in a GSP:

```
<g:if test="${flash.message}">
   <div class="flash">${flash.message}</div>
</g:if>
```

For objects that you want to survive longer than a single redirect, you'll need to explore session scope.

SESSION SCOPE

The next longest lived scope is session scope. Objects that you place in session scope remain until the user closes their browser. Internally, servers use a session cookie called JSESSIONID to map a user to their session, and the cookie expires when they close their browser (or when the server times out the session due to inactivity).

Sessions are replicated in a clustered environment, so it's best to keep their contents to a minimum. A common use case is putting a logged-in User object into the session, so be sure you understand how detached domain objects work (see the sidebar).

Session gotchas: the mystery of the detached object

If you're storing a domain object in the session (such as the logged-in User object), the object will become *detached* from your Hibernate session. That means you won't be able to access any uninitialized lazy-loaded relationships the object holds. For example, you won't be able to call session.user.following.each {}. To reattach the object (so you can walk its object graph of relationships, for instance), use the attach() method that is available on all domain classes. For our User example, it would look like this:

```
def user = session.user
if (!user.isAttached()) {
   user.attach()
}
user.following.each { nextFollowing -> /* do stuff */ }
```

SERVLETCONTEXT (APPLICATION) SCOPE

The final scope available is *servletContext scope*, sometimes called *application scope*. This map is shared across your whole application, and it's handy for storing state that's not dependent on any particular user (such as the number of logins since the application was started). This scope is also useful for loading resources from within your web application itself (for example, servletContext.getResourceAsStream("/images/my-logo.gif")). Consult the standard servletContext Javadoc for details.

NOTE   There are also flow and conversation scopes, but we won't cover those until chapter 9, which deals with Grails webflows.

We now have a good handle on how scopes work, and we've explained the mystery of that flash object. We store data in request scope for rendering in the view, in flash scope for surviving a redirect, in session scope for long-lived user-specific data, and in application scope for long-lived application-specific data.

It's time to explore how controllers can talk to other controllers to route the user around the application. When we introduced our addPost() action, we called redirect() methods, so it's time to learn about controller redirects and flows.

5.1.4 Handling default actions

Grails lets you supply a default index() action for each controller that you implement. When the user accesses the controller without specifying an action name (such as when accessing /hubbub/post), the index() action will handle the request (typically redirecting the user to some other action).

Let's retrofit an index() action to our PostController, so that when the user navigates to /hubbub/post, they're immediately redirected to the timeline() action of our scaffold. Listing 5.5 shows the updated PostController code.

Listing 5.5 Catching the index() action and redirecting the user

```
package com.grailsinaction

class PostController {

    def scaffold = true

    def index = {
        if (!params.id)
            params.id = "chuck_norris"
        redirect(action: 'timeline', params: params)     ◁── Passes params when redirecting
    }
    // other code removed here
}
```

One of the gotchas when redirecting is that you lose your params map if you don't explicitly pass it through to your redirected action. If we hadn't passed params from the index() action, then had the timeline() action made use of any incoming param values, they would have been null.

A world of default-action alternatives

We've discussed using the index() action to perform default actions when hitting the base controller URL. But there are many ways to handle default actions.

For example, if your controller has only one action on it, that will be interpreted as the default action. In listing 5.5, if timeline() were the only action in the controller, we could have omitted the index() action and the controller would have handled requests for /hubbub/post.

If you have multiple actions in your controller, you can explicitly declare your default action at the top of your controller:

```
def defaultAction = 'timeline'
```

> **A world of default-action alternatives (continued)**
>
> Using an `index()` action is very common, so we showed you that technique first. But in most of these sorts of scenarios, using `defaultAction` makes a lot more sense, because you don't have to repackage your `params` and there's no client redirect involved.

The typical role of an `index()` action is redirecting, but we haven't explained the options for handling redirects. It's time to get acquainted with the many redirect options.

5.1.5 *Working with redirects*

We've used `redirect()` calls throughout our code. For example, after we call `addPost()`, we redirect back to the timeline. When a default `index()` action is called, we redirect to another one.

All of our `redirect()` uses so far have followed a particular pattern, like this:

```
redirect(action:'timeline')
```

For this form of redirect, the target action name must exist on the current controller.

But what if you want to refer to an action on a different controller? Perhaps after registering a user on the `User` controller, you want to send them to the timeline on the `Post` controller. For those situations, you can use the extended version of `redirect()`:

```
redirect(controller: 'post', action:'timeline', id: newUser.userId)
```

The `id` field is optional, as is the action name. If you don't specify an action, it will go to the default action on the controller (as discussed in the previous section).

If you need to pass parameters during the redirect, you can pass in a map of parameters to be sent:

```
redirect(controller: 'post', action:'timeline',
    params: [fullName: newUser.profile.fullName,
        email: newUser.profile.email ]
        )
```

Finally, you can also redirect using the `uri:` or `url:` params to redirect to relative or absolute addresses. For example, instead of this,

```
redirect(controller: 'post', action:'timeline')
```

you can use the URI option:

```
redirect(uri: '/post/timeline')
```

And if you need to go to an external address, use the URL version:

```
redirect(url: 'http://www.google.com?q=hubbub')
```

That's about all you need to know about redirects. We'll be using them a lot, so it's good to be familiar with their many flavors.

Our next step is to take what we've implemented in this chapter, and move it to a more maintainable application architecture. One of the most powerful tools Grails offers for doing that is the *Grails service*.

5.2 Services: making things robust and maintainable

We've learned a lot of powerful techniques so far in this chapter: all sorts of data binding, controller routing, and redirect magic. But before things get unmaintainable, we'd better learn some techniques to keep a clean application for the long haul. In this section, we'll explore how services can dramatically simplify your controllers.

So far in our `PostController`, we've implemented an `addPost()` action to handle the creation of new `Posts`. But later we'll want to create `Posts` from many different entry points (specifically from a REST service and a Jabber gateway). That means our `Post` logic will need to be repeated in all those places. And because we're DRY (Don't Repeat Yourself) people, that repetition sounds like a bad thing.

In this section, we'll extract all of our new-post functionality into a Grails service that we can call from anywhere we like. It will make things a whole lot tidier and more maintainable.

5.2.1 Implementing a PostService

It's time to abstract our `Post` operations into a `PostService` that we can access from anywhere in our application. We first saw services in chapter 1, where we wrote a simple quote service to abstract the lookup process for quote generation. Services offer a simple, maintainable, and testable way of encapsulating reusable business logic. Services can participate in transactions, can be injected almost anywhere in your application, and are easy to develop.

Let's create a `PostService` for Hubbub. It won't surprise you that the process starts on the command line:

```
grails create-service com.grailsinaction.post
```

This will create a starter PostService.groovy file in /grails-app/services/com/grails-inaction.

In listing 5.6, we add some logic to our service so that we can add posts by supplying the `userId` and `content` of the post.

> **Listing 5.6 PostService.groovy defines `PostService` and a related exception class**

```
package com.grailsinaction
                                                     ❶ Forces transactions to roll
class PostException extends RuntimeException {            back if exceptions occur
    String message
    Post post
}                          ❷ Places Post-
                              related logic into
class PostService {           reusable service    ❸ Rolls back
                                                     database changes
    boolean transactional = true                     if errors occur
```

```
Post createPost(String userId, String content) {          Wraps Post-creation
    def user = User.findByUserId(userId)               ❹ logic in method
    if (user) {
        def post = new Post(content: content)
        user.addToPosts(post)                        ❺ Validates Post object
        if (user.save()) {                              during save
            return post
        } else {                                                      Throws
            throw new PostException(                             ❻ exception if
                message: "Invalid or empty post", post: post)         validation fails
        }
    }
    throw new PostException(message: "Invalid User Id")
}
}
```

In listing 5.6, we first define a new `Exception`, `PostException`, to handle any errors that we encounter with the save ❶. We'll use this exception to store an error message and any `Post` objects that fail validation. Groovy lets you define more than one class in a .groovy file, so we do that here to keep the exception with the service.

Next, we define our service, which, following Grails conventions, always ends in the name "Service" ❷, and we mark it `transactional` ❸. (We'll explore transactional semantics in depth in chapter 14.) Our `createPost()` method takes a `userId` and the post's `content` ❹ and returns a `Post` object or throws a `PostException` if things go bad.

NOTE Because `PostException` extends `RuntimeException` in listing 5.6, Grails will automatically roll back any database transactions that happen inside the method. You'll learn more about how this works in chapter 14.

This is a transactional service, so we can attempt the `save()` ❺, which will return `null` if there are any validation errors, triggering our invalid-post exception ❻. With the exception, we pass back the `Post` object itself, because clients might want to inspect and display the exact validation errors. If the `save()` goes well, we return the persisted `Post` object.

5.2.2 *Wiring our PostService to our PostController*

With our `PostService` in place, we now need to wire it up to the `PostController`. As you saw in chapter 1, this injection happens by declaring a property in the controller with the same name as the service (but with a lowercase first letter).

Listing 5.7 shows the updated `PostController` code, which now does all posting through the `PostService`.

Listing 5.7 An updated `PostController` that uses our new `PostService`

```
package com.grailsinaction

class PostController {                    ❶ Injects postService
                                             into the controller
    def postService
    def scaffold = true
```

```
def timeline = {
   def user = User.findByUserId(params.id)
   [ user : user ]
}

def addPost = {
   try {
      def newPost =
         postService.createPost(params.id,          ❷ Invokes service
                        params.content)                  methods
      flash.message = "Added new post: ${newPost.content}"
   } catch (PostException pe) {                        Catches errors
      flash.message = pe.message                     ❸ for display in UI
   }
   redirect(action: 'timeline', id: params.id)
}
}
```

In listing 5.7, our controller has been updated to inject the PostService automatically ❶. With our service in place, all we have to do is invoke the createPost() method ❷ and deal with any fallout from invalid posts ❸.

Creating the PostService involved quite a bit of refactoring, but the result is a tidy, reusable service that we can use in later chapters for posting from REST services and message queues, so it was worth the effort.

There's still lots to explore about services (such as whether they're injected as singletons or prototypes, how transactions are preserved, and how to test them), and we'll come back to them in chapter 14. We gave you a taste of services here because controllers are the most common place to use them, and this means we can take advantage of them later in the chapter.

Logging: a special case of injection

One special case of injection is the Grails logger. We haven't used it yet, but every controller, service, and domain class is automatically injected with a Log4j log object (which happens through some MetaClass magic in the Grails bootstrap process rather than through classic Spring injection, but the result is the same).

You can use a log object wherever it makes sense:

```
log.debug "The value of user is: ${user}"
```

The log object can be particularly useful in exception scenarios. If you pass the exception as the second parameter to the log method, you get a full stack trace in your logs:

```
try {
   user.punchChuckNorris()
} catch (e) {
   log.error "Failed to punch Chuck Norris", e
}
```

Logging configuration is controlled by entries in your /grails-app/conf/Config.groovy file. You can even use the runtimeLogging plugin to change log levels while your application is running.

With our posting functionality now tidily abstracted in its own service, it's time to explore other aspects of our controller that we can implement in more satisfying and maintainable ways.

The next vital area of controller operation that we need to be familiar with is *data binding*—how form data is parsed and validated and ends up in the database. We've used simple techniques so far, but it's time to introduce you to a range of more powerful features.

5.3 Data binding

Now that you understand how services work, it's time to revisit the way we get form parameters into domain objects. So far we've either manipulated data in the `params` map or bound incoming parameters with a `new Post(params)` style constructor, but what about cases where you don't want to bind all parameters? Perhaps you don't want the user to be able to supply their own `/user/update?password=secret&userId=admin` style overrides.

The process of marshaling parameters into object properties is known as *data binding*. We haven't given you many approaches to this topic, so it's time to delve a little deeper.

5.3.1 Binding to an existing object

Most of our data-binding explorations have focused on creating new domain objects from an incoming `params` object. But the update scenario is another common case—perhaps you're letting the user change their profile with an updated email address.

Let's say our user `update` action performs an update like the one in listing 5.8.

Listing 5.8   Data binding with properties can be perilous

```
def update = {
    def user = session.user.attach()       ① Attaches existing
    user.properties = params                   user from
    if (user.validate()) {                     session scope
        flash.message = "Successfully updated user"
    } else {                                ② Updates fields
        user.discard()                         based on
    }                                          matching params
    [ user : user ]
}                                           ③ Validates user is
                                               still current

                                            ④ Discards user on
                                               failed validation
                                               (Grails 1.0)
```

In this example, we reattach a `User` object that we stored in session scope during login ① to the current thread's Hibernate session. We then bind the `params` object to the user's `properties` ②, so any parameter that matches the name of a user property will be updated on the `User` object. Finally, we validate the object to make sure all our constraints still hold ③, and we roll things back if they fail ④.

This updates the `User` properties as we intended. Notice the explicit `discard()` if validation fails ④. In Grails 1.0, if you didn't explicitly `discard()` an object that failed validation, GORM would still persist it back to the database with the bad value. Under Grails 1.1, the explicit `discard()` is no longer required—Grails itself will mark any object failing validation as read-only, and it will never be persisted back to the database. If you're switching between Grails 1.0 and 1.1, this is an important gotcha.

We now have a strategy for updating existing domain classes, but we haven't looked at how we can exclude or include specific parameters in the binding. For that, we need to introduce you to `bindData()`.

5.3.2 Whitelist and blacklist bind params

The `bindData()` method available in controllers lets you blacklist certain parameters from the marshalling process.

The two-argument version of `bindData()` is equivalent to a standard property assignment:

```
bindData(user, params)
```

This has the same result as the more-familiar assignment style of data binding that you've already seen:

```
user.properties = params
```

But `bindData()`'s blacklisting power is introduced when using the three-argument version of the command, which takes a list of properties to exclude from the binding process. If we wanted to exclude our `userId` and `password` parameters from the update, we could do something like this:

```
bindData(user, params, ['userId', 'password'])
```

That solves half the problem—the blacklisting of certain properties. What if we want to specify certain parameters to be included in the bind? Since Grails 1.1, the `properties` object supports a subscript operator that you can use in whitelist binding scenarios.

For example, if we only let the user update their `email` and `fullName` values, we can do things like this:

```
user.profile.properties['email', 'fullName'] = params
```

This will only update the `email` and `fullName` properties on the user's `Profile` object, discarding all other parameters that match `User` property names.

Now that we've explored data binding for single domain classes, let's explore how we can perform data binding on entire graphs of objects.

5.3.3 Complex forms: binding multiple objects

All of our examples so far have concentrated on binding a single domain class, but Grails also gives you the option of handling form submissions for nested objects. Consider user registration, for example. We need a `User` object (to handle the `userId` and `password`), and a `Profile` object (to handle the `fullName`, `bio`, `homepage`, `email`, and other attributes).

In listing 5.9, we implement a form that references fields on a User object and its Profile in a null-safe way. Submitting a form like this will allow you to create both the User and attached Profile in a single save.

Listing 5.9   A form that will update multiple domain objects in a single submit

```
<html>
   <head>
      <title>Register New User</title>
      <meta name="layout" content="main"/>
   </head>
   <body>

      <h1>Register New User</h1>

      <g:hasErrors>
         <div class="errors">
           <g:renderErrors bean="${user}" as="list" />
         </div>
      </g:hasErrors>

      <g:form action="register">
         <dl>
            <dt>User Id</dt>
            <dd><g:textField name="userId"
               value="${user?.userId}"/></dd>
            <dt>Password</dt>
            <dd><g:passwordField name="password"
                   value="${user?.password}"/></dd>
            <dt>Full Name</dt>
            <dd><g:textField name="profile.fullName"
                   value="${user?.profile?.fullName}"/></dd>
            <dt>Bio</dt>
            <dd><g:textArea name="profile.bio"
                   value="${user?.profile?.bio}"/></dd>
            <dt>Email</dt>
            <dd><g:textField name="profile.email"
                   value="${user?.profile?.email}"/></dd>
            <dt><g:submitButton name="register" value="Register"/></dt>
         </dl>

      </g:form>

   </body>
</html>
```

The registration form in listing 5.9 contains a number of fields from both the User and Profile objects. Notice that the profile-related fields are kept in form controls with the prefix "profile": profile.fullName, profile.bio, profile.email. Grails makes use of this prefix when the form is submitted to bind the field to a relation on the saved object. Figure 5.7 demonstrates how the single set of parameters are split off into the User object and its nested Profile object.

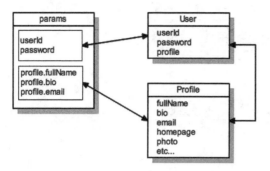

Figure 5.7 Parameters are split into bound objects based on their prefix.

Listing 5.10 shows the new `register()` action, which we've added to the `User-Controller`. Creating and saving a `User` object based on the incoming `params` object binds all those `Profile` fields as well.

Listing 5.10 Implementing a `register()` action for the `UserController`

```
def register = {
  def user = new User(params)
  if (user.validate()) {
    user.save()
    flash.message = "Successfully Created User"
      redirect(uri: '/')
    } else {
      flash.message = "Error Registering User"
      return [ user: user ]
    }
  }
}
```

If `user.validate()` fails, we return to the registration form, passing the failing `User` object. If we have an object with validation errors, we use the `<g:hasErrors>` and `<g:renderErrors>` tags to display them. Recall the `errors` div in our registration form (listing 5.9):

```
<g:hasErrors>
  <div class="errors">
    <g:renderErrors bean="${user}" as="list" />
  </div>
</g:hasErrors>
```

The `<g:renderErrors>` tag renders validation messages for the named bean as an HTML unordered list (`<ul>`), which is convenient for informing the user what's wrong. This is the same mechanism scaffolds use to display validation errors (which you saw in chapter 4). Figure 5.8 shows our new registration form in action, rendering appropriate error messages.

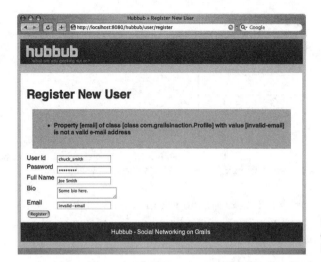

Figure 5.8   You can bind multiple domain objects on a single form and include error handling.

We've now implemented a basic registration process, and even thrown in some error handling to keep it tidy. But you might be wondering how the error handling works behind the scenes. It's important to get a handle on how errors work, in case your application needs custom layout and rendering of error messages for particular fields. Let's take a look.

5.3.4   *Error handling*

In the previous section, we passed a `User` object that had failed validation through to the view. The view then made use of the `<g:hasErrors>` and `<g:renderErrors>` tags to display the error messages (as in figure 5.8). You might be curious how those tags know what the failing validations are.

In chapter 3 (section 3.3), we saw that calling `user.validate()` populates a `user.errors` object with failing validations. The `hasErrors()` and `renderErrors()` methods use this object to iterate through the errors.

But what if you want to highlight the individual field values that are failing validation, rather than listing them all at the top of the page? You can take advantage of a special version of the hasErrors tag that specifies a domain object in request scope as well as the field you're rendering. Listing 5.11 shows an example of rendering the email validation errors next to the `email` field.

Listing 5.11   Implementing field-level errors is hard work at the moment.

```
<dt>Email</dt>                                    Displays block when  ❶
<dd>                                                  field is invalid
   <g:textField name="profile.email" value="${user?.profile?.email}"/>
   <g:hasErrors bean="${user}" field="profile.email">
      <g:eachError bean="${user}" field="profile.email">       Iterates
         <p style="color: red;"><g:message error="${it}"/></p>  through
      </g:eachError>                                            errors on
                                                          ❷  email field
```

Displays error text ❸

```
    </g:hasErrors>
</dd>
```

In listing 5.11, we use the `<g:hasErrors>` tag to find any validation errors for the email field on the user's `Profile` object ❶. If any errors exist, we use the `<g:each-Error>` tag to iterate through them ❷. Remember that a given field may fail more than one validation. Finally, we resolve the error message from our resource bundle by using the `<g:message>` tag ❸.

After seeing all that, you probably feel that `<g:renderErrors>` is pretty nice after all. Hopefully a future version of Grails will make marking-up field-level errors much less painful.

Figure 5.9 gives you an idea of the kind of markup generated by the techniques in listing 5.11. As you can see, you can co-locate the errors, but it's a lot of work, and a red asterisk next to the failing field is probably as effective.

Figure 5.9 Field-level markup of errors is difficult but achievable in Grails 1.1.

Now that you understand some of the power of Grails' data binding, and you've learned how errors work, it's time to introduce you to one last technique for data binding that makes the whole operation a lot more maintainable: Grails' *command objects*.

5.4 Command objects

All of this data binding and manipulation is wonderful, but what happens when there isn't a one-to-one mapping between the form data and a domain object? For example, a registration screen might have both "password" and "confirmPassword" fields that need to match to ensure the user hasn't made a mistake entering the password.

For these sorts of scenarios, Grails offers the *command object*. The command object's purpose is to marshal data from form parameters into a non-domain class that offers its own validation.

5.4.1 Handling custom user registration forms

User registration involves subtle validations that only make sense during the registration process (like the example of matching passwords). Let's cook up a `UserRegistrationCommand` object to see how you might capture both sets of data in a single command object.

Typically, command objects are single-use objects, so by convention they're created inside the same .groovy file as the controller that uses them. For our example, let's enhance the `UserController` class with the new command class, as shown in listing 5.12.

Listing 5.12 A `UserRegistrationCommand` class

```
class UserRegistrationCommand {

    String userId
    String password                      Introduces field for
    String passwordRepeat            ◁⌐ password confirmation

    byte[] photo
    String fullName
    String bio
    String homepage
    String email
    String timezone
    String country
    String jabberAddress

    static constraints = {
        userId(size: 3..20)

        password(size: 6..8, blank: false,
             validator: { passwd, urc ->
                 return passwd != urc.userId
             })                             ⌐ Checks confirmation field
        passwordRepeat(nullable: false, ◁⌐ matches first password
             validator: { passwd2, urc ->
                 return passwd2 == urc.password
             })
        fullName(nullable: true)
        bio(nullable: true, maxSize: 1000)
        homepage(url: true, nullable: true)
        email(email: true, nullable: true)
        photo(nullable: true)
        country(nullable: true)
        timezone(nullable: true)
        jabberAddress(email: true, nullable: true)
    }

}
```

There's quite a lot of validation going on there! We've incorporated all the validation from both our `User` and `Profile` objects, which won't be new to you. We've also added a custom field and validation that's specific to the registration process (specifically, that `password` and `passwordRepeat` must match).

Command objects are particularly useful in scenarios where you have different or augmented validation rules firing for the form submission that aren't in your domain model. A password-confirmation field is a classic example.

The neatest part of the command object process is writing a controller action to consume the form submission. Reference the command as the first argument to the action closure, and the binding occurs automatically. Listing 5.13 shows our custom action `register2()` for handling our command object.

DRY strategies for reusing validators

You might be wondering if there is a more DRY (Don't Repeat Yourself) way to reuse the constraints from domain classes in your command objects. There are no built-in mechanisms, but people have been creative in the way they approach the problem. There are three basic options. By using standard assignments between classes, you can share:

- the `constraints` closure in its entirety
- the map of constraints for a single field
- custom validator closures

None of these solutions are elegant, and we look forward to seeing a better DRY validation mechanism in a future Grails release.

Listing 5.13 A register action that uses command objects

```
def register2 = { UserRegistrationCommand urc ->
    if (urc.hasErrors()) {
        return [ user : urc ]
    } else {
        def user = new User(urc.properties)
        user.profile = new Profile(urc.properties)
        if (user.save()) {
            flash.message =
                "Welcome aboard, ${urc.fullName ?: urc.userId}"
            redirect(uri: '/')
        } else {
            // maybe not unique userId?
            return [ user : urc ]
        }
    }
}
```

❶ Binds data from params to command object

❷ Uses hasErrors to check validations

❸ Binds data to new User object

❹ Saves and validates new user

In listing 5.13, the command object is passed in as the first argument to the action's closure ❶, causing Grails to attempt to bind all incoming `params` entries to the command object's fields. Validations are then applied, and we can check the results by calling `hasErrors()` on the command object itself ❷.

If the data looks good, we can bind the command object's fields to the various domain classes. In listing 5.13, we bind to both `User` and `Profile` ❸ and then attempt to save the new user.

We have to confirm that the `save()` is successful ❹, because some constraints only make sense in a domain class, not in a command object. (For example, our `User` class has a `unique` constraint on the `userId`). Although you could attempt to simulate a unique constraint on your command object with a custom validator, even then the user isn't guaranteed to be unique until the real `save()` is committed to the database.

Command objects are great for this sort of form, where you don't have a one-to-one mapping with a domain class. But they also offer other features. Command objects can participate in injection, for example.

5.4.2   *Participating in injection*

Command objects aren't dumb value objects with a little validation. They're subject to the same bean-injection features as controllers, which means they can make fantastic encapsulators of business logic.

In our `UserRegistrationCommand` example, the user enters a clear-text password, but let's imagine we wanted to store it encrypted in the database. If we had defined a `cryptoService`, we could inject it directly into the command object. We might do something like this:

```
class UserRegistrationCommand {

    def cryptoService

    String getEncryptedPassword() {
        return cryptoService.getEncryptedPassword(password)
    }

// our other properties and validators

}
```

We could then use the `cryptoService` to do the heavy lifting to ensure that there's only one class that knows how password encryption is implemented. Adding a convenience routine like `getEncryptedPassword()` to our command class makes consuming the command class in our controller code a lot tidier.

Now that we've covered data binding and controller logic, all that's left for this chapter is the sweet stuff. We'll move on to handling photo uploads, creating a basic security file, and customizing the site's URLs.

Let's start by looking at how we'll upload user profile photos.

5.5   *Working with images*

We've now seen nearly every controller trick that you're likely to want to use in your next Grails project. There are, however, a few outliers—you won't need them in every application, but when you need them, you really need them.

In this section, we're going to explore how to handle file uploads (our user's profile photo) and how to render custom content types (image data, in our case). Although your next application might not have much use for photos, the techniques are useful for whatever kind of content you want to render.

5.5.1   *Handling file uploads*

What's a social-networking site without the ability to upload photos and avatars? But if you've ever added file-upload capabilities to a Java web application, you know the complexities involved (not only the mess involved when handling byte streams, but also handling security issues, such as limiting file sizes to prevent denial-of-service attacks). Grails puts that complexity behind you. Let's set to work implementing a photo-upload capability for Hubbub.

We'll start by creating an `ImageController` to handle image uploading and rendering:

```
grails create-controller com.grailsinaction.Image
```

There are two ways to handle file uploads in a controller, and which one you select depends on what you want to accomplish. If you want to store the image in a domain class, your best option is to use a command object. Listing 5.14 shows how to use a command object for photo uploads.

Listing 5.14 Handling image uploading via a command object

```
package com.grailsinaction

class PhotoUploadCommand {          Holds uploaded
   byte[] photo                     photo data
   String userId
}

class ImageController {

   def upload = { PhotoUploadCommand puc ->
      def user = User.findByUserId(puc.userId)
      user.profile.photo = puc.photo
      redirect(action: 'view', id: puc.userId)
   }
   def form = {
      // pass through to upload form          Passes list of
      [ userList : User.list() ]              users to the view
   }

   def view = {
      // pass through to "view photo" page
   }
}
```

The upload process for images using a command object binds the uploaded image data to a byte array.

To actually be able to select a photo for upload in our browser window, we need a view with an Upload control. The form also needs to be tagged to tell the browser that the form contains a file upload, so we'll use the <g:uploadForm> tag, as shown in listing 5.15.

Listing 5.15 An image-upload form

```
<g:uploadForm action="upload">
   User Id:
   <g:select name="userId" from="${userList}"
      optionKey="userId" optionValue="userId" />
   <p/>
   Photo: <input name="photo" type="file" />
   <g:submitButton name="upload" value="Upload"/>
</g:uploadForm>
```

Remember, the upload form needs to use <g:uploadForm> instead of <g:form>, and it needs an input box with type="file" to hold the image upload data.

The browser will render the form in listing 5.15 with an upload box as shown in figure 5.10.

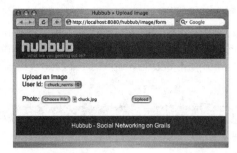

Figure 5.10   Our image-upload form in action

With our command object backing the upload, users are only a click away from getting their profile pictures into the database.

5.5.2   Uploading to the filesystem

If you want to store the uploaded image in the filesystem rather than the database, you need access to the raw Spring `MultipartHttpServletRequest` object that backs the upload process.

For this case, you have more options for storing the byte array:

```
def rawUpload = {

    // a Spring MultipartHttpServletRequest
    def mhsr = request.getFile('photo')
    if (!mhsr?.empty && mhrs.size < 1024*200) {      ⟵  Ensures file size
        mhsr.transferTo(                                less than 200Kb
            new File(
                "/hubbub/images/${params.userId}/mugshot.gif"
            )
        )

    }
}
```

The `MultipartHttpServletRequest` class has a `transferTo()` method for moving the picture data directly to a file, which is convenient if you're averse to storing BLOBs in your database. For a detailed discussion of `MultipartHttpServletRequest`, consult the Spring Javadoc.

5.5.3   Rendering photos from the database

Now that our photos can be uploaded to the database or filesystem, we need a way to display them. We'll create `<img>` tags in our application and have Grails retrieve our profile photos and render them.

First, we'll create a new profile view, so the `UserController` can view a profile, and we'll include a link to the user's profile picture. Let's call the view /views/user/profile.gsp and give it an HTML image tag:

```
<div class="profilePic">
    <g:if test="${profile.photo}">
        <img src="
```

```
            <g:createLink controller='image'
                action='renderImage' id='${userId}'/>
        "/>
    </g:if>
    <p>Profile for <strong>${profile.fullName}</strong></p>
    <p>Bio: ${profile.bio}</p>
</div>
```

Creates link to
render image

This code fragment creates a link back to /image/renderImage/id based on the userId of the current user. Once we've implemented our `renderImage()` action in `ImageController`, we can link our image tags to /image/renderImage/chuck_norris or any other user ID.

Listing 5.16 shows how we can send image data to the client.

Listing 5.16   Sending image data to the browser

```
def renderImage = {
    def user = User.findByUserId(params.id)
    if (user?.profile?.photo) {
        response.setContentLength(user.profile.photo.length)
        response.outputStream.write(user.profile.photo)
    } else {
        response.sendError(404)              <--| Sends 404 error
    }                                            | if no photo
}
```

As listing 5.16 shows, to write to the browser, you write the bytes directly to the response's output stream, and you also need to tell the browser the size of the data.

With our backend rendering implemented, figure 5.11 shows the result for /user /profile/chuck_norris.

We now have a basic profile screen running, which completes our explorations of image rendering and all the UI functionality we'll be doing in this chapter. We'll learn a lot more UI techniques in chapter 6, but for now there are still two more important controller features to learn about: filters and URL mappings. Both affect how a user navigates your application, and an understanding of both is essential for developing powerful Grails applications.

Let's start with exploring filters.

Figure 5.11   Rendering a profile picture

5.6   *Intercepting requests with filters*

So far in this chapter, we've spent a lot of time looking at the frontend user experience. But there are also important techniques that you need to implement at the backend. In this section we'll explore the use of filters for augmenting the Grails request/response pipeline with your own custom processing.

5.6.1   *Writing your first filter*

Grails *filters* give you a powerful tool for intercepting every request (or a subset of requests) and for performing business logic before or after the controller action fires. If you've worked with Java Servlet filters, you might recognize Grails filters as providing similar functionality, although Grails filters only intercept controller requests, not static file requests for JavaScript, CSS, image files, and the like.

A classic example of where you might want this sort of approach is a security filter—you want to check that a user has access to a target resource (some popular Grails security plugins use Grails filters for this purpose). Let's put a simple security filter together to show you how it can be done.

First we'll create a shell for our filter:

```
grails create-filters LameSecurity
```

This command will write a starter template in /grails-app/conf/LameSecurityFilters.groovy (note the plural "Filters"; if you name it with the singular form, it won't fire).

Next we'll modify our filter to perform some simple checks, as shown in listing 5.17.

Listing 5.17 A basic security filter implementation

```
import com.grailsinaction.*

class LameSecurityFilters {

    def filters = {
        secureActions(controller:'post',                    ❶ Names
                action:'(addPost|deletePost)') {               security rules    ❷ Limits filter to
            before = {                                                             two actions
                                                            ❸ Tests for presence
                if (params.logonId) {                          of logonId param
                    session.user = User.findByUserId(params.logonId)
                }                                           ❹ Tests for existing
                                                               user in session
                if (!session.user) {
                    redirect(controller: 'login', action: 'form')
                    return false
                }                   ❺ Stops subsequent
            }                          filters from firing
            after = { model->

            }
            afterView = {
```

```
      log.debug "Finished running ${controllerName} -
   ➥${actionName}"        ◁─┐  Logs diagnostic data
      }                      ❻  after view completes
   }

 }
}
```

You can name the filters that you put into the file (for documentation purposes only), so it's good to choose names that summarize your filter logic. In listing 5.17, we've chosen to call our set of rules secureActions ❶.

You can put as many filters as you like in the file, and all matching rules will fire in order from the top until one returns false from its before() closure. As you'll learn soon, you can apply filters to wildcards (controller: '*' action: '*'), but in listing 5.17, we only want the filter to fire for the addPost or deletePost actions ❶. Using Boolean operators lets you fine-tune the application of the filter.

Inside the body of the filter, you can provide closures for before, after, or after-View. Table 5.2 outlines the filter lifecycle phases and their typical features.

Table 5.2   Lifecycle phases and their usage

Closure	Fires when?	Useful for
before	Before any controller logic is invoked	Security, referrer headers
after	After controller logic, but before the view is rendered	Altering a model before presentation to view
afterView	After the view has finished rendering	Performance metrics

Our before closure checks that the user provided a logonId parameter ❸, and if so, and the corresponding user exists, it stores the User object in the session to signify a login. Otherwise it redirects to the login screen ❹.

If any before closure returns false, as happens at ❺, no other filters will fire and the controller action won't be invoked. This is typically done when you have a filter (such as a security filter) that has redirected the request.

We've also added an afterView closure ❻ to demonstrate some diagnostic options, and to show you some of the variables that Grails provides in filters. Although filters don't have all of the functionality of controllers, they expose the common controller variables that we covered earlier in the chapter (request, response, params, session, flash, and a few filter-specific extras). They also have two methods: redirect() and render(). Table 5.3 shows you some additional filter variables that we haven't made use of.

Although we haven't made use of it in listing 5.17, there's also a special case for the after closure that takes a model as an argument. That's the model map that the controller returns from the action that handled the request. You can augment that model in your filter, and modify it if you must.

Table 5.3 Variables exposed to filters

Variable	Description
`controllerName`	Name of the currently firing controller
`actionName`	Name of the currently firing action
`applicationContext`	The Spring application context—useful for looking up Spring beans, but filters support dependency injection, which is much cleaner
`grailsApplication`	The current `grailsApplication` object—useful for finding out run-time information, such as the Grails version or application name

TIP Modifying existing model values in your filters is a bad idea—it makes your code difficult to follow and will inevitably introduce subtle bugs in your controller logic. Augment them, by all means, but leave your existing model values alone, lest you get support calls in the wee small hours and have to debug things.

Handling injection in filters

What if you need a service inside your filter? Filters have the same injection rules as other Grails artifacts, so you can declare the service (or other artifact) as a property in your filter and it will be injected for you. Here's an example:

```
class SecurityFilters {
    def authService
    def filters = {
        // then somewhere inside one of your filters
        authService.checkAccess(params.userId,
                        controllerName, actionName)
    }
}
```

5.6.2 *Filter URL options*

You've already seen filters applied to controllers and actions, but there are plenty more options for both fine- and course-grained filtering. First, both controller and action names are subject to wildcarding (and you can wildcard either or both). You can also use Boolean operators to be selective about what you capture.

Let's look at a few common filtering use cases. This example filters for all actions on all controllers:

```
myGreedyFilter(controller:'*', action:'*') {
}
```

This one filters for all actions on the User controller:

```
myControllerFilter(controller:'user', action:'*') {
}
```

And the following one filters for just a few actions on the User controller:

```
mySelectiveFilter(controller:'user', action:'(update|edit|delete)') {
}
```

But if thinking in terms of controllers and actions is not your bag (perhaps because you've done some URL mapping magic for permalinking), you can also use a URI style of mapping in your filters:

```
myGreedyUriFilter(uri:'/**') {

}

mySelectiveUriFilter(uri:'/post/**') {

}

myParticularUriFilter(uri:'/post/supersecret/list') {

}
```

The URI-matching mechanism uses Ant-style wildcarding. If you've never seen those double asterisks before, they mean "all subdirectories nested to unlimited levels". One thing to note is that URL mappings fire before filters, so if you were depending on a filter to catch a nonexistent URL, think again. It will return a 404 error and not get to your filter.

That's quite an arsenal of tools for selective filtering. You've now learned the skills to create all sorts of backend intercepting logic for your next application. Whether you're implementing a custom security mechanism or a stats-tracking filter, or you're doing some debugging and profiling, filters give you lots of power for fine-grained request interception.

There's one final feature of controllers that we need to cover: URL mappings.

5.7   Creating custom URL mappings

So far, we've followed Grails convention, with URLs translating to /controllerName /actionName/id. But even this convention is configurable through URL mappings.

The /grails-app/conf/UrlMappings.groovy file is shown in listing 5.18. This file is where you configure rules for routing incoming requests to particular controllers and actions.

Listing 5.18   UrlMappings.groovy holds all the URL routing information for your app.

```
class UrlMappings {
    static mappings = {
        "/$controller/$action?/$id?"{
            constraints {
                // apply constraints here
            }
        }
        "/"(view:"/index")
        "500"(view:'/error')
    }
}
```

The $ variables in the UrlMappings file can be confusing, so let's add a static mapping (permalink) to the file to see how things work:

```
"/timeline/chuck_norris" {
    controller = "post"
    action = "timeline"
    id = "chuck_norris"
}
```

With our permalink in place, we can now access the URL /hubbub/timeline/chuck _norris, and it will route us to the `PostController` and fire the `timeline` action with an `id` parameter of `"chuck_norris"`. Note that this isn't a redirect: the browser's URL will stay the same, but the controller and action specified in the permalink will fire.

You can also use a more concise version of the syntax:

```
"/timeline/chuck_norris"(controller:"post",
        action:"timeline", id:"chuck_norris")
```

We find the block-based version more readable, and it also gives you more flexibility (as we'll see shortly).

Now that we've seen mapping blocks, it's time to get back to those variables we saw earlier.

5.7.1 *myHubbub: rolling your own permalinks*

You can define how custom variables in URL mappings are passed through as parameters to the controller. For example, it would be great to have a permalink on the Hubbub site to give users a page for their recent posts. Maybe a URL like /hubbub /users/glen could map to all of Glen's posts, and /hubbub/users/peter could send you off to Peter's.

One way to achieve this style of permalink is to create a URL mapping like this:

```
"/users/$id" {
    controller = "post"
    action = "timeline"
}
```

This will still call the `timeline` action of the `PostController`, but with a `params.id` value of "glen", "peter", or whatever forms the last part of the URL.

5.7.2 *Optional variables and constraints*

When you define custom variables in your mapping string, you can provide constraints to make sure the value matches a particular string or list.

Suppose we want to provide permalinks for a user's RSS or Atom feeds. We can implement a feed permalink with an entry like this:

```
"/users/$userId/feed/$format?" {
    controller = "post"
    action = "feed"
    constraints {
```

```
        format(inList: ['rss', 'atom'])
    }
}
```

There are two important things to notice here. We've made the format portion of the URL optional (by suffixing it with ?), so the user can omit it. If they do supply it, we've added a `constraints` section to ensure that they can only specify "rss" or "atom" as the format. This means /hubbub/users/glen/feed/atom is fine, as is /hubbub/users /glen/feed, but /hubbub/users/glen/feed/sneaky will return a 404 page-not-found error. You can use these constraints to define permalinks with fine-grained URLs.

The rules in your URLMapping file are applied in the order in which they appear, so you can start with more specific rules and fall back to more general ones.

5.7.3 Handling response codes

While we're on the topic of 404 pages, UrlMappings also gives you great flexibility in mapping response codes to custom pages. If you look in the default mapping file, you'll notice this entry:

```
"500"(view:'/error')
```

This maps the "Error 500: Internal Server Error" code to /views/error.gsp. You can use this mechanism to map any of the HTTP response codes to one of your pages. For example, you could map the standard 500 error to a page inspired by the classic "tweet of death" Twitter 500 page:

```
"500"(view:'/failWhale')
```

If you want your errors to be handled by a controller action instead of directly by a GSP, that's supported too. This might be convenient for keeping stats on which URLs keep 404ing on your site. Here's how you could configure the 404 error code to be handled by a dedicated errors controller:

```
"404"(controller: "errors", action: "notFound")
```

5.7.4 Mapping directly to the view

There are situations where you might want to map a URL directly to a view and bypass any controller logic. The classic example is your application's home page, which you might implement like this:

```
"/"(view:"/homepage/index")
```

Notice that you don't include the .gsp extension when you construct the mapping.

5.7.5 Wildcard support

URL mappings can also support greedy wildcards using Ant-style wildcards. This is particularly useful when you impersonate filenames in your backend.

For example, if you generate PDFs dynamically, but want to provide permalinks on your site, you might do something like this:

```
"/documents/$docname**.pdf"(controller:"pdf", action:"render")
```

The wildcard option lets you match /documents/release-notes/myproject.pdf as well as /document/manuals/myproject.pdf. In both cases, you'll get a docname parameter that you can use in the controller action. The docname will contain the relative path that $docname matches (for example, release-notes/myproject and manuals/myproject). This capability is convenient for developing content management systems (CMS) where you generate the PDF based on dynamic data in a domain object.

And that's the end of our exploration of UrlMappings. We've finished all you need to know about controllers. It's time to review what we've taken in.

5.8　*Summary and best practices*

In this chapter, we've explored a mountain of skills and techniques related to controllers.

We started by implementing a timeline and addPost feature for Hubbub. We then refactored our posting operations into a PostService that we'll reuse later in the book. After tidying up our posting logic, we looked at all sorts of data-binding techniques, including whitelisting, blacklisting, error handling, and command objects.

We then had some fun with custom controller content types while we implemented our profile page and handled photo uploads. Finally, we learned about backend logic and using filters and UrlMappings.

Let's pull out some of the key practices to take away from the chapter:

- *Use flash scope.*　Flash scope is ideal for passing messages to the user (when a redirect is involved).
- *Use the errors object wisely.*　Make use of the errors object on your domain class to display validation messages. Take advantage of resource bundles to make error messages relevant to your application use cases.
- *Use command objects.*　Take advantage of command objects for form submissions. Don't just use them for validation—they can also be handy for encapsulating tricky business logic.
- *Understand data binding.*　Data-binding options in Grails are plentiful and subtle. Understand how data binding works for child objects when form parameters are prefixed. Use whitelisting to ensure that data binding doesn't compromise sensitive fields.
- *Be forgiving with URLs.*　Use default actions to make URLs more forgiving, and do the same for custom URL mappings. Permalink-style URLs are much easier to remember and not difficult to implement.
- *Apply filters.*　Employ filters when you need to selectively fire backend logic based on URLs or controller-actions combos.

We've learned a lot about the internals of controllers in this chapter, and in the next chapter we'll build on our knowledge by implementing some fine-looking views to give Hubbub some visual sizzle.

Developing tasty views, forms, and layouts

We've spent most of the book so far building the heart of Hubbub: processing incoming requests, interacting with the data model, calling business logic, and creating posts, users, and timelines. It's been a lot of fun, but not visually satisfying. It's time to leave the core functionality behind and do some work on the user interface (UI) of our web application.

A great-looking UI has all sorts of subtle impacts on the user. People think that a visually pleasing application is more robust, more performant, and more productive than a bare-bones application, even though none of that may be true.

In this chapter, we'll focus on the frontend. We'll cover the basics of putting forms together, and we'll investigate how to support multiple browsers by using reusable layouts. We'll also turn our attention to visual effects and implement some slick animations and Ajax interactions. By the time we're done, Hubbub will sparkle.

We first need to get a good grasp of Grails' primary view technology: Groovy Server Pages (GSP), so our UI adventure will begin with a tour of the core GSP form tags.

6.1   Understanding the core form tags

We've been making use of GSPs to handle our HTML output since chapter 1, but we haven't given you a solid introduction to them. GSP is an evolution of view technology from Java Server Pages (JSP). The things that were difficult in JSP (particularly tag libraries) are much simplified and accessible in GSP. When you catch yourself developing custom taglibs while your application is running (and not requiring a restart), you'll fall in love.

In this section, we'll cover all the basic GSP tags you'll use from day to day when designing forms and user interactions. Whether it's flow control, iteration, or complex form management with error handling, you'll find it all here. But it all starts with getting a feel for "if" tests.

6.1.1   A handful of essential tags

You'll spend most of your time working with Grails views, using a few core GSP tags. It's time to learn a few of the most common tags.

The first tags you need to learn are the logical and iteration tags. Every programmer loves a good `if()` test, so listing 6.1 introduces `<g:if>` being used to test usernames.

Listing 6.1   The basic `if` tag

```
<g:if test="${user?.name == 'Chuck Norris'}">
  Roundhouse Kicks welcome here.
</g:if>
<g:elseif test="${user?.name == 'Jack Bauer'}">
  Lock up your Presidents.
</g:elseif>
<g:else>
  Take a number. We'll call you when we're ready.
</g:else>
```

The else and elseif blocks are optional. Use if, if ... else, or if ... elseif ... else in whatever combinations you want.

Another common tag is `<g:each>`, which iterates through a collection or array. It is often used when accessing a domain class member collection, such as iterating through followers:

```
<g:each var="nextUser" in="${following}">
    <li>${nextUser.userId}</li>
</g:each>
```

The `<g:if>` and `<g:each>` tags are the bread and butter of select and iteration, and you'll use them a lot. But you'll also need to combine them with some basic link tags to keep your user moving through the application. Let's look at how we can introduce some workflow with the versatile `<g:link>` tag.

6.1.2 A pocketful of link tags

Another common set of tags is the linking tags. These give you convenient ways to generate URLs that link to controller actions.

Here's an example:

```
<g:link controller="post" action="global" >Back to Hubbub</g:link>
```

You can omit the `action` attribute if you're linking to the default action.

Similarly, if you're linking to another action in the current controller, you can omit the `controller` attribute. For example, if the previous action was /post/edit, you could link back to the `timeline` action (/post/timeline) with this link:

```
<g:link action="timeline" >Back to Timeline</g:link>
```

But sometimes you don't want a full anchor tag—you want the target URL. This can be handy for Ajax, where you need to work in URL terms, but it's also handy in generating `<img>` tags. When generating thumbnail tags for your followers, you could use something like this:

```
<img src="<g:createLink action="renderImage" controller="image"
    id="${nextUser.userId}"/>" alt="${nextUser.userId}"/>
```

This will create a URL like /image/renderImage/glen. Remember that the last part of the URL forms the `params.id` attribute in your controller. All of the linking tags support `action`, `controller`, and `id` attributes, so you have a lot of flexibility.

Although `<g:link>` and `<g:createLink>` are the most common link tags, there is another one that you'll use less frequently: `<g:createLinkTo>` (yes, the names are confusing). The `<g:createLinkTo>` tag is handy for generating links to files within your application, and its most common use is with CSS and static images. Here's an example:

```
<link rel="stylesheet"
    href="${createLinkTo(dir:'css',file:'hubbub.css')}" />
```

That's not a tag; that's a method call!

You can reference all tags using a method-style syntax—with attribute maps as an argument—rather than using the more classic JSP-style invocation. The preceding code line is equivalent to this:

```
<link rel="stylesheet" href="
    <g:createLinkTo dir='css' file='hubbub.css'/>
"/>
```

Some people find this method-style invocation easier to read when nesting tags within other tags. In this example, it gets tricky to work out which /> belongs to which tag, but a good IDE goes a long way to making this clear.

The link tag names are similar, and this can be confusing. They're summarized in table 6.1.

Table 6.1   Link-related tags

Tag	Description
link	Generates an `<a href>` around the enclosed content
createLink	Generates a URL for embedding in another tag
createLinkTo	Generates a URL to a local file

TIP   In chapter 5, we explored URL-mapping tricks with entries in UrlMappings.groovy. The good news is that the link tags are aware of your rewrite rules and will honor those mappings.

Our next core set of tags involves form handling. Let's explore the flexibility available with the Grails form tags.

6.1.3   A tour of the form tags

Forms are the bread and butter of web interactivity. You'll be spending a lot of time generating forms in GSPs, and processing their results in controller actions, so it's important to understand how to use the HTML form-field tags in GSPs. You're free to mix and match regular by-hand HTML form fields with Grails tags, but you'll find that the form tags make things simpler and more maintainable.

At the end of the last chapter, we showed you how to use command objects to process a user registration, but we didn't use any form tags in the registration form. Listing 6.2 shows a revised attempt at a registration form using the standard Grails form tags. We've introduced a few fake fields so we can demonstrate what is available.

Listing 6.2   Our new registration form demonstrates many of the core form tags.

```
<dl>                                          Marks form to
   <g:uploadForm>                        ⬅   support file uploads
      <dt>User Id: </dt>
      <dd><g:textField name="userId" /></dd>    ⬅ Creates plain text field

      <dt>Password:</dt>                               Creates obscured
      <dd><g:passwordField name="password" /></dd>  ⬅ password field
      <dt>(repeat)</dt>
      <dd><g:passwordField name="passwordRepeat" /></dd>

      <dt>Country:</dt>                                 Creates country
      <dd><g:countrySelect name="country"              selection box
        noSelection="['':'Choose your country...']"/>  ⬅
```

```
<dt>Photo:</dt>                                              Creates file
<dd><input type="file" name="photo"/></dd>    ◁┘       upload field

<dt>Timezone:</dt>                                           Creates timezone
<dd><g:timeZoneSelect name="timezone"/></dd>   ◁┘      select box

<dt>Who introduced you to Hubbub?</dt>
<dd>
<g:select name="referrer"
  from="${com.grailsinaction.Profile.list()}"
  optionKey="id"                                             Populates select
  optionValue="fullName""                                    box from database
  noSelection="${['null':'Please Choose...']}" />

</dd>

<dt>Spam me forever:</dt>
<dd>
  <g:checkBox name="spamMe" checked="true"/>   ◁—   Creates check box
</dd>

<dt>Email Format:</dt>
<dd>
<g:radioGroup name="emailFormat"
    labels="['Plain','HTML']"
    values="['P', 'H']"                          Creates group of
    value="H">                                   radio buttons
  ${it.label} ${it.radio}
</g:radioGroup>
</dd>

<dt>                                                         Submits to
  <g:actionSubmit value="Register" />   ◁┘       selected action
</dt>
<dd>
  <g:actionSubmit value="Cancel" action="cancelRegister" />
</dd>
</g:uploadForm>
</dl>
                                                             Navigates
<p>                                                          around
  <g:link controller="post">Back to Hubbub</g:link>   ◁┘     the app
</p>
```

That's a lot of tags. We'll be spending the rest of this section discussing these core tags, but this gives you a chance to see them in use first. Figure 6.1 shows how the form is rendered.

The form needs some layout work, but functionality-wise we're progressing well. That's a pretty comprehensive survey of all the basic form tags. Let's take a look at them each in turn.

THE BASIC FORM TAG

All Grails forms start with a `<g:form>` or `<g:uploadForm>`, depending on whether you're supporting file uploads or not. You configure the form tags with an optional `action` and `controller` name:

```
<g:form controller="user" action="register">
```

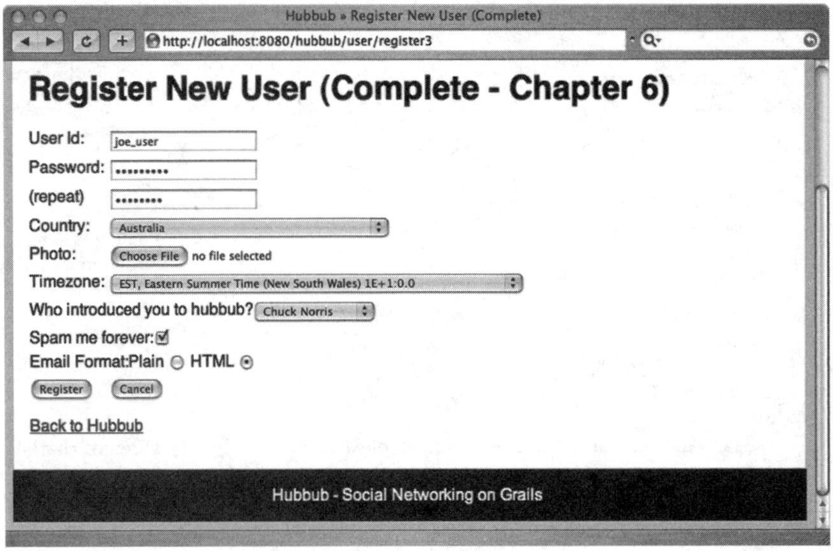

Figure 6.1   A registration form that uses the core form tags

As with the <g:link> tag we discussed earlier, you can usually rely on conventions. For instance, if you're inside another User action (such as /user/list), you can describe your form in terms of the target action, and it will default to the current controller:

```
<g:form action="register">
```

If you want the form to submit to the current action, you can even omit the action name.

BASIC TEXTFIELDS, TEXTAREAS, AND PASSWORDFIELDS

The cornerstone of web form development is making use of text fields. The three basic variants include <g:textField> (single line), <g:textArea> (multiline), and <g:passwordField> (single line with asterisk placeholders).

Our registration form uses the single-line versions:

```
<g:textField name="userId" value="${newuser?.userId}"/>
<g:passwordField name="password" value="${newuser?.password}"/>
```

The name attribute refers to the name of the field in the params object being submitted to the target action. In this example, we'll have params.userId and params.password holding the values.

All form fields support a value element that represents the prepopulated value of the form. In the preceding example, we use the safe dereference operator (?.) to keep our values null-safe for the initial form display.

Although we didn't use a textArea in listing 6.2, they follow the same basic format as the other text-based fields:

```
<g:textArea name="bio" value="${newuser.bio}" rows="10" cols="60"/>
```

This will render a textArea with the specified size, prebound to the target value of `newuser.bio`.

> **How can I pass custom HTML attributes to Grails taglibs?**
>
> The textArea tag only explicitly supports `name` and `value` attributes, but it passes through unknown attributes to the generated HTML tag. This means you can use the standard `rows` and `cols` attributes of HTML TextAreas.
>
> This passthrough mechanism exists for all Grails tags, so if there are specific HTML attributes you want rendered in the final tag output (perhaps a class attribute for CSS styling), just add them to the tag's attributes and they will be passed through.

THE DROP-DOWN JOY OF SELECT

One of the most complex (and sophisticated) Grails form tags is `<g:select>`. The select tag lets you generate drop-down boxes populated from backend data sources or embedded lists and ranges.

The tag expects the `from` attribute to contain a list of objects (or a range if you prefer). You then supply an `optionKey` and `optionValue` that represent the property on each object that should be used to generate the drop-down list.

Let's revisit our registration example from listing 6.2:

```
<g:select name="referrer"
          from="${com.grailsinaction.Profile.list()}"
          optionKey="id"
          optionValue="fullName"
          noSelection="${['null':'Please Choose...']}" />
```

The `from` attribute retrieves a list of profiles from a backend domain class. The `optionKey` attribute represents the `Profile` object's `id` field, and it is the value that will be submitted for the `referrer` parameter. The `optionValue` attribute represents the string that will be displayed in the drop-down list itself—it displays the `Profile` object's `fullName` field.

The special case in which nothing is selected is handled by the `noSelection` attribute, which takes a map with a key of `'null'` (the string, not the value).

The `from` field is a piece of Groovy code, so you can use any sort of dynamic finder you like to generate the list, or you can provide a static list if that makes sense:

```
<g:select from="['Groovy', 'Java', 'Python']" name="preferredLanguage"/>
```

If you don't supply `optionKey` and `optionValue`, the tag does a `toString()` on each element in the list for both the key and the value, which is perfect for when you need a static list.

CHECK BOXES AND RADIO BUTTONS

Check boxes are supported through a simple tag that consists of a name and a value representing the checked status:

```
<g:checkBox name="spamMe" value="${newuser.spamMe}"/>
```

Radio buttons give you a little more flexibility. The most common way to work with radio buttons is via a radioGroup. In listing 6.2, we implemented `emailFormat` using the radioGroup tag:

```
<g:radioGroup name="emailFormat"
          labels="['Plain','HTML']"
          values="['P', 'H']"
          value="H">
    ${it.label} ${it.radio}
</g:radioGroup>
```

Notice that you have to supply both `labels` and `values` for the buttons.

The radioGroup tag is also a little different from checkBox in that the tag iterates through its contents once for each entry. That's why we need to supply those `${it.label}` and `${it.radio}` elements, which get rendered once for each radio button. This iterating approach gives you a lot of flexibility in how the radio buttons are marked up, but it's a bit of a corner case amongst the Grails form taglibs.

Grails also provides a `<g:radio>` tag for cases when you want to generate your radio buttons without iteration, but you have to set the same `name` attribute for each button in the group. For this reason, it's often safer to go the radioGroup approach.

HIDDEN FIELDS

Although we didn't demonstrate hidden fields in listing 6.2, they're a special case of a `<g:textField>` that doesn't display in the browser. Here's an example:

```
<g:hiddenField name="dateRendered" value="${new Date()}" />
```

You're free to put whatever text values you like in a hiddenField, and they will end up in the `params` map when the form is submitted.

HANDLING MULTIPLE SUBMIT BUTTONS

Having multiple buttons on one form can make form handling awkward. Traditionally, you had to submit the form to one controller, then have a big `switch` statement to route to the appropriate action based on which button was clicked.

Grails provides the `<g:actionSubmit>` button, which makes it easy to send the form to the right action, handling the messy routing stuff for you. Here's an example:

```
<g:actionSubmit value="Register" />
<g:actionSubmit value="Cancel" action="cancelRegister" />
```

You'll notice that we've specified the `action` on one button and not the other. If you don't specify an action name, Grails will assume the action is the lowercased name of the button (/user/register for the first button). If you use a different convention, you're free to specify the action name (as we did in the second line, which submits to /user/cancelRegister).

HANDLING DATE SELECTIONS

One of the least-documented Grails tags is the datePicker. This tag creates a series of controls that allow the user to select a date value.

The tag renders a series of combo boxes for the user to select the day of the month, month name, and year (and optionally values for hours, minutes, and seconds) making it ideal for applications that take care of things like hotel booking or flight dates. When the user submits the form, the Grails data binder turns the collection of controls into a Java `Date` object, making date-handling very straightforward.

Creating a datePicker is very straightforward:

```
<g:datePicker name="arrivalDate"
        value="${myBooking.arrivalDate}"
        precision="day"/>
```

The `precision` field specifies which fields you want the user to be able to enter. In the preceding example, the value of `day` will provide fields for the day, month, and year. Setting the precision to `minute` would create additional fields for both hours and minutes in the datePicker. See the Grails reference guide for a complete set of configuration options.

One common gotcha when working with the datePicker is that your controller must use Grails' data binding mechanism (either a `bindData()` or a properties assignment) in order for the conversion of the datePicker controls to work. In practice, that means you must not use Groovy-style property binding to do your initial save. For example, `new Booking(params).save()` won't work when processing forms containing datePickers. Also, don't expect `params.arrivalDate` to return a date—the actual date is built up during data binding from the several HTML controls that the datePicker tag generates.

TAG SUMMARY

We have covered a lot of ground so far, and introduced many of the common tags that you're likely to use. Tables 6.2 and 6.3 summarize both the common and less common tags that you'll encounter when developing with Grails.

Table 6.2 Summary of basic form tags

Tag	Description
g:form	Creates a standard HTML form element
g:uploadForm	Creates a form that supports nested file upload elements
g:textField	Creates a single-line text field
g:passwordField	Creates a single-line text field with opaque characters
g:textArea	Creates a multiline text field
g:checkbox	Creates a check box that returns a `true` or `false` value
g:radio and g:radioGroup	Creates a radio button that can nested in a radio group for scenarios where only one option can be selected
g:select	Creates a drop-down box with prepopulated elements
g:hiddenField	Creates a field that isn't visible in the browser
g:actionSubmit	Creates a button that submits the form to a particular controller action

Table 6.3   Less-common UI-related form tags

Tag	Description
g:datePicker	Creates a series of drop-down lists for current time and date selection
g:currencySelect	Displays a user-selectable list of currencies
g:paginate	Displays a series of page navigation links for multipage datasets
g:timezoneSelect	Displays a user-selectable list of Java time zones
g:countrySelect	Displays a user-selectable list of countries
g:message	Displays a message from a message-bundle
g:hasErrors	Tests whether an object has validation errors
g:renderErrors	Renders all validation errors on an object as a list
g:javascript	Embeds a JavaScript inline or a link to a JavaScript file or library

TIP   Grails lets you use legacy JSP taglibs in GSPs. If you have existing validation or utility taglibs, there's no need to rewrite them—just add a `<%
@taglib %>` directive to your GSP. Check out the online docs at http://
grails.org/doc/1.1.x/ for examples.

That completes our whirlwind tour of the core Grails form tags. We'll spend the rest
of the book applying those tags, so don't feel too overwhelmed—you'll get plenty of
practice!

There's one other tag that deserves special consideration because it implements
the tricky concept of pagination—datasets that you can browse through over multiple
pages. In the next section we'll use it to add pagination to Hubbub's timeline feature.

6.1.4   Adding pagination to the timeline

One of the most unusual and useful core tags is `<g:paginate>`. It renders a series of
navigation links so you can move through multiple pages of results.

Our global timeline in Hubbub will have entries for all the posts in the system, so
it's going to grow rapidly. Adding a `<g:paginate>` tag allows us to add navigation links
to older posts, as shown in figure 6.2.

Provided that your controller has populated a count of the entries that can be pag-
inated, using the tag is as simple as passing on this total. You can also tell it how many
results you want displayed per page using the `max` parameter (`max` is optional, and it
defaults to 10).

```
<g:paginate total="${postCount}" max="25" />
```

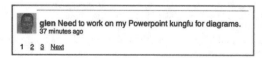

**Figure 6.2   The `<g:paginate>`
tag in action**

The tag divides the total number of entries by the maximum per page and creates links for each page. Each page link is sneakily marked up to point to the current controller, with max and offset values (for example, max = 25, offset = 50). When you click on the link for the third page in the timeline, you'll navigate to /post/global?max=25&offset=50.

Dynamic finders know about the max and offset variables, so when an action like the following one executes, the params collection passes max and offset values to Post.list():

```
def posts = Post.list(params)
def postCount = Post.count()
[ posts, postCount ]
```

This means list() will honor those values in the query, offsetting the query result list and returning the next "page" of posts. Try out the paginate tag in the Hubbub global timeline so you can see the magic at work (and understand exactly what's happening).

You now have a good grasp of all the core Grails form UI elements. But there are situations when none of the standard tags will do, and you need to write your own. We'll look at that next.

6.2 Extending views with your own tags

We've used a lot of the standard Grails tags for form elements, conditional branching, error handling, and even iteration. But what about when the built-in options aren't specific enough? There are options for developing your own tags, so let's write a few of our own.

Grails supports three different types of custom tags, as listed in table 6.4.

Table 6.4 Types of custom tags supported by Grails

Type	Description	Example
Simple Tags	Outputs HTML	`<g:button>`
Logical Tags	Performs a conditional output based on a test	`<g:if test="">`
Iterative Tags	Iterates through a collection, rendering content for each element	`<g:each in="">`

The good news is that you can write whatever simple, logical, and iterative tags you need. We'll write one of each type to give you some ideas.

6.2.1 Simple tags

Our Hubbub timeline could use a date upgrade. Most Web 2.0 apps support those "5 minutes ago" dates, which look cool and solve time-zone issues. Let's implement a dateFromNow tag that will take a date and output a nice format.

It will come as no surprise that we start with a template:

```
grails create-tag-lib date
```

This will generate the shell of a taglib in /grails-app/taglib/DateTagLib.groovy. Implementing simple tags involves processing the `attrs` parameter and rendering HTML to the output stream.

We'll invoke our tag like this:

```
<g:dateFromNow date="${post.created}"/>
```

Implementing the dateFromNow tag in the `DateTagLib` class involves creating a closure called `dateFromNow` and processing the `date` attribute. Listing 6.3 shows a first draft of the implementation.

Listing 6.3   Creating a custom dateFromNow tag

```
class DateTagLib {

    def dateFromNow = { attrs ->        Accesses date attribute
        def date = attrs.date           from custom tag
        def niceDate = getNiceDate(date) // implement this somehow...

        out << niceDate                 Writes formatted date
                                        to the page
    }

}
```

We access `date` using `attrs.date`, and pass it to our `getNiceDate()` method to turn it into "x minutes ago" format, and then we output the result to the stream. Groovy overloads the `<<` operator for streaming objects to perform a `write()`, so there's nothing more to do than implement our `getNiceDate()` business logic, as shown in listing 6.4.

Listing 6.4   Implementing a much nicer date format for Hubbub

```
static String getNiceDate(Date date) {

    def now = new Date()

    def diff = Math.abs(now.time - date.time)
    static final long second = 1000
    static final long minute = second * 60
    static final long hour = minute * 60
    static final long day = hour * 24

    def niceTime = ""

    long calc = 0;

    calc = Math.floor(diff / day)
    if (calc) {
        niceTime += calc + " day" + (calc > 1 ? "s " : " ")
        diff %= day
    }

    calc = Math.floor(diff / hour)
    if (calc) {
        niceTime += calc + " hour" + (calc > 1 ? "s " : " ")
        diff %= hour
    }
```

```
calc = Math.floor(diff / minute)
if (calc) {
   niceTime += calc + " minute" + (calc > 1 ? "s " : " ")
   diff %= minute
}

if (!niceTime) {
   niceTime = "Right now"
} else {
   niceTime += (date.time > now.time) ? "from now" : "ago"
}

return niceTime
```

}

We now have a reusable tag we can use wherever we need to render a date in "x min-utes ago" format. We've used a single attribute (date) for our example, but your tags can have multiple attributes.

> ### What's the g:? Using custom namespaces
>
> All our sample tags have taken the form <g:tagName>. The g: prefix is referred to as the tag's *namespace*. If you don't specify a custom namespace for your taglibs, they will use the <g:> prefix. How do you customize this? Add a new declaration to your DateTagLib.groovy file:
>
> ```
> static namespace = "hubbub"
> ```
>
> If you do this, you can refer to your tags as <hubbub:dateFromNow ...>. It's best to use short namespaces to reduce typing, so let's use a namespace of "h" for Hub-bub tags so we can specify <h:dateFromNow>.
>
> You should always declare a namespace for your tags so they're less likely to collide with other tags—particularly with future Grails built-ins.

Now that we've implemented a simple tag, let's explore Grails' support for building logical tags.

6.2.2 Logical tags

Sometimes you want to display a block of content conditionally. Let's say we only want to display certain content to Internet Explorer users. We might do something like this:

```
<h:lameBrowser userAgent="MSIE">
    <p>Dude, Firefox really is better. No, really. </p>
</h:lameBrowser>
```

We want IE users to see this message, but all other browsers will pass on by. Let's implement a UtilTagLib as shown in listing 6.5.

Listing 6.5   A lameBrowser tag demonstrating logical tags in action

```
class UtilTagLib {

    static namespace = "h"

    def lameBrowser = { attrs, body ->

        if(request.getHeader('User-Agent')          Checks User-Agent header
                    =~ attrs.userAgent ) {           matches tag attribute
            out << body()          ◁──┐ Displays any content that
        }                             │ was inside original tag
    }

}
```

Notice that logical tags take two arguments: `attrs`, which you've already seen, and `body`, which contains the `content` block inside the tag. If the test evaluates to `true`, we render the `body()` to the output stream; otherwise we send nothing.

This sort of tag is common for security scenarios. For example, when using the JSecurity plugin, you'll often employ convenience tags like `isLoggedIn` for conditional output:

```
<jsec:isLoggedIn>
    <div>Logged in as: <jsec:principal/>
        (<g:link controller="auth" action="signOut">
          sign out
        </g:link>)</div>
</jsec:isLoggedIn>
```

Notice that the contents of your logical tags may themselves be complex GSP fragments that call other tags in other taglibs.

With our exploration of logical tags complete, let's turn to the last style of custom tags Grails supports: iteration tags.

6.2.3   *Iteration tags*

The most complex of the custom tag types is the iteration tag. This type of tag performs multiple invocations of its `body()` with different input values for each iteration.

The Hubbub sidebar should contain images for the friends that we're following. We could implement it as a standard `<g:each>` tag, like this:

```
<!-- People I am following -->
<div id="friendsThumbnails">
    <g:each var="followUser" in="${following}">
        <img src="
          <g:createLink action="tiny" controller="image"
            id="${followUser.userId}"/>
          "alt="${followUser.userId}"/>
    </g:each>
</div>
```

An eachFollower tag, on the other hand, would give us a more visually pleasing approach and let us do something like this:

```
<h:eachFollower in="${following}">
   <img src="
      <g:createLink action="tiny" controller="image"
         id="${followUser.userId}"/>
      " alt="${followUser.userId}"/>
</h:eachFollower>
```

The eachFollower tag can be implemented with an iterating call to the body method:

```
def eachFollower = { attrs, body ->

   def followers = attrs.followers
   followers?.each { follower ->

      body(followUser: follower)

   }

}
```

But that's a lot of work to replicate the standard behavior of <g:each>. To be honest, we can't think of too many scenarios where you're not better off using the more explicit semantics of <g:each>. A smarter use of your time would be implementing a tag for user thumbnails, which we'll explore next.

6.2.4 *Calling one tag from another*

When you're developing your own custom tags, you often want to reuse standard Grails tags from within your own implementation. For example, if you were building a custom tag that incorporated links to a standard controller action, you'd probably want to take advantage of the existing createLink tag.

Let's apply that thinking to a new custom tag so you can see this reuse in action. Take the example of generating URLs for those tiny follower images. As you saw in the last section, we're currently doing this in HTML with dynamic URL construction:

```
<img src="
   <g:createLink action="tiny" controller="image"
      id="${followUser.userId}"/>
   " alt="${followUser.userId}"/>
```

It would be much nicer to be able to hide that all in a custom tinyThumbnail tag, like this:

```
<h:tinyThumbnail userId="${followUser.userId}"/>
```

When we implement our tinyThumbnail tag, we want to be able to reuse the functionality built into the standard g:createLink tag. And we can! Here's our custom implementation:

```
def tinyThumbnail = { attrs ->

   def userId = attrs.userId
   out << "<img src='"
   out << g.createLink(action: "tiny",
      controller: "image", id: userId)       | Reuses existing Grails tag
   out << "' alt='${userId}'"
}
```

As we saw earlier, you can invoke an existing tag using method-style invocation. The namespace must be used as the object of the method call ("g" for the standard taglibs, as shown previously).

Now that you've learned how to create your own custom tags, the next step is to learn how to improve application layouts.

6.3   *Adding delicious layouts*

We've spent plenty of time implementing functionality for Hubbub, but we've spent none on its appearance. Grails doesn't just make implementing features fast, it also enables you to make your application look and feel good. At the heart of look-and-feel matters is Grails' support for layouts.

We've been using templates since chapter 4 (and we even touched on them in chapter 1), but we never explained how they work. All of the heavy lifting for layout functionality in Grails is done via a popular Java layout library called SiteMesh (http://www.opensymphony.com/sitemesh/). You may not have been exposed to SiteMesh before, so let's take a look at it.

6.3.1   *Introducing SiteMesh*

SiteMesh operates as a page decorator. You render plain HTML for your page, and it is passed through a SiteMesh decorator (to add the header, footer, sidebars, and so on), and the final merged page is rendered to the browser. You might like to think of it as shown in figure 6.3.

One of the most powerful and sophisticated features of SiteMesh is merging elements from your target page into your decorator. This will make more sense with an example, so let's explore how SiteMesh is used to implement Hubbub's common look and feel.

EXPLORING THE MERGING PROCESS

Let's review our template from chapter 4—a simple layout that adds a title field and a basic footer. We placed our layouts in /grails-app/views/layouts, but because we want

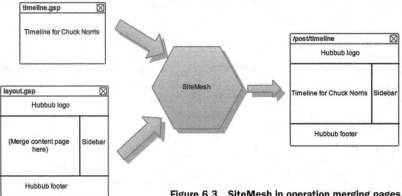

Figure 6.3   SiteMesh in operation merging pages

our template to apply to our scaffolding code too, we edited the standard template, called /grails-app/views/layouts/main.gsp. Listing 6.6 reproduces that template.

Listing 6.6 A basic custom template for Hubbub

```
<html>
  <head>
    <title>Hubbub &raquo;
      <g:layoutTitle default="Welcome" />        ❶  Merges title element
    </title>                                          from content page
    <link rel="stylesheet" href="
      <g:createLinkTo dir='css' file='hubbub.css'/>
    "/>
    <g:javascript library="application" />      ❷  Merges head element
    <g:layoutHead />                                 from content page
  </head>
  <body>
    <div>
      <div id="hd">
        <a href="<g:createLinkTo dir="/"/>">
          <img id="logo" src="
            ${createLinkTo(dir: 'images',
                 file: 'headerlogo.png')}
          " alt="hubbub logo"/>
        </a>
      </div>
      <div id="bd"><!-- start body -->        ❸  Merges body element
        <g:layoutBody/>                              from content page
      </div>  <!-- end body -->
      <div id="ft">
        <div id="footerText">
          Hubbub - Social Networking on Grails
        </div>
      </div>
    </div>
  </body>
</html>
```

We start by laying out the title. We prefix all title elements with "Hubbub >>", followed by the title value from the target page ❶ . If the target page doesn't have a custom <title> element, we display "Welcome". This gives us a convenient way of changing all our titles in one place.

We use the SiteMesh <g:layoutHead> tag ❷ to merge any content from our target page's <head> element, and the <g:layoutBody> tag ❸ to merge in the contents of our target page's <body> element.

Once all those tags fire, our target view page will be merged with our layout template to give us a consistent layout throughout the application. This approach to markup offers a double win. Your content pages become simple and uncluttered, and your layout pages make it easy to change the look and feel of your application with a single edit.

Displaying application versions in footers

The `<g:meta>` tag gives you access to all the entries in your Grails application.properties file in the root directory of your project. It's often convenient to display the version of your application in the footer, for reporting issues against, and to confirm that a new version has deployed successfully. You might display your current application and Grails version in a footer using code like this:

```
Version <g:meta name="app.version"/>
on Grails <g:meta name="app.grails.version"/>
```

You can change the version of your application at any time by using the `grails set-version` command from the command line, or by editing the application.properties file directly. The version number of your application affects the naming of your target WAR file, so it can be handy to bump the number with each deployed version, so you can keep old copies of WAR artifacts around for an immediate rollback if things go bad. (This isn't a substitute for version control, but it's a cheap rollback option nonetheless.)

APPLYING LAYOUTS BY CONVENTION

In chapter 1, we introduced you to a simple way of applying layouts by convention. It's time to review the options and dig deeper into some applications of them.

For example, if we were dealing with the Post controller, we could control its decoration with the techniques listed in table 6.5.

Table 6.5 Conventions for applying layout templates

Apply template to ...	Example of convention or technique
All actions in a controller	Create layout in /layouts/post.gsp
A specific action in a controller	Create layout in /layouts/post/list.gsp
A portion of a target page	Include tag in target page: `<g:applyLayout name="postFragment">Hi</g:applyLayout>`
Override any conventions explicitly for a single page	Include tag in target page: `<meta name="layout" content="vanilla"/>`

Using conventions eliminates the need to specify the `<meta>` tag and makes your application more maintainable at the same time. When we open a GSP file and don't see any meta magic, we know exactly where to look for a decorator (/views/layouts /<controllerName>), which makes maintenance a lot more straightforward.

While we're on the subject of real-world approaches to page layouts, it's time to explore other ways to make them simpler.

6.3.2   *Standardizing page layouts*

If you've done any work laying out multicolumn web applications, you already know how complex a standard CSS layout can be. Some browsers won't float the divs correctly to give you the right gutter, it's hard to get some sections of your page to grow while others stay static, there are all sorts of font-size issues, and the page never looks good in Internet Explorer.

You need to address all of these issues in your application layouts, and it's time we showed you the best way to go about it. First, let's sketch out how we want Hubbub to look. Figure 6.4 shows a rough sketch for the app.

Figure 6.4   **A mockup of our Hubbub UI**

As you can see, we've got a top header followed by a tabbed area with a right sidebar, followed by a full-width footer. If you were coding this by hand, you'd be in for a shock. These kind of CSS layouts involve a massive amount of work and are very difficult to keep consistent across browsers. In Grails, the smartest way to handle CSS layouts is with YUI Grids.

YUI Grids gives you a simple CSS-based mechanism for fine-grained control of browser layouts. It's a 4 KB CSS file that you can add to your application and that will solve your cross-browser layout dramas for good.

You can download the CSS file and view comprehensive documentation from the YUI Grids page (http://developer.yahoo.com/yui/grids/), where you'll also find the YUI Grids Builder. You can even use the online builder to generate your basic template layout for you. Figure 6.5 shows a sample of the YUI Grids Builder in action, building our layout from the sketch above.

Once you've got the layout you want, click the Show Code button and you'll be presented with your template ready to customize. Listing 6.7 shows the YUI code generated from the layout in figure 6.5.

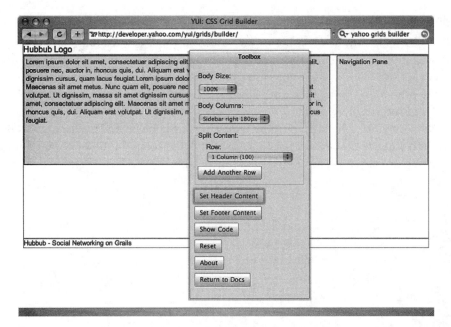

Figure 6.5   **The YUI Grids Builder makes cross-browser CSS layouts easy.**

Listing 6.7   The YUI-generated code

```
<!DOCTYPE HTML PUBLIC "-//W3C//DTD HTML 4.01//EN"
 "http://www.w3.org/TR/html4/strict.dtd">
<html>
<head>
  <title>YUI Base Page</title>
  <link rel="stylesheet"
     href="http://yui.yahooapis.com/2.5.1/build/
     ➥ reset-fonts-grids/reset-fonts-grids.css" type="text/css">
</head>
<body>
<div id="doc3" class="yui-t4">
  <div id="hd"><h1>Hubbub Logo</h1></div>
  <div id="bd">
   <div id="yui-main">
    <div class="yui-b"><div class="yui-g">
    <!-- YOUR DATA GOES HERE -->
    </div>
</div>
   </div>
   <div class="yui-b"><!-- YOUR NAVIGATION GOES HERE --></div>

   </div>
   <div id="ft">Hubbub - Social Networking on Grails</div>
</div>
</body>
</html>
```

With a few tagged YUI divs, we have a cross-browser, safely degrading CSS layout that will look the same on any browser. All we need to do now is incorporate our <g:layout> tags to merge in the head and body, and add some CSS styling to give us a better idea of what it might look like.

You'll notice that there are some portions of our layout that we'll want to reuse in several places. For example, our sidebar on the right should display for several of the tabs, and it might be useful elsewhere in the app as well. Rather than encode that stuff directly in the layout, we can take advantage of Grails templates.

6.3.3 Fragment layouts with templates

When you want to reuse portions of your application layout throughout your application, you have a candidate for a template. Templates encapsulate fragments of GSP functionality and can be incorporated in your pages using the <g:render> tag.

Take the example of the static login fragment shown in listing 6.8.

Listing 6.8   A sidebar fragment to include

```
<div id="sidebar">

   <h3>Login</h3>
   <div id="loginForm">
      <g:form controller="login">

        <ul>
           <li>User Id: <g:textField name="userId" size="12"/></li>
           <li>Password:
              <g:passwordField name="password" size="12"/>
           </li>
           <li><g:submitButton name="login" value="Login"/></li>
        </ul>

      </g:form>
   </div>

</div>
```

There may be several pages in your application that require this small piece of content. If you save the fragment in /views/_sidebar.gsp (note the underscore), you can reference it in your GSP pages or layouts with this tag:

```
<g:render template="/sidebar"/>
```

Better still, the templates themselves can contain model references that you can pass by using the model attribute:

```
<g:render template="/sidebar" model="[defaultUser: 'name-here']"/>
```

This makes templates great self-contained pieces of view functionality. You can even use templates in controllers when rendering Ajax fragments—we'll get into that in section 6.4.

With our standard layouts now in place, it's time to let the user choose their own look and feel for Hubbub. This is called *skinning*, and Grails makes it easy to implement.

6.3.4 *Adding skinning*

Hubbub looks great with its standard blue and grey design. But social-networking sites generally let users skin their own timelines. Let's add skinning to Hubbub.

First, we'll need a way to select a preferred skin, and for that we'll need to add a new optional field to the Profile object:

```
package com.grailsinaction

class Profile {

   static belongsTo = User

   String fullName
   // ... other fields omitted          Adds support for per-
   String skin                          user skinning

   static constraints = {
      fullName(nullable: true)
      // ... other constraints omitted
      skin(nullable: true, blank: true, inList: ['blues', 'nighttime'])
   }
}
```

NOTE   You'll want to update the profile-editing screens to support the new skin types, but we'll leave that as an exercise for you (or you can grab the example source from github).

With the skin in place, we need to customize the user's timeline page to take advantage of it. If the user has a skin for their timeline, we'll apply it using CSS. Listing 6.9 shows an extract of the updated timeline.gsp file.

Listing 6.9   Applying a skin via CSS

```
<html>
   <head>
      <title>Timeline for ${user.profile.fullName}</title>
      <meta name="layout" content="main"/>
      <g:if test="${user.profile.skin}">                    Checks whether
                                                            user has a skin
         <link rel="stylesheet" href="
            <g:createLinkTo dir='css'
                file='${user.profile.skin}.css'/>           Applies user's
         "/>                                                 preferred skin
      </g:if>
   </head>
   <body>
```

The updated timeline checks to see if the user has a skin configured, and, if so, it adds a link to the appropriate stylesheet from the CSS directory. The CSS skin files work by overriding the background colors of body elements and heading styles. For skinning to work well, it's important that you make good use of CSS classes and IDs to mark up your view pages.

Figure 6.6 shows our "nighttime" skin in action. If you need to support skinning site-wide rather than for individual pages, you're better off making use of filters, which we introduced in chapter 5. Set up your skin name in a filter and pass it using a

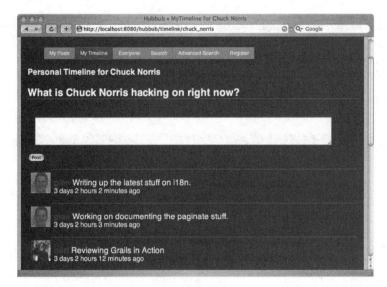

Figure 6.6 The nighttime theme in action

session-scoped variable. Then configure the CSS skin in your main layout page, and you're set.

6.3.5 *Implementing navigation tabs*

With the skinning in place, it's time to turn our attention to navigation. Which UI elements will we provide to allow the user to navigate around the application? The most recognizable option is to display a series of navigation tabs at the top of the page.

In the early days of Grails, all of this tab-style navigation was done by hand. Typically you would write a tag to generate menu items, and do the hard work of highlighting the appropriate tab based on the current controller action. Things got messy quickly.

But since Marc Palmer's Navigation plugin came on the scene, generating navigation tabs has become straightforward. We're going to cover third-party plugins in depth in chapter 8, but for now we'll walk you through the basics of installing and using the Navigation plugin.

To install the Navigation plugin, change to the root directory of your project and run the following command:

```
grails install-plugin navigation
```

Grails will inform you that it's downloading the plugin and installing it into your application.

Once the plugin is installed, you can mark your controller classes with a new `navigation` property and tell the plugin which actions from your controller to display in your menu. We want to generate a menu for Hubbub that looks something like figure 6.7.

Figure 6.7 Our planned navigation menu

Although that looks like a lot of work, the Navigation plugin makes generating the menu straightforward. Listing 6.10 shows extracts of the updated `UserController` and `PostController` with new navigation blocks that specify what to include in the menu.

Listing 6.10 Defining menu options in your controller

```
class PostController {

    static navigation = [
        [group:'tabs', action:'timeline', title: 'My Timeline', order: 0],
        [action: 'global', title: 'Global Timeline', order: 1]
    ]
    // ... other code omitted
}

class UserController {

    static navigation = [
        [group:'tabs', action:'search', order: 90],
        [action: 'advSearch', title: 'Advanced Search', order: 95],
        [action: 'register', order: 99, isVisible: { true }]
    ]
    // ... other code omitted
}
```

For each navigation block, you provide a series of maps, each representing one item in the menu. In each map, you provide the action that should fire when the menu is clicked, along with an optional title. If you don't specify a title, the plugin will use a nicely formatted name of the action (`register` becomes "Register" and `advSearch` would default to "Adv Search").

You can use the `order` property to control where in the menu your items are positioned. (In the future, third-party plugins might make use of this field to include their own items in your menus automatically.) You can even supply an `isVisible` property that will be tested when the menu is rendered. For example, you might control the register menu to only show if the user isn't logged in.

Now that our menu blocks are all defined, we have to make two entries in our template to display the menu. In the `head` element of our main layout, we'll add a `<nav:resources/>` element:

```
<head>
    <nav:resources/>
</head>
```

This will incorporate the menu CSS elements. (You can override them all with your own styling, but the defaults look great.)

In the body of our layout, we'll position the menu in the page with a `<nav:render/>` tag specifying the group attribute that appeared in our navigation block:

```
<div id="bd"><!-- start body -->
    <nav:render group="tabs"/>
    <g:layoutBody/>
</div>
```

With those two changes, our menu is ready to roll. Figure 6.8 shows the new menu in operation.

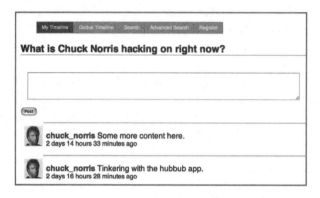

Figure 6.8   The Navigation plugin painlessly handles all your menu needs.

With our menu looking slick, it's time to explore some other ways to raise our UI to the next level. One obvious way is to use Ajax to update the user's timeline in-place when they add a new post. But before we get started, you need to learn a little about how Grails integrates Ajax.

6.4   Applying Ajax tags

We've done a lot of UI work so far, but we've saved the best for last. In this section, we'll use Ajax to take the Hubbub UI experience to a whole new level. We'll get a taste for dynamically changing our Hubbub page in-place using remote calls to backend code. Then we'll create some visual sizzle with JavaScript animation and effects.

But first we need to lay the foundation by choosing a JavaScript library to do the heavy lifting for us.

6.4.1   Choosing a JavaScript library

Grails implements all of its built-in Ajax functionality through *adaptive* tag libraries. That means that all of the standard Ajax tags can be backed by whatever JavaScript library you prefer and still expose the same API to the client and server. Prototype is supported out of the box, and Dojo, YUI, and jQuery are supported using plugins. That means you're free to start with one library, and change to a different one as your application fills out.

Not all JavaScript libraries play nicely together, so if some of your GSPs use a particular library, it makes sense to use that for your Ajax implementation too. For instance, if you're planning on doing any animation effects with Scriptaculous, it makes sense to choose Prototype (because that's what Scriptaculous uses under the hood). If you're planning on using YUI autocomplete, you might as well use YUI for your Ajax remoting too (because you've already burned the page-load time bootstrapping the YUI infrastructure).

Prototype seems to be the most widely used by Grails developers (though jQuery is starting to develop a big following for its unobtrusiveness and great effects library), so we'll use Prototype for our examples.

6.4.2   *Essential Ajax form remoting*

It's time to get to work on our user's timeline action to apply a little Ajax style. We'll restyle our posting form to submit post contents using Ajax, then update our timeline with the latest entries.

The first step in using an Ajax call is importing your preferred library. We'll start by updating our timeline.gsp `head` element to tell Grails that we want to use Prototype as our remoting library. Using the `library` attribute of the javascript tag generates HTML tags for the multiple source JavaScript files that comprise the specified library:

```
<head>
    <title>Timeline for ${user.profile.fullName}</title>
    <meta name="layout" content="main"/>
    <g:javascript library="prototype"/>
</head>
```

With our library selected, we can now update the posting form to submit the `Post` contents remotely. Grails provides the `<g:submitToRemote>` tag to bundle up the contents of a form and send it via Ajax to a backend service. Listing 6.11 shows the updated form definition.

Listing 6.11   Adding a new `Post` via Ajax

```
<g:form                                                     Creates Ajax link ❶
    action="ajaxAdd">
  <g:textArea id='postContent' name="content" rows="3" cols="50"/><br/>
  <g:submitToRemote value="Post"
      url="[controller: 'post', action: 'addPostAjax']"           Specifies Map of
      update="allPosts"                                       ❷  params to submit
      onSuccess="clearPost(e)"          Sets id of HTML
      onLoading="showSpinner(true)"  ❸  element to update
      onComplete="showSpinner(false)"/>            ❹  Handles events
  <img id="spinner" style="display: none"              generated by the tag
      src="<g:createLinkTo dir='/images' file='spinner.gif'/>"/>
</g:form>                                            Adds the spinner image ❺
```

The `<g:form>` and `<g:textField>` tags remain unchanged. Only a `<g:submitTo-Remote>` tag has been introduced ❶. Its only required attribute is `url`, which is a map with `controller` and `action` values ❷. We'll add a new `addPostAjax()` action in the `PostController` to handle the new submission.

If the `update` attribute is specified ❸, it should be the `id` of the div to be updated when the call is complete. In our case, the `addPostAjax()` call will return the updated HTML for the timeline, which is in a div with `id` `allPosts`.

If the onSuccess attribute is specified ❹, it should contain the JavaScript function that should be called once the form submission has finished successfully (no backend 404s or other errors). Whatever function you supply to onSuccess should take an argument (e) that is the XMLHTTPResponse that represents the backend call. In our case, we use clearPost to clear the textArea when the user has successfully posted the new item.

Finally, onLoading and onComplete are called before and after the Ajax call, which we take advantage of to show and hide an animated *spinner* image ❺.

If you're curious about those clearPost and showSpinner JavaScript calls, there's no magic in them—just a few lines of Prototype to keep the UI responsive. It's always good to show and hide an image when doing Ajax calls, so the user knows that something is happening. Listing 6.12 shows the JavaScript we're using to keep the user up to date.

Listing 6.12 Keeping the user updated with JavaScript

```
<g:javascript>
   function clearPost(e) {
      $('postContent').value='';
   }
   function showSpinner(visible) {
      $('spinner').style.display = visible ? "inline" : "none";
   }
</g:javascript>
```

With our client interface implemented, we need to implement the addPostAjax() action in PostController. Listing 6.13 shows the backend code we'll need.

Listing 6.13 Implementing the addPostAjax() backend

```
def addPostAjax = {                                    ❶ Creates post
   try {                                                  via service
      def newPost = postService.createPost(      ◁─┘
         session.user.userId, params.content)          ❷ Queries 20 most
      def recentPosts = Post.findAllByUser(      ◁─┘     recent posts
         session.user,
         [sort: 'dateCreated', order: 'desc', max: 20])
      render(template:"postentries",    ◁─┐
         collection: recentPosts,          Renders postentries template
         var: 'post')                    ❸ for each query result
   } catch (PostException pe) {
      render {                                ◁─┐
         div(class:"errors", pe.message)        Handles bad situations
      }                                       ❹ with error message
   }
}
```

Because we did the hard work of abstracting the PostService in chapter 5, we can reuse it for our Ajax implementation here ❶. After we create our new Post, we retrieve the latest posts to send back to the timeline ❷. Then it's a matter of reusing the `postentries` template we developed earlier and passing it our collection of recent posts ❸. This will send the HTML of the timeline body back to the client for updating the `allPosts` div.

If an error happens in the process, we'll use the markup builder (discussed in chapter 2, section 2.4.4) version of `render` ❹ to send back a div with the error message (styled as an error, so the big pink warning box is displayed).

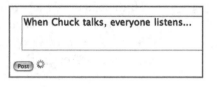

Figure 6.9   Our Ajax spinner in action

Figure 6.9 shows our Ajax timeline in progress with our stylish Ajax spinner giving the user feedback to indicate that things are underway.

The submitToRemote tag we used in listing 6.11 has other options that we haven't explored yet, including the ability to handle server response codes such as `on404` and other event options. It can also handle JSON return values, and we'll use this later in the chapter. For full coverage of its capabilities, check out the Grails online docs at http://grails.org/doc/1.1.x/.

With our basic Ajax functionality in place, it's time to explore how we can use animation libraries to make the whole app more visually stunning.

6.4.3   Sizzle++: going further with animation and effects

We've already given Hubbub quite a makeover in this chapter, but it's time to go the whole nine yards and add some animation effects for true Web 2.0 sizzle. If the last time you used JavaScript effect libraries was doing marquees in the late '90s, there's good news: things have come a long way.

Through libraries like Scriptaculous, YUI, and jQuery, visually stunning and cross-browser JavaScript has become a reality. A whole new level of engineering has created reusable libraries that degrade gracefully and integrate unobtrusively into your application.

We'll be using Scriptaculous for our visual effects. It comes with Grails, so there's nothing to install, and you can get straight to business. It also has lots of effects that can usually be implemented as one-liners.

INTRODUCING SCRIPTACULOUS

Scriptaculous is a JavaScript library for adding impressive visual effects to your application. Fading, appearing, flashing, resizing, and animating are all common UI interactions that Scriptaculous offers.

If you've never used a JavaScript animation library before, you might be intimidated by the thought of complex animation coding. Be comforted: Scriptaculous provides good defaults for an incredible amount of behavior, making everything look great, even for the artistically challenged.

The first step in using the library is to include it in your page header:

```
<head>
    <title>Timeline for ${session.user.userId}</title>
    <g:javascript library="scriptaculous" />
</head>
```

Because Scriptaculous already includes Prototype, there's no need to import both.

With the library imported, using animation effects is a simple matter of invoking one of the numerous Scriptaculous `Effect` methods (for example, `Effect.Fade('myDiv')`). Let's take it for a test drive by adding a TinyURL bar to Hubbub.

SLICK FADES ON TINYURLS

If you've ever used Twitter, you'll notice that any URLs you place in your messages are automatically *compressed* via URL shrinking sites like TinyURL.com. Because URLs can get quite long, this URL-shrinking process helps keep posts that incorporate URLs under the 140-character limit that Twitter imposes. It's high time we added a TinyURL feature to Hubbub. And while we're at it, we'll add some JavaScript effect know-how to make it look slick.

We want to make it easy for users to add URLs to their posts, so we'll add a TinyURL entry box to the posting form. But users don't need a TinyURL entry box onscreen all the time—just when they want to include a URL in their post. So let's make a div to hold the TinyURL entry form, but have it fade in and dissolve out as required.

First, we'll make the div invisible by default, using a `display: none;` CSS tag:

```
<div id="tinyUrl" style="display:none;">
   <g:form>
      TinyUrl: <g:textField name="fullUrl"/>
      <g:submitToRemote action="tinyurl" onSuccess="addTinyUrl(e)"
         value="Make Tiny"/>
   </g:form>
</div>
```

Then we'll add a JavaScript link on our form to fade the div in and out as required. A simple link next to the Post button will be fine:

```
<a href="#" id="showHideUrl" onClick="return toggleTinyUrl()">
   Show TinyURL
</a>
```

Then we need a little JavaScript to implement the appearing and dissolving:

```
<g:javascript>

function toggleTinyUrl() {
   var tinyUrlDisplay = $('tinyUrl').style.display;
   var toggleText = $('showHideUrl');
   if (tinyUrlDisplay == 'none' ) {
      new Effect.BlindDown('tinyUrl', { duration: 0.5 });
      toggleText.innerText = 'Hide TinyURL';
   } else {
      new Effect.BlindUp('tinyUrl', { duration: 0.5 });
      toggleText.innerText = 'Show TinyURL';
   }
}
</g:javascript>
```

The Scriptaculous calls are one-liners, `Effect.BlindDown()` and `Effect.BlindUp()`, passing the div id of our TinyURL form. This effect pair causes the TinyURL bar to smoothly appear and disappear from the top down.

You can also customize the time it takes for the effects to complete. We like to keep effects fairly quick to ensure they don't distract from the workflow. For example, we tuned the `BlindDown()` to take half the default time like this:

```
new Effect.BlindDown('tinyUrl', { duration: 0.5 })
```

Consult the Scriptaculous documentation (http://script.aculo.us/) for the details of the effect parameters. There's also a fantastic showcase page that gives you a chance to play with each of the available effects and see what they look like in a browser (http://wiki.github.com/madrobby/scriptaculous/combination-effects-demo).

Scriptaculous has shortcuts for most of the common UI features you'll want to animate. For example, now that you know how effects work, let's refactor our example with a one-liner:

```
<a href="#" id="showHideUrl"
   onclick="Effect.toggle('tinyUrl', 'blind',
➥ { duration: 0.5 }); return false;">
   TinyURL Bar
</a>
```

`Effect.toggle()` does all of the appear and fade work we implemented in our custom JavaScript, and it even gives you a variety of mechanisms for toggling (`slide`, `blind`, `appear`). Notice that we explicitly return `false` from `onclick` to ensure the browser doesn't follow the "#" link.

HANDLING JSON RETURN VALUES

It's all very well to have ourTinyURL bar fading in and out, but what about when the user wants to use it? We'd like them to be able to enter a URL, click the Make Tiny button, and have the post field automatically append the tiny URL to the current post textArea.

To implement that, we're going to need a way to do the following:

1 Bundle up the current full URL from the text field and send it to the backend via Ajax.

2 Calculate theTinyURL in some backend controller action, and return the value.

3 Catch the return value in our view, and append it to the textArea of the post.

The easiest way to implement the first step is by defining a `submitToRemote` button. This will bundle up the form values and submit them to a backend controller using Ajax. Here's what it would look like in our /views/posts/list.gsp file:

```
<g:form>
   TinyUrl: <g:textField name="fullUrl"/>
   <g:submitToRemote action="tinyurl"
      onSuccess="addTinyUrl(e)" value="Make Tiny"/>
</g:form>
```

The `<g:submitToRemote>` tag will invoke the `tinyurl()` action on the `Post-Controller`, passing it a `params` object with all the form fields in it. In our case, we only have one parameter (`fullUrl`), which we have to shrink. When the remote call completes, the `onSuccess` attribute contains the JavaScript function to be called on success.

The gee-whiz aspect is that the `onSuccess` target gets passed the result of the remote action. If our action returns text, xml, or JSON, we can use it in our client-side JavaScript function.

Let's now implement our controller—listing 6.14 shows our TinyURL implementation. We take the `fullUrl` the user passes in, and hand it off to the TinyURL website for shrinking.

Listing 6.14   A TinyURL action to shrink URLs via JSON

```
def tinyurl = {
   def origUrl = params.fullUrl?.encodeAsURL()
   def tinyUrl =
      new URL("http://tinyurl.com/api-create.php?url=${origUrl}").text
   render(contentType:"application/json") {
      urls(small: tinyUrl, full: params.fullUrl)
   }
}
```

A Groovy enhancement to the URL class lets you access the contents of a URL by calling on the `text` property. In listing 6.14, we call the TinyURL endpoint, which returns a compressed version of the incoming `${origUrl}` value. Once we have the compressed URL, we take advantage of the versatile `render()` method to return a small piece of JSON. The returned JSON will contain properties for both large and small versions of the URL. We're only interested in the small version for display, but we wanted to demonstrate how to return multiple values.

Let's complete the picture by implementing the client-side JavaScript to process the returned JSON in our `addTinyUrl(e)` callback. Listing 6.15 shows the JavaScript for our handler.

Listing 6.15   Implementing a callback to handle the JSON return values

```
<g:javascript>

function addTinyUrl(e) {
   var tinyUrl = e.responseJSON.urls.small;
   $("postContent").value += tinyUrl;
   updateCounter();
   toggleTinyUrl();
}

</g:javascript>
```

When the backend returns a content type of application/JSON, Prototype automatically `evals()` the return value into a native JavaScript object. From there, we can access the `small` property value we returned from our controller in listing 6.14 to display our tiny URL. Figure 6.10 shows the new feature in operation.

We've now got a good handle on Scriptaculous eye candy, and we've even combined it with some funky backend Ajax and JSON magic.

That completes our tour of Grails' Ajax functionality. We've covered an incredible amount about Grails UI features in this chapter, so let's wrap up.

What are you hacking on right now?   68

This is not the coolest site in the world. This is just a tribute:
http://tinyurl.com/5vdm53

Post TinyURL

TinyUrl: http://www.grailsinaction.com/
Make Tiny

Figure 6.10   Our TinyURL
feature in action

6.5   *Summary and best practices*

We started this chapter by touring the basic Grails form tags and learned about more form tags than you'll probably ever need to use in one application. We also looked at how to develop our own custom tags for situations where the standard tags don't provide enough flexibility.

We then toured all the different options Grails gives you for layouts and templates, and we even implemented our own skins and navigation menus.

Finally, we explored some advanced Grails Ajax concepts, implementing a dynamic timeline and aTinyURL codec that uses JSON to communicate with backend services. Along the way, we picked up some JavaScript animation skills to make it all sizzle.

We learned a lot and developed a few best practices:

- *Apply pagination.*   Paginating large datasets creates a much better user experience and it's easy to implement.

- *Develop custom tags.*   Take the time to develop reusable tag components for common parts of your UI. It will save you time, simplify maintenance, and enable you to reuse them in future projects.

- *Use convention-based layout.*   Favor convention-based layouts over explicit meta tags. Often a specific layout for one particular action can make things much more maintainable than doing meta-magic branching. Take advantage of meta tag styles when you need to style a subset of pages for a controller, but use convention layouts for the rest.

- *Layout smarter.*   Handle basic flash message display in your layout rather than repeating it for each view. Use templates for common HTML fragments, passing in explicit model elements. Inside Ajax calls, resist the urge to render HTML directly, and do any rendering via a template call.

- *Pick a JavaScript library.*   Gain an appreciation of the strengths and weaknesses of the various JavaScript libraries. They all have different approaches and are worth exploring. Choose an Ajax library that makes sense for the rest of your app. It takes time to download libraries, so minimize the number of libraries in play.

- *Use a layout library.* When developing complex CSS layouts, use YUI Grids. It will save you time and look great on all browsers.

We've now learned a lot of core Grails concepts, but there's one important area that we really haven't given much consideration to: testing. In the next chapter, we'll dive deep into Grails support for testing controllers, validators, taglibs, and more.

Building reliable applications

In this chapter

- Why you should do testing
- How to test different parts of your application
- Choosing between different testing strategies

We've introduced all the main components of a Grails application, and you have learned more than enough to start developing some useful and usable applications. You're probably highly motivated to get coding and experimenting! And while your motivation is high, it makes sense to take a step back and look at how you can improve the quality and reliability of your applications through testing.

7.1 Why should we test software?

There are two approaches to writing software that works as it should: *correct by design* and *correct through testing*. Those in the former camp believe that you can design software to be correct from the outset. This philosophy has yet to penetrate the commercial sector to any great extent, but its counterpart, demonstrating correctness through testing, has become immensely popular in recent years.

The principle is quite simple: for every line of code that we write, we should have a test that makes sure the code works as expected. When all the tests are passing, we know that the software is working correctly, and that gives us confidence when we release the software. The key is to automate as many of the tests as possible, so that they can be run frequently and reliably. Testing also allows you to refactor software with a far higher degree of confidence than would otherwise be possible. One of the many problems in software development is that changes can have unintended side effects, so anything that mitigates that is a significant benefit.

Tests take on even greater significance within Grails. As you know, the Groovy compiler can't pick up the same sorts of type errors that the Java compiler does because Groovy is a dynamic language. That means tests are the first line of defense against class cast exceptions and missing properties or methods.

Some would argue that this means you gain productivity in writing application code at the cost of a greater testing burden. We disagree. If you follow a strategy of light (or no) testing in Java, you'll certainly find the level of testing required for Grails applications to be higher. But this is a poor comparison; you should be aiming for full test coverage in all your applications, whether they be written in Java or Groovy. Doing otherwise runs the risk of introducing far more bugs into the software than can possibly be justified.

There are several benefits to testing, but in the end it comes down to a simple question: Do you want to write software that runs reliably? If the answer is yes (and we sincerely hope it is), there is no avoiding testing. But before you start going weak at the knees thinking about the extra burden of writing tests, we'd like to allay your fears. Even if you're not used to writing tests, you'll find that the process becomes easier the more you do it. Not only that, you'll almost certainly see your confidence in the code grow, and the tests will become an indispensable safety net.

We'll take a bottom-up approach to testing that starts with the unit tests and then moves on to functional testing. Another perfectly valid approach is top-down, in which you start with the feature-based testing and work down to the unit-testing level as you implement each feature. Which approach suits you or your team best is worth investigating, but whichever process you follow, the techniques we describe here are equally applicable. If you're unfamiliar with the terms "unit testing" and "functional testing," don't worry; we'll explain them as we go.

TEST-DRIVEN DEVELOPMENT

In recent years, the status of testing has changed. Once it was something that you did after the code was written, if at all. Now there is a movement that says, "Tests are important. In fact, they're so important that they should be written first!" The process championed by this movement is known as test-driven development (TDD). The principle is simple: write a test before you write any corresponding implementation code.

TDD offers several benefits. First and foremost, this approach guarantees that you have tests for all your classes. Second, you're able to develop code faster than otherwise because the test gives you early feedback on whether that code works or not—the "code a bit, test a bit" cycle becomes more efficient. Third, if you write the tests first, you're far more likely to design your classes and systems so that they're easily tested. Bolting tests on after the code has been written can be difficult without redesigning the code. Finally, TDD forces you to think about what behavior you want from your class at the outset. Focusing on the *what* rather than the *how* can improve the design of your classes and speed up code writing. Knowing where you're going helps you get there sooner.

> **Fixing bugs**
>
> We're sure that you're well versed in the art of fixing bugs, but we'd like to encourage you to follow a particular process when doing so. The first stage of fixing a bug should be to write a test for it. This test should be written in such a way that it fails until the bug is fixed.
>
> You could fix the bug and then write a test afterwards, but how could you be sure that the test fails with the bug in place? You would have to revert the changes and run the test again. Far better to write the test first and retain the benefits of TDD.

Because of these benefits, we think that TDD should be actively encouraged. We could even take TDD further by following the top-down testing approach, which starts with writing functional tests, then writing unit tests, and only then writing the code. If you choose to take this route, make sure you build up the functional tests gradually, only testing the parts of the feature (or features) that relate to the specific classes you're working on. Attempting to write a functional test that covers the whole feature up front is something of a fool's errand.

7.2   *Unit testing*

Testing a Grails application can initially seem an intimidating prospect. Grails itself provides much of the plumbing and also seems to sprinkle many of your classes with magic, so it may seem next to impossible to test those classes in isolation. Never fear, though! Grails provides a testing framework to help you navigate these waters and make unit testing easy.

Why are we starting with unit tests? One reason is that we're taking a bottom-up approach, so it's the logical place to begin. But as you'll see later, you can also use Grails integration tests for "unit testing" if you want. There are two primary advantages of unit tests over integration tests:

- They're quicker to run.
- You can run them from within your IDE.

Reducing the length of your "code a bit, test a bit" cycles is crucial to maintaining focus and momentum, so unit tests are ideal at this stage.

That's enough of the background—let's take a look at some real code. Just as we started with the domain model back in chapter 3, we'll start with testing domain classes.

7.2.1 Testing domain classes

It might strike you as a bit strange to test domain classes—what is there to test? This is a valid question if your domain classes have no behavior (methods). But all domain classes contain logic that qualifies them for testing: their constraints. Because of this, Grails provides explicit support for testing constraints via `GrailsUnitTestCase`.

WRITING THE UNIT TEST

Let's take a look at how this works by writing a test for Hubbub's `User` class, which has some interesting constraints. All unit tests are stored under the test/unit directory, so create the file test/unit/com/grailsinaction/UserUnitTests.groovy if it doesn't already exist. Listing 7.1 shows the test case implementation.

Listing 7.1 Our first domain class unit test

```
package com.grailsinaction

class UserUnitTests extends grails.test.GrailsUnitTestCase {
    void testConstraints() {
        def will = new User(userId: "william")              ❶ Mocks the
        mockForConstraintsTests(User, [ will ])                 domain class

        def testUser = new User()                           ❷ Validates the
        assertFalse testUser.validate()                        test object
        assertEquals "nullable",
                testUser.errors["userId"]
        assertEquals "nullable",                            ❸ Checks validation
                testUser.errors["password"]                    errors

        testUser = new User(userId: "william", password: "william")
        assertFalse testUser.validate()
        assertEquals "unique", testUser.errors["userId"]
        assertEquals "validator", testUser.errors["password"]
        ...
        testUser = new User(userId: "glen", password: "passwd")
        assertTrue testUser.validate()
    }
}
```

One of the first things you might notice is how much code there is in the test. You'll find that thorough tests often contain more code than what is being tested, but the benefits far outweigh the cost. You can see from the example that the test code itself is quite simple, albeit rather repetitive. Also note that we've named the class `UserUnit-Tests`: the `UnitTests` suffix isn't a requirement of Grails but it's a useful convention for easily distinguishing between unit and integration tests in your IDE.

The first thing that happens in listing 7.1 is that the test case extends a helper class provided by Grails: `GrailsUnitTestCase`. This is the granddaddy in the family, and you'll probably use it either directly or indirectly in all your unit tests. Not only does it make your life easier, but it's essential for creating mock objects—it prevents certain side-effects that make tests fail for no apparent reason.

Who are you mocking?

The process of *mocking* involves providing fake versions of classes or methods that can be used in place of the real implementations. The cool thing is that you can control the behavior of the mock object or method, so you can pass known data to the object under test.

Mocking can be used at any level of testing, but it's most commonly associated with unit tests. Many of the methods provided by `GrailsUnitTestCase` are used to mock the dynamic properties and methods that would normally be injected into classes by Grails.

Next we use a special method provided by `GrailsUnitTestCase` to mock our domain class so that we can test its constraints ❶. Remember that the domain class has no knowledge of the constraints—it's Grails itself that interprets and processes them.

Once `mockForConstraintsTests()` has been called for a domain class, you can start testing the validation. All you have to do is create instances of the mocked domain class and call `validate()` on them ❷. If all the field values of the domain instance pass validation, the return value is `true`, otherwise `false`.

Under the hood

All of the `mock*()` methods provided by `GrailsUnitTestCase` use metaclass programming to add mock properties, methods, and objects. That means you can add your own or override the existing ones to fine-tune the behavior.

In addition, the mock validation performs real Spring data-binding, so the `errors` property is a real instance of Spring's `Errors` interface. This allows you to check for multiple constraint violations on a single field, for example.

At this point, you'll find that your domain instance also has an `errors` property, which you can use to find out what fields failed and why. This property, created by the testing framework, behaves almost identically to the one automatically created by Grails, so you won't get confused when switching between tests and application code. The one difference is that you can't treat the `errors` property as a map in your application code. The big advantage of this extra behavior in tests is that you can easily check whether a constraint has been violated by passing the name of a field as the map key and testing the return value ❸. That value will be the name of the first constraint violated by the corresponding field, or null if the field passed validation. If the field values in our User instance are null, we can check for the string "nullable" (that is, the name of the constraint).

RUNNING THE TEST

Let's try our test now. One way to do this is to run the test directly from within your IDE, if that's supported, but for now we'll use the Grails command:

```
grails test-app -unit
```

This will run all the application's unit tests (those under the test/unit directory) and generate reports for them. In our case, there is only one unit test, so the output looks like this:

```
...
Running 1 Unit Test...
Running test UserUnitTests...
SUCCESS
Unit Tests Completed in 1514ms ...
...
```

Not only do you get a summary of results printed to the console, but Grails also generates an HTML report in the test/reports/html directory. Fire up your browser and open the index.html file in that directory to see a breakdown of the tests by package and class.

How does Grails know which methods to execute for the tests? For example, you might have a checkErrors() method that's called from several of your test methods, but you wouldn't want it run as a test itself. Not a problem: Grails will only execute public methods that are explicitly declared to return void, whose name starts with "test", and that have no arguments. The testConstraints() method in listing 7.1 is an example.

It's straightforward so far. Let's now take a closer look at ❶, because we have yet to explain a rather important feature of mockForConstraintsTests(). You'll see that we pass a list of User instances as its second argument, albeit a single-item list in this case. To test the unique constraint on the userId field, we need some existing domain instances to compare the new value against, and the list we pass to mockFor-ConstraintsTests() counts as the set of "existing" records. As you can see from the test case, userId fails validation when its value is "william" because the list already contains a domain instance with that value.

To see this in action, change the fourth line of the unit test to this:

```
mockForConstraintsTests(User)
```

Now run the tests again. This time you'll see the following line in the console output:

```
testConstraints...FAILURE
```

If you look at the HTML report, you'll see that the test failed because it expected unique but found null. The unique constraint was *not* violated.

At this point, you may be wondering whether the effort of testing constraints is worth it. If you aren't yet convinced, consider this: a typo in the name of the constraints field introduces a subtle and difficult to diagnose bug that people often spend hours trying to resolve. Surely the 5 to 10 minutes it takes to write a test is worth it, just for that?

Only one question remains: where do those assert*() methods come from? JUnit users will find them familiar, and for good reason.

BEHIND THE SCENES: JUNIT

JUnit is the de facto standard unit-testing framework for Java, so not only does Grails use it as the basis of its own testing framework, but Groovy itself comes with direct support for it. Figure 7.1 shows the relevant class hierarchy from JUnit, through Groovy, to Grails. Don't worry about the top three classes in the diagram—we'll get to them in due course.

Every Grails unit-test class you write will be one of these JUnit test cases, so you can use exactly the same techniques you would with plain JUnit. It's not only those classes that Grails takes advantage of either: the test-app command uses Ant's JUnit tasks to generate the reports.

Most of the assert*() methods are provided by JUnit's TestCase, but GroovyTestCase also contains some extra ones. Of particular note are the set of shouldFail() methods that allow you to check that a particular block of code throws an exception. For example, this code checks that a method throws an exception when it's passed an empty string:

```
shouldFail(IllegalArgumentException) {
   myService.testMethod("")
}
```

In this case, we specified the type of exception that we expect to be thrown, but you can also leave that argument out if you don't care what the type of the exception is.

Table 7.1 lists some of the more common and useful assertions that you have access to when your tests extend GroovyTestCase. Note that all the methods shown also have versions that take a string as the first argument. This allows you to specify a message

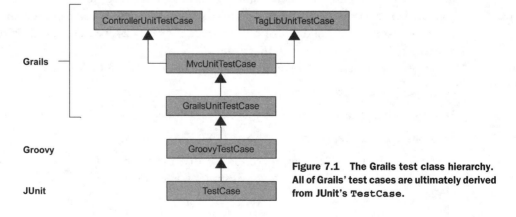

Figure 7.1   The Grails test class hierarchy. All of Grails' test cases are ultimately derived from JUnit's TestCase.

that will be reported when the assertion fails, allowing you to easily determine from the reports why a particular test failed. For example, if this assertion fails,

```
assertEquals "Unique constraint should have triggered, but didn't",
    "unique",
    testUser.errors["userId"]
```

the message "Unique constraint should have..." will appear in the test report.

Table 7.1 Useful assertions available to your test cases

Method	Description
assertEquals(expected, actual)	Compares two values or objects for equality using the equals() method
assertTrue(value)	Checks that the given value is true after being coerced to a Boolean
assertFalse(value)	Checks that the given value is false after being coerced to a Boolean
assertNull(value)	Checks that the given value is null
assertNotNull(value)	Checks that the given value is *not* null
assertSame(expected, actual)	Checks that two objects are the same instance
assertArrayEquals(expected, actual)	Compares two arrays for equality, checking that they have exactly the same elements
shouldFail(type, closure)	Checks that the given closure throws an exception of the given type, or any exception if type is omitted

That was a quick look at the JUnit framework, but you can find more information in books and online articles. One good place to start is http://www.junit.org. Most of that knowledge applies equally to Grails tests—that's one of the great things about reusing other frameworks!

Many domain classes include more than fields and constraints—people often enrich their domain model with methods, which obviously need testing. Methods on domain classes aren't much different from methods on any other class, so they can be tested in the normal way. We'll show you the techniques available by looking at testing a service, but remember that the approach taken applies to any class, including domain classes.

7.2.2 *Testing services*

It's a common (and recommended) practice to place the business logic of an application in services. We'll see more of services in later chapters, but from a testing perspective they're interesting because they're so ordinary. Grails doesn't inject any dynamic properties or methods into them (except for the log property), so the techniques we'll use to test them can be applied to any class.

Let's test a simple service. The following class is a rather contrived example (entirely unrelated to Hubbub), but it allows us to demonstrate a variety of Grails' unit-testing features:

```
class BasketService {
   def userService

   def listItems() {
      def user = userService.getCurrentUser()
      if (!user) { throw new NoUserException() }
      else {
         log.info "Retrieving basket items for ${user.name}"
         return Item.findAllByUser(user)
      }
   }
}
```

The idea is that the listItems() method returns all the items in the current user's shopping basket, or throws an exception if there is no user.

There are some nasty obstacles in the way of testing this class, such as the query, the log property, and the field. At runtime, Grails provides all three itself, so you don't have to worry about setting them up. This isn't the case during a unit test, though, so we have to mock them ourselves either by using metaprogramming tricks (for the dynamic properties and methods) or by creating mock objects (for the service dependency). That's quite a bit of work to do for a single test, and it's not easy either.

Fortunately, Grails' testing support provides you with the tools you need to solve these problems easily and concisely. Listing 7.2 contains a unit test for the example service. Notice how the test case extends GrailsUnitTestCase? It provides all the mocking methods we're about to discuss.

Listing 7.2   Testing a Grails service

```
package com.grailsinaction

class BasketServiceUnitTests extends grails.test.GrailsUnitTestCase {
   void testListItems() {
      mockLogging(BasketService)          ❶ Mocks log property

      def currUser = new User(name: "lucy")
      def otherUser = new User(name: "alan")
      mockDomain(Item, [                   ❷ Mocks
         new Item(user: currUser, name: "orange"),    domain
         new Item(user: otherUser, name: "lemon"),    class
         new Item(user: currUser, name: "apple") ])

      def userControl = mockFor(UserService)
      userControl.demand.getCurrentUser(1..1) = {->    Mocks a
         currUser                                       dependency
      }

      def testService = new BasketService()
      testService.userService = userControl.createMock()

      def items = testService.listItems()
```

```
        assertEquals 2, items.size()
        assertEquals "orange", items[0].name
        assertEquals "apple", items[1].name

        userControl.verify()
    }
}
```

⤶ **Checks mock methods were called**

Let's take the `log` property first: by calling the `mockLogging(Class)` method ❶, any subsequently created instance of the given class will magically gain a working `log` property that echoes all log messages to the console. By default, debug and trace messages aren't included, to avoid excess output, but you can enable the debug messages by passing `true` as an optional second argument to `mockLogging()`.

A similar scheme exists for domain classes ❷, although it's more powerful and consequently more complicated. First of all, `mockDomain(Class, List)` adds dummy implementations of almost all the dynamic domain class methods. The most notable exceptions are criteria and Hibernate Query Language (HQL) queries. But dynamic finders are fully supported and behave as the real methods do.

Most of the `static` methods that Grails adds dynamically only make sense if there are existing database records to find and work with, but this is a unit test, so there isn't even a database. Fortunately, this is taken care of by the second argument to `mockDomain()`. Just as with `mockForConstraintsTests()`, that argument is a (potentially empty) list of domain instances representing existing database records that acts as the backing store for the dynamic finders and other related methods. For example, `Item.list()` will return all the items in the list passed to `mockDomain()`. What's more, the search methods will always return domain instances in the same order as they're defined in the list, which means guaranteed and consistent ordering for your tests. There is almost nothing worse than a test failing because the ordering of a collection has changed.

While we're talking about that second argument, what about `id` values? You can give each of the domain instances in the list an explicit `id` value if you want, but you don't have to. By default, each domain instance will be given an ID matching its position in the list, starting from 1.

---

id and version fields, and IDEs

As you'll have noticed by now, domain classes don't have explicit `id` and `version` fields, but you can still set their values from your code. This is because the Grails compiler adds those two fields to the generated class files.

Unfortunately, not all IDEs use the Grails compiler when compiling your application's domain classes, so the fields may not be added. If that's the case and you try to give either field a value in your unit test, the IDE will complain of a missing property when it attempts to run the test. Not surprising, because neither of them exist.

You can work around this problem by explicitly declaring `Long id` and `version` fields in the domain classes. It might also be a good idea to suggest to the IDE developers that they use the Grails compiler or inject the fields themselves.

Even if the method that you're testing doesn't use the search or object retrieval methods, it can still be worth passing a list into `mockDomain()`. The `save()` implementation will add the domain instance to the list, whereas `delete()` will remove it. This allows you to check whether those methods have been called correctly or not.

We've dealt with the `log` property and the domain classes, but we still need to work out a way of mocking those dependencies. None of the methods we've seen so far help us because they're far too specialized. What we need is a more general mocking system, and that's where `mockFor()` comes in.

7.2.3   General mocking in Grails

A mock object should look and behave like the class it's mocking. For example, if the class implements an interface, you could create a new class that also implements the interface but has mock implementations of the methods. But if you have lots of classes to mock and not all of them implement interfaces, this involves a lot of overhead. You can also run into problems with properties and methods that would normally be dynamically added to the target class.

What we need is a lightweight approach that enables us to add a mock implementation of any method and would allow us to mock only those methods that are called by the code under test, keeping the burden of testing low. The `mockFor()` method does exactly what we need.

The first step in mocking a dependency (or *collaborator*, in testing parlance) is to call `mockFor()` with the class you want to mock. You saw this in listing 7.2, but here's the relevant line again:

```
def mockControl = mockFor(UserService)
```

Why do we assign its return value to a variable called `mockControl`? Because the object returned by the method isn't a mock instance of `UserService` itself, but one that allows you to set up the mock methods and create the mock instance. Its behavior is similar to the `MockControl` class from the EasyMock 1.x library; hence the name of the variable.

Once we have the control object, we can start specifying the methods we expect to be called and providing mock implementations for them. In listing 7.2, we expect the service we're testing to call the `getCurrentUser()` method on the `userService` collaborator, so we declare that expectation using the `demand` property on the control object. Figure 7.2 breaks the call down into its component parts.

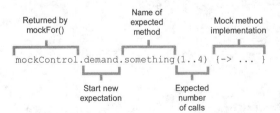

Figure 7.2   Setting an expectation on the object returned by `mockFor()`

This syntax will be familiar if you have ever used Groovy's `MockFor` or `StubFor` classes. The expected method appears as a call on the `demand` property with a range as its argument. This range specifies how many times you expect the method to be called. For example, `2..2` states that the method should be called exactly twice, whereas `1..4` states that the call should be called at least once, but no more than four times. If no range is given, an implicit value of `1..1` is assumed, which means the method should be called exactly once.

Why not use Groovy's MockFor class?

There are several reasons for not using `MockFor`, but the main one is that it doesn't fit as nicely with the metaprogramming system used by Grails as it could. Also, its syntax gets ugly if you need to mock more than one collaborator in any given test.

That doesn't mean you can't use `MockFor` in Grails unit tests, but we think you'll find the `mockFor()` method easier to use and a little more flexible.

The closure is the mock implementation. You can use it to check the values of the arguments and return a particular value or object to the code under test. The number and types of the closure's arguments should match those of the method being mocked, or your mock implementation won't be called.

What if the method under test accesses a property on one of its collaborators? Easy. As you know, property access in Groovy translates to calls on the corresponding getter and setter methods, so all you have to do is mock those methods. For example, say your collaborator has a property called `length`—mocking access to it is as simple as this:

```
mockControl.demand.getLength(1..2) {-> ... }
```

You can take the same approach with the setter method too.

We've now set up the expectations on the control object, so what's next? That depends. If the class under test creates the collaborator itself, there is nothing more to be done at this point. The collaborator will automatically have the mock method implementations that we defined. But in listing 7.2 we have to provide the collaborator ourselves, so we use the mock control's `createMock()` method:

```
testService.userService = userControl.createMock()
```

This has all been preparatory work. We still need to call the method that we're testing and check that it behaves as we expect. The main idea is to verify that its behavior corresponds to the values returned from the mocked methods. In many cases, it also makes sense to check that the method under test passes the appropriate argument values to those mocked methods.

After the method has been executed and we've tested its behavior, we're still not quite finished. How do we know whether the mocked methods have been called the correct number of times, or at all? It's quite possible that you don't care, and in some scenarios that's appropriate. But what if the real implementation of one of the mocked methods persists some data somewhere, or sends an email? You'll want to make sure that the method is called.

Behind the scenes, the mock control counts the number of times a particular method has been called. As soon as one is called more times than expected, an assertion error will be thrown. That doesn't help us if the method is never called, but that problem is easily solved. Once you have executed the method under test, you can call `mockControl.verify()`. This method will throw an assertion error if any of the expected methods have been called fewer than the expected number of times.

Figure 7.3 illustrates the basic sequence of steps followed by a typical unit test. This is a common pattern that's effectively fixed by the way the mocking system works, so almost all of your own unit tests will look similar.

Before we move on, there are a couple of extra features of `mockFor()` that you might be interested in. The first involves mocking static methods, which can be achieved by inserting `static` after the `demand` property:

```
mockControl.demand.static.list() { Map args -> ... }
```

That's it. Nothing else needs to be done to get the mock static method working.

The second feature relates to the order in which the mocked methods are called. It might be important in certain scenarios for the method under test to call the various methods in a fixed order, and for any deviation to result in a test failure. This is known as *strict* mode, and it's the default behavior for `mockFor()`. On the other hand, the order may not be important at all, in which case you don't want tests failing because the methods are called in a different order. Fortunately, `mockFor()` has a *loose* mode for such cases, and you can enable it by passing `true` as the second argument:

```
def mockControl = mockFor(OtherService, true)
```

As you can see, `mockFor()` is a powerful and yet easy-to-use testing tool that can be used to mock almost anything. When it comes to controllers, though, you want

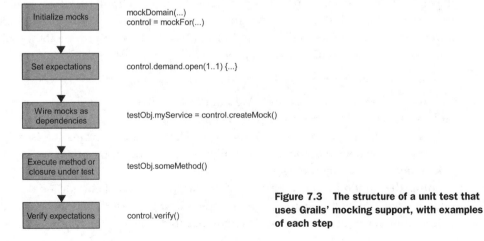

Figure 7.3 The structure of a unit test that uses Grails' mocking support, with examples of each step

something that will handle all the standard dynamic properties and methods. Manually doing it with mockFor() would be verbose and tedious in the extreme.

7.2.4 Testing controllers

Controllers are tricky beasts to test because they have so many dynamic properties and methods, as well as several ways they can render a page. They can return a model, render a view, render arbitrary text, or redirect to another URL. That's why Grails comes with a support class for controllers: ControllerUnitTestCase.

Let's take it for a spin by testing one of Hubbub's controllers. We'll start with one of the actions that returns a model. All we want to know is whether the model contains the data that it should, given the parameters passed in to the action. To do this, we need to set up some test parameters, execute the action, and inspect the map that it returns. Listing 7.3 shows how we go about that.

Listing 7.3 Testing a controller action that returns a model

```
package com.grailsinaction

class PostControllerUnitTests extends grails.test.ControllerUnitTestCase {
    void testShow() {
        mockDomain(User, [
            new User(userId: "glen"),
            new User(userId: "peter") ]                   ❶ Sets request
        this.controller.params.id = "peter"                 parameter

        def model = this.controller.show()                ❷ Tests action's
                                                             model
        assertEquals "peter", model["viewUser"]?.userId
    }
}
```

The ControllerUnitTestCase class instantiates a test controller at the start of each test, so we can start using it straight away ❶. How does it know which controller class to instantiate? By convention. It looks at the name of the unit-test class and uses the string up to and including "Controller", so PostControllerUnitTests becomes Post-Controller. If this convention doesn't work for you, you can pass the controller class directly to the super constructor:

```
PostControllerUnitTests() {
    super(PostController)
}
```

Often your controller actions work with parameters, so you want to pass those in somehow. That's easy—add them to the params map on the controller ❶. This is one of several special properties that you have access to from your tests, all of which are listed in table 7.2.

We then invoke the action and assign the return value to a variable so that we can check the entries it contains ❷.

Table 7.2   Mock controller properties available in unit tests

Property name	Description
request	The mock request (GrailsMockHttpServletRequest)
response	The mock response (GrailsMockHttpServletResponse)
session	The mock HTTP session (Spring's MockHttpSession)
flash	A map representing flash scope
params	A map representing and containing the action parameters
redirectArgs	A map of the arguments passed to the redirect() method by the action under test
renderArgs	A map of the arguments passed to the render() method by the action under test
template	A map of template arguments if render() has been called for a template; contains the name of the template under the map key name and an entry with a map key of bean, collection, or model (depending on which named argument was passed to render())
modelAndView	A Spring ModelAndView instance that can be queried for both the name of the target view and the view's model

That's it—nice and painless. But controller code is rarely this simple, and actions that return a model are the easiest to test. What if the controller performs a redirect or uses the render() method?

How you handle these other cases depends on what mechanism the controller uses. Consider a redirect, for example:

```
redirect(controller: "post", action: "list")
```

To check whether the method is called correctly, look at the redirectArgs map on the controller:

```
assertEquals "post", this.controller.redirectArgs["controller"]
assertEquals "list", this.controller.redirectArgs["action"]
```

A similar approach can be used for the render() method, although you'll want to check the renderArgs property rather than redirectArgs. But not all forms of render() can be tested like this—some of them write to the response directly, including the following:

- render ... as XML/JSON
- render { ... }
- render "..."
- render text: "..."

Rather than check the renderArgs map, you can examine the content generated by these methods via the contentAsString property on the response object. Here we make sure that the start of the XML response begins with the post element:

```
assertTrue response.contentAsString.startsWith("<post>")
```

The main thing to be careful of when checking the response content directly is unexpected whitespace and ordering of text elements. For example, when you're rendering a Hubbub post as XML, how you do it affects what text is generated. Remember, most whitespace can be safely ignored by XML parsers, and the order of attributes isn't significant. So you may initially use an approach that generates nicely formatted and indented XML and later replace that implementation with one that uses no whitespace at all. Any pure string comparisons you make in your tests would then fail.

Under the hood

As you know, controllers have several dynamic methods and properties available to them at runtime, which makes them tricky to test. `ControllerUnitTestCase` makes life easier for you by using the `mockController()` method on `GrailsUnitTestCase` to add those methods and properties during test setup. These mock implementations are the ones that populate those `...Args` maps and render content to the mock response so that you can check it via the `contentAsString` property.

Controllers have quite a few unique features, and we could probably fill a whole chapter on the various techniques for testing them. Fortunately, you can read about the full gamut in the Grails user guide. Two items, though, deserve special mention: command objects and tag libraries.

COMMAND OBJECTS

Testing controllers that use the `params` object directly is easy enough, but using the same technique for actions that take command objects won't work. The problem is that the magic that binds parameters to the command objects at runtime isn't available to unit tests. But don't worry, the solution is surprisingly simple.

Say you have a `login` action that accepts a command object containing a username and password:

```
def login = { LoginCommand cmd ->
   ...
}
```

All you need to do in the test is create an instance of that command object and pass it to the action:

```
def testLogin() {
   def testCmd = new LoginCommand(username: "peter", password: "pass")
   this.controller.login(cmd)
   ...
}
```

It's that easy. The only fly in the ointment is with validation errors. Because you're creating the command object yourself, no validation is being performed on the data. That makes it difficult to test that your action is handling validation errors correctly.

Never fear—the Grails developers are one step ahead, and in this case you can call `validate()` directly on your command object:

```
def testLogin() {
   mockCommandObject(LoginCommand)

   def testCmd = new LoginCommand(username: "peter", password: "pass")
   testCmd.validate()
   this.controller.login(cmd)
   ...
}
```

If any of the fields in the command object contain invalid values, the `validate()` method will populate the associated `errors` property appropriately. The action under test won't be able to tell the difference: it will see a command object with validation errors.

TAG LIBRARIES

Testing with tag libraries is a bit less straightforward than with command objects. Unlike command objects, you can't pass tag libraries into a controller action, which means we need a different approach.

Let's take a look at some arbitrary controller code that uses the `link` tag:

```
def show = {
   ...
   render link(controller: "post", action: "list") { "Home" }
}
```

Notice how the tag invocation looks like a method call? That's our way in! We can mock the tag "method" using `mockFor()` on the controller, like so:

```
def mock = mockFor(MyController)
mock.demand.link(1..1) { Map args, Closure c ->
   ...
}
```

When the test runs, the controller will invoke this mock version rather than the tag. This approach will work regardless of whether the controller uses `link(...)` or `g.link(...)`. The notable missing feature is support for other tag namespaces, so if your controller calls tags that are in a custom namespace, you'll need to use integration tests.

It's all very well mocking tags when testing controllers, but it might be a good idea to test the tags themselves. They do contain code, after all.

7.2.5   *Testing tag libraries*

At first, the prospect of testing tag libraries might fill you with dread. You usually see them in Groovy Server Pages (GSP) files, so how do you test them from a simple class? Easy. A tag library is a class with some closures, and you can treat those closures like methods. In fact, tag libraries share a lot of aspects with controllers, from Dependency Injection to the dynamic properties that are available.

It won't come as a surprise to you that Grails provides a unit-test support class for tag libraries: `TagLibUnitTestCase`. This class behaves in almost exactly the same way as its controller counterpart, using convention to determine which tag library to instantiate. It also provides access to mock request, response, and session objects.

To demonstrate how to write a unit test for tag libraries, let's start with a simple tag that only writes its content out to the response if a user is logged into Hubbub:

```
class SecurityTagLib {
    def isLoggedIn = { attrs, body ->
        if (session.user) {
            out << body()
        }
    }
}
```

The tag would be used like this:

```
<g:isLoggedIn>You are logged in!</g:isLoggedIn>
```

It's simple, but it will help us demonstrate an important technique in testing tags.

Listing 7.4 contains the implementation of our unit test for this tag library. It tests both conditions: if a user is logged in and if no user is logged in.

Listing 7.4   A sample unit test for a tag library

```
package com.grailsinaction

class SecurityTagLibUnitTests extends grails.test.TagLibUnitTestCase {
    void testIsLoggedIn() {
        String testContent = "You are logged in!"
        mockSession["user"] = "me"
        tagLib.isLoggedIn([:]) {-> testContent }          ❶ Calls tag as a
                                                             method
        assertEquals testContent, tagLib.out.toString()   ❷ Checks tag
    }                                                        output
    void testIsLoggedInNoUser() {
        String testContent = "You are not logged in!"
        tagLib.isLoggedIn([:]) {-> testContent }

        assertEquals "", tagLib.out.toString()
    }
}
```

There isn't anything too earth-shattering here. In one case, we add a `user` entry to the mock session, which the tag library can access via the dynamic `session` property. The more interesting aspects concern how we invoke the tag and then check the output it generates.

First of all, the unit-test support class automatically instantiates the tag library and assigns it to the `tagLib` property ❷. We then call the tag as if it were a method. One oddity is the empty map (`[:]`) as an argument, which is required because the tag expects an attribute map as the first argument. If we were passing in at least one attribute value, we could use the implicit syntax instead:

```
tagLib.isLoggedIn(attr1: "value") { ... }
```

Much nicer, but not an option if you have no attributes.

The real key to this unit test is the next bit on line ❶, where we pass a simple, zero-argument closure to the tag. As you saw in the previous chapter, the content inside a GSP tag is passed to the implementation as a closure, so here we provide a mock one that returns a simple string. If the tag writes out its content, which in this case happens if the session contains a `user` object, that string is streamed to the magic `out` property.

In order to check whether the appropriate text has been generated by the tag, we then perform a `toString()` on the `out` property and compare it to the expected value ❷. That's all there is to it, although it might be worth noting that the `out` property is an instance of `StringWriter`.

Not all tags are as simple as `isLoggedIn`, but all the features we've used so far in this chapter also apply to testing tag libraries. You can use `mockFor()` to mock dependencies and calls to other tags, and you can use `mockLogging()` if your tag uses the `log` property.

That pretty much covers everything you need to know about unit testing. It was a lot to digest in one go, so well done for making it this far! As you have seen, there aren't many things that you can't unit test with the classes provided by Grails. Sometimes, though, you can find yourself writing terribly complex mocks to test a simple method. This may be a sign that the method itself needs refactoring, but in many cases it's the nature of the beast. At that point, it's worth contemplating an alternative approach.

7.3   *Integration testing*

Where unit tests are about testing individual, atomic *units* of functionality (like classes and their methods), integration tests are designed to test larger parts of an application, such as a controller *and* its dependencies together. The main focus is on ensuring that the units work together correctly—that they *integrate* properly.

In Grails, integration tests appear on the surface to be unit tests. In fact, if you create a new integration test with this command,

```
grails create-integration-test Book
```

the only apparent difference is that the test is created in the test/integration directory rather than in test/unit. But as we all know, appearances can be deceptive.

The fundamental difference is that integration tests run inside a full Grails environment, with a running database and all those dynamic methods and properties that you're used to. You don't have to mock any of them. For all intents and purposes, the tests run against a real instance of your application. The main thing missing is the servlet container, the lack of which has certain repercussions.

Here is a summary of what works and what doesn't:

- All plugins that don't exclude the test environment are loaded.
- `BootStrap` is executed. Spring application context is fully populated.
- Domain classes work against a live database (an in-memory HSQLDB, by default).

- All dynamic methods and properties are available.
- Mock versions of the servlet request, response, and session are used.
- No Grails or servlet filters are executed.
- URL mappings have no effect.
- Views can't be tested.

Some of these may not mean much to you at this point, but we suggest you refer back to this list as you become more familiar with the trappings of Grails, such as the services and the Spring application context. You'll also get a better feel for integration tests as we work through some examples.

> **Under the hood**
> Each integration test is run inside a transaction that's rolled back at the end of the test. This means that no changes are committed to the database. Also, the default Grails environment for tests is "test".

You're probably now wondering when you should use integration tests and how to write them. It would be great if we could draw on some solid best practices from the Grails community, but few guidelines have emerged so far. Nonetheless, we'll endeavor to provide you with a useful starting point.

There are three main situations in which you'll need to write integration tests:

- When you can't test something with unit tests.
- When you want to test the interactions between objects.
- When it's easier to test with real data than to mock everything.

We'll look at some of the situations in which unit tests won't work in section 7.3.2, but first we'll look at the second and third points.

7.3.1 Filling the gaps

You have probably seen the "mind the gap" sign many a time, a helpful hint that you risk tripping or falling headfirst into a hole. It may surprise you, but that warning has a special resonance when it comes to testing applications. Unit tests are tremendously useful and help ensure that classes and methods are doing what they should *in isolation,* but there are plenty of things that can go wrong when they start interacting with each other. Those interactions constitute the "gaps" in the unit testing coverage that you need to be mindful of.

Let's look at a concrete example. Say you have a simple controller that uses a service to get a list of items associated with a user. It then extracts the names of the items into a new list and passes them to the associated view. The code would look something like this:

```
class MyController {
    def myService
```

```
def show = {
   def items = myService.fetchItemsFor(params.userId)
   [ itemNames: items.collect { it.name } ]
}
}
```

Let's also assume that the unit tests for the controller and service are both passing, so there's nothing obviously wrong with the controller code. Does that mean the code is fine?

Whether there's a problem or not depends on the behavior of the service method: if it returns an empty list when there are no items, everything works fine. But what if the service method returns `null` instead? There's no reason it can't do so, but now you can see that the controller will throw a `NullPointerException` because of the code `items.collect {...}`. This bug has materialized because of a faulty assumption on the part of the controller: that the service method will return an empty list rather than `null` (which is why methods should return empty collections rather than `null`).

TIP   Bugs often manifest themselves in the boundary conditions of applications, when collections are empty, values are missing, or numbers are zero or negative. That's why it's crucial to test as many of these conditions as possible, particularly because they tend to be ignored during manual testing.

This example demonstrates the kind of issues that can crop up when classes that pass their unit tests start working together. When you add in dynamic methods and properties, you'll find that there are plenty of things that can go wrong. A simple integration test would have picked the problem up quickly, and you can see an example test in listing 7.5. This test not only covers the case where there are no items, but also the one where there are a few.

> **Listing 7.5 Your first integration test—including domain objects and a service**

```
import grails.test.GroovyPagesTestCase

class MyControllerTests extends GroovyTestCase {
   def myService                                    ◁──┐ ❶ Injects MyService
                                                         instance
   void testShowNoItems() {
      def myController = new MyController()          ❷ Creates object
      myController.myService = myService                to test

      myController.params.userId = "glen"            ◁──┐ Sets action
      def model = myController.show()                ❸ parameters

      assertEquals 0, model["itemNames"].size()
   }

   void testShow() {
      new Item(userId: "glen", name: "chair").save()    ❹ Initializes data
      new Item(userId: "peter", name: "desk").save()
      new Item(userId: "glen", name: "table").save(
            flush: true)
```

```
    def myController = ...
    ...

    def names = model["itemNames"]
    assertEquals 2, names.size()
    assertNotNull names.find { it == "chair" }
    assertNotNull names.find { it == "table" }
  }
}
```

⑤ Checks results

On the surface, the test looks like the unit tests we looked at earlier. The differences are profound, though, so let's take a closer look. The first "oddity" you'll see is the myService property ❶, like the one in MyController. When you run the test, Grails will set this property to a fully configured instance of MyService. It might seem strange to inject dependencies into a test like this, but the reason will be made clear as we look at the test method itself.

As with unit tests, if you want to test a particular class, be it a controller, a service, or whatever, you instantiate it with new ❷. The problem with this approach is that any dependencies that would normally be injected at runtime (myService, in this case) are left empty. As you'll see in chapter 14, the dependencies are only populated if the object is managed by Spring. (Integration tests and BootStrap are exceptions to this rule, but they're instantiated by Grails.) To work around this problem, we manually set the myService property on the controller to the value of the test's myService field. This may look like a hack, but it's the 100 percent certified way to handle such dependencies in integration tests.

Fed up with mocking?

Sometimes it can be tiresome to mock class after class in your unit tests, at which point integration tests become appealing. Beware, though: the effort required to set up the data in such a way as to test all boundary conditions in integration testing can be more than that required to mock collaborators. On the other hand, sometimes it can be far easier.

Unfortunately, there are no hard and fast rules, so it's worth experimenting. If an integration test proves easier to write, then go for it! The harder the tests are to write, the less likely they are to be written.

Once the test controller is created and initialized, it's time to provide some test parameters ❸. Note that we used exactly the same syntax in our unit tests, so you shouldn't get too confused when switching between unit and integration tests. One notable difference is with command objects: in integration tests you populate the params object as we have done in this example. Grails automatically instantiates any command objects declared by the controller action and binds the parameters to them. This means you can add a command object to an action without impacting its test.

Finally, we come to the issue of test data. With unit tests, the data is either passed into the object or method under test, or it's provided by mock collaborators. The approach for integration tests is different: the tests are run against a live database, so you create data via the domain classes ❹ as you do in the live application. But because you are working against a database, there are no guarantees that data will be returned in the order you expect, unless it's explicitly sorted. Bear that in mind when you assert results, and try to come up with order-independent ways of testing the data ❺.

Hopefully you now have a reasonable idea of what an integration test is and why they come in handy. You now know enough to write integration tests for any controller or service. For further information, check out the Grails user guide, which has more specific information on testing controllers, tag libraries, and other types of Grails artifacts.

For services and controllers, you have a choice of which road to go down, but there are some situations in which unit tests don't cut it.

7.3.2 *When only an integration test will do*

Grails' unit test support will get you a long way in your testing endeavors, but there *are* gaps in its coverage you need to be aware of. In particular, it doesn't give you any help with either criteria or Hibernate Query Language (HQL) queries, nor does it have any support for testing URL mappings. You'll also see in chapter 9 that web flows require integration tests.

When it comes to criteria and HQL queries, you can use the integration-testing approach you saw in listing 7.5. Grails will take care of everything for you. You could even switch between dynamic finders, criteria, and HQL queries without needing to touch a line of the test case.

Testing URL mappings is a simple matter of leveraging the GrailsUrlMappings-TestCase support class. Let's say, for the sake of argument, that we have these mappings:

```
class UrlMappings {
    static mappings = {
        "/basket/$username"(controller: "basket", action: "show")
        "/$controller/$action?/$id?"()
        "500"(view: "error")
    }
}
```

Our test case would look something like the code in listing 7.6, which makes sure that the correct mapping is used for particular URLs. It will also test the reverse mapping—from controller and action to URL.

Listing 7.6 Testing URL mappings

```
class UrlMappingsTestCase extends grails.test.GrailsUrlMappingsTestCase {
    void testMappings() {
        assertUrlMapping("/item/edit/123",        ❶ Tests URL
                controller: "item",                   mapping
                action: "edit") {
            id = 123
        }
```

```
assertUrlMapping("/basket/fred",
            controller: "basket",
            action: "show") {
    username = "fred"          ◁── Checks that parameter
}                                   is mapped
assertForwardUrlMapping(500, view: "error")   ◁── ❷ Tests status code
    }                                              mapping
}
```

As you can see, setting up the test is quite straightforward. The superclass automatically loads all the application's URL mappings and does all the necessary preparation in setUp(), so we can go straight into the tests themselves. The foot soldier of URL mapping tests is the assertUrlMapping() method ❶, which accepts a URL as the first argument, and a controller and action as named ones. In the first test, we make sure that the URL "/item/edit/123" maps to the item controller and edit action, with the value 123 mapped to the id parameter. This method also checks that the reverse mapping works.

The second test is similar to the first, but we're making sure that the more specific URL mapping ("/basket/$username") overrides the more general one.

Finally, we test that the 500 status code mapping works ❷. We use the assert-ForwardUrlMapping() method here because the support class doesn't support reverse mappings for status codes.

There is also a corresponding assertReverseUrlMapping() method that accepts the same arguments as the other assertion methods.

There isn't any more to integration tests than that. Writing them is surprisingly simple. The trick is determining when to use them. Hopefully we've given you enough information that you can make an informed decision.

The next stage of testing involves making sure that the application works as a whole, particularly the user interface. To do that, we need to use a system of testing that runs the application in a servlet container and interacts with it. We need functional tests.

7.4   *Functional testing*

A combination of unit and integration tests can give you a great deal of confidence that your application is working, and they're fairly easy to develop and run. Yet there are gaping holes in their coverage: views, filters, and controller interceptors. How do we go about plugging those gaps?

The answer is to test the whole application, including the user interface. That's what end users see and interact with, so it's important to make sure it's working as expected. We call this "functional testing," and there are several different ways to do it. You could, for example, sit a person in front of a computer screen and get him to exercise the application by following some written instructions: click on this link, enter this data, click on that button, and so on. This is a perfectly valid approach and one that's probably still widely used.

The reason companies often do manual testing is because functional tests can be difficult to write, and user interfaces are particularly troublesome. But with manual testing you lose the benefits of automation: regular feedback, reproducibility, and so on. We don't want that, so it's good to know that there are several Grails plugins that can help us out. We'll start by looking at a way to exercise our UI without a browser.

7.4.1 Introducing the Functional Test plugin

The natural environment for a Grails application is a servlet container. The only way to test the application in that environment is by communicating with the server via HTTP. Several Grails plugins allow you to do this, and the most mature one is the WebTest plugin from Canoo. But we're going to give a relatively new kid a chance to strut its stuff: the Functional Test plugin.

We begin by installing the plugin:

```
grails install-plugin functional-test
```

Although it doesn't have a particularly catchy name, the Functional Test plugin more than makes up for it in use.

Before we can write a test using our freshly installed plugin, we first need something to test. For this example, we're going to look at the Hubbub page containing the user's timeline, because it has plenty of content we can test, and it also includes a form. Creating a skeleton test for this page is as simple as this:

```
grails create-functional-test PostList
```

This command creates the test/functional/PostListTests.groovy file, which you'll find is pretty spartan.

Our next step is to flesh it out with some test code. Listing 7.7 contains two tests: the first checks that the application generates a server error if the client attempts to access the timeline page without first logging in; the second tests that the page is displayed correctly when a user *is* logged in.

Listing 7.7 Functional test for Hubbub's timeline page

```
package com.grailsinaction

class PostListTests extends functionaltestplugin.FunctionalTestCase {
    void testTimelineNotLoggedIn() {
        get("/post/timeline")              ◁── ❶ Sends GET
                                                  request to URL
        assertStatus 500   ◁── Checks HTTP
    }                          status
    void testTimeline() {
        post("/login/index") {    ❷ Sends POST with data
            userId = "peter"
            password = "password"
        }

        assertTitle "Hubbub » New Post"       ❸ Checks page content
        assertContentContains(
            "What are you hacking on right now?")
```

```
    }
}
```

The test may not look like much, but it does a surprising amount. We start off by sending a GET request to the timeline page's URL ❶. In this case, the URL is relative to the servlet context because it starts with a slash (/) but you can also specify either of the following:

- absolute URLs (of the form "http://...")
- relative URLs (such as "post/timeline")

URLs of the second form are interpreted as relative to the *last URL loaded* or, if this is the first request, a default value (specified by the config option `grails.functional.test.baseURL`).

> **Under the hood**
> The Functional Test plugin uses the HtmlUnit library under the covers, so if you're familiar with it, you can access the HtmlUnit `Page` object via the `page` property:
>
> ```
> assertTrue page.forms["userDetails"]
> ```
>
> You might also notice that `get()`, `post()`, `put()`, and so on, don't return anything. That's because the plugin (or more specifically, HtmlUnit) saves the response in memory—all subsequent actions and assertions apply to that response until the next request is sent.

We know that a user can't access this page directly without logging in, so we expect that the response will have a status of 500, which we check. And that's it for the first test.

The second one starts by logging a user into the application with a POST to the login controller ❷. This is similar to our earlier GET, but we can populate the POST data by passing a closure to the `post()` method. Each property assignment with that closure corresponds to a parameter value in the POST data. It's simple and easy to read—just how we like it. And you aren't limited to GET and POST—the plugin supports `put()` and `delete()` methods too.

Getting back to the test, the login action redirects to the timeline page for the user, so we check that the page title and contents ❸ match that page. You can also check that the page is a result of a redirect by using this approach:

```
redirectEnabled = false
post("/login/index") { ... }

assertRedirectUrl("/post/timeline")
followRedirect()
redirectEnabled = true
```

The `redirectEnabled` property allows you to control whether the plugin "follows" redirects. By setting it to `false`, you can assert the URL of the redirect and get the plugin to load the target URL via the `followRedirect()` method. In our case, though, we're only interested in whether the timeline page is displayed, not whether it happened via a redirect.

Now that the test has been written, we can run it:

```
grails functional-tests
```

The tests take a while to run because the command first has to start your application in a servlet container. Once it has finished, you'll find that it generates the same types of reports in exactly the same place (test/reports) as the `test-app` command.

In this brief example, we've demonstrated only a few of the assertions you can use, but the plugin supports quite a collection, and we've listed many of them in table 7.3. You can find the full selection documented at http://www.grails.org/Grails+Functional+Testing.

Many of the assertions have variations with "Contains" and "Strict" in the name, so there is some flexibility there.

Table 7.3 Common assertions in the Functional Test plugin

Assertion	Description
`assertStatus(int)`	Checks the status code of the HTTP response
`assertContent(String)`	Checks the content of the page (case-insensitive comparison and whitespace is ignored)
`assertTitle(String)`	Checks the page title
`assertHeader(String, String)`	Checks the value of the named HTTP header
`assertContentType(String)`	Checks the content type of the response

By this point, you may be thinking that it all looks like too much hard work and that the test code is too low-level. True, the feature set may be small, but it gives you a great deal of power and flexibility. You can easily group fragments of tests into your own methods and reuse them. For example, say we need to check the timeline page in several tests. We don't want to repeat the code over and over again, so instead we can factor out the assertions into a method, like so:

```
def checkTimelinePage() {
    assertTitle "Hubbub » New Post"
    assertContentContains "What are you hacking on right now?"
    ...
}
```

We can call this method from anywhere in our tests to perform a complete check on the page. By building intermediate blocks of code like this, we begin to create a suite of robust and thorough tests.

This is all good stuff, but a word of warning: UI tests are inherently fragile because the user interface tends to change frequently, if only in small ways. The key to overcoming this fragility is to strike a balance between checking enough aspects of the UI to ensure it's working correctly and not being so specific that the tests regularly break. Experience counts for a lot here, but we suggest you err on the side of being too strict with the tests, because you can easily loosen them if they break too often. Erring the other way means that bugs get through.

And that (almost) completes our stack of tests covering (almost) every aspect of the application. Functional tests provide that last element of confidence that things are working. You can use them for system integration testing too, so if and when you deploy the application to staging or production, you can run the functional test suite to check that all is well.

We've "almost" completed our testing coverage, so what's left? That would be JavaScript and other client-side technologies.

7.4.2 *Other testing tools*

Both the WebTest and Functional Test plugins use the Rhino JavaScript engine, and although it's improving, the engine still struggles with some JavaScript libraries. That leaves a gap for some other tools.

SELENIUM

Where the Functional Test plugin uses a Java library to send HTTP requests and handle the responses, Selenium piggybacks on the browser. This has two distinct advantages over the other approach:

- You can check that your application works with the browsers your users prefer.
- You can get the browser's JavaScript handling for free!

Differences between browsers are the bane of a web developer's life, so the ability to run a full suite of automated tests on multiple browsers isn't to be sniffed at. And if the other functional testing plugins choke on your beautiful, dynamic user interface because they can't handle the JavaScript, using the browser to do the tests becomes a no-brainer.

A nice feature of this tool is the Selenium IDE—a plugin for the Firefox browser. This gives you a point-and-click interface for writing your tests. You'll almost certainly want to customize the generated tests, but it makes getting started that much easier. You can find out more on the plugin's web page: http://www.grails.org/Selenium+plugin.

This raises an interesting question: should you use Functional Test (or WebTest) or Selenium? Maybe even both? This is a difficult question, and it pretty much comes down to personal preference. You may be more comfortable with the user interface presented by Selenium IDE, but the Functional Test and WebTest plugins generally run quite a bit faster.

Being code junkies, we like the expressiveness of the Functional Test plugin and the control it gives us in writing the tests. We prefer to start with that and only consider Selenium if we need cross-browser testing or if the JavaScript is causing problems.

JSUNIT

Speaking of JavaScript, isn't that code? Shouldn't we be testing it too? Yes, and maybe. Although it's code, you can effectively test it via Selenium if you want. But then you're talking about functional tests for your JavaScript rather than unit tests.

If you have non-trivial JavaScript in your application, it makes sense to unit test it. That's where JsUnit comes in and, as you can probably guess, it's a member of the xUnit family of testing frameworks. Install the jsunit plugin for Grails and away you go!

You can check out the plugin documentation on the Grails website and the JsUnit documentation at http://jsunit.berlios.de/.

FIXTURES

As you know, Grails already has a mechanism for setting up data on startup: the Boot-Strap class. You may think this is more than enough for your needs, but if that's the case, we'd like you to reconsider.

The main problem relates to functional tests: although your BootStrap class is called when the server starts up, there's no way to reset the data in the middle of the tests. That means your database starts filling up with records, and your later tests have to account for all the extra data added by earlier ones. Nightmare!

As an example, imagine we have a test that expects the timeline page to display five posts. Then another developer comes along and creates a test that adds a post to that timeline. Suddenly our test breaks because the timeline page is now displaying *six* posts.

The solution to this problem lies in another of Grails' wonderful plugins: fixtures. It allows you to configure a set of data (using domain classes rather than SQL) that you can load at any time. You can see an example of its use in integration tests on its web page: http://www.grails.org/Fixtures+Plugin.

Using fixtures in functional tests is trickier, because your tests are running outside of the server. One option is to set up a dedicated controller that drops the existing data from the database and then loads the fixture data. Just be careful that you don't make the controller available in the production system.

That concludes our quick look at alternative testing tools and also our coverage of testing in Grails. You should now have a solid foundation in unit and functional testing and the knowledge to build on that foundation. You'll find that there are many options to make testing easier and more fun, including tools like easyb for behavior-driven development (http://www.easyb.org/) and the Code Coverage plugin for seeing how much of your code is exercised by tests (http://www.piragua.com/ or http://www.grails.org/Test+Code+Coverage+Plugin). So, keep on testing!

7.5   *Summary and best practices*

Testing is an essential part of ensuring product quality. Without it, how can you be confident that your application works? It also has a massive impact on the process of refactoring, because without testing you have no idea whether you have broken something.

The first aim of this chapter was to instill a testing habit. Once testing becomes a habit, you'll find it much easier to keep it going. The second was to show you how to write tests at all levels: unit, integration, and functional. You need to utilize testing at all these levels to ensure maximum reliability. The tools are there, and they will only get better, so why not make use of them?

The following guidelines will help you get the most out of your testing:

- *Test first, test often* By writing your tests first, you not only ensure that your code is covered, but you also have to think clearly about what you want the code to do. If you run the tests often, you get quicker feedback when something breaks, which makes it easier to fix. This helps speed up the development cycle.

- *Make testing easy* You might think making testing easy is the responsibility of the testing framework, and you would be partly right. But making your code easy to test can go a long way to ensuring that it does have tests. Such things as allowing test cases to inject collaborators, using interfaces, and avoiding static variables and methods can be a great help.

  In addition, if you do find something difficult to test, look for a solution that can be reused for similar code. Otherwise, none of it will have associated tests.

- *Maintain test coverage* It can be easy to skip tests or postpone writing them, but that's the start of a slippery slope. There is a theory that neighborhoods with visible broken windows are more susceptible to crime, because people think that no one cares so they don't either. Something similar happens with tests: if there are gaps in the testing coverage, developers form the impression that tests don't matter much. Try to avoid gaps in test coverage as much as possible.

- *Use continuous integration* When you're working with a team, you'll quickly find that code committed by one person breaks when it's combined with changes from someone else. Use a continuous integration (CI) system to ensure that these breakages are picked up early and often. In fact, CI can even be useful for a one-person team, by detecting files that haven't been committed, for example.

- *Test at all levels* We can't stress this enough: make sure that you're testing at both the unit and functional levels. Even if there is some overlap and redundancy, that's better than having gaps in your test coverage.

And so the lecture finishes. As a reward for persevering, you now get the opportunity to have some fun with cool plugins.

Everyday Grails

In part 2 of this book, you learned about the basic building blocks of Grails applications. In part 3, you'll apply that knowledge to building all the necessary pieces of a real-world application.

Chapter 8 introduces Grails plugins—ways of extending your applications using third-party code modules. We'll use plugins to give Hubbub an extreme UI makeover introducing you to charting, graphics, tooltips, rich text editors, and a wealth of other UI enhancements along the way. We'll also add some important functional enhancements, like email integration and full text search.

In chapter 9, we'll take a tour of Grails Webflow—a lightweight state engine that lets you easily add wizard-like flows to your applications. By building a basic shopping-cart feature for Hubbub's online store, you'll learn how Grails makes it easy to walk your user through a series of steps, branching to special subflows as required. You'll also learn how to thoroughly test it all.

Security is a vital topic in deploying any kind of application on the internet, so chapter 10 will give you a thorough grounding in web security issues. After learning about the common vulnerabilities in web applications, you'll learn how to mitigate them and keep everything secure. We'll also take you on a tour of a popular Grails security plugin that allows you to add all sorts of access-control features to Hubbub.

Exposing your application to the world via a RESTful API has become standard practice for most successful Web 2.0 applications. In chapter 11, we'll talk about the ideas behind RESTful APIs and give you all the tools to quickly build REST-style features into your application. But REST isn't the only game in town for remoting, so we'll also survey many other popular remoting technologies, including SOAP and RMI.

Message-oriented architectures have become extremely popular for developing highly scalable applications. In chapter 12, we'll introduce you to messaging by adding an instant-messaging gateway to Hubbub. You'll learn about messaging queues and topics, and find out how the JMS plugin makes interacting with messaging systems very productive. For those after a lighter-weight asynchronous option, we'll also look at scheduling using the Quartz plugin.

Upon completing part 3, you'll have all the knowledge required to deliver robust, full-featured Grails web applications.

Using plugins: adding Web 2.0 in 60 minutes

8

Few things in life do exactly what you want, and unsurprisingly Grails is no different. Fortunately, there's a wealth of Java tools and libraries out there that will help you implement almost any feature you could want. Because Grails is inherently a Java-based framework, you can use pretty much any Java library out there. Many of them are robust and mature, so why reinvent the wheel?

You can use Java libraries as is, but there can be big benefits to having an adapter between Grails and the library that makes it easier to use and quicker to set up. This is the purpose of the Grails plugin system. The idea is that *functionality* is bundled into modules that can be loaded by the framework and integrated into the system. That functionality may be full-text search, tag clouds, or a fancy new UI technology. In fact, many of the features of Grails are implemented as plugins themselves, including GORM.

You can see how the plugins relate to Grails and each other in figure 8.1. If you're familiar with Eclipse or any of the other Java-centric IDEs, their plugin systems are analogous to Grails' own.

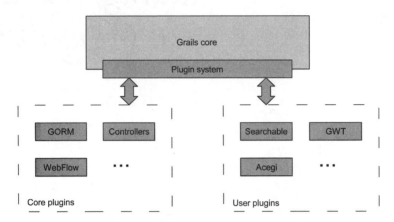

Figure 8.1   The plugin architecture

The upshot of all this is that anyone can provide extra functionality by writing a plugin, and that's what many people have done. You'll see how easy it is to install these plugins into your applications, effectively giving them a shot of steroids. From section 8.2 onwards, we'll explore some of the popular and cool plugins that are available.

8.1   *Taking advantage of others' hard work*

When might you want to install a plugin? If you find yourself with a feature requirement that doesn't sound specific to your application—one that's not directly related to your business logic—look out for existing plugins that promise to do the job for you. If you would use a separate library or tool to do the job in a plain Java project, then a plugin is probably the best solution in Grails. Remember, it's rarely a good idea to reinvent the wheel.

Take Hubbub, for example. We'll want to send emails from various parts of the application, such as a user registration module or a daily email digest module, but emailing isn't what Hubbub is about. The feature is outside the core of Hubbub and is common to lots of different types of applications. That makes it an ideal plugin candidate, and you won't be surprised to learn that an email plugin already exists.

Once you've decided that there might be a plugin that does what you need, it's time to find the appropriate one.

8.1.1 Finding plugins

There are two main sources of information about plugins: the Grails Plugin repository and the Grails website.

THE GRAILS PLUGIN REPOSITORY

Grails has a couple of commands that can be used to query for plugin information, both of which work against what is known as the *Grails Plugin repository*. This is a centralized online storage area that hosts many of the available Grails plugins, making it easy for Grails to query for, install, and upload them. As you will see a bit later, you can even set up your own local repository.

For now, we're interested in the querying capabilities:

```
grails list-plugins
```

This command will produce output similar to this:

```
Plug-ins available in the Grails repository are listed below:
-----------------------------------------------------------

acegi            <0.5.1>          --  Grails Spring Security 2.0 Plugin
aop              <no releases>    --  No description available
audit-logging    <0.4>            --  adds hibernate audit logging
...
```

As the `list-plugins` name suggests, this command will list all the plugins currently available in the repository. For each one, it will display the name, latest version, and a short description. You may notice that some plugins show both "<no releases>" and "No description available." In many cases, this is a sign that the plugin was added to the repository before Grails 1.0, and it hasn't been updated. Proceed with caution.

> **Under the hood**
>
> The Grails Plugin repository is implemented as a Subversion repository accessible via HTTP, so you'll need to be able to access the internet from your computer. The structure of the directories and files in the repository follows conventions that allow Grails to download specific versions of a plugin.
>
> If you need to configure an HTTP proxy, run this command:
>
> ```
> grails set-proxy
> ```
>
> Enter the details as requested. The list of plugins will be cached locally in a file called plugins-list.xml, which is typically located in `$HOME/.grails/1.1/plugins`.

The list of plugins is quite long. If you're running on a Unix-like system, such as Mac OS X or Linux, we suggest that you pipe the output through grep, like so:

```
grails list-plugins | grep "mail"
```

This isn't possible on Windows (unless you use Cygwin), but the plugins are listed alphabetically, so you shouldn't have much trouble browsing through the list.

Now that we have the list, what's next? We want to find out whether there's a plugin that will make sending emails from Hubbub easy, so we look for anything to do with "mail." It shouldn't take you long to find an entry in the list for the "mail" plugin, which according to its description "provides mail support to a running Grails application." That looks like the ticket.

Once you have the name of a plugin, you can find out more about it with this command:

```
grails plugin-info mail
```

You'll receive results something like this:

```
-------------------------------------------------------------------------
Information about Grails plugin
-------------------------------------------------------------------------
Name: mail    | Latest release: 0.5
-------------------------------------------------------------------------
Provides Mail support to a running Grails application
-------------------------------------------------------------------------
Author: Graeme Rocher
-------------------------------------------------------------------------
Author's e-mail: graeme@g2one.com
-------------------------------------------------------------------------
Find more info here: http://grails.org/Mail+Plugin
-------------------------------------------------------------------------
This plug-in provides a MailService class as well as configuring the necessary
beans within the Spring ApplicationContext.
...

-------------------------------------------------------------------------
Available full releases:  0.1 0.1-ALPHA 0.3 0.4 0.5 0.6-SNAPSHOT
...
```

The important information here is the location of online documentation (http://grails.org/Mail+Plugin, in this example) and the long description, which should provide you with enough information to decide whether the plugin is suitable or not.

Although the Grails Plugin repository makes life easy for the user, not all plugins are available through it. Those that aren't can often be found via the Grails website.

THE GRAILS WEBSITE

Along with plenty of other useful information for the discerning Grails developer, the main Grails website has a page that lists plugins by category. It also has documentation for many of them, which means that searching for plugins on the website can be fruitful. The downside to the website is that it relies on users and plugin authors to keep it up to date, so its information may be out of date, incorrect, or nonexistent for some plugins.

You can find the categorized list at http://grails.org/plugin/home. This section of the site is known as the Plugin Portal, where you can browse and search for plugins and their reference information. The site also supports RSS feeds for staying up to date with new and changed plugins. You can even vote for the plugins you think are the best.

What should you do if you can't find what you're looking for either via the Grails commands or the website? As a last resort, you can always ask on the Grails user mailing list (http://grails.org/Mailing+lists)—the community is friendly and responsive.

Once you've found a plugin you want to use, you can install it into your application.

8.1.2 Installing plugins

As with almost any piece of software, you have to install a plugin before you can use it. Fortunately, Grails has a simple command that will do this for you:

```
grails install-plugin <plugin name>
```

Provide the name of the plugin you want, and Grails will fetch the latest version from the Grails Plugin repository and install it locally. Use the name displayed by the `list-plugins` command—in our previous example, the name is "mail".

When you install a plugin, Grails stores a local copy of the plugin's zip archive. This means that when you install the plugin in another project, Grails can reuse this cached version rather than downloading the plugin from the repository again. When a new version of the plugin is released, the `install-plugin` command has to retrieve it from the repository. You can see an overview of the logic that Grails uses in figure 8.2.

What if you want to use the same plugin version for all your projects? It can be time-consuming to keep upgrading your projects if you have more than a few, particularly if the new plugin version requires changes to your code. Or perhaps you have tested a particular version thoroughly, and upgrading represents an unnecessary risk. Whatever the reason, specifying an explicit version often makes sense. You can achieve this in a variety of ways, but the simplest is to pass the version to the `install-plugin` command, like this:

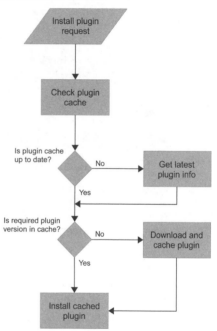

Figure 8.2 Grails plugin installation logic

```
grails install-plugin mail 0.1
```

An alternative approach is to specify the location of the plugin package file, which conventionally has the name grails-<name>-<version>.zip, such as grails-mail-0.1.zip. The location could be a URL, like this:

```
grails install-plugin http://somewhere.org/plugins/grails-mail-0.1.zip
```

Or it could be a local file path if you've downloaded the package manually or someone has sent it to you:

```
grails install-plugin /home/ben/plugins/grails-mail-0.1.zip
```

The file path can either be absolute, as in the preceding example, or relative. Some plugins are exclusively distributed this way, in which case they won't appear in the output of the list-plugins command.

In chapter 16, we'll cover another approach that involves setting up your own plugin repository, but first we need to cover a few more details of plugin installation.

Where are my plugins?

You've installed a plugin or two, but where has Grails put them? Although you don't need to know where they are, they can be a great source of instruction and inspiration when you decide to write your own plugins.

By default, Grails stores plugins in,

```
$HOME/.grails/<grailsVersion>/projects/<project>/plugins
```

where $HOME represents the current user's home directory, <grailsVersion> is the version of Grails used to install the plugin, and <project> is the name of the project you installed it into.

Global plugins go into a slightly different place because they aren't associated with a particular project:

```
$HOME/.grails/<grailsVersion>/global-plugins
```

In chapter 16 we show you how to control where Grails stores project plugins.

PROJECTS REMEMBER THEIR PLUGINS

Once a plugin has been installed into a project, that project remembers the fact. If you're the sole developer of the application, this doesn't really matter, but imagine you're in a team and someone else has added a plugin to the project and committed the changes to your version control system (VCS). Because the project remembers which plugins have been installed, Grails will automatically fetch and install any that are missing from your local copy. You don't have to do anything. When you run the application, it will work, at least as far as the plugins are concerned.

GLOBAL PLUGINS

Some plugins are universally useful, and you'll want to install them in all your projects. Consider the debug plugin, which enables you to track the information that flows through a Grails application. Rather than adding a feature required by an application, it aims to support your development process. That makes it an ideal candidate for *all* projects.

Because installing the same plugin into every project is pretty tedious, Grails allows you to install it globally by supplying the -global option to the install-plugin command:

```
grails install-plugin -global debug
```

As we explained, a project normally remembers what plugins have been installed. In the case of global plugins, though, no such link is maintained, so if you install a plugin globally and commit the project changes to your VCS, Grails won't automatically download and install that plugin for your teammates.

TIP When deciding whether to install a plugin globally, ask yourself this: do the projects *require* the plugin? If the answer is yes, you should *not* install it globally.

PLUGIN DEPENDENCIES

Many plugins are self-contained. This means that everything they require is either available through Grails or packaged in the plugin. Some are more complex and require features provided by other plugins—they *depend* on those other plugins, which might in turn depend on other plugins.

Figure 8.3 shows a (rather contrived) example of plugin dependencies for a Grails application. As you can see, managing the plugins and their dependencies yourself would be a lot of work. That's why Grails manages them for you. When you install a plugin, it automatically checks what plugins it depends on and installs those that haven't been installed already.

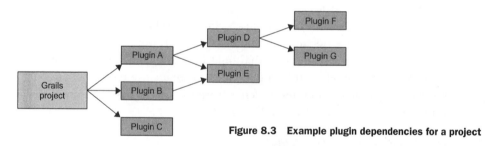

Figure 8.3 Example plugin dependencies for a project

Consider figure 8.3 and imagine you want to install plugin A into your project. When you run the `install-plugin` command, Grails will automatically fetch and install plugins D, E, F, and G because plugin A either directly or indirectly depends on them. Alternatively, if you already have plugin B installed, then Grails will only install plugins D, F, and G—plugin E is already installed because of B.

As a user of plugins, all of this is transparent to you. Even if you don't quite understand what is going on at this stage, that's OK. One thing to be aware of is that if you install a plugin from a zip archive rather than a plugin repository, Grails will still attempt to install its dependencies from the repository. This may not be a problem for you, but it's useful to know, just in case.

UNINSTALLING PLUGINS

Once something is installed, it can be irritating if there isn't an easy way to remove it. Grails provides the imaginatively named `uninstall-plugin` command to remove an existing plugin from your system. Pass it the name of the plugin, and it will do the rest:

```
grails uninstall-plugin mail
```

In addition, recall that projects remember what plugins are installed. This means that Grails will automatically remove a plugin if it's installed for a project that doesn't use it. Again, this makes life easier in team environments.

APPLYING OUR KNOWLEDGE: THE HUBBUB EXTREME MAKEOVER BEGINS

Now that you have a feel for how plugins are installed, uninstalled, and otherwise managed, it's time to apply all of that theory to a real project. We're going to spend the rest of this chapter introducing you to several popular Grails plugins and giving Hubbub an extreme makeover, adding popular Web 2.0 user-requested features like graphs and charts, email integration, full-text search, and a host of other UI goodies.

Once you get a feel for how plugins can be used to quickly add features to your application, you'll find yourself addicted to the near-instant gratification that this style of functionality reuse provides. Let's get started with charting.

8.2   *Adding charts and graphs*

Creating charts and graphs in web apps has traditionally been a bit of a pain. Most libraries pregenerate or autogenerate images on the fly, which is time-consuming and somewhat inflexible. And when it comes to aesthetics, only a mother could love some of those charts. If you want great visuals, you have to use Flash, which has its own issues with performance and accessibility.

When Google Chart came out, the world of web-charting suddenly became a whole lot simpler and more elegant. The way Google Chart works is conceptually simple: you create an <IMG> tag in your page that links to a Google Chart URL. You add parameters to a URL to configure the type of chart to create, the data to display, and the size of the chart. Google generates the chart with the typical instant Google performance you're used to, and the charts look slick.

8.2.1   *Installing the Google Chart plugin*

For Grails developers, the charting story is even better. The Google Chart plugin offers a set of simple tags that make adding charts to your pages easy. Let's install it and create some charts:

```
grails install-plugin google-chart 0.4.8
```

We're specifying a particular version here, but you can leave the version out to get the latest one. The Google Chart plugin ships with a sample page that demonstrates the available charts. If you want to explore what you can do, run your application and open http://localhost:8080/hubbub/plugins/google-chart-0.4.8/. Note that you have to change the version number to match the version of the Google Chart plugin you installed.

Let's take a tour of the basic charting tags and learn how to use them.

8.2.2 *Creating your first chart*

For our first chart, we'll add some basic statistics tracking to Hubbub. We'll create a stats page for each user that shows some details about their posting frequency.

As a first step, we'll create a URL mapping so we have a friendly way to get to our user stats page:

```
"/users/$userId/stats" {
    controller = "user"
    action = "stats"
}
```

With our `stats` permalink in place, let's add a `stats` action to our `UserController`. We'll start with pie and bar charts showing which days of the week the user most frequently posts messages on.

In our action, we need to generate a map that contains the day name (Mon, Tues, and so on) and the number of posts on that day. This is demonstrated in listing 8.1.

Listing 8.1 Adding a `stats` action to the `UserController`

```
def stats = {
    User user = User.findByUserId(params.userId)
    if (user) {
        def sdf = new java.text.SimpleDateFormat('E')    ⟵  Converts date to
        def postsOnDay = [:]                                   day of week
        user.posts.each { post ->                        ⟵  Converts post date
            def dayOfWeek = sdf.format(post.dateCreated)        to day of week
            if (postsOnDay[dayOfWeek]) {      ⟵  Maps day of week to count
                postsOnDay[dayOfWeek]++              of Posts for that day
            } else {
                postsOnDay[dayOfWeek] = 1
            }
        }
        return [ userId: params.userId, postsOnDay: postsOnDay ]
    } else {
        flash.message = "No stats available for that user"
        redirect(uri: "/")
    }
}
```

The only unusual thing here is the use of `SimpleDataFormat` to format the date of the post. It's a sneaky way of passing in a date and converting it to a day name. We then key a map from the day name to a count of posts on that day. We could do this calculation more efficiently with a Hibernate projection (which we covered in chapter 4, section 4.3.3), but let's go for a simple programmatic solution for now.

With our map set up, we next need to render the chart in our GSP. The Google Chart plugin offers a taglib with convenience tags for all the common chart types. Let's start with the pie chart, as shown in listing 8.2.

Listing 8.2   Generating a 3-D pie chart

```
<g:pieChart type="3d"
        title='Posts Per Day'
        size="${[600,200]}"
        labels="${postsOnDay.keySet()}"
        dataType='text'
        data='${postsOnDay.values().asList()}' />
```

We use the `<g:pieChart>` tag, and supply it with our titles, labels, and data. As you might expect, the `labels` attribute is a list of strings, and the `data` attribute is a list of numbers. Google Chart handles the rest. That `dataType` field is important, and we'll get to it shortly, but first let's take a look at the output in figure 8.4.

That's a pretty fine-looking chart for a one-liner! The colors are defaulted here, but you can customize them as you like—we'll explore this shortly. Before we do, though, it's time to explain how those data types work.

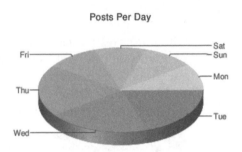

Figure 8.4   **Our 3-D pie chart in action**

8.2.3   *What's the story with dataType?*

Google Chart supports three types of `dataType`: `text`, `simple`, and `extended`. The one you use depends on the type and size of data you need to chart. Depending on the value you set for `dataType`, the Google Chart plugin will normalize your data and encode the result to send to Google.

Table 8.1 shows the available data types.

The bottom line is that the `simple` `dataType` is often the best option for data sets of more than a few elements, because the `text` `dataType` can result in a verbose URL.

Table 8.1   Data types supported by Google Chart

Data type	Discrete values	Cost/benefit
text	100	This gives you an easy-to-debug URL, but a long one. You can see each data value as plain text.
simple	63	This is perfect for most small charts, and it gives the smallest URLs. Data values are compressed using a special encoder: 1=A, 2=B, and so on.
extended	4096	This is only useful for large charts that have a fine-grained scale. It uses a similar encoder to the `simple` type: 0=AA, 1=AB, 2=AC, and so on.

8.2.4 *Bar charts: setting custom colors and gridlines*

With our pie chart done and a basic knowledge of data types under our belt, let's look at how we might implement the same data in a bar chart. Like our pie chart, it all starts with a custom charting tag, as shown in listing 8.3.

Listing 8.3   Our Google-generated bar chart

```
<g:barChart type="bvs"
        title="Posts Per Date (bar)"
        size="${[200,200]}"
        colors="${['00FF00']}"
        fill="${'bg,s,efefef'}"
        axes="x,y"
        axesLabels="${
            [0:postsOnDay.keySet(),
            1:[0,postsOnDay.values().max()/2,
                postsOnDay.values().max()]
            ]
        }"
        dataType="simple"
        data="${postsOnDay.values().asList()}" />
```

Things are getting a little more complex now, but we're starting to take advantage of some of the more advanced features of the library. First, let's check out the results, shown in figure 8.5.

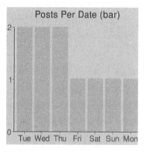

Figure 8.5   Our Google bar chart in action

Most of the new attributes we added are necessary because we're working with a chart that has axes. We need to specify the axis labels, which have a format of [bottom, middle, top] label. The values for the labels are generated algorithmically to ensure that they work for charts with any data value. In our example, we only ever have two posts for a given day, so the calculated labels for min, middle, and max resolve to 0, 1, and 2 respectively.

Axis labels also have their own format that can be confusing. The labels are expressed as 0: (list of labels), 1: (list of labels), with 0 being the *X*-axis and 1 being the *Y*-axis.

Setting the type to bvs tells Google Chart we want a "Barchart Vertical Stacked" style. You can use this field to select horizontal or vertical bars, and you can use stacking or grouping for multiple data sets. Check out the Google Chart Developer's Guide (http://code.google.com/apis/chart/) for the available types (there are dozens, depending on the type of chart you're using).

We've also added a few customizations. The most obvious change is that we're starting to customize the colors. We've added a light grey background fill color (fill="${'bg,s,efefef'}"), and we've changed the color of the bars to green rather than the default yellow (colors="${['00FF00']}"). You'll notice that Google Chart uses hexadecimal-style colors, which you'll be familiar with from CSS. The fill color is expressed as bg,s,efefef which translates as "background, solid fill, light gray."

Google Chart is full of these magic codes—far too many to document here—so check out the online docs for the full set of options. You can customize almost any part of the chart's appearance.

8.2.5 *Line charts: handling multiple datasets and line styles*

The third common type of chart is a line chart. Generating a line chart will also give us a chance to explore charting multiple data sets.

We only have one statistic at our disposal right now, so let's fabricate a second one. We'll copy our `postPerDay` values into a `doubleData` list that contains a doubled set of values. Listing 8.4 shows our updated stats.gsp file with the new `lineChart` calls.

Listing 8.4 Generating a multiseries line chart

```
<%
def doubleData = postsOnDay.values().collect { it * 2 }
def seriesData = [ postsOnDay.values().asList(), doubleData ]
%>

<g:lineChart type="lc"
        title="Posts Per Date (line)"
        size="${[600,200]}"
        colors="${['FF0000','0000FF']}"
        axes="x,y"
        lineStyles="${[[2,2,2],[2,8,4]]}"
        legend="${[ 'Original', 'Doubler' ]}"
        gridLines="16.6,25"
        axesLabels="${[0:postsOnDay.keySet(),
                   1:[0,doubleData.max()/2,
                        doubleData.max()]]}"
        dataType="simple"
        data="${ seriesData }" />
```

In this example, we've passed our data attribute as a list of lists, with each sublist being a separate data series. We've also customized the line styles and colors—notice that both calls take a list, with each value pertaining to a different data set. To sweeten the deal, we've added a legend for our data series and some gridlines, which make everything easier to read. Figure 8.6 shows our output.

Other than passing a list of lists for the dataset, there's nothing more that you need to be aware of when handling multiple datasets. You can pass in a list of colors and styles (one per series), and add your own legend by passing in a list of strings (again, one per series).

Gridlines can be a little confusing at first. The two values (16.5, 25) refer to the percentage points of the graph where gridlines appear. In our example, the *X* values appear in 16.5 percent intervals (that is, splitting the chart into seven pieces), and the *Y* values are in 25 percent intervals (splitting the chart into four). You probably want to calculate the *X* values dynamically if you have a variable number of categories.

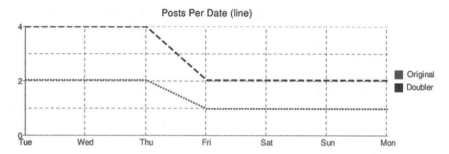

Figure 8.6 A multiseries line chart

The final thing you might want to customize is the line styles. The triplet values (2,2,2 and 2,8,4) represent line thickness, length on, and length off. Our first example is two pixels thick, and two pixels on, then two off, which gives us the nice dotted-line effect.

Space forbids us from covering every conceivable charting option, and Google offers a wealth of them, but these examples should get you started. You'll have your first charts up and running in no time.

It's time to consider what you can do when your users don't have internet access.

8.2.6 *Intranet charts: Google Chart without Google*

Google Chart is great, but what if you're deploying to your intranet and your users don't have access to the internet? All your Google charts are unavailable, right? Wrong.

The good folks at JFreeChart (a nice, standalone Java-charting library) have created a servlet that mirrors the Google Chart API. It's called Eastwood, and there's even a Grails plugin to integrate the servlet with your Grails application:

```
grails install-plugin eastwood-chart
```

With the plugin in place, you tell Google Chart to use your local `eastwood` servlet rather than the remote Google Chart address. The Google Chart taglib exposes this via a static `apiString` property that you can set in BootStrap.groovy:

```
GoogleChartTagLib.apiString = "http://localhost:8080/hubbub/chart?"
```

If you're sneaky, you could even make the switch between Google Chart and Eastwood conditional, depending on whether your app is running on an internal or external server.

Our exploration of charting is now complete. The next application feature we'll add is mail support, and there's a mail plugin waiting to be explored.

8.3 *Adding mail support*

If your application offers any sort of user sign-up capability, it won't be long before you'll need to look at implementing email support. Whether you need to send signup welcome emails, respond to forgotten-password messages, or support a daily digest, having email capability is now a pretty standard requirement. Grails offers the Mail plugin to make sending email simple. You can send mail from controllers or services, and even use complex GSP views to create fancy HTML emails.

Let's install the plugin and get under way:

```
grails install-plugin mail
```

After you've installed the plugin, you need to add two lines of configuration to tell the plugin where to find your mail server and what the default From address should be. Let's update our /grails-app/conf/Config.groovy file:

```
grails.mail.host="192.168.1.9"
grails.mail.default.from="hubbub@grailsinaction.com"
```

The default From address is optional. You can always specify your own From address each time you invoke the mail plugin, but it makes sense to set it here because there's less maintenance later on if you need to change it.

If you have different mail servers for different environments, you can nest this value inside the development/test/production sections of Config.groovy so that you have environment-specific values.

Adding configuration properties for your own code

You might be wondering how the Mail plugin reads values from Config.groovy and how you can add your own property settings to your application.

Let's imagine Hubbub had a setting for enabling a proxy server. In our Config.groovy file we'd add a value for the property:

```
hubbub.proxy.enabled = true
```

If you need access to settings from a controller, you can reference the implicit `grailsApplication` object to get your setting, with a line like this:

```
if (grailsApplication.config.hubbub.proxy.enabled) {
    /* do proxy stuff */
}
```

But `grailsApplication` isn't available inside services, so you need to do a bit more work. First, you need to import the underlying `ConfigurationHolder` object, then access the code statically like this:

```
import org.codehaus.groovy.grails.commons.ConfigurationHolder
class MyService {
    def doStuff {
        if (ConfigurationHolder.config.hubbub.proxy.enabled) {
            /* do proxy stuff */
        }
    }
}
```

TIP   You might be worried whether the Mail plugin is up to supporting your mail server setup. Fear not, there are ample configuration options available for the plugin, including custom ports and SSL connections. Consult the Mail plugin page for the complete set of configuration options.

With our configuration all done, it's time to send our first email.

8.3.1   Sending mail inline

The Mail plugin gives you two basic options for invoking the mail service:

- Via a `sendMail()` method dynamically added to each controller
- By calling the `mailService.sendMail()` method from within a service that has `mailService` injected

TIP   MailService is automatically injected into each controller, so there's no need to `def mailService`.

Let's start with the controller-based mechanism, because that gives us a few options that aren't available in a service. For our first email, let's send a "welcome aboard" signup message, as shown in listing 8.5.

Listing 8.5   Sending a welcome email

```
def welcomeEmail = {
    if (params.email) {
        sendMail {              Added by the
            to params.email     mail plugin
            subject "Welcome to Hubbub!"
            body """
            Hi, ${params.email}. Great to have you on board.    Uses multiline
                                                                string to send mail
            The Hubbub Team.                                    body inline
            """
        }
        flash.message = "Welcome aboard"
    }
    redirect(uri: "/")

}
```

Using the inline version of Mail is a matter of passing in a closure with the appropriate values for `to`, `subject`, and `body`. You can also provide `cc` and `bcc` fields, and you can comma-delimit a list of addresses. In listing 8.5, we use a Groovy multiline string (`"""`) so we can lay out the email inline with our controller code.

That's fine for simple scenarios, but we don't want layout logic embedded in a controller. It's time to move all our layout logic into a GSP to make things more maintainable.

8.3.2   *Using a view as your mail body*

Having an embedded email layout in your controller classes means you can't take advantage of the HTML editor in your IDE. It also makes it harder to get your graphic designer's input into the process. Fortunately the Mail plugin lets you delegate your UI output to a view. Let's take it for a spin.

First, let's create a standard Grails view to host our content. We'll include some CSS styling too, because it's available, and set the content type to text/html so a rich HTML email is sent. Listing 8.6 shows our email template.

Listing 8.6   A template view for our email, with CSS styling

```
<%@ page contentType="text/html"%>
<html>
<head>
   <title>Welcome Aboard</title>
   <style type="text/css">              ◁─┐ Provides CSS style
      body {                                 for our mail
         font-family: "Trebuchet MS"
      }
   </style>
</head>
<body>
   <h1>Howdy!</h1>
   <p>
      Hi, ${email}. Great to have you on board.    ◁─┐ Uses variables provided
   </p>                                                 by the controller
   <p>
      <strong>The Hubbub Team.</strong>
   </p>

</body>

</html>
```

With our content in place, we need a way of wiring it up to our controller action. This is handled by some custom attributes on the sendMail tag. Listing 8.7 shows the updated action.

Listing 8.7   An updated welcome action that defers to the view for rendering

```
def welcomeEmail = {

    if (params.email) {
       sendMail {
          to params.email
          subject "Welcome to Hubbub!"
          body(view: "welcomeEmail", model: [ email: params.email ])
       }
       flash.message = "Welcome aboard"
    }
    redirect(uri: "/")

}
```

Figure 8.7   A new message arriving with suitable markup

We pass the `view` name and the `model` attributes via the body tag. We're already inside the `UserController`, so we can use a relative `view` name for the corresponding GSP (minus the .gsp extension). If you're sending email from a service or a Quartz job, you need to specify the full path to the view (in this example, it would be `"/user/welcomeEmail"`) because Grails has no servlet request to work with.

Figure 8.7 shows our welcome email in action, sending our rich HTML email to the user's inbox.

That completes our tour of the Mail plugin. Next on the list is adding full-text search capability. Let's look at the Searchable plugin.

8.4   Full-text search: rolling your own search

With users flocking to its social networking goodness every day, Hubbub post volumes are going to skyrocket. And users will want to search.

In the good old days, people implemented website search logic using SQL queries (such as `post.content like '%grails%'`), but that isn't sufficient for today's requirements. Using SQL `like` queries can be highly inefficient, and it's increasingly complex as the number of searched fields grows. For most full-text searches, the user wants to search multiple fields, which effectively rules out SQL.

Fortunately, clever folks have implemented full-text indexing and search engines that handle indexing database contents and provide convenient ways to search. One of the most popular Java full-text solutions is Lucene, and its higher-level abstraction library Compass.

The Grails Searchable plugin wraps these full-text search libraries to give you a simple and transparent way to implement searching. Whenever you save a domain object (such as with `post.save()`), the plugin adds the object to the full-text index. When you delete or update an instance, the plugin alters the index accordingly. When you want to search, you just call `Post.search("your search terms")` and you have yourself a list of hits. There's also a completely customizable domain-specific language (DSL) for specifying which domain class properties are indexed.

Let's kick things off by installing the plugin:

```
grails install-plugin searchable
```

With the plugin installed, we're ready to start configuring which objects we want to be searchable. That will require some thinking.

8.4.1   *Making objects searchable*

The first step in making use of the Searchable plugin is determining which objects to index. In the case of Hubbub, users will want to search on Post object content (to see posts matching a term), and also on the User object (does my friend "Joe Cool" have an account?).

The simplest way to add our Post and User objects to the searchable index is to add a searchable property, like this:

```
class User {
    static searchable = true
    ...
}

class Post {
    static searchable = true
    ...
}
```

When a domain class is marked searchable, the plugin indexes its primitive fields (strings, dates, numbers, and collections of those). Later on, we'll customize which fields get indexed, but for now we'll stick with the defaults.

That's it—your basic search capability is implemented. If we now startup Hubbub, we can use the provided Searchable page to search our index. Open http://local-host:8080/hubbub/searchable and take it for a spin, as demonstrated in figure 8.8.

Figure 8.8   The default Searchable interface is pretty usable from the get-go.

Not too bad for five minutes effort, but there's still some work to do. The data is being searched, but the output is not what we want. It found the user and post information relating to "glen", but we need to skin the output with our Hubbub style, and it would be nice to format the link results to use our preferred permalink format (/user/profile/glen for profile info, and /users/glen for all the posts). Also, the user probably only wants to search for posts (Find a Post) or users (Find a Friend).

Let's step outside the default search page and create a custom search page. We'll create a custom search controller first, and then put some effort into the view:

```
grails create-controller com.grailsinaction.search
```

We'll start our implementation by offering a search of all posts, because that's the more common option. Listing 8.8 shows our first attempt at a custom search controller.

Listing 8.8 custom search controller

```
package com.grailsinaction

class SearchController {

   def search = {
      def query = params.q

      if (!query) {
         return [:]
      }

      try {
         def searchResult = Post.search(query, params)       ← ❶ Invokes new
         return [searchResult: searchResult]                      search method
      } catch (e) {
         return [searchError: true]
      }
   }
}
```

As we saw earlier, Searchable adds a dynamic `search()` method ❶ to each domain class. It has two parameters: the query string and a map of options. Typically the options map will contain values for maximum hits per page, offset for pagination, and sorting order. For now, we'll pass in the `params` object, and we'll worry about passing in explicit options later.

The `search()` method returns a map containing metadata about the search, along with a list of domain classes matching the criteria. Table 8.2 gives a breakdown of what's available.

Typically, in the view, you iterate over the results field, displaying each of the hit objects (and perhaps get fancy with a little keyword highlighting). You can also use the `total` and `max` values to display the diagnostics ("returned 10 of 326 hits," for example).

With our controller ready to go, we just need to put together a small /views /search/search.gsp file to let the user enter some values and to display the results from the search. We'll ignore pagination for now and get started with a bare-bones approach, as shown in listing 8.9.

Table 8.2 The `searchResult` return value gives you a wealth of query information.

Field	Description
total	The total number of matching results in the index
results	A List of domain class instances matching the query
max	The maximum number of hits to return (typically used to paginate; defaults to 10)
offset	The number of entries to skip when returning the first hit of the result set—used for pagination
scores	A list of raw result confidence for each hit (a floating point value between 0.0 and 1.0)

Listing 8.9 A first custom search form

```html
<html>
   <head>
      <title>Find A Post</title>
      <meta name="layout" content="main"/>
   </head>
   <body>

      <h1>Search</h1>

      <g:form>
         <g:textField name="q" value="${params.q}"/>
         <g:submitButton name="search" value="Search"/>
      </g:form>
      <hr/>

      <g:if test="${searchResult?.results}">
         <g:each var="result" in="${searchResult.results}">    ⟵┘ Iterates over search results

            <div class="searchPost">
               <div class="searchFrom">
                  From
            <g:link controller="users"
              action="${result.user.userId}">    Creates links to user profile
                  ${result.user.userId}
            </g:link>
               ...
               </div>
               <div class="searchContent">    Displays matching post content
                  ${result.content}
               </div>    ⟵┘
            </div>

         </g:each>
      </g:if>

   </body>
</html>
```

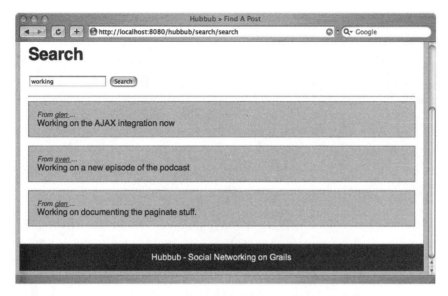

Figure 8.9 Our first custom search form in action

If there are results, we iterate over them and render them in divs. That lets us apply CSS styles to the results. Figure 8.9 shows our first customized search in action.

Those results look pretty nice, but there's no keyword markup. It's time to explore what Searchable offers us to help out.

8.4.2 *Highlighting hit terms*

If you're displaying search results, the user will probably want the keyword hits highlighted. Searchable gives you the power to implement this, but it requires some work with closures. Listing 8.10 shows the updated controller code that highlights the hits.

Listing 8.10 An updated search controller with hit-term highlighting

```
package com.grailsinaction

class SearchController {

    def search = {
        def query = params.q

        if (!query) {
            return [:]
        }

        try {
            params.withHighlighter = {highlighter, index, sr ->    ←❶
                // lazy-init the list of highlighted search results
                if (!sr.highlights) {    ←
                    sr.highlights = []    ❷
                }
```

```
            // store highlighted text;
            // "content" is a searchable-property of the
            // Post domain class
            def matchedFragment = highlighter.fragment("content")    ◁━❸
            sr.highlights[index] = "..." +
                (matchedFragment ?: "") + "..."    ◁━❹
        }

        def searchResult = Post.search(query, params)
        return [searchResult: searchResult]

    } catch (e) {
        return [searchError: true]
    }
  }
}
```

The updated search code uses the `withHighlighter` closure ❶, which takes a high-lighter object (used to hold the word that was highlighted along with its surrounding text), an `index` counter (used to track the hit number), and the search result object itself.

We create a new `highlights` object on each search result if it doesn't already exist ❷, and we use it to hold the marked-up version of the search result (the version with the keyword highlighted).

For each result, we retrieve the fragment of the `Post`'s `content` field that matched the search ❸, and we surround it with ellipses ❹ to show it's an extract. The matched fragment will contain the word that was matched plus a few surrounding words for context. The matched word will be surrounded in <b> tags by the plugin.

Listing 8.11 shows our updated view code that will extract those matching phrases and render them in the browser.

Listing 8.11   Updated view code for handling hit terms

```
<g:each var="result" in="${searchResult.results}" status="hitNum">

    <div class="searchPost">
        <div class="searchFrom">
            From
            <g:link controller="users" action="${result.user.userId}">
                ${result.user.userId}
            </g:link>
            ...
        </div>
        <div class="searchContent">
            ${searchResult.highlights[hitNum]}
        </div>
    </div>

</g:each>
```

This code uses a `status` attribute in the `<g:each>` tag. Then it accesses the hit-num.Hits marked up with <b> tag. Figure 8.10 shows the results of searching for "work". With hit-term highlighting set up, the search is starting to look useful. But we don't want our search page to display thousands of hits, so it's time to implement pagination.

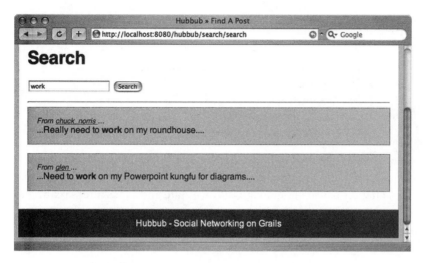

Figure 8.10 Hit-term highlighting in action

8.4.3 *Implementing pagination*

So far, we've only explored the first page of our results. We haven't specified the max property for our searches, and the Searchable plugin has defaulted to returning the first ten. It's time we gave users control over how many results are returned per page. The good news is that we can use the same pagination control you saw in chapter 6.

Let's first add a combo box to let the user choose the number of hits to be displayed per page. If we call the field max, Searchable will pick it up for free, which means no changes to our controller code. Here's the updated form:

```
<g:form>
    <g:textField name="q" value="${params.q}"/>
    <g:select name="max" from="${[1, 5, 10, 50]}"
            value="${params.max ?: 10}" />
    <g:submitButton name="search" value="Search"/>
</g:form>
```

Our backend controller is unchanged, but we'll need to make some UI changes to the results section of our page to use the paginating aspects of the output (the total number of matching results, which page we're on, and so on).

Handling the case when there's only one page of results makes this trickier than it should be. Listing 8.12 shows the updated GSP.

Listing 8.12 Displaying marked up hit terms

```
Displaying hits
    <b>${searchResult.offset+1}-
        ${searchResult.offset + searchResult.max}</b> of
    <b>${searchResult.total}</b>:

    <g:set var="totalPages"
        value="${Math.ceil(searchResult.total / searchResult.max)}"/>
```

```
<g:if test="${totalPages == 1}">
   <span class="currentStep">1</span>
</g:if>
<g:else>
   <g:paginate controller="search" action="search"
      params="[q: params.q]"
      total="${searchResult.total}"
      prev="&lt; previous" next="next &gt;"/>
</g:else>
<p/>
```

If there's only one page to display, we don't need to invoke the paginate tag at all. But if we're spanning pages, we need to tell the tag the total size of the result list. As you'll recall from chapter 6, the tag manages its own state and looks after creating the necessary links to navigate to next and previous pages.

Figure 8.11 shows it in use.

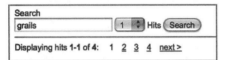

Figure 8.11   Implementing pagination on our search

Our paginating search capability is done. With that feature implemented, we've learned enough of the basics to implement the most common features you'll need in your own search facilities. But there's still more Searchable power to explore: it's time to look at some advanced features.

8.4.4   Customizing what gets indexed

So far in our exploration of search, we've relied on the default indexing rules: we've marked our domain classes as searchable. But when you index lots of data, it's useful to control what gets stored—it's pointless indexing a million password fields, because you never want them exposed in a search. You also want to be careful not to index data that's under high concurrency (for example, a clickCounter field stored on every domain object) because you'll open yourself up to a lot of complex locking and exception handling around concurrent updates to the index.

Fortunately Searchable exposes a more complete DSL for fine-grained index creation, so you can configure what is searchable. Let's upgrade our User object to make sure passwords never get indexed:

```
class User {

   static searchable = {
      except = ['password']
   }
   // more stuff...
}
```

Two common operations on the Searchable DSL are except (index all fields except these) and only (only index these).

Customizing the index location

When you install the Searchable plugin, it adds a new command to install its config-uration file. If you don't install a custom version, it will use default values. Most of these defaults are fine, except that the index file location defaults to the current user's home directory. This isn't what you want in production.

To install a custom config file, use the following command:

```
grails install-searchable-config
```

This will create the /grails-app/conf/Searchable.groovy file, which lets you customize the location of your index files (and other options—see the comments in the created file). For example, you might have a special location for index files on your production servers:

```
compassConnection = new File(
      "/var/indexes/${appName}/${grailsEnv}"
   ).absolutePath
```

You can override the locations for the development, test, and production environments like in Config.groovy.

8.4.5 Query suggestions: did you mean "Grails"?

One of the coolest features in Google is the suggest-query capability. Can't remember how to spell zucchini and spell it zukini? Google will show you results, but it'll also prompt you, "Did you mean zucchini?" Searchable gives you that feature for free, if you tell it which domain classes are subject to the check.

To enable this, you use the Searchable DSL we introduced in the previous section. Let's change our `Post` domain class to mark it searchable for the suggest-query option, which uses the `spellCheck` option:

```
static searchable = {
   spellCheck "include"
}
```

Once the domain class is marked to use the suggest feature, you pass in the `suggest-Query` option to your search code. Here's our updated search action using the new parameter:

```
params.suggestQuery = true
def searchResult = Post.search(query, params)
```

Although the controller changes were fairly painless, we're in for a bit more work in the view to display the suggested terms. We'll use some internal Searchable classes to do this. Perhaps one day this will be wrapped up in a Searchable taglib, but for now here's how to display the search term:

```
<g:if test="${searchResult?.suggestedQuery}">
<%@ page import="org.codehaus.groovy.grails.plugins.
        ➥ searchable.util.StringQueryUtils" %>
<p>Did you mean
```

```
<g:link controller="search" action="search"
    params="[q: searchResult.suggestedQuery]">
        ${StringQueryUtils.highlightTermDiffs(
            params.q.trim(), searchResult.suggestedQuery)
        }
</g:link>?
</g:if>
```

We've done all the work, so it's time to run our app and give it a test. Figure 8.12 shows a search for a popular competing web framework.

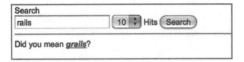

Figure 8.12   The Searchable suggest-query feature in action

Although `suggestQuery` makes for a great demo, there's one more core feature of search that we haven't explored yet. What if we want to constrain the query to only match items within the current user's posts? To implement that, we need to explore how search subcomponents work.

8.4.6   *Searching across relationships*

We've already explored how the indexing process handles domain classes that are in relationships with one another. We discovered that if a domain class has a relationship to another (a `User` has many `Posts`) and the related domain class is also marked `searchable`, the index will also contain that relationship data. That's good, because we can navigate from parent to child without concern.

But what if we want to search all `Posts` that belong to a particular user? We need some way of storing fields from the related `User` object in the index related to the `Post` data. Searchable handles that relationship with `component`.

We'll show you the syntax first, and then break down what's happening behind the scenes. Listing 8.13 shows our updated `Post` object's searchable mapping.

Listing 8.13   An updated `Post` object with more custom search tuning

```
class Post {
    static searchable = {
        user(component:true)       Allows searching of Post objects
        spellCheck "include"       based on User criteria
    }
    static belongsTo = [ user : User ]
    // ...other stuff
}
```

We've told Searchable that we want to store all of the fields of our `User` object with the index for each `Post`. When the index is stored in this manner, we can search against the `Post` object, using constraints from the `User` object (for example, to find all posts where `userId` is "glen").

In order to implement this, let's update the search UI to handle the new option:

```
<g:if test="${session.user}">
   Just My Stuff:
   <g:checkBox name="justMine" value="${params.justMine}"/>
</g:if>
```

We'll also update our search controller to handle the check box. The simplest way to do this is to append a constraint to the submitted query. You can do this with Google-style restrictions, by appending +userId:glen at the end of the query, for example.

The following code updates our controller to automatically add the constraint when the check box for justMine is checked:

```
if (params.justMine) {
   query += " +userId:${session.user.userId}"
}
def searchResult = Post.search(query, params)
```

We now have our constrained user search. Using strings to do this is fine for simple search restrictions, but it can open up all sorts of security issues when trying to restrict sensitive searches. There's all kinds of evil the user could work on the submitted queryString, and you have to be careful to remove all the nasties by hand-crafted regular expressions.

For those scenarios, a better option is to use the full-blown Searchable Search-Builder DSL. You could, for example, rework the preceding search using must() specifiers, which the user can't tinker with. For example, you could do something like this:

```
def searchResult = Post.search params, {
   must(queryString(query))
   must(term("userId", session.user.userId))
}
```

Using the SearchBuilder DSL offers a much "safer" approach for guaranteeing the constraint will apply to the final query. Check out the Searchable SearchBuilder DSL on the Grails wiki for more information (http://www.grails.org/Searchable+Plugin+-+Searching+-+Query+Builder). Be warned, though, the DSL can be tricky to use, so you might want to familiarize yourself with the Compass API that it's built on first.

Debugging indexes with Luke

Luke (http://www.getopt.org/luke/) is a tool for viewing your index files to see exactly what's being stored. If you've having trouble working out how all of the component settings affect index creation, download (or Web Start) Luke, and point it at your index directory.

The Documents tab is handy for debugging search DSL issues—it lets you step through each element in the index and see exactly which keywords are stored, as shown here:

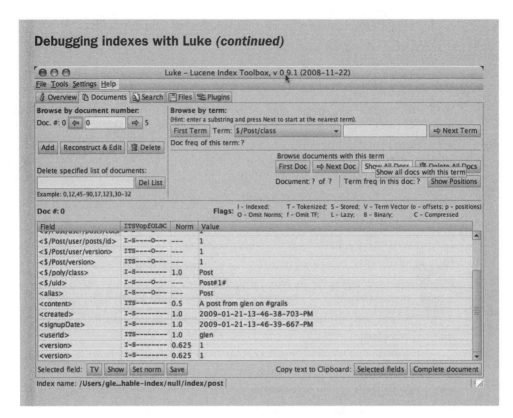

The Searchable plugin is complex but powerful. Take the time to explore the online docs and see the configuration options available.

It's now time to look at our last UI plugin: GrailsUI.

8.5   *GrailsUI makeover*

With our full-text search capability in place, it's time to polish our UI. There are numerous Grails plugins for adding more UI sizzle to your app, but one of the most popular (and easy to use) is the GrailsUI plugin.

GrailsUI is a wrapper for YahooUI (YUI)—the poplar JavaScript UI toolkit from Yahoo!—but the plugin's Grails integration is what makes it so attractive. It includes everything from tooltips to date pickers, rich-text editors, dialog boxes, data tables, and even Ajax autocomplete fields—all with fantastic Grails integration to make consuming the service straightforward. Our goals for Hubbub are modest: some tooltips, rich-text editing, a nicer date picker, and some fancy Ajax autocomplete fields.

To get started, we first need to install the plugin:

```
grails install-plugin grails-ui
```

With the plugin up and running, it's time to start working on our new features.

8.5.1 *Adding tooltips*

Tooltips are the easiest UI feature to implement, so let's start there. For our tooltips, we'd like the user to be able to hover over a friend's icon and see the person's name.

All components in the GrailsUI plugin follow the same implementation pattern:

1 Declare which components you want to use in your page in the header section.
2 Use a GrailsUI tag to create the component.
3 For fine-grained customization, supply any special YahooUI tags that you want passed through to the rendered control.

We start by declaring that our /post/timeline.gsp page will use the hover tag. We'll add the definition to the head section of the page using a special GrailsUI `gui:resources` tag:

```
<gui:resources components="['tooltip']"/>
```

With our resource declared, we can enhance our sidebar to use the hover element, which is invoked with `<gui:tooltip text="your tooltip">`. We have already developed a custom tag to render the thumbnail itself (`h:tinyThumbnail`), but let's enhance things to add the user's ID when the user hovers over their thumbnail:

```
<div id="friendsThumbnails">
  <g:each var="followUser" in="${following}">
    <gui:tooltip text="${followUser.userId}">
      <h:tinyThumbnail userId="${followUser.userId}"/>
    </gui:tooltip>
  </g:each>
</div>
```

We've set the tooltip text to be the user's ID, which should be enough to let the user know who they are following. Figure 8.13 shows the tooltip in action.

Our tooltip tag has given you a taste for the basics of how GrailsUI handles components. It's time to set our sights a little higher, and look at how we might use our newfound knowledge to implement a rich-text editor for our registration page.

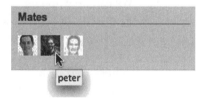

Figure 8.13 Applying a tooltip to our followers section

8.5.2 *Implementing rich-text editing*

The rich-text editor component of GrailsUI is used to edit HTML content fields, and it's useful for adding basic CMS (content management system) functionality to your application.

In the case of Hubbub, we'd like to let the user add an HTML bio field on registration, and we'd like to give them the freedom to use whatever markup they'd like. Users aren't particularly fond of hand-editing HTML, so let's give them the full bells and whistles of an HTML editor to play with.

As with our tooltip integration, everything starts with a resource definition. Here's the definition for including the rich-text editor into /user/register.gsp:

```
<gui:resources components="['richEditor']"/>
```

With the definition in place, using the editor is a simple matter of invoking the tag with any default value you'd like included. Typically the value comes from an existing form field. Listing 8.14 demonstrates our updated `bio` field editor.

Listing 8.14   Implementing a rich-text `bio` field editor

```
<dt>Bio:</dt>
<dd>
   <p style="margin-top: 3em"/>
   <gui:richEditor id="bio"
             height="100px"
             width="600px"/>
   <script type="text/javascript">
      GRAILSUI.bio.defaultToolbar.titlebar =      Changing custom properties
         'Enter your bio';                        of the underlying YUI object
   </script>

</dd>
```

This will render a full editor for the user to interact with. All the rich-text support you'd expect is in there: bold, italic, underlines, fonts, and hyperlinks. The only values you must supply to the richEditor tag are `id` and `value`, but we've chosen to pass in the `height` and `width` as well. For more advanced attributes, you need to invoke some JavaScript, so we've also taken advantage of the customization options to supply a custom toolbar title.

We can now update our bios with some new info, as shown in figure 8.14. That's as full-featured a text editor as you're likely to need. YUI gives you a large number of configuration options (including the ability to remove and add your own buttons, modify the look and feel, and set all sorts of event options). We won't get into the details here, but check out the extensive YUI documentation available online (http://developer.yahoo.com/yui/) to see all the available attributes.

With our rich-text editor working, let's turn our attention to giving our dates a makeover.

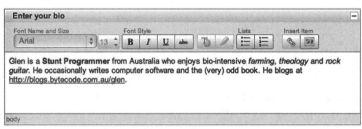

Figure 8.14   Using a rich-text editor to enter bio data

8.5.3   *Implementing calendar-style dates*

The standard Grails date-picker is functional, but in terms of UI beauty and ease of use, let's just say "it's got *character*". It will happily let the user specify date and time values, but they need to select from a range of combo boxes, and the user experience not very inviting. In most cases, when the user selects a date, they expect a calendar-style view that's been made popular by hotel and flight-reservation sites.

GrailsUI ships with one of these, and it's a one-line change to switch between the standard and GrailsUI versions of the date picker. Let's use it to add a feature to Hubbub that allows users to schedule the publishing of a post—the post won't be displayed until a certain date is reached.

First, we need to update our header definition in /user/post.gsp to include the new control. Notice that you can supply a list of control names to the tag if your page uses more than one component:

```
<gui:resources components="['tooltip','datePicker']"/>
```

With our definition in good order, the next step is to include the tag itself in the view:

```
Schedule Post:
<gui:datePicker id='postOn' value="${new Date()}" includeTime="true"/>
```

In this example, we've included the time portion of the date, so the user can select the exact moment the post is released. The control looks better without the time portion, but if you need the granularity for a straight replacement for a Grails date, it's good to have that power.

One final trap is in store for us, though. YUI components can be picky about their styling. For certain components, you need to change the body style on your page to include the YUI skin definition class, and the YUI Calendar component that GrailsUI Calendar is built on is one of them.

We'll update the body class on our Post template directly (/layouts/user/post.gsp) rather than the target GSP file (/views/user/post.gsp)—that will let us avoid any special SiteMesh ${pageProperty(name: "body.style")} coding to merge tag attributes between layout and view. Here's the updated definition in the layout:

```
<body class="yui-skin-sam">
```

With the skin definition in place, the calendar is ready to use. You can see the rendered view in figure 8.15.

The text box still needs some CSS styling, but the fly-out calendar looks great. With our new date control implemented, it's time to move on to our last control—Ajax autocomplete.

Figure 8.15   Using a calendar picker for date selection

8.5.4   *Introducing autocomplete*

We're going to finish with one of the most complex controls in the GrailsUI suite: autocomplete. We're going to enhance Hubbub to allow the user to select a tag from the UI by typing a few characters and being presented with a list of available tags to select from. Implementing autocomplete requires changes in both the frontend and backend because the autocomplete drop-down list needs to be populated from our backend data source.

Let's start with the client changes first. We include autocomplete in our header definitions for /views/user/post.gsp:

```
<gui:resources components="['tooltip','datePicker','autoComplete']"/>
```

Once our resource definition is in place, we can safely reference the autocomplete tag in the view. There's a lot of configuration that goes with autocomplete. Let's look at the tag first:

```
Tags: <gui:autoComplete
             id="tags"
             resultName="tags"
             labelField="name"
             idField="id"
             controller="post"
             action="autoTags"
             delimChar=" "
        />
```

That's quite an invocation. As you might expect, `controller` and `action` point to the backend controller that returns the data to populate the drop-down list. The `delim-Char` parameter lets you separate several entries with the same control. In our case, we want to be able to tag things like "groovy grails news" and get separate drop-down lists for the tag name each time we press the space bar.

The remaining attributes, `resultName`, `labelField`, and `idField`, relate to the JSON data returned by the backend controller. In a moment we'll see that our backend action will return JSON data that looks like this:

```
{"tags":[{"id":1,"name":"grails"},{"id":2,"name":"groovy"}]}
```

The `resultName` field refers to the name of the JSON root element. The `idField` and `labelField` refer to the elements within the JSON data that contain the values for the autocomplete field (`id` and `name`). In this example, we only care about the name field, but the `idField` is a requirement of the control because it creates hidden fields (in the preceding example, `tags` and `tags_id`) containing the label and IDs respectively.

The last step is to implement the backend logic that does the query based on the user's keypresses. Take a look at the code in listing 8.15.

> **Listing 8.15 The backend implementation for autocompleting tags**

```
import grails.converters.JSON

class PostController {

    ...
    def autoTags = {
        def queryTerm = params.query          ①  Extracts query term
        User user = session.user.attach()         from params

        def matchingTags = Tag.findAllByUser(user).     ②  Collects all tags
           ➥ findAll { tag ->                               matching the term
            tag.name.toLowerCase().startsWith(queryTerm)
        }
        def tagList = matchingTags.collect { tag ->     ③  Creates list matching
            [id: tag.id, name: tag.name]                    tag id to name
        }
        def jsonResult = [
            tags: tagList
        ]                                          ④  Returns results as
        render jsonResult as JSON                      JSON object
    }
}
```

The user's keypresses will be in `params.query` ①, so we need to search the user's tags to find any that match. We need case-insensitive searching, so we retrieve all the user's tags and iterate through them to find the ones that begin with the keypresses ②.

Once we've got our target set of responses, we need to convert them into a format suitable for the autocomplete control. First, we create a list of id/name pairs for each tag ③, and then we return our result as a JSON object ④. Notice that the name of the root element of our `jsonResult` object (`tags`) is the element that matches the `resultName` attribute on our original view tag.

With all the plumbing done, there's nothing more to do than sit back and enjoy our autocomplete control in action. You can see the results in figure 8.16.

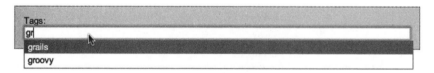

Figure 8.16 Our autocompleting tags in action

With autocomplete in place, we've concluded our tour of popular Grails plugins and given Hubbub a complete makeover.

8.6 *Summary and best practices*

We've covered a lot of plugins in this chapter, but we've given you a thorough grounding in a host of popular features that you're likely to want to add to your next application.

We introduced you to the basics of how plugins are installed and bundled, and we covered creating graphs and charts and integrating email into your application. We also explored numerous searchable options for making your app's full-text search facility hum.

Finally, we gave Hubbub a complete makeover using the GrailsUI plugin, adding tooltips, a rich-text editor, a date picker, and an autocomplete capability. It was a lot to take in, but our app's usability has increased tremendously.

Here are a few best-practices to take away from the chapter:

- *Keep it simple.*   Prefer the `simple dataType` when generating charts. The URLs are much shorter, which gives you space for a lot more data.
- *Use Mail config.*   Set the `mail.grails.default.from` attribute in Config.groovy so there's a single place to maintain your From address. You then no longer need to use the From field when invoking mail services.
- *Customize search config.*   Always install a custom searchable config file so you can place your index data somewhere sensible.
- *Index selectively.*   Be careful which fields you include in your index. Watch out for sensitive data, as well as data that's under high concurrency (if you index your `clickCounter` field, only bad can come of it).
- *Explore GrailsUI.*   The GrailsUI plugin has a wealth of custom components you can use. You know all the basics now, so adding new components to your library will be easy. Take the time to browse the GrailsUI documentation to see what UI features are available.

We've spent a lot of time focusing on the UI in this chapter, so it's time to balance that frontend work with some backend work. In the next chapter, you'll have a chance to develop your frontend and backend Grails skills as you handle wizard-style workflows by developing a basic online store for Hubbub products.

Wizards and workflow
with webflows

In this chapter

- What webflows are, and what they're useful for
- Implementing basic wizard-style flows
- Making use of branching for complex conditions
- Simplifying logic with subflows
- Leveraging flow-scoped stateful services
- Testing webflows

We've covered a lot of territory so far, and learned a lot about the basics of controllers, views, and models—how they work together and how to test them. We've given our application a great UI makeover, and learned plenty about core Grails application development in the process. But we haven't explored basic workflow yet.

What if you have a signup process that spans several pages? Or what if your shopping cart checkout needs to optionally give the user shipping preferences based on their location? You can solve these issues with your current knowledge of

255

controllers and a bunch of redirects with hidden form variables, but you'd be writing your own state engine, and depending on the complexity of the flow, things can get complex quickly.

Grails webflows are designed for exactly this kind of scenario, and they make implementing multipage wizards with optional steps clean and maintainable. Webflows offer an easy-to-use and highly-configurable state engine—perfect for your next web-based workflow, and without all the overhead of a heavyweight rules engine.

Let's learn how webflows can make implementing a Hubbub store an afternoon's work.

9.1   *What is a webflow?*

A Grails webflow is a series of logical steps displaying various screens through which the user progresses to arrive at a final destination. Users might skip steps depending on the data they've entered (for example, if they do or don't want custom shipping), and they might end up at entirely different end pages as a result of their selections (such as if their order is complete or their items are out of stock).

Let's look at an ideal multistep application flow in flowchart form. We'll use Hubbub for our example and have the user select some items from the store and enter their shipping details. We'll then validate their credit card and give them a confirmation page. Figure 9.1 shows our first draft of an order flow for the Hubbub shop. We'll implement the flow basics in a webflow and then add some more complex steps and subflows as the chapter progresses.

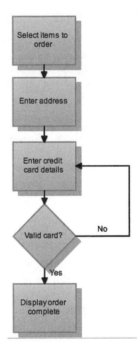

This first flow is pretty simple, but even at this stage it illustrates a few key advantages of having a webflow engine. What will a webflow give us that a standard Grails controller solution wouldn't? A webflow will do several things:

- Track what stage of the workflow the user is at (so the Next and Previous buttons will be context sensitive)
- Provide a simple domain-specific language (DSL) to express what happens at each stage of the process, so it's easy to see which step happens where
- Make it easy to insert new steps into the process without refactoring a lot of controller actions
- Give us a lot of power for expressing decision states simply and elegantly (like our card-validation step) and for handling routing based on the outcome of the decision
- Introduce two new scopes—*flow* and *conversation*— that allow us to store variables that can only be accessed within the flow, and which will be removed automatically at the conclusion of the flow

Figure 9.1   Our basic workflow as a flowchart

Webflows offer a lot of power for any part of an application that lends itself to a multi-step interaction.

But one thing that you should know up front is that webflows aren't suited for every application setting—they're targeted to basic wizard-style multistep operations. They're perfect for breaking a complex 100-field form into multiple sequential pages, or for tricky checkout features where you have to validate credit cards, collect address and shipping options, and then offer a confirmation page. But don't try to force your new Flickr-clone site into a webflow style of interaction—you'll spend more time fighting the framework than solving real problems.

9.1.1 Writing your first flow: a checkout wizard

Now that you have a basic understanding of the situations where webflows do and don't make sense, it's time to write our simple order flow and learn how all the pieces fit together.

You'll be pleasantly surprised to find that all webflow definitions happen in the context of a standard controller. Let's start by creating a Hubbub shop controller for purchasing Hubbub-approved swag:

```
grails create-controller com.grailsinaction.shop
```

With our shop controller in place, it's time to start defining our first flow. As outlined in figure 9.1, we'll use the Webflow DSL to define actions for each of the steps in the workflow. We'll call our flow `orderFlow`—flow definitions, by convention, always start with an action ending in "Flow". This tells Grails that it's a Webflow DSL definition. Flows also get their own endpoint, so our `orderFlow` will have a URL of /hubbub /shop/order.

We can now define the flow. Listing 9.1 defines the parent-level flow element.

Listing 9.1 Our empty flow definition waiting for some workflow steps

```
package com.grailsinaction

class ShopController {

    def index = {
        redirect(action: "order")
    }

    def orderFlow = {

    }
}
```

That's quite bare bones. You'll notice we've included an `index` action on our controller. As you'll recall, if there's only one action in a controller, it becomes the default action, but given the special nature of webflow URLs, that rule doesn't apply. If you want a tidy URL (/shop redirecting to /shop/order), you have to take matters into your own hands.

Also notice that although the definition of the flow is `orderFlow`, we refer to the action without the "Flow" part from within controllers—so the redirect from `index()` is to `"order"`, not `"orderFlow"`.

Our flow is defined in listing 9.1, but it doesn't do anything yet. An easy way of getting started with flows like this is to develop skeleton code for the entire flow first, and then fill in the logic later. Without further ado, let's throw together a bare-bones definition of the flow, and then put some meat on each step. Listing 9.2 shows a skeleton flow definition ready for some flow-step logic.

Listing 9.2 A skeleton flow definition

```
def orderFlow = {

    displayProducts {                         Processes Next button
        on("next") {                          on form submit
            // capture products
        }.to("enterAddress")                  Transitions to
        on("cancel").to("finish")             enterAddress state
    }

    enterAddress {
        on("next") {
            // capture address
        }.to("enterPayment")
        on("previous").to("displayProducts")
    }

    enterPayment {
        on("next") {
            // capture payment details
        }.to("validateCard")
        on("previous").to("enterAddress")
    }

    validateCard {
        action {                    ←— Acts as branching point
            // do some logic here
            if (params.validCard) {
                log.debug "Valid Card!!"
                valid()
            } else {
                log.debug "Invalid Card!!"
                invalid()
            }
        }
        on("valid").to("orderComplete")       Branches based on
        on("invalid").to("enterPayment")      return value of action
    }

    orderComplete {
        // display order
        on("finished").to("finish")
    }
    finish {                        Terminates flow
```

```
        redirect(controller:"homePage", action: "index")
    }

}
```

Even though this is a bare-bones workflow, there's still some basic wizard-like logic going on. You can see how each webflow state matches a step in our flowchart diagram (figure 9.1). After each on() step, the webflow transitions the flow to() a new state. We'll get into the details shortly, but for now see if you can get the gist of the flow as a whole, and how it maps to our flowchart.

Now that you have a feel for how flows are implemented, it's time to learn how flows transition from state to state. Let's start our exploration with a few of those on().to() things.

The execution param: back-button and permalinking issues

As you start working with webflows, you'll notice a constantly changing state-tracking parameter that the webflow appends to each URL in your flow (execution=e1s1, with the value changing on each state change).

Suppose a user bookmarks a flow in the middle of your page, or links to it from an external resource, or uses the browser's back button after the flow has ended and tries to resubmit a form from the middle of the flow. In these cases, Grails intercepts a request to an expired or finished flow and redirects the user to the first state in the flow. If you look at the webflow logs (see the sidebar on "Debugging bizarre webflow errors"), you'll see the framework catch them:

```
[6431198] servlet.FlowHandlerAdapter Restarting a new execution of
            previously expired/ended flow 'order'
```

Normally, heading back to the start of the flow is the best way to handle this kind of error. If you need to perform custom expired-flow management, your best bet is to create a custom filter for the error.

9.1.2 Anatomy of a flow state

Each step in the flow is referred to as a *state*. The first flow state encountered in a webflow is known as the *start state*, which, in our case, is displayProducts.

When the user first hits /shop/order, Grails will invoke displayProducts to get things going. Let's have a closer look at its definition:

```
displayProducts {
    on("next") {
        // capture products
    }.to("enterAddress")
    on("cancel").to("finish")
}
```

How does displayProducts fire those "next" and "cancel" rules? The answer lies in how view conventions work. In the case of displayProducts, Grails will first render a view page called /views/shop/order/displayProduct.gsp, and then wait for the user to submit the page. Based on the buttons clicked on that page, the flow can progress.

Listing 9.3 creates a basic `displayProduct` page to get us started. (Remember, this is in an "order" subdirectory of /views/shop, so we're one level deeper than normal.)

Listing 9.3   Triggering flow steps from a view

```html
<html>
  <head>
    <title>Shop for Official Merchandise</title>
    <meta content="main" name="layout"/>
  </head>
  <body>

    Display Products Details Here
    <g:form action="order">
      <g:submitButton name="next" value="Next"/>
      <g:submitButton name="cancel" value="Finished Shopping"/>
    </g:form>

  </body>
</html>
```

❶ Matches form name to flow name
❷ Matches button with flow transitions

This looks like a pretty standard Grails form GSP, with only a few items that relate to webflow. First, notice that the form submission target is `"order"`, not `orderFlow` ❶. Views in the flow always point to the same target action, and the webflow engine handles which state the user should be sent to based on their progress (via the execution parameter that the webflow adds to each URL, as discussed in the previous sidebar on the execution param).

The other thing to note is that the button names are now important ❷. The name of the button will invoke the appropriate action in the backend, so be careful not to misspell them.

The final part of an action is the `.to()` clause, which tells the webflow which state to fire next. When the user clicks on a Cancel button, things start to fire. The form is submitted, the webflow follows the `on()` clause and ends up at the `finish` state, which sends the user back home. Listing 9.4 demonstrates the flow transition.

Listing 9.4   The `on()` clause maps the Cancel button name to the next logical action.

```
displayProducts {
    on("next") {
        // capture products
    }.to("enterAddress")
    on("cancel").to("finish")
}

finish {
    redirect(controller:"homePage", action: "index")
}
```

Terminates flow by omitting on() clauses

You'll notice that the `finish` state has no `.to()` clauses. Any state without a `.to()` clause is referred to as an *end state*. These states are special because once an end state fires, all flow state data is discarded (such as which step the user is at in the flow, and anything in flow scope, which we'll discuss shortly).

Breaking conventions: using custom view rendering

Webflow view names follow the standard convention (view filename matches the state name), but you're free to break from that convention when you need to via a custom `render()` call. For example, our `displayProducts` state in listing 9.4 could be directed to a different view name as follows:

```
displayProducts {
    render(view: "standardProducts")
    on("next") {
        // capture products
    }.to("enterAddress")
    on("cancel").to("finish")
}
```

9.2 *Working with webflows*

Now that you understand a little about how webflows handle states and routing, let's apply that knowledge to implement our order flow. In this section, we'll learn the basics of implementing a useful flow:

- How to store objects in flow scope
- How to perform data binding and error handling in a flow
- How to implement decision states to route the user to different states programmatically

We'll start with an exploration of *flow scope*—a new scope that Grails provides for storing objects that are accessed throughout the lifetime of a webflow.

9.2.1 *Flow scope: better than Flash scope, cheaper than session scope*

Grails webflows add a new scope to your repertoire: *flow scope*. Items put in flow scope live for the life of the flow (that is, until the user transitions to an end state, as in our previous `finish` example). Using flow scope is a effective way to share data across a flow, and it's perfect for storing objects that are built up throughout the flow. In our Hubbub example, we could store a product selection in the first step of the flow, and use it in a later step to confirm the order and work out the bill.

You can reference flow scope explicitly, like the other scopes, from within any state in your flow. Here's an example:

```
displayProducts {
    on("next") {
        flow.order = new Order(params)    ◁── Places object in flow
    }.to("enterAddress")                         scope explicitly
    on("cancel").to("finish")
}
```

This is an explicit way of accessing flow scope, but there are even better options. When you return objects from flow states (via a map style commonly used in controllers), they implicitly end up in flow scope. You can do things like this:

```
displayProducts {
    on("next") {
        def orderDetails = new Order(params)
        [ order: orderDetails, orderStartDate: new Date() ]   ◁──┐  Places objects
    }.to("enterAddress")                                           in flow scope
    on("cancel").to("finish")
}
```

This will automatically place `orderDetails` and `orderStartDate` in flow scope for you. But flow scope has its own gotchas, and they're significant. The biggest one is that every object you place in flow scope must implement `Serializable`.

What's the deal with Serializable?

The requirement that all flow-scoped objects implement `Serializable` means that basic types like `Strings` and `Dates` work fine, but domain object that are stored in flow scope must implement `Serializable`. Worse still, to satisfy the `Serializable` contract, any domain classes it holds a reference to need to be `Serializable` too. That can lead to a lot of `Serializable` changes!

If you haven't worked with the `Serializable` interface in Java before, you might want to start with the Javadoc for `java.io.Serializable`. For most of your webflow uses, you'll simply need to add `implements Serializable` to your domain class definition. But there are some complex and subtle use cases for `Serializable` that can trip up new Grails developers—particularly when `Serializable` objects are placed in collections.

A lot of the items you'll store in flow scope are objects you've validated in previous steps, and you won't want to go back and mark all domain objects `Serializable` just to store them in flow scope. Fortunately, using `Serializable` command objects offers us a neat solution to this problem.

Let's continue our webflow exploration by digging a little deeper into the practical ways we can handle validation in a webflow setting.

9.2.2   *Strategies for binding and validation*

We've discussed some of the complexities of persisting domain objects in flow scope, but webflows give you some other options for handling and validating forms. One of the nicest is support for command objects in flows. We saw command objects in chapter 5, when we were looking at ways to handle form submissions—they should be the perfect solution for our current problem of avoiding the need to make domain classes `Serializable`.

Imagine that our `displayProducts` view gives us options for the numbers of shirts and hats to purchase. It might be as simple as this:

```
<g:form action="order">
   Shirts: <g:textField name="numShirts" value="0"/>
   Hats: <g:textField name="numHats" value="0"/>
   <g:submitButton name="next" value="Next"/>
   <g:submitButton name="cancel" value="Finished Shopping"/>
</g:form>
```

We'd like to ensure that when the user submits a value for the form, they don't order more than 10 shirts or 10 hats. That sounds like a classic validation problem, right? The example `Serializable` object in listing 9.5 specifies a range of 0 to 10 for the order values, and we can add any other validation logic that's relevant to the task at hand.

Listing 9.5   Command objects in flow steps must implement `Serializable`.

```
class OrderDetailsCommand implements Serializable {

   int numShirts
   int numHats

   boolean isOrderBlank() {
      numShirts == 0 && numHats == 0
   }

   static constraints = {
      numShirts(range: 0..10)
      numHats(range: 0..10)
   }
}
```

Listing 9.6 shows how we can wire up our command object to our `displayProducts` state.

Listing 9.6   Mapping a command object to a flow step

```
displayProducts {
   on("next") { OrderDetailsCommand odc ->      ①  Binds form data to          ②  Ensures
      if (odc.hasErrors() || odc.isOrderBlank()) {     command object                  order is
         flow.orderDetails = odc                                                       valid
         return error()         ④  Stops user progressing       Keeps invalid
      }                             in the flow                   orders in flow
      [ orderDetails: odc, orderStartDate: new Date() ]     ③  scope
   }.to("enterAddress")
   on("cancel").to("finish")
}
```

Like standard (non-webflow) actions, webflow states that require a marshaled command object specify the object as the first closure argument ①. Grails marshals the request parameters into the command objects and sets the errors if there are validation errors ②.

One thing you haven't seen before is the call to the `error()` method ④. Returning `error()` tells the webflow to return to the previously rendered view so the user can fix any failing validations, but the user will need access to the validation errors to fix the invalid fields. To support this, we put the failing command object back in flow scope ➌ so we can make use of its errors collection in the rendered view page.

This all makes more sense when you see it in action. Listing 9.7 shows an updated `displayProducts` view, this time with more-robust error handling.

Listing 9.7   An updated `displayProducts` view with error handling

```
<g:hasErrors bean="${orderDetails}">
   <div class="errors">
      <g:renderErrors bean="${orderDetails}"/>
   </div>
</g:hasErrors>

<g:form action="order">
   Shirts: <g:textField name="numShirts"
                  value="${orderDetails?.numShirts}"/>
   Hats: <g:textField name="numHats" value="${orderDetails?.numHats}"/>
   <g:submitButton name="next" value="Next"/>
   <g:submitButton name="cancel" value="Finished Shopping"/>
</g:form>
```

Notice that we're now rendering any error collection that's present on our flow-scoped `orderDetails` object. We also prepopulate the default field values with the flow-scoped object so we can repopulate the incorrect values for the users. Figure 9.2 shows the error messages in action.

This is what we wanted. You might have noticed that the error messages have been customized, too. The same i18n message bundle support we introduced in section 4.1.2 is available when using webflows. We added the following entries to /grails-app/i18n/messages.properties to generate the errors in figure 9.2:

```
OrderDetailsCommand.numShirts.range.toosmall=
     You may not order less than {3} shirts.
OrderDetailsCommand.numShirts.range.toobig=
     You may not order more than {4} shirts.
OrderDetailsCommand.numHats.range.toosmall=
     You may not order less than {3} hats.
OrderDetailsCommand.numHats.range.toobig=
     You may not order more than {4} hats.
```

NOTE   For a refresher on i18n message bundle support, look back to chapter 4.

With our flow now validating, and our flow-scope populated with command objects, it's time to look at a flow state that doesn't have any UI at all: the *action state*.

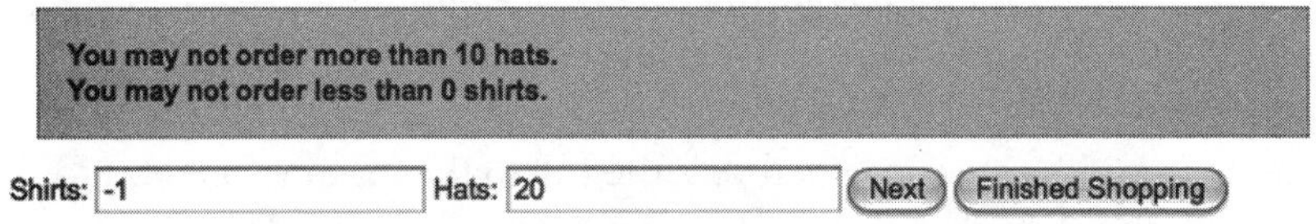

Figure 9.2   Our form displays errors and repopulates failing fields.

9.2.3   *Making decisions programmatically with action states*

So far, our flow-routing decisions have been UI-driven: the user clicks the Next or Previous button, or the form submission fails validation. But we haven't yet looked at altering the flow programmatically. We might want to check stock levels, or validate a credit card, or offer special shipping options for people living in remote places.

This kind of decision step in a flow doesn't have a UI, just the ability to change the flow based on some backend processing. In the context of webflows, these are called *action states*, to separate them from the more common *transition states* we've been dealing with so far.

Let's use credit card handling as an example. After the user submits their credit card details, we want to verify them against a merchant service. If the card number and balance are OK, the flow can continue, but if the card fails validation, we want to return to the card-input form. We can implement this kind of decision flow with an action state.

Let's implement a simple credit card validation step that fails whenever a user presents a card in the morning. We want to end up with a result like that in figure 9.3. A form like this will normally go through a standard view-state action to validate the basic field entries. It would look something like this:

```
enterPayment {
    on("next") {  PaymentCommand pc ->
        flow.pc = pc
        if (pc.hasErrors()) {
            return error()
        }
    }.to("validateCard")
    on("previous").to("enterAddress")
}
```

We do the basic validation checks, and if things are fine, we transition to our new action state: validateCard.

Action states start with the action keyword, so that Grails knows there's no view to render. From there, the body of the flow is like any other flow state. Action states typically define and return custom transition names to make the body of the flow more readable. In listing 9.8, we return invalid() or valid() depending on the processing of the credit card.

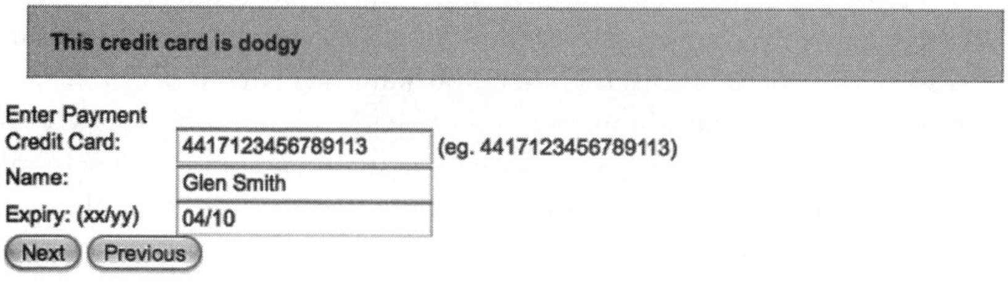

Figure 9.3   Flows support custom error messages created with message bundles.

Listing 9.8 Implementing a credit card validation action step

```
validateCard {
   action {
      def validCard = new Date().hours > 11 // PM is nice
      if (validCard) {
         valid()
      } else {
         flow.pc.errors.rejectValue("cardNumber",    | Rejects value
            "card.failed.validation",                | with custom
            "This credit card is dodgy")             | error code
         invalid()
      }
   }
   on("valid").to("orderComplete")
   on("invalid").to("enterPayment")
}
```

In listing 9.8, when the validation fails, we add a custom error object to the `Payment-Command` (pc) in flow scope. This enables our views to use the existing Grails `has-Errors` tags to conditionally display the contents of our message.

That pretty much covers what action states do and how you use them. Action states are great for representing complex decision logic without cluttering up already over-worked transition actions. They're also great for branching to kick off subflows, which we'll look at shortly.

You have now seen all the common webflow features that you're likely to use in your next Grails application. In the next section, we'll cover a number of advanced webflow concepts—you'll use these less frequently, but they are convenient for specific webflow scenarios.

9.3   *Advanced webflows*

You should now have a solid understanding of all the basics of implementing application flows, but there are a few advanced webflow features that come in handy for particular flow scenarios. In this section, we'll explore some of them, including subflows and conversations. We'll start by looking at flow-scoped services.

9.3.1   *Flow-scoped services*

So far we've learned about storing `Serializable` objects in flow scope so they can be passed along to subsequent flow states. We haven't yet introduced you to using flow-scoped services to give you the equivalent of lightweight stateful session beans.

Flow-scoped services are useful when you want a service object that you can use throughout a flow, but that will maintain data that's relevant only to the current flow. Our credit-card validator is a good example. We use it early in the flow to validate the credit card, and then later in the flow we might access an error code or validation number stored statefully in the service.

Let's clean up our earlier example and experiment with generating a flow-scoped credit-card validator. Flow-scoped services are like regular services and are created in the standard way:

```
grails create-service com.grailsinaction.CreditCard
```

This is the same as every other service you've created. But unlike standard services, you explicitly specify the scope of service via the scope attribute:

```
class CreditCardService implements Serializable {

    static scope = "flow"
    static transactional = false
}
```

Like all objects stored in flow scope, these services must implement Serializable. Once the service is defined in this manner, the standard service injection rules apply for controllers that use the service (review chapter 4 if you need a refresher on services).

It's important to note that, although the service definition happens in the controller (and not in the flow DSL), each new flow will get a new instance of the injected service—the service is created per flow, not per controller.

Here's our updated ShopController with the service injected:

```
class ShopController {

    def creditCardService

    // ... rest of controller actions

}
```

Once the service is defined in the controller, making use of the service within any of your flow states will ensure that you access an instance of the service that's created uniquely for that flow. This means you can use the service in action steps. Listing 9.9 shows our validateCard action reworked to use our flow-scoped service.

Listing 9.9   Invoking a stateful service to validate the card

```
validateCard {
    action {
        def validCard = creditCardService.checkCard(
            flow.pc.cardNumber,                     Invokes flow-
            flow.pc.name,                           scoped service
            flow.pc.expiry)
        if (validCard) {
            valid()
        } else {
            flow.pc.errors.rejectValue("cardNumber",
                "card.failed.validation",
                "This credit card is dodgy")
            invalid()
        }
    }
```

```
    on("valid").to("orderComplete")
    on("invalid").to("enterPayment")
}
```

Notice that we reference our `creditCardService`, and Grails takes care of all the flow-scoped state management behind the scenes. No magic `flow.creditCardService` is required.

The biggest advantage of flow-scoped services is that you can safely access the service in a stateful way in subsequent flow states. That freedom means we can implement our `CreditCardService` as a stateful bean, confident we'll never have concurrency issues from webflow states that consume the service. Listing 9.10 shows a basic stateful implementation of the service.

Listing 9.10   Abstracting credit-card validation to a stateful service

```
package com.grailsinaction
                                              Ensures flow-scoped
class CreditCardService implements Serializable {  ◁──┘ service is Serializable

    static scope = "flow"          ◁─┐ Marks service as
    static transactional = false     │ flow-scoped

    boolean cardChecked = false
    String cardNumber
    String name
    String expiry
    Date checkedAt

    boolean checkCard(String aNumber, String aName, String anExpiry) {
        (cardNumber, name, expiry) = [ aNumber, aName, anExpiry ]
        log.debug "Validating ${cardNumber} for
                ${name} with expiry ${expiry}"
        // do remote service here
        checkedAt = new Date()
        cardChecked = true
        println "Card is ${cardChecked}"
        return cardChecked

    }
}
```

As we explained in Chapter 4, you typically write stateless services because by default they're shared singletons. But in listing 9.10, we store the card details statefully in the service. Later in the flow, we can safely reference that data or call other methods on the service that reference those internal attributes, confident that nothing will have been overwritten in the meantime.

Because flow-scoped services are serialized in the flow, they need to implement `Serializable`, like everything else that is stored in a flow. This is different from standard services, so when you see errors that say "object in flow state could not be serialized," you know what to do.

> ## What if I want a service that's flow- and controller-scoped?
>
> I know what you're thinking—you want to use your service in flow scope, but also use some of its methods from a standard controller. Sorry, but that's almost always a code smell.
>
> The main reason for using flow-scoped services is to keep stateful data. If you want to mix and match stateful and stateless methods, you're probably talking about methods that belong in two different service classes.
>
> One solution is to move your flow-specific stateful code into its own service, and then inject your stateless service into that. This means you can reuse your stateless business logic, use a stateful bean, and keeps things DRY at the same time.

9.3.2 Subflows and conversations

So far we've looked at branching and stepping through a single flow. But when your flow grows, things can get complex. You'll be branching in and out of various parts of your flow, your workflows will become confusing, and your flow state can start to get cluttered. For these scenarios, Grails provides the option of subflows, which let you group some related flow functionality in a separate standalone flow.

Subflows offer several advantages:

- You can reuse a subflow in several different parent flows.
- Your flow state is cleaner because it's scoped only to your subflow, and it's cleaned up on subflow termination
- Grouping logic into subflows makes your flows shorter and more self-contained, and your logic is easier to follow
- You can share data between parent flows and subflows, so you don't sacrifice or duplicate flow data

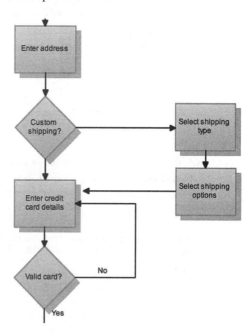

Our postage and shipping calculations are a logical place to use subflows. We'll give the user the option of choosing custom shipping, and if they do, we'll send them off to a subflow that handles shipping options. Figure 9.4 shows an updated section of our flowchart (from figure 9.1), with our new subflow appearing after the address step.

Figure 9.4 Adding a new custom shipping subflow after the address step

On the address page, we'll give the user a Custom Shipping check box, and we'll use that flag to trigger our subflow. We'll need a command object to hold the shipping details: listing 9.11 shows this `ShippingCommand` class. We'll add constraints later, but for now we'll use it as a simple DTO.

Listing 9.11   A `ShippingCommand` object holds the user's shipping preferences

```
class ShippingCommand implements Serializable {

    String address
    String state
    String postcode
    String country
    boolean customShipping
    String shippingType
    String shippingOptions

}
```

Let's get set up to trigger the subflow from our main `orderFlow`. To do that, we need to share our shipping details from the parent flow to the subflow. At the moment, we store our `ShippingCommand` data in flow scope, but flow scope doesn't get passed to subflows. For that, we need *conversation scope*, which covers data shared between the current flow and all subflows. Let's make the modifications to put our shipping details in the conversation, as shown in listing 9.12..

Listing 9.12   Storing details in conversation scope means the data can pass to subflows.

```
enterAddress {
    on("next") { ShippingCommand sc ->        ┐ Places command objects
        conversation.sc = sc            ◁─────┘ in conversation scope
        if (sc.hasErrors()) {
            return error()
        }
    }.to("checkShipping")
    on("previous").to("displayProducts")
}
```

With our shipping details in conversation scope, we're ready to do some branching based on whether the user has any custom shipping requirements. This is a great chance to put our knowledge of action flows to work. Listing 9.13 introduces a check-Shipping action to localize our shipping logic.

Listing 9.13   Using an action step to determine whether we need custom shipping

```
checkShipping {                              ❶ Accesses
    action {                                   conversation-
        if (conversation.sc.customShipping) {  ◁── scoped variables
            custom()
        } else {                           ◁─ ┐ Triggers custom
            standard()     ◁─ ┐             ❷ shipping transition
        }                   ❸ Triggers standard
                              shipping transition
```

```
   }
   on("custom").to("customShipping")          ◄┐  ④  Transitions to
   on("standard").to("enterPayment")   ◄┐         customShipping state
}                                        └── ⑤  Transitions to
                                                enterPayment state
```

In listing 9.13, we first check our shipping command object to see if the user has requested custom shipping ❶. If they have, we invoke the custom() transition ❷ which will transition them to the customShipping state ④. If the user wants standard shipping, we invoke the standard() transition ❸, and the flow continues to enter-Payment as usual ⑤.

It's now time to introduce our customShipping flow state. This new flow state handles branching to a new subflow, and there are a few things you need to know about the process. First, we'll look at the definition in listing 9.14 to give you a taste of the new construct: subflow().

Listing 9.14   Triggering a subflow from the parent flow

```
customShipping {
   subflow(customShippingFlow)            ◄─────┐  ◄──┐  Defines state
   on("goBack").to("enterAddress")              │  ❶   that starts a
   on("standardShipping") {          Ensures    │      subflow
      conversation.sc.customShipping = false    │
   }.to("enterPayment")              subflow name
   on("customShipping").to("enterPayment")  ❷  matches
}                                            current state
                                             name with
                                             Flow suffix
```

The first thing you need to know about subflows is that naming is important. The subflow name ❶ must match the state name ❷ without the "Flow" suffix—the subflow branch to customShippingFlow must happen in a state called customShipping. This is a bit of a tedious convention that will probably go away in some future Grails version, but for now that's the deal.

But where do all those state results come from (goBack, standardShipping, customShipping)? The short answer is that they're the values of the end state returned from the subflow. That will make more sense when you've seen the subflow definition, so let's do that next.

In listing 9.15 we add a new definition to our OrderController for the new customShipping subflow.

Listing 9.15   Implementing a custom shipping subflow

```
def customShippingFlow = {
                                ❶  Allows user to
                                   choose shipping type
   selectShippingType {       ◄─┘
      on("next") {
         conversation.sc.shippingType = params.shippingType
      }.to("selectShippingOptions")
      on("standardShipping").to("standardShipping")
      on("previous").to("goBack")
   }
                                ❷  Defines optional step
                                   for shipping options
   selectShippingOptions {    ◄──┘
```

```
        on("previous").to("selectShippingType")
        on("next") {                              ❸ Saves shipping
           conversation.sc.shippingOptions =         options in
               params.shippingOptions                conversation
        }.to("customShipping")
    }
    customShipping()         ❹ Specifies value
    standardShipping()          to return to
    goBack()                    parent flow
}
```

As you saw in our flowchart (figure 9.4), custom shipping is straightforward. It's a two-step process with the user first choosing a shipping type ❶ and then continuing on to select shipping options ❷. Then they're done.

A subflow looks exactly like any other flow. There are only two differences in a sub-flow:

- The use of conversation-scoped variables (rather than flow-scoped variables) to share and update data from the parent flow
- The use of end states to trigger state change in the parent flow

In listing 9.15, when the user clicks the Next button in the selectShippingOptions flow ❸, the customShipping() end state is triggered. This ends the flow ❹ because there are no more .on() triggers to that state, so the value is returned to the custom-Shipping action in the parent OrderFlow, which looked like this:

```
customShipping {
    subflow(customShippingFlow)
    on("goBack").to("enterAddress")
    on("standardShipping") {
       conversation.sc.customShipping = false
    }.to("enterPayment")
    on("customShipping").to("enterPayment")
}
```

customShipping fires the transition to the next state, enterPayment, and the flow continues as normal. By moving all of that shipping logic into its own flow, we've managed to move a lot of logic out of orderFlow, and we've made a reusable shippingFlow in the process.

But there's still a piece of the puzzle missing. We've covered the logic of subflows, but you might be wondering where the GSP files go for this new subflow. They follow the same convention as for parent flows. If customShippingFlow is defined in Order-Controller (as was the case here), the selectShippingType.gsp file goes in /views /order/customShipping/.

We've covered a lot of advanced information about webflows and subflows, but there's one area we haven't explored: testing. How are we going to test all those flows and subflows to ensure that everything works as we expect? It's time to explore web-flow testing support.

Debugging bizarre webflow errors

When you have a complex graph of flows and subflows, you will inevitably end up with some kind of bizarre serialization error, 404 error, or other problem. In these situations, there are two important options to work through.

First, you can run `grails clean`. You might just have a compilation issue, so clearing out classes and recompiling will often resolve your issue.

If that doesn't work, you can try the second option and configure logging levels in /grails-app/conf/Config.groovy so you can see all of the webflow's internal debug logs. Add a line like this:

```
log4j = {
    debug 'org.springframework.webflow'
}
```

Then restart your server. You'll get verbose output, but it will give you clues as to what states are triggering and what is being serialized in the process. It will take some time to work through it all, but at least you'll have a better idea of what the problem is.

If your problem relates to view resolution (for example, you're getting 404 errors), try configuring log levels for org.springframework to debug. Better still, install the runtime-logging plugin and change your log levels on the fly via /hubbub/runtimeLogging. It gets noisy, but you will get to the bottom of the issue (or possibly raise a JIRA in the process).

9.4   Testing webflows

As with all your other Grails artifacts, you should be giving some thought to how you can test your webflows. The state-tracking side of a webflow makes testing trickier than for your standard controller, but Grails offers some built-in support for mocking the required pieces of the puzzle. Let's take a look at a basic test case to give you an idea of how to get started.

Our work so far has been in the order controller, so we'll start our testing there. All webflow testing must be done in integration tests, so let's create a skeleton integration test case:

```
grails create-integration-test com.grailsinaction.OrderFlowIntegration
```

With our integration test in place, we'll update it to extend `WebFlowTestCase`—the base class for all webflow-related tests. Listing 9.16 shows a simple test case.

Listing 9.16   A simple integration test for our flow

```
package com.grailsinaction

import grails.test.*

class OrderFlowIntegrationTests extends WebFlowTestCase {

    def shopController = new ShopController()
```

**Extends ❶
WebFlowTestCase
to test our flow**

**Returns handle to ❷
flow being tested**

```
def getFlow() { shopController.orderFlow }
void testBasicOrder() {

    startFlow()
    assertCurrentStateEquals "displayProducts"

}
}
```

❸ Specifies flow to test

❹ Starts flow and enters default state

As we said, all webflow test cases are integration tests that extend `WebFlowTestCase` ❶. Extending `WebFlowTestCase` requires that you create a `getFlow()` method ❸ to return the closure action that represents your webflow. In our case, we're working with the `orderFlow`. We then create an instance of `ShopController` that we can keep around for later ❷, because we'll need to simulate supplying `params` to our actions. Finally, we start our `testBasicOrder()` implementation by triggering the `startFlow()` method ❹.

As the name suggests, `startFlow()` is the first action on your flow, and it's one of several methods added by `WebFlowTestCase` that you use to trigger actions on your flows. The most important of these methods are listed in table 9.1.

Table 9.1 Flow-related methods available in `WebFlowTestCase`

Method	Description
startFlow()	Triggers the first state in the current flow
signalEvent(String)	Simulates a user triggering a flow event
setCurrentState(String)	Starts a new flow, moving immediately to the specified state
getFlowScope()	Obtains the current flow scope
getConversationScope()	Obtains the current conversation scope

After starting the flow, we can assert that the current state has been moved to `displayProducts()` using `assertCurrentStateEquals()` ❹. This assertion and others are also added by `WebFlowTestCase` to ensure that your flow is tracking to the correct state. Table 9.2 lists some of the most important assertions available in webflow tests.

Table 9.2 Flow-related assertions available in `WebFlowTestCase`

Assertion	Description
assertCurrentStateEquals(String)	Checks that the current state is active, and that the state name matches the specified string
assertFlowExecutionActive()	Asserts that the flow hasn't reached an end state
assertFlowExecutionEnded()	Asserts that the flow has reached an end state and terminated

Table 9.2 Flow-related assertions available in `WebFlowTestCase` *(continued)*

Assertion	Description
`assertFlowExecutionOutcomeEquals(String)`	When a flow has ended, ensures the outcome name matches the supplied string

Now that you've seen the basics of webflow tests, let's create a more complete test case for our order flow.

9.4.1 Handling input parameters

You learned a lot about testing controllers in chapter 7, so passing parameters in to controllers should be nothing new. But testing in a webflow setting gives you a few more corner cases to deal with.

We'll submit some invalid parameters to our `displayProducts` state, and see how we can enhance our test case to give the flow a lot more test coverage. Listing 9.17 shows our test case with code to submit product order numbers and handle error conditions when the order numbers exceed the maximum allowed.

Listing 9.17 Submitting values and handling error conditions

```
void testBasicOrder() {

    startFlow()
    assertCurrentStateEquals "displayProducts"         ❶ Simulates
                                                          invalid form
    shopController.params.numShirts = 1                   field value with
    shopController.params.numHats = 1000    ◁┐            params object
    signalEvent('next')

    assertTrue getFlowScope().orderDetails.hasErrors()   ❷ Confirms error
    assertCurrentStateEquals "displayProducts"              condition

    shopController.params.numHats = 1      ┌─ ❸ Corrects failing field
    signalEvent('next')                              and resubmits
    assertCurrentStateEquals "enterAddress"    ◁
                                              ┌─ Confirms flow
}                                          ❹   progressed
```

After starting our flow, we start the test by simulating a user submitting an order form with an invalid quantity of hats ❶. The constraint on the command object is that order quantities for items must be between 0 and 10.

Signaling the `next` event submits our parameters to the `displayProduction` action (shown earlier in listing 9.6), resulting in a validation error, and redirecting back to the `displayProducts` state. To refresh your memory, these are the actions we're testing:

```
displayProducts {
    on("next") { OrderDetailsCommand odc ->          ┐ Places failing
        if (odc.hasErrors() || odc.isOrderBlank()) {   order back in
            flow.orderDetails = odc     ◁              flow scope
```

```
        return error()
    }
    [ orderDetails: odc, orderStartDate: new Date() ]
}.to("enterAddress")
on("cancel").to("finish")
}
```

Notice that when validation fails, we place the command object back in flow scope so
we can preserve the previous form values when we rerender the order form. Because
the failed order ends up in flow scope, it means that our test case can assert that the
resulting `orderDetails` object appears in flow scope with the relevant errors attribute,
and the user has been routed back to the `displayProducts` step ❷.

With our error handling tested, we correct the invalid hat quantity and retrigger
the submit ❸. This time, all validations should pass, and we should end up at the
`enterAddress` action ❹.

That's quite a comprehensive test, and it will no doubt give you lots of ideas about
how to write your own. We've toured signaling events, learned how to handle parameters, and even dealt with errors. But we haven't explored subflows and flow termination yet. Let's look at those now.

9.4.2   *Testing subflow transitions*

You'll recall that we moved the custom-shipping logic into a subflow in section 9.3.2.
We'll now write a test for that subflow. But we should first test that when the Custom
Shipping check box is checked, the user is sent to the subflow, and when it isn't
checked, they go straight through to `enterPayment`.

Listing 9.18 shows the updated test code for skipping the custom shipping, then
backing up and selecting it, which should leave you in the subflow.

Listing 9.18   Tripping a subflow

```
void testSubflowTrigger() {

    setCurrentState('enterAddress')          ❶ Moves to enterAddress state

    shopController.params.customShipping = false      ❷ Simulates standard shipping
    signalEvent('next')
    assertEquals false, getConversationScope().sc.customShipping   ❸ Confirms custom shipping is skipped
    assertCurrentStateEquals "enterPayment"

    signalEvent('previous')                  ❹ Simulates clicking Previous button
    assertCurrentStateEquals "enterAddress"

    shopController.params.customShipping = true     ❺ Confirms custom shipping page is displayed
    signalEvent('next')
    assertEquals true, getConversationScope().sc.customShipping
    assertCurrentStateEquals "selectShippingType"
}
```

We start our test by jumping directly to the `enterAddress` state ❶. We then simulate
checking the Custom Shipping check box and clicking the Next button ❷. Without

custom shipping, the user should end up at the `enterPayment` state, so we explicitly check that the subflow has been skipped ❸.

We then simulate clicking the Previous button and check that this returns us to the `enterAddress` state ❹. This time, though, we simulate checking the `customShipping` check box, which starts the subflow and leaves us on the first step of the subflow—the `selectShippingType` page ❺.

We could go on submitting params to the subflow to exercise the entire order process, but we'll leave that as an exercise for you.

With our subflow integration now comprehensively tested, it's time to write a test case to fully test the subflow itself. This will give us a chance to explore flow-termination testing.

9.4.3 Testing flow termination

The last thing we need to test is that flows terminate correctly. Our custom shipping flow has interesting termination characteristics, so it's a good candidate for experimentation. Listing 9.19 reproduces the flow in its entirety.

Listing 9.19 Our custom shipping flow terminates in lots of interesting ways.

```
def customShippingFlow = {

    selectShippingType {
        on("next") {
            conversation.sc.shippingType = params.shippingType
        }.to("selectShippingOptions")
        on("standardShipping").to("standardShipping")
        on("previous").to("goBack")
    }

    selectShippingOptions {
        on("previous").to("selectShippingType")
        on("next") {
            conversation.sc.shippingOptions = params.shippingOptions
        }.to("customShipping")
    }

    customShipping()
    standardShipping()
    goBack()
}
```

First, we need to create an integration test:

```
grails create-integration-test
        com.grailsinaction.CustomShippingFlowIntegration
```

With our shell test case in place, it's time to add some testing logic to exercise our new subflow. Listing 9.20 demonstrates the logic to simulate the user submitting a shipping type and shipping details and ending up at the `customShipping` endpoint.

Listing 9.20 A test case for custom flow termination

```
package com.grailsinaction

import grails.test.*

class CustomShippingFlowIntegrationTests extends WebFlowTestCase {

    def shopController = new ShopController()

    def getFlow() { shopController.customShippingFlow }

    void testFlowTermination() {

        startFlow()
        getConversationScope().sc = new ShippingCommand()
        shopController.params.shippingType = "express"
        signalEvent("next")
        shopController.params.shippingOptions = "same-day"
        signalEvent("next")
        assertFlowExecutionEnded()
        assertFlowExecutionOutcomeEquals(
                    "customShipping")
    }
}
```

❶ Confirms flow
terminated in
correct state

Our test case starts the subflow, and then submits shipping type and custom shipping options. Once those flow events have fired, we can assert that the flow has completed and that the final state of the flow is customShipping ❶. The assertFlowExecution-Ended() call is redundant, because the final assertFlowExecutionOutcomeEquals() assertion ensures that the flow is in an end state, but we include it here for completeness.

That concludes our tour of webflow testing techniques. It's time to review what we've learned.

9.5 *Summary and best practices*

This chapter has taken you on a comprehensive tour of Grails webflow—a highly configurable state-engine for handling Grails UI workflows. You've learned the basics of how states and transitions work, and you've implemented plenty of features that are common to wizard-style checkouts.

We've introduced you to the unique webflow states, *flow* and *conversation*, and used them to store validated command objects that are passed through the flow. We've also explored some of the advanced webflow features, such as subflows and session-scoped services.

We concluded the chapter with a thorough introduction to webflow testing, including all the basics of trigger flows, testing error conditions, and examining flow-termination states.

It's been a comprehensive tour, and we've seen plenty of webflow best practices along the way:

- *Apply webflows selectively.* Know what kinds of problems webflows are useful for, and only use them where they make sense. The most productive webflow features are specific state-engine style interactions, so don't over-apply them.

- *Tame complex forms.* Use webflows for complex form handling—splitting your form over multiple pages and skipping steps that aren't applicable for every user.

- *Favor flow scope.* Favor flow scope over session scope. Webflows will clean up the storage for you and give you more efficient use of server memory.

- *Understand execution params.* Learn the impact of the execution param and how it influences Back buttons and permalinks. Design your flows to minimize that impact.

- *Use command objects.* Make use of command objects to handle form validation for each state of your flow. Use validators on command objects to make them self-describing, and add custom routines to clarify business intent (like isOrderBlank()).

- *Simplify with action states.* Simplify your decision states by using action states. Make good use of transition names to make the logic clearer.

- *Utilize flow-scoped services.* Use flow-scoped services for stateful beans in your flows. The concurrency model is simple, and the services can be cleaned up on flow termination.

- *Write tests.* As with all of your Grails artifacts, write test cases to ensure that your flow works the way you think it does. Writing tests is much quicker in the long run than continuous human-driven UI testing in the browser, and it will help regression testing when new Grails versions come out.

By completing the Hubbub online store, we've given you a thorough introduction to Grails Webflows and added a host of new features to Hubbub. In the next chapter, we'll turn our attention to applying security constraints to Hubbub—ensuring users can only access the features in Hubbub they're permitted to.

Don't let strangers in— security

In this chapter

- Why you need to consider security
- How to protect your application from attacks
- Implementing access control

Hubbub's user interface has improved dramatically in the last couple of chapters, so it's time to consider the implications of releasing Hubbub into the wild. That means understanding what might happen to the application when it's public, and making sure nothing horrible happens. Welcome to the world of security.

10.1 Why security matters

We're sure that you're aware of some of the security issues related to web applications and perhaps some of the techniques for mitigating the risk. We'll cover most of them in relation to Grails, so you'll know what measures you can take to harden your applications against attack and unauthorized access. By the end of the chapter, you'll have the confidence to publish a web application in the real world with real users.

Before we go into the details, though, we'll tell a short story. Company A was a successful bank that wanted to provide an internet service for their customers. They realized that such a system would be under constant threat from villainous rogues trying to gain access to customers' details and their money, so they brought in a system that would turn their internet portal into the virtual equivalent of Fort Knox. No man-in-the-middle attacks would fool it, customers never sent their credentials in full to the server, and everything was done over SSL. For all intents and purposes, it was impregnable.

Then, one day, an employee copied the details of thousands of customers to a laptop to continue working at home. The next morning, the employee accidentally left the laptop on the train, and it was gone. The details on that computer, all unencrypted, were worth far more than the laptop itself. It was a huge embarrassment to the company, which had to contact all the affected customers and inform them of the incident. Many of them closed their accounts and went elsewhere. The bank's reputation suffered almost irreparable damage.

This is a fictional story, and we hope that no bank would ever allow employees to copy customer data (particularly unencrypted data) and carry it around. Yet there have been several high-profile incidents in which laptops have been left in public places and confidential information has been lost in the mail!

The point behind the story is that security isn't a product or a technology; it isn't something you can buy off the shelf. Making your application accessible only via SSL doesn't magically make it secure. Security is a process and a mindset. We don't expect you to push for a change of organizational mindset at your company, but we do think it's important to keep the moral of that story in your mind when developing applications, even if you're just working on a personal project in your spare time.

Let's explore some of the threats that your applications face and the ways that you can protect against them.

10.2 *Protecting against malicious intent*

You have probably heard of the internet worms that travel the world in minutes and infect website after website, and of websites that have been defaced and applications that have been tricked into giving confidential information to people who shouldn't have access to it. There's certainly no shortage of people who are willing to invest a bit of time in these nefarious activities. Your job is to stop them from doing something similar to your own applications.

The most important thing you can do is think about what you're developing and always consider the security aspect. If we can also get you thinking like an attacker, then so much the better! Just don't turn into one and then blame us. We like to avoid legal entanglements.

In this section, we'll take you through some simple steps and thought processes that will considerably reduce your risk of exposure and protect you against the majority of potential attacks. Although our examples are presented in the context of Grails, you can apply the concepts to any development in any language.

We'll start by considering one of the biggest areas of weakness in software: dealing with external inputs.

10.2.1 *Validate all your inputs*

Imagine that you want to search in Hubbub for all posts that have been tagged "grails". There are millions of such posts because it's such a cool topic to discuss, and if Hubbub attempted to return *all* of them, the request would punish both the server and the client. To prevent this, Hubbub returns 50 by default. But suppose you only want the 10 most recent results.

We can deal with that in Hubbub by accepting a max parameter (which would contain the value 10) and passing that through to the underlying query:

```
def search = {
   def max = params.max?.toInteger() ?: 50
   def results = Post.findAllByTag("grails", [ max: max ])
   ...
}
```

Note that this code doesn't match the Hubbub application as it stands, but it serves to illustrate an important point. You might look at it and think there's nothing wrong, but there's a fundamental flaw: it trusts the user. Consider what would happen if the user tried this URL: http://localhost:8080/hubbub/post/search?query=grails&max =1000000000.

That's a max value of one billion! Our action will now attempt to return and display all the posts with the tag "grails" (there aren't *quite* a billion such posts). A few requests like that, and your server will grind to a halt. It's a classic denial of service (DoS) scenario.

The moral is simple: never trust external sources of data—validate everything you use. A simple solution in this particular case is to cap the value of max:

```
def max = params.max?.toInteger() ?: 50
max = Math.min(max, 500)
```

This small change will allow a user to request up to 500 posts, but no more. This is a simple case, but what if you have several parameters to check across lots of actions?

An alternative approach is to use command objects, which allow you to declare validation constraints and check whether there are errors. Because you can reuse command objects in different actions, you end up with a system that's much easier to maintain than if you manually validated the parameters. You also get all the other benefits of command objects that you saw earlier in the book.

Alternatively, if you don't want the hassle of creating a command object, try the multitalented bindData() method instead. The following example binds all parameters except any named "created":

```
def update = {
   def post = new Post()
   bindData(post, params, ["created"])
   ...
}
```

Chapter 5 introduced this blacklist version of the method, in which the third argument to `bindData()` is a list of the domain class fields that must not be bound.
Because a user should not be able to affect the time at which a post is created, we
exclude that field. `bindData()` also excludes some default properties: `id`, `version`,
`metaClass`, and `properties` (the last two are related to Groovy, so don't worry about
them). Note that this method is dynamically injected into controllers, so you can't use
it from services or domain classes.

The dangers of binding to domain classes

As you have seen, you can also bind parameters directly to domain objects. This is
dangerous, because any parameter value matching a domain class field will be
bound. An attacker could modify a property that you don't want them to.

You can use a command object instead, and then bind its properties to the domain
object, like so:

```
def update = { PostCommand cmd ->
   if (!cmd.hasErrors()) {
      def post = new Post(cmd.properties)
      ...
   }
   ...
}
```

"Aha!" we hear you cry. "What if I do the validation on the client? Then I don't have to
bother with it on the server." Validation on the client is definitely useful for the user,
but it would be a mistake to then leave it out of the server.

DOUBLE VALIDATION

Whenever you develop a web application, remember that the interface to the application isn't a browser: it's the HTTP protocol. Anyone can send requests to your application from any client. They can even use telnet and manually craft the HTTP requests;
after all, HTTP is a pretty simple text-based protocol. Your client-side validation won't
be activated in such a situation. Alternatively, the user may disable JavaScript in their
browser.

What this means for your application is that it could receive anything from a client—and probably will. This is why you have to do validation on your server as well as
in the client. We know it's not DRY (Don't Repeat Yourself), but unfortunately it's the
price you have to pay for a rich client backed by a publicly accessible server. This rule
holds no matter what type of client you use, whether it be JavaScript in a browser, a
Flash application, or a Java applet.

It's not just the stuff in the `params` object you have to worry about, either. What if you're handling requests that contain data that you need to read from the request directly?

OTHER TYPES OF REQUESTS

As you'll see in the next chapter, you may have requests that contain XML, JSON, or even custom data. In such cases, the information is usually not added to the `params` object, so the data-binding techniques we've shown so far won't work. What can you do?

If it's possible with the data you're receiving, you could parse it into a map of parameters and values that you could then use with the `bindData()` method. JSON data is particularly amenable to this approach. Alternatively, if you're dealing with XML, you should consider using XML Schema. This allows you to add constraints to attribute values and element content, so you can provide input validation in a declarative manner.

If all else fails, you'll have to roll your own validation, even if that means checking the values manually as we did with the `max` parameter in the example earlier. Using no validation at all isn't an option, or at least not a safe one.

You should now see that validating input is crucial to protecting your application. Fortunately, with simple data checks, careful data binding, and constraints, you can easily protect yourself against malign HTTP requests. As you'll see in the Hubbub source code for this chapter, we've implemented the necessary changes in the controllers.

Such code will get you a long way to ensuring that your web applications remain safe in a dangerous world, but don't think the story is over. You'll almost certainly write an application in the future that gets information from a different source or in a format that doesn't fit the data-binding mechanisms. At that point, the most important thing to remember is that the input should be validated, come what may.

Usually, input validation isn't enough on its own. Dangerous input isn't always obvious and can be difficult to detect. That means you need to be careful about what you *do* with any input data you receive.

10.2.2 *Escape all your outputs*

Imagine that we have a controller action in Hubbub that displays all the posts for a given user. For example, here's a useful query that does this:

```
def userId = "peter"
Post.findAll("from Post as post WHERE post.user.userId = '${userId}'")
```

This query uses a local `userId` property to control which posts are returned. Looks pretty innocent, doesn't it?

Go ahead and try it in the Grails console—copy the two lines of the example, and execute. Depending on how much data you have, you should see something like the first screenshot in figure 10.1.

Figure 10.1 **An HQL query run first with a perfectly safe input value (on the left) and a second time with an example SQL injection attack (on the right). In the latter case, all posts in the database are returned by the query.**

Data and the console

If your database is configured for `create-drop` or has no data in it, the examples in this section won't be particularly helpful. You can quickly populate the database with some sample data by running these two lines in the console:

```
def bs = new BootStrap()
bs.init()
```

Now imagine that an attacker modifies the URL of the request so that the `userId` parameter has the value in this example:

```
def userId = "' or 'test' = 'test"
Post.findAll("from Post as post WHERE post.user.userId = '${userId}'")
```

The query is the same, but this time `userId` doesn't look like an ID at all. Look what happens when we substitute the value into the query:

```
... WHERE post.user.userId = '' or 'test' = 'test'
```

Oooh, sneaky! What the attacker has done is modify the query so that all posts are returned, which could quite easily bring your server to a grinding halt! This is an example of what is known as a SQL injection attack. The second screenshot in figure 10.1 shows its effect.

Input validation may stop the request from ever getting to the point where the query is executed, but in many cases validation can't prevent dangerous values from getting through without blocking valid ones as well. Fortunately, there's a simple solution: by escaping the input value before inserting it into the query, you foil the attack.

NOTE You'll rarely suffer from this problem in your Grails applications because both dynamic finders and criteria queries automatically escape their arguments.

We'll finish off this little example with a modified version of the HQL query that's safe from the attack because it escapes the value of userId:

```
def userId = "' or 'test' = 'test"
Post.findAll("from Post as post WHERE post.user.userId = ?", [ userId ])
```

This is the Hibernate equivalent of a JDBC parameterized query.

We'll now consider another, related scenario. Start the Hubbub server, log in to the application, and then try to post this message (verbatim!):

```
<script type="text/javascript">alert("Got ya!")</script>
```

What happens? A dialog pops up showing the message "Got ya!" Now every time you refresh your timeline page, that message will pop up. Oops, that doesn't look good. You have just demonstrated how a cross-site scripting (XSS) attack works. It's another form of injection attack, but in this case it targets HTML and JavaScript rather than SQL.

Not surprisingly, the solution is the same as for SQL injection: escape the user input before displaying it in a web page. This can either be done manually, by calling the encodeAsHTML() method on the text you want to display, or automatically, by adding (or changing) this entry in grails-app/conf/Config.groovy:

```
grails.views.default.codec = "html"
```

With this setting, Grails will escape all expressions in your GSP files for HTML—and you don't have to lift a finger!

WARNING Although the grails.views.default.codec setting works in most cases, it won't escape any values in GSP tag attributes, nor will it escape the output of tags themselves. Tags should perform any required escaping or encoding themselves.

To see the effect of the setting in practice, consider this fragment of GSP code:

```
<div>${post.content}</div>
<g:textField name="test" value="${post.content}"/>
```

The post's content is escaped automatically in the first line, because it's referenced from inside a standalone expression. But Grails won't do the same for the value attribute on the second line. That's why the implementation of the textField tag does the equivalent of this:

```
attrs["value"].encodeAsHTML()
```

In general, though, if you use HTML as the default GSP codec and the standard Grails GSP tags, you don't have to worry. Just be aware that any custom GSP tags you write should take account of escaping issues if they write any of their input directly to the output.

We're almost done here, but we think it worth mentioning that escaping or encoding user input won't work if you don't pick the right codec for the job. For example, if an input value is going into a URL link, use the `encodeAsURL()` method; if it's going elsewhere in an HTML page, use the HTML codec.

We've only given examples of two types of injection attack here, but there are others, such as code injection (say, if you allow users to provide Groovy code that you then run), OS command injection (anything passed to `Runtime.exec()` or equivalent), and file-path injection. In all these cases, be aware whether you're dealing with untrusted input or not, and if so, escape it or cleanse it some other way.

Along with input validation, escaping your output appropriately protects you from a whole class of potential attacks. Although the potential consequences are severe, we hope that you'll gain confidence from how simple it is to shield your application from those attacks. Awareness is the key: always think, "am I using untrusted input, and if so, what am I doing with it?"

We've so far concerned ourselves with dealing with inputs from untrusted sources, but if your application were to hold sensitive information about users, you'd face another issue. How do you transfer that information without people being able to read it?

10.2.3 SSL, encryption, and message digests

Imagine that your bank's internet portal allowed you to send your user ID and password (or other credential) unencrypted. Does that sound like a safe thing to do? We certainly don't think so, and that bank would lose customers pretty quickly. The problem is that although you think you're sending information directly to the website, its route is often far from straight, and this gives attackers the opportunity to look at that information.

The standard solution is to use the HTTPS protocol, which encrypts all communication between the browser and the server by using Secure Sockets Layer (SSL). As an added bonus, SSL requires the server to publish an SSL certificate, which gives users confidence that they're using the real website rather than a fake.

Running your Grails application in HTTPS mode is as simple as passing the `--https` argument to the `run-app` or `run-war` command. You'll then be able to access the application via an https://localhost:8443/... URL as well as with the more usual http://localhost:8080/... one.

If you do run Hubbub or your own application like this, you'll notice that your browser doesn't seem too happy when accessing it. Figure 10.2 shows you what Firefox thinks of Hubbub over HTTPS. The problem is that Grails creates a *self-signed* SSL certificate on demand. In effect, your application is saying, "trust me, I am who I say I am." In this case, you know that you can trust it because you started the server, but how can real users do so?

In order to avoid such messages from the browser, you need to get your SSL certificate signed by what is known as a Certificate Authority (CA), like VeriSign, Thawte, Comodo, or Go Daddy. Most (if not all) browsers recognize and trust these providers by default, so when users access websites that have certificates signed by one of them,

Figure 10.2   Trying to access Hubbub via HTTPS with Firefox 3. The browser doesn't like the self-signed certificate, but you can accept it by adding it as an exception (see the link at the bottom of the screen).

they see the locked padlock (or some other indication that the site is secure) and no warning or error messages.

So how do you get your certificate signed by one of these CAs? All the providers will give you explicit instructions for doing this, but the general procedure is something like this:

1 Create a private key for your server using the JDK's `keytool` command.
2 Generate a Certificate Signing Request (CSR).
3 Send the CSR to the CA.
4 Wait for them to send you a signed certificate back, and then import it into your keystore.

SSL may be the closest most web application developers get to encryption, but that doesn't mean it's the only time you'll ever need it. In case you ever find yourself contemplating using manual encryption or signing (a relative of encryption), here are a few guidelines that may help:

- Use industry-standard encryption and hashing algorithms—don't try to roll your own!
- Don't use algorithms with known vulnerabilities, such as DES, SHA-1, and MD5.
- Don't transfer private keys!

You'll see that we mentioned SHA-1 and MD5 in that list. These aren't encryption algorithms but hash functions that create a fixed-length representation of some given data. That representation is called a "hash" or "digest." The idea is that if the data were to change, then so would its hash. This allows you to detect whether data has been tampered with if you know what its original hash was. Instead of SHA-1 and MD5, consider using SHA-256 or SHA-512. These have no known weaknesses at this time and can be used in the same way as the older hash functions.

NOTE   If you are interested in why SHA-1 and MD5 are considered vulnerable, the Wikipedia articles for the two functions are a good starting point.

We're already using a hash function in Hubbub to store the users' passwords, and this is quite a common technique. Any website that will reset your password instead of sending it to you is probably storing passwords like this—there's no way for it to get the original data (the password, in this case) from the hash. It's a one-way algorithm. The main reason for using hashing in this way is so that even if people have access to the data in the database, they can't then use the password to impersonate another user.

That's a pretty quick tour of cryptography, and we've barely touched the surface. For most people, using SSL will solve any confidentiality requirements that they have. Just make sure that users can't access confidential information via (unencrypted) HTTP. Before we move on, we'd like to mention The Legion of the Bouncy Castle (http://www.bouncycastle.org/), who have an incredibly useful open source Java Cryptography Extension (JCE) provider with quite a few encryption algorithms, such as Blowfish. They even have classes for working with OpenPGP.

We've now covered three areas of concern, but there's one more left. It's not a vulnerability, but it's nearly as important.

10.2.4   Don't give away information

Imagine for a moment that you're one of those unscrupulous types who wants to hack into an application. What would you do? You could try some of the injection attacks we've already seen, but the developer has closed those holes. That means you have to try a lot of different attacks to find a vulnerability.

An alternative approach is to find out what platform the web application is based on. If you know that, you can narrow your hacking attempts to known vulnerabilities of the platform. Finding out that information can be trivial. Take a look at this URL: http://www.somecompany.com/orders/buy.php.

Unless the company is being clever, it's a pretty safe bet that PHP is the underlying technology on this website.

Grails applications don't make it quite so obvious, but there are still weaknesses. Try pointing your browser at this URL while Hubbub is up and running: http://localhost:8080/hubbub/path/unknown.

You can see the result in figure 10.3: any attacker now knows that Hubbub is a Java web application running on Jetty. Even worse, if your application throws an exception, Grails will display its standard error page. Then the attacker also knows that your application uses Grails.

Back in chapter 5, we introduced you to a feature that helps in this situation: mapping response codes to controllers. Ideally, we want to map all the error response codes that Grails typically generates to our own views:

Figure 10.3   Hitting an unknown page displays information about the platform by default. Try to avoid gifting attackers such useful information.

```
class UrlMappings {
    ...
    "403"(controller: "errors", action: "forbidden")
    "404"(controller: "errors", action: "notFound")
    "500"(controller: "errors", action: "internalError")
}
```

You'll see in the next chapter that there are plenty of other HTTP status codes you could map, but it's only worth mapping the ones that your application uses. If any part of the application uses a different status code from those listed here, add an entry for it to the URL mappings.

Unfortunately, that's not quite the end of the story. Certain parts of the GSP infrastructure are currently hard-coded to display the view grails-app/views/error.gsp if an exception is thrown by a GSP page. This completely bypasses the mechanism we just used, declaring to the whole world that your application is implemented with Grails. To work around this issue, we recommend that you modify the GSP to send a "500" error if the environment is set to production:

```
<%@ page import="grails.util.Environment" %>
<g:if test="${Environment.current == Environment.PRODUCTION}">
    ${response.sendError(500)}
</g:if>
<g:else>
    ...
</g:else>
```

This change means that your production application won't be divulging information about its platform, but you still get the benefits of the error message and stack trace when running in development and test environments.

You can breathe a sigh of relief now—we've completed our coverage of typical web application vulnerabilities and the techniques you can use to remove them. You now know enough to make sure that your application isn't as leaky as the typical website, plus you have the mindset and tools to tighten the security further.

All of the information we've discussed in this section and more is covered in the "CWE/SANS Top 25 Most Dangerous Programming Errors" (http://cwe.mitre.org/top25/) and the OWASP "Top 10" (http://www.owasp.org/index.php/Top_10_2007). These websites are a must-read—they give you lots of information about the hazards that await the application developer with regard to security. You'll also find some useful tools at OWASP such as Scarab, a tool that will automatically test your application for common vulnerabilities.

Before we move on to another essential aspect of application security, we should mention that code reviews are a great way of preventing vulnerabilities from slipping into your code. So long as the whole team is always reviewing code with one eye on security, your applications will stay secure.

Protecting against malicious intent is a major part of application security, and by considering whether your code is vulnerable as you write it, you can mitigate a lot of the risk. Yet, that's only part of the puzzle. If any part of your application is restricted to specific users or groups of users, you need to make sure that people can't see or do what they shouldn't.

10.3 Access control

Many applications need to know who the user is, either because they're storing information that should only be visible to certain (known) people, or because they need to restrict access to some or all of their functionality. Maybe they need to track who does what. In Hubbub, for example, we're not interested in anonymous posts: when a user posts a new message, Hubbub needs to know who posted it. We also want to make sure that only a user can modify his or her own profile. Nobody else should be allowed to do so, except perhaps a system administrator.

This is what access control is all about. It can range from simply making sure that only real people (as opposed to "bots") can access an application, to using complex rules based on multiple permissions, projects, and groups. Hubbub falls firmly into the first category, but we'll try to provide enough information that you can readily go beyond the basics.

A question of terminology

The phrase "authentication and authorization" is fairly common and means pretty much the same thing as "access control," but the latter is currently the preferred term in security circles. Different security frameworks also tend to have their own jargon, which can make comparing them quite difficult. If in doubt, pick one that you understand.

Access control breaks down into two main aspects:

- Is the person you're communicating with who they say they are (authentication)?
- Do they have the rights to perform a given action (authorization)?

Simple access control can be implemented via standard Grails filters and the session, but you're almost invariably better off using one of the available security plugins. Why reinvent the wheel? These are the main candidates:

- *Authentication plugin* The Authentication plugin is a lightweight authentication implementation with no dependencies on any third-party libraries. It's good for websites that require registered users but don't have complex authorization requirements.
- *JSecurity plugin* The JSecurity plugin provides full-featured access control and cryptography via the Apache JSecurity library (currently an Incubator project). Although JSecurity isn't widely known yet, it has been used in production systems for several years.
- *Spring Security (Acegi) plugin* Formerly known as Acegi Security, Spring Security is a well-known and widely used framework for Java web applications. It provides the most comprehensive suite of authentication options of the three plugins listed here. Newcomers often find it difficult to understand, but the plugin does a great job of hiding much of the complexity.

A couple of options we haven't listed here are the standard Java Authentication and Authorization Service (JAAS), which comes as part of the JDK, and J2EE access control as provided by J2EE containers. Although standards, they aren't widely used in the Grails community, and JAAS is quite difficult to use and understand. That said, if you find yourself using them, documentation for both should apply to Grails applications.

The plugins operate as gatekeepers to the web application, as illustrated in figure 10.4. They decide whether a particular request is allowed through to the application, based on configured rules. If a request is allowed, the plugin displays the application's response. Otherwise, it may require the client to log in, or it may display an "access denied" page.

We can't cover all of these plugins in this chapter, so we'll concentrate on the Spring Security plugin. Many of the ideas we'll discuss apply equally to the other plugins, so you should have no trouble using them in combination with their online documentation.

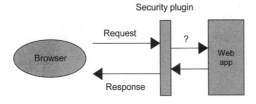

Figure 10.4 How the typical Grails security plugin fits into the request/response cycle. The "?" highlights where the request may or may not be forwarded to the application at the plugin's discretion.

10.3.1 *Getting started with Spring Security*

Access control is impossible without determining who the current user is. Hubbub currently does this by requiring users to enter their user ID and password on the login page and then storing the corresponding `User` instance in the HTTP session (assuming authentication is successful). We want to replace this basic mechanism with the more full-featured Spring Security.

The first step is to install the plugin:

```
grails install-plugin acegi
```

You may find the name of the plugin a little confusing, but it makes sense when you realize that the plugin was first created while the framework was still called Acegi Security.

With that done, you now have access to a small collection of useful scripts, one of which generates the domain classes that the Spring Security plugin needs. Without them, you'll have no access control.

If you were creating an application from scratch and using Spring Security from the start, this process would be straightforward:

```
grails create-auth-domains org.example.User org.example.Role
➥ org.example.Requestmap
```

This would create three classes in grails-app/domain/org/example: `User`, `Role`, and `Requestmap`. We'll explain what these are for in due course, but first we have to deal with the fact that we already have a `User` class, and we'd quite like to keep it. So, rather than using the preceding command, we use this one:

```
grails create-auth-domains DummyUser
➥ com.grailsinaction.Role Requestmap
```

In this case, our existing `User` class won't be overwritten, but now the plugin is configured to get user information from the `DummyUser` class.

Not to worry, that's easily fixed. The plugin can use any domain class for the user as long as it contains fields for the username, password, whether the account is enabled or not, and a collection of authorities, or roles. Our `User` domain class already has the first two, so all we have to do is add the other two:

```
class User {
    String userId
    String password
    boolean enabled

    static hasMany = [ authorities: com.grailsinaction.Role,
                    ... ]
    static belongsTo = com.grailsinaction.Role
    ...
}
```

We also need to fix the `Role` class, because it's currently linked to `DummyUser`, so we change the relationship like so:

```
class Role {
   static hasMany = [people: User]
   ...
}
```

Because we have our own user class, we don't need `DummyUser` any more. Removing it helps keep the application uncluttered. Because the associated scaffold pages won't work without the domain class, we should also remove `DummyUserController` and its views (grails-app/views/dummyUser).

The `User` and `Role` classes form the basis of our access-control system, determining who can do what. It's a simple model, as demonstrated in figure 10.5. One last thing we need to do is update the code in `BootStrap` so that all the preconfigured users are assigned a role, or authority. Users who have none can't log in. What the code for this looks like is unimportant at this stage, but you can see the changes in the sample Hubbub code for the chapter. You'll also see in the code that we use the plugin's `authenticateService` object to encode passwords before storing them in the database:

```
authenticateService.encodePassword("password")
```

Although we'll move on now, don't worry. We'll come back to this service a little later.

Next, we need to configure Spring Security to work with our custom `User` class. When you ran the `create-auth-domains` command, it sneakily added an extra file to your grails-app/conf directory:

Figure 10.5   The relationship between the core access-control domain classes. The model is simple.

SecurityConfig.groovy. This one file allows you to control many aspects of the plugin and Spring Security—it even has an extensive reference page: http://www.grails.org/ AcegiSecurity+Plugin+-+Customizing+with+ SecurityConfig.

The copy of SecurityConfig.groovy in Hubbub currently looks like this (give or take a comment or two):

```
security {
   active = true
   loginUserDomainClass = "DummyUser"
   authorityDomainClass = "com.grailsinaction.Role"
   requestMapClass = "Requestmap"
}
```

You should recognize the last three values because they were the ones you passed to the `create-auth-domains` command. You can probably guess what we do next: change the `loginUserDomainClass` value to `com.grailsinaction.User`. Voila! Spring Security is now using our own `user` class.

WARNING   Be careful with the `active` configuration option: setting it to `false` will disable Spring Security, and you'll lose your access control! Even more important, the same will happen if the option is removed from the file or the file itself is deleted.

We're not quite done yet. By default, the plugin expects the `user` domain class to contain fields named `username` and `passwd`, but ours are `userId` and `password`. To fix this, we add the following two options to SecurityConfig.groovy:

```
userName = "userId"
password = "password"
```

So far so good. Spring Security isn't doing anything for us yet, but it's primed and ready. All we have to do is point and shoot, or, more specifically, configure the URLs that we want protected.

10.3.2 Protecting URLs

We're going to start with a simple security model for Hubbub: all pages will require an authenticated user *except* the home page, which anyone will be able to view. The plugin gives us three options for specifying this information:

- *Static config*—The rules are declared in SecurityConfig.groovy.
- *Dynamic*—The rules are stored in the database as `Requestmaps`.
- *Annotations*—The rules are declared using annotations in controllers and services.

Now you know what the `Requestmap` domain class is for! It maps URLs to permissions, or "authorities" in Spring Security terminology. This approach is useful if you want to change the security settings after the application has been deployed. Annotations allow you to secure controllers regardless of the URL used to access them. They're also convenient for securing service methods.

For Hubbub, though, we're going with the old-fashioned static-config approach, partly because it keeps all the security information together, and partly because we need to talk about the ordering of rules. Because we aren't using dynamic URL rules, we can delete the `Requestmap` domain class, its corresponding controller, and the associated views.

Let's now look at the configuration we'll be using to implement the required access control. Listing 10.1 shows you the SecurityConfig.groovy file that we end up with once the URL rules are added. This ensures that all users have access to the home and login pages, but only authenticated users can see the rest of the application. We also make sure that all JavaScript, CSS, and image files are unsecured.

Listing 10.1 Spring Security configuration for Hubbub's simple access-control model

```
security {
    active = true
    cacheUsers = false         ⟵┘ Disables Hibernate cache

    loginUserDomainClass = "com.grailsinaction.User"
    authorityDomainClass = "com.grailsinaction.Role"
    userName = "userId"
    password = "password"                    ❶ Disables
                                               dynamic rules
    useRequestMapDomainClass = false   ⟵┘
```

```
    requestMapString = """\
CONVERT_URL_TO_LOWERCASE_BEFORE_COMPARISON
PATTERN_TYPE_APACHE_ANT
/=IS_AUTHENTICATED_ANONYMOUSLY
/login/auth=IS_AUTHENTICATED_ANONYMOUSLY
/js/**=IS_AUTHENTICATED_ANONYMOUSLY
/css/**=IS_AUTHENTICATED_ANONYMOUSLY
/images/**=IS_AUTHENTICATED_ANONYMOUSLY
/plugins/**=IS_AUTHENTICATED_ANONYMOUSLY
/**=IS_AUTHENTICATED_FULLY
    """
}
```

❷ **Configures URL rules**

The first half of the file is mostly stuff you've seen already—it's the second half that we're interested in right now. In order to use the static config, we first disable the dynamic `Requestmap` handling ❶. Then come the URL rules themselves, in a multi-line string assigned to the `requestMapString` option ❷. Note that the configuration is line-based, so make sure every entry is on its own line.

The first two lines of the configuration are general settings and are typically included in all Spring Security configurations. The first one forces Spring Security to lowercase the URLs of requests before comparing them to the rules. A URL like

```
http://localhost:8080/hubbub/starPost/showAll
```

would become

```
http://localhost:8080/hubbub/starpost/showall
```

before the comparison. That means your URL rules in `requestMapString` should be all lowercase. The second general setting specifies that Spring Security will use standard Ant path-matching behavior when comparing request URLs to rules. This means that to create a rule that matches all .js files, you could use `/**/*.js`, which specifies any file with a .js extension in any directory.

After the general settings, we declare the rules we want in order. Because we want the home page accessible to anyone, the first rule assigns IS_AUTHENTICATED_ ANONYMOUSLY to the root URL (/). We also need to allow everyone access to the login page (/login/auth) provided by the plugin—otherwise no one could log in! The static resources, such as JavaScript, CSS, and image files (provided by the application and plugins), are also configured this way. Finally, we restrict access to all other URLs to authenticated users—those who have successfully logged in.

You have to be careful with the order of these rules, because Spring Security uses the first one that matches the request URL. For example, if you put the last rule first (/**), all pages of your application would require an authenticated user regardless of the rules that come after. The more specific the URL pattern in a rule, the earlier it should go in the list.

Hubbub is now secured against anonymous access. If a user doesn't have an account, he can't post any messages. Try it out by starting the server and pointing your browser at http://localhost:8080/hubbub/post/timeline. You'll automatically be redirected to the plugin's login page, shown in figure 10.6.

Figure 10.6   The Spring Security plugin's standard login page, with the "Remember me" check box

You can log in using one of the existing users, such as `glen` with a password of `password`, but this will generate a server error. We still need to integrate the login with the rest of the application, which currently expects to find the `User` instance in the session.

Before we do that, let's take a quick look at that "Remember me" option on the plugin's login page. It's a feature we're sure you're familiar with from various websites, and it suits Hubbub quite well. The application doesn't need a high degree of security, so allowing the user to access the application without logging in every time is a big win. The problem is, if you come back to Hubbub after some time, you'll find you can't access the application. In fact, the browser gets confused because it keeps being redirected to the same page again and again. Spring Security sees that the user is remembered and bypasses the login page. Unfortunately, most of the application's pages require a fully authenticated user, so the user is redirected to the /login/denied page. This also requires a fully authenticated user, so we get stuck in a loop!

WARNING   Never allow the user to select the "Remember me" option if the application doesn't support it. If you're using the default login page provided by the plugin, remove the "Remember me" check box.

For Hubbub, we want to support "Remember me," and to do that we change this URL rule

```
/**=IS_AUTHENTICATED_FULLY
```

to this:

```
/**=IS_AUTHENTICATED_REMEMBERED
```

That's it! The "Remember me" feature now works, and the browser won't get stuck.

Now that we've sorted out that problem, let's make the access control work better for Hubbub.

10.3.3 *Getting hold of the current user*

The access control is looking promising so far, and we haven't had to do much work. It's not quite working for us yet, but that won't take long to fix. The first thing we need to do is fix the user's timeline page, which is currently generating a "500" error because it can't access the logged-in user.

We have a couple of options available to us. First, we could store the User instance in the session when the user logs in, because we can edit the login controller that the plugin created for us (grails-app/controllers/LoginController.groovy). But this would be a bit of a waste because we can get it from Spring Security directly. Why use up valuable session space if we don't have to? So instead, we'll go with the second option: change the application code to get the user from Spring Security.

One way to do this would be to get the current Spring Security context from the SecurityContextHolder class and extract the user. This context represents all the security information related to the current user, so it can provide you with pretty much anything you need. It's not particularly pleasant to deal with, though, so it's fortunate that the plugin provides the authenticate service. This service contains lots of useful methods, most of which are listed in table 10.1.

Table 10.1   A summary of useful methods provided by the plugin's authenticate service

Method	Description
isLoggedIn()	Returns true if the current user is logged in, otherwise false
ifAllGranted(roles)	Returns true if the current user has all the given roles, otherwise false; roles is a comma-separated list of role names as a string
ifNotGranted(roles)	Similar to ifAllGranted, but only returns true if the user has none of the given roles
ifAnyGranted(roles)	Similar to ifAllGranted, but returns true if the user has at least one of the given roles
userDomain()	Returns the domain instance for the current user
encodePassword(pwd)	Encodes the given password with the configured hash algorithm and returns the hash; this hash can be stored in the password field of the user domain class
isAjax(request)	Returns true if the given HttpServletRequest appears to be an AJAX one

As you can probably guess, we want to use the userDomain() method to get hold of the User instance. One thing to bear in mind is that the method returns a *detached* instance, which means it isn't bound to the underlying Hibernate session. That means we can't access any of its collections or save any changes to it until we reattach it to the session. In this case, because we want to make sure we have the user's latest details, we refetch the user from the database.

Here are the changes we need to make in the post controller:

```
class PostController {
   def authenticateService
   ...
   def list = {
      def user = authenticateService.userDomain()
      user = User.get(user.id)
      ...
   }
   ...
   def add = {
      def content = params.postContent
      if (content) {
         def user = authenticateService.userDomain()
         user = User.get(user.id)

         if (user) {
            ...
         }
      }
      ...
   }
   ...
}
```

The plugin's authenticate service will be injected into the `authenticateService` property by Grails, and we can then use it to get hold of the current user.

That fixes the controller, but if you try to access the /post/timeline page, you'll still get an error. Our sidebar GSP template still grabs the user directly from the HTTP session. Your first thought may be to access the authenticate service from the template (an ugly solution, and a bad idea) or add the user to the model returned by the action (a better idea). Unfortunately, the sidebar template is referenced from a layout, so all views that use that layout will require the model to contain the user instance.

Fortunately, we don't have to worry about that problem because the plugin provides us with a tag library that does what we need. Instead of code like this

```
<dd>${session.user.userId}</dd>
```

our grails-app/views/post/_sidebar.gsp can use a special tag that allows us to print out any field of the user instance:

```
<dl>
  <dt>User</dt>
  <dd><g:loggedInUserInfo field="userId">Guest</g:loggedInUserInfo>
</dl>
```

We can also use this tag as a method, as in this example fragment:

```
<g:createLink action="following" controller="friend"
         id="${loggedInUserInfo(field: 'userId')}"/>
```

Once we've implemented these few changes, Hubbub will come roaring back to life.

While we're on the subject of GSP tags, we can add the following block to any of our layouts so that users can log out at any time:

```
<g:isLoggedIn>
  <g:link controller="logout" action="index">sign out</g:link>
</g:isLoggedIn>
```

The `isLoggedIn` tag is another one provided by the plugin. It only writes out its contents if the user is logged in via Spring Security. In this case, the content is a link to the logout controller created by the plugin earlier (in our application's grails-app /controllers directory).

The access control is working nicely now. Only authenticated (or remembered) users can access the /post/timeline page, and new posts are correctly associated with the currently logged-in user. We can even provide a link allowing the user to log out. What more do we need?

One problem is that we now have two login pages, so it would be good to get rid of one. Let's keep the old one that sits on our home page.

10.3.4　*Using a custom login page*

The process of configuring the plugin to use our home page as its login page is easy—we add these entries to SecurityConfig.groovy:

```
loginFormUrl = "/"
defaultTargetUrl = "/post/timeline"
```

The first option makes sure that Spring Security redirects to the home page when authentication is required, and the second tells Spring Security to load the user's timeline page by default after a successful login. If the user is redirected to the home page to authenticate, Spring Security will then redirect back to the original page.

Unfortunately, that's not quite all we have to do. Our existing login form won't work as it is because the fields need to have special names—ones that are recognized by Spring Security. On the bright side, this gives us an opportunity to add a "Remember me" box. Here is the new form in grails-app/views/_sidebar.gsp:

```
<form action="${resource(file: 'j_spring_security_check')}" method="POST">
  <table>
    <tr><td>User Id:</td><td><g:textField name="j_username"/></td></tr>
    <tr>
      <td>Password:</td>
      <td><input name="j_password" type="password"/></td>
    </tr>
    <tr>
      <td>Remember:</td>
      <td><input type="checkbox" name="_spring_security_remember_me"/></td>
    </tr>
    <tr><td colspan="2"><g:submitButton name="login" value="Login"/></td>
  </table>
</form>
```

The critical parts of this code are the form's action URL and the names of the user ID, password, and remember fields.

Now that everything is working and we have basic access control in place, it's time to consider how we can test this. We do want to make sure that it's working properly and that future changes don't break anything!

10.3.5 *Testing access control*

Spring Security, like other security frameworks, uses a combination of servlet filters and other types of interceptors to control access to an application. This makes it particularly tricky to test, because there are no classes that you can unit test nor do filters take part in integration tests. Both types of test are redundant when it comes to testing access control. Functional tests are the only game in town.

Figure 10.7 shows the logic that we want to test. It's not comprehensive, but it does illustrate what we're trying to achieve with our tests. We want to make sure that all the conditions work and that application pages are displayed when we expect them to be.

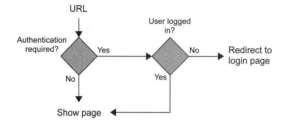

Figure 10.7 A simple access-control logic flow that we want to functionally test. The expected behavior depends on the URL of a request and whether the user is logged in or not.

Writing a test to confirm the behavior shown in the diagram is straightforward, and you can see the resulting code in listing 10.2. As in chapter 7, we're using the Functional Test plugin to access particular URLs, but now some of those URLs are protected.

Listing 10.2 A functional test to verify the access-control behavior

```
package com.grailsinaction

class AccessControlTests extends functionaltestplugin.FunctionalTestCase {
    void testAnonymousAccess() {
        get("/")                              ❶ Allows anonymous access
        checkHomePage()
    }

    void testTimeline() {
        get("/post/timeline")                 ❷ Denies anonymous access
        checkHomePage()

        login("peter", "test")                ❸ Checks login failure
        checkHomePage()

        login()
        checkTimelinePage()
```

```
        post("/logout")                    ❹ Checks that logout works
        get("/post/timeline")
        checkHomePage()
    }

    void checkHomePage() {
        assertTitle "Hubbub » Howdy"
    }

    void checkTimelinePage() {
        assertTitle "Hubbub » New Post"
        assertContentContains "What are you hacking on right now?"
    }

    void login(userId = "peter", password = "password") {
        post("/j_spring_security_check") {
            j_username = userId
            j_password = password
        }
    }
}
```

We start by ensuring that users have access to the login or home page ❶. You should also make sure that any other pages that allow anonymous access are checked in this way. We then check the behavior of a protected page, which in this case is the user's personal timeline. An unauthenticated user should be redirected to the login page ❷, and a failed login attempt ❸ should result in the same.

We finish up by checking a successful login and then making sure that the logout URL does log the user out ❹. This serves two purposes: first, we ensure that the logout code works; and second, we make sure that subsequent tests don't start with an authenticated user. We try to leave the application in the same state as it was at the start of the test.

NOTE   The code in listing 10.2 demonstrates the usefulness of factoring out code into utility methods, such as `login()`. These can also be collected into a base class so that all your functional tests can benefit from them.

Congratulations! Everything is now working, and we have a system in place that we can grow as we need. And remember, a lot of the work involved has come from using our existing domain classes and views. The process is much simpler and quicker if you accept the defaults that the plugin provides. That said, by doing it the hard way, we've explored several facets of Spring Security and the plugin that will stand you in good stead for the future.

In the remainder of the chapter, we'll look at more advanced techniques that will help you with a variety of security requirements and add some useful refinements to Hubbub.

10.4 *Further exploration of Spring Security*

Spring Security is a powerful framework with various options for authentication and authorization, many of which the plugin exposes to you. It would be impossible to discuss everything you can do with Spring Security in a single chapter—a book would be more appropriate. So rather than attempt the impossible, we'll introduce you in this section to some common scenarios that require special treatment. First, we need to fill some gaps in Hubbub's current access-control setup.

10.4.1 Adding user registration

You may already have spotted a problem with the user management in Hubbub: we don't have any! Although the `BootStrap` currently creates a few standard users, Hubbub as an application isn't much good if we can't add more.

One option would be to build a user-management UI around the `User` and `Role` classes. The plugin even helps you do so by providing a `generate-manager` command. Hubbub isn't that kind of application, though. Users won't want to send emails to a system administrator to get an account set up. The typical solution is to allow users to register, so that's what we'll do.

Again, the plugin helps out here by providing a command that will get us started on the road to user registration:

```
grails generate-registration
```

This one command will set up the necessary controllers and views, and even download JavaMail and Activation JARs so that the plugin can send confirmation emails. Not only that, but the registration screen includes a captcha to help prevent spam bots from signing up.

That's almost all we need to do, but the user-registration feature provided by the plugin has a few extra requirements we need to satisfy. First, we need to add these fields to our `User` class:

```
class User {
    ...
    String email
    String userRealName
    boolean emailShow = false
    ...
    static constraints = {
        ...
        email(nullable: true, blank: true)
        userRealName(nullable: true, blank: true)
    }
    ...
}
```

We add the extra constraints because `BootStrap` is currently not giving the users it creates values for the new fields, so we need to make them optional. It's a case of expediency. Note that the user domain class generated by the plugin includes these extra fields by default.

One more thing we mustn't forget is that the user registration adds some extra URLs that need to be accessible to users who aren't authenticated. We need to add these two rules to the security configuration:

```
/captcha/**=IS_AUTHENTICATED_ANONYMOUSLY
/register/**=IS_AUTHENTICATED_ANONYMOUSLY
```

It's not much good having a screen for registration if the users can't access it. Remember, these rules should go before the one for `/**`; otherwise the captcha and registration pages will require an authenticated or remembered user.

With that last change, you can start up Hubbub again and access the user-registration screen at http://localhost:8080/hubbub/register/. You'll see that the interface is pretty basic, but you can register a new user ID and then log in with it straight away. Also, because the plugin generates the controllers and views in your project directory, you can customize the pages and behavior to your heart's content.

An extra feature of the user registration that we haven't mentioned yet is email confirmations. You can configure the plugin to send an email to any user who successfully registers. This feature is disabled by default, but you can enable it via this option in the security configuration:

```
useMail = true
```

You then need to configure an SMTP server so that the plugin can send the emails. You'll find a complete listing of the email options at the URL for SecurityConfig settings (http://www.grails.org/AcegiSecurity+Plugin+-+Customizing+with+SecurityConfig).

Note that the email feature is quite basic and only handles notification messages. It can't send an email containing a code or link to activate the corresponding user account, so if you want this behavior, you'll have to implement it yourself. Nonetheless, the user registration does a reasonable job for little effort and gives you a good starting point from which to take it further.

That almost completes the security infrastructure for Hubbub, but there are still a couple of concerns regarding who can do what. It's also about time you found out what that `Role` class is for.

10.4.2 *Tightening restrictions on access*

Spring Security uses the concept of *authorities* for assigning and determining *rights*: who can do what. Its implementation is surprisingly powerful, but because the concept of authorities is quite abstract, it's difficult for people to understand.

The plugin sidesteps this problem by only dealing with named authorities called *roles*. These are simple—they're names. A user is assigned any number of said roles, which gives him or her the right to access any URLs restricted to any of those roles. Table 10.2 demonstrates how rule requirements combine with role assignments to determine whether a user has access to a particular URL. If any of the roles the user has match any of the required roles, access is granted. Note that in these examples, `ROLE_USER` and `ROLE_ADMIN` are strings. Also, if a user has no role, then he or she can't even log in.

So how are roles assigned? By linking a `Role` instance to a `User` instance either programmatically, as we do in `BootStrap` in the example Hubbub source code, or via a

Table 10.2 How role requirements and role assignments relate to each other

Rule requires	User has	Access granted?
ROLE_USER	ROLE_USER	Yes
ROLE_ADMIN	ROLE_USER	No
ROLE_USER, ROLE_ADMIN	ROLE_USER	Yes

user-management UI. The latter is ideal if you want to assign or revoke user privileges at runtime.

A typical `Role` instance might have a name of `ROLE_USER` and a description of "A known, registered user of the system." You can then make that role a requirement for any given URL by adding it to the corresponding rule:

```
/profile/**=ROLE_USER
```

This begs the question, what is the difference between `IS_AUTHENTICATED_REMEM-BERED`, `IS_AUTHENTICATED_FULLY`, and `ROLE_USER`?

- `IS_AUTHENTICATED_REMEMBERED`—Built into Spring Security. Allows any user that's authenticated or remembered.
- `IS_AUTHENTICATED_FULLY`—Built into Spring Security. Allows any user that's authenticated. Does not allow *remembered* users.
- `ROLE_USER`—User-defined role that only allows access to users that have been assigned it. Applies whether the user is authenticated or remembered.

Let's consider a more concrete example. Say you have created a user-management UI using the plugin's `generate-manager` command. You don't want just anybody to have access to it because modifying user information and adding, deleting, or disabling accounts are highly sensitive operations. What do you do?

First, you create a new role, in `BootStrap`, for example, with the name `ROLE_ADMIN`, and assign it to a user:

```
def role = new Role(authority: "ROLE_ADMIN", description: "A super user.")
def admin = new User(userId: "dilbert", ...).save()
role.addToPeople(admin)
role.save()
```

Then, you restrict access to the user-management URLs to that role:

```
/user/**=ROLE_ADMIN
/role/**=ROLE_ADMIN
/requestmap/**=ROLE_ADMIN
```

That's it! Your user-management UI is now restricted to administrators only.

All straightforward, we think you'll agree. But there is one fly in the ointment. Imagine that users can edit their profiles. We can limit access to the Edit Profile page by role, but then anyone with the required role can access everyone's profile—

definitely not what we want! This is where we hit the limits of Spring Security and have to implement a solution ourselves.

The easiest way to add this kind of feature is via Grails filters. All we have to do is configure a `before` interceptor on the profile controller that checks whether the current user is the owner of the requested profile. Listing 10.3 contains such a filter, which goes into grails-app/conf/SecurityFilters.groovy. If the current user's ID doesn't match the one given in the request URL, access is blocked.

Listing 10.3 Restricting access using a filter

```
package com.grailsinaction

class SecurityFilters {                     ❶ Injects
    def authenticateService    ◁┘            required service

    def filters = {
        profileChanges(controller: "profile", action: "edit,update") {
            before = {
                def currUserId = authenticateService.userDomain().userId
                if (currUserId != params.userId) {              ◁───┐
                    redirect(controller: "login", action: "denied")   ❷ Compares
                    return false                                         user IDs
                }
                return true
            }
        }
    }
}
```

The filter is surprisingly simple. The first point to make is that we use the authenticate service ❶ to get hold of the current user's information. Inside the filter, we compare the current user's ID to the `userId` parameter from the request ❷. If they don't match, we redirect to the plugin's standard "access denied" page and return `false` to prevent Grails from going further with the request. Otherwise we let the request go through. You can't get much easier than that!

We've now finished with the authorization side of things. You have certainly learned enough to cover many of the situations you're likely to encounter; but for those occasions when you need finer-grained control, you might want to look into Spring Security's Access Control Lists (ACLs). Although the plugin doesn't support them directly at the time of writing, it may well do so in the near future. Alternatively, you might consider the JSecurity plugin, which has a large degree of flexibility and power. For more information, visit their home pages on the Grails website.

If we're done with authorization, what's left? There are some interesting scenarios regarding authentication that we think you might be interested in.

10.4.3 *Other authentication options*

The authentication we've used so far is based on storing users and their passwords in the database. Although this is one of the most common approaches, it isn't the only one. Spring Security (and, by extension, the plugin) supports many schemes via what it calls "authentication providers." You may be surprised to learn that Hubbub is already using three of them:

- `AnonymousAuthenticationProvider`
- `RememberMeAuthenticationProvider`
- `GrailsDaoAuthenticationProvider`

It's the last of these that uses our `User` domain class for authentication.

In most cases, enabling a provider is straightforward because it simply involves adding a few entries to the security configuration. We'll now take a walk through some of the more useful providers. You can find more information about them on the plugin's website, which includes tutorials as well as reference information.

LDAP

Most commonly used in corporate environments, the Lightweight Directory Access Protocol (LDAP) is an API for accessing any type of hierarchically structured data. One of its most popular uses is for storing user accounts, and it has its own authentication scheme. If your company keeps all its user data in an LDAP server, you probably need to authenticate users of your application against it. Microsoft's Active Directory implements LDAP, so you can access it in the same way.

OPENID

The holy grail of web application authentication is to allow the user to authenticate once and immediately have access to a vast array of different applications. OpenID is one technology that's seeking to fulfill that goal. At the moment, user IDs are URLs and are often difficult to remember, but it's becoming more widely used with support from Yahoo!, Microsoft, Google, and MySpace, to name a few.

When you log into an application with OpenID, you're authenticating against an OpenID provider, which then redirects you back to the original application. There are already several providers from which to choose.

FACEBOOK CONNECT

If you haven't heard of Facebook, where have you been? It takes a similar approach to OpenID except that there's only one provider: Facebook. It means that you can log into an application with your Facebook account, providing the application with some of the social network information.

BASIC AUTHENTICATION

This is the granddaddy of authentication on the web. It uses HTTP headers and status codes for its implementation, and Spring Security supports it via a filter rather than an authentication provider.

It isn't often used by websites these days, particularly as the user credentials are passed to the server in clear text. It also adds some overhead because the credentials are sent with every request. In many cases this is unnecessary, but it does make sense for software clients that don't want to mess around with cookies. In fact, when used over HTTPS, it's ideal for REST clients when your application requires access control. You'll find out more about REST in the next chapter.

By default, the plugin and its login controller only support one authentication provider at a time, but you can change this fairly easily. In the security configuration, add an option called `providerNames` and set its value to a list of the authentication providers you want:

```
providerNames = ['facebookAuthProvider',
        'daoAuthenticationProvider',
        'anonymousAuthenticationProvider',
        'rememberMeAuthenticationProvider']
```

All you then have to do is modify your login controller and form to support these multiple authentication types.

As I'm sure you can see, Spring Security provides many options, and we've barely scratched the surface in this section. It has even more authentication providers that you can choose from, it supports access control on service methods, and it also has an event mechanism. For more information on all these features, check the online documentation for both the plugin and Spring Security itself.

You can now breathe a sigh of relief—you've made it! We've covered a lot of material in this chapter, and yet there is even more to the whole subject area. Don't worry, though; we've given you a solid foundation on which to build your knowledge in this area.

10.5 *Summary and best practices*

Security is a complex subject that often requires the average developer to think in new ways. You have seen several examples of the types of attacks that your Grails applications might face, but the focus has been more on the techniques you should apply, rather than the attacks that they counter. While developing, it's easier to remember to "validate all your inputs" rather than to "protect against SQL/code/ whatever injection attacks."

Thought also needs to be applied to the access-control rules you set up. A framework like Spring Security can make it easy to add access control to an application, but it's no more secure than the rules you define. Make sure you understand the application's specific requirements before implementing its access control.

Another important point to think about is how secure the application needs to be. How sensitive is the information in it? What are the consequences if an attacker manages to masquerade as a genuine user? You can put a lot of security checks in, but are they worth the associated cost in development time and possibly user inconvenience? For example, Hubbub doesn't contain particularly sensitive information, but it should make it difficult to post messages as other people. On the other hand, a banking application requires far more checks and should make sure that no one can even see user-specific information.

Here are some ideas and guidelines to help you protect your application:

- *Remember the motto: "strength in depth."* If you only have a single layer of security around your application, an attacker who gets through has untrammeled access to the whole application. You should also perform input validation in your controllers and use the query options that auto-escape parameters, for example.

- *Know your trust boundaries.* A trust boundary is a point of communication where one side is trusted and the other is not. It's at these trust boundaries that you must be particularly vigilant, scrubbing data that comes in and making sure data going out is safe.

- *Test, test, test!* Make sure that the application isn't susceptible to common types of attack by using functional tests and automated tools like OWASP's Scarab.

- *Obfuscation isn't a substitute for proper security.* Hiding or mangling information can be useful—after all, there's no point in advertising anything that might help an attacker. But if you rely on obfuscation, you run a high risk of compromise. It's complementary to other techniques, not a substitute.

- *Develop with security in mind.* Remember that security is a process and a mindset. In order for your application to be secure, you have to consciously consider the potential effects of the code you write.

- *Perform code reviews.* Just as code reviews help weed out coding mistakes and movements in the direction of the "ball of mud" design pattern, they can also pick up security flaws. There's nothing like a second pair of eyes when it comes to catching these things.

- *Use existing tools and frameworks.* No matter how vigilant you are, errors will creep in. Security tools and frameworks are battle tested and in wide use. That means vulnerabilities are quickly found and quashed. Why risk your application by using homegrown solutions?

Lastly, we'd like to reiterate that there are several security frameworks available for Grails, so if you need one, we think it's worth a little research to make sure you pick the right one for you.

With all this security knowledge under your belt, you can now consider opening up your applications a bit and allowing access to software clients, and not just human users via their web browsers.

Remote access

In this chapter

- Making your application available to software clients
- Leveraging HTTP via the REST pattern
- Exporting services to remote clients

Now that you have a good grounding in securing an application from attack and unauthorized access, it's time to look at how other software (other than web browsers) can use and interact with your Grails applications.

The prominence of controllers and GSPs shows how heavily geared Grails is toward browser-based web applications, but there's often no reason to limit yourself to a single UI—anyone who has used Twitter knows that you can use a variety of different clients to view and post tweets. An HTML interface isn't much use for such software clients because they usually control the presentation of the information themselves. What we need is a way for software clients to interact with the data in the system—in effect, a public API to the application.

Such an API can be exposed in many different ways, and this chapter will introduce you to a few of the more common ones. The primary focus will be on a mechanism that has become popular in recent years and that suits web applications well:

REST. Grails has core support for this technique, and that's another reason to look at it closely. We'll also take a peek at a couple of plugin options that may suit your requirements better: remoting (with RMI) and Web Services via the SOAP protocol.

By the time you have finished this chapter, you'll understand how to design and implement a public API in Grails quickly and easily, while avoiding some of the pitfalls. You'll also know enough to make an informed decision on what implementation to use based on your requirements and the nature of the application.

We'll start by adding a simple API to Hubbub that will allow software clients to view and post messages.

11.1   Using a RESTful solution

The first step in creating an API for an application is deciding what it should allow clients to do. After all, if a feature isn't available in the API, a client can't use it. Working out what should go into the API isn't always an easy task, but during development you have scope to experiment. Once the API is published, that's it. You have to avoid changes that will disrupt those software clients that rely on it.

TIP   Adding elements to an API often causes fewer problems than changing or removing existing elements. A good strategy is to start minimally and grow the API as required.

Hubbub could have quite an extensive API, but for now we'll keep it simple. Clients should be able to do the following:

- List existing posts
- Create new posts
- Retrieve the content of existing posts

Note that these statements don't contain any information about implementation, and that's the best way to start. Once you have your API in this form, it's time to look at the implementation.

In Java, an API is typically expressed as a set of public interfaces with well-defined behavior, but this isn't much use for a web application whose clients may not be written in Java. What other options are there? Consider how a web browser communicates with your web applications. They talk to each other via the platform-neutral HTTP protocol—why not try using that?

11.1.1   Your first steps in REST

You may think HTTP is just the language of the web, but it embodies the REST (short for representational state transfer) architectural style that works for any client/server communication, not just web browsers. The idea is that an application should be viewed as a collection of resources that can be operated on by a few methods. Take, for example, a wiki: each page is a single resource that you can fetch, modify, or delete. You can even create new pages.

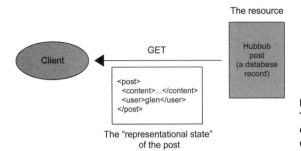

Figure 11.1   The key concepts of REST. The Hubbub post (a domain instance) is our resource, and the XML returned to the client is a representation of that resource.

Why the name *REST*? Each method (except delete) involves transferring the contents of a particular page between the client (the browser) and the wiki. The page contents are a representation of the state (data) of that page. You can see another example in figure 11.1, where a Hubbub post is the resource.

The sheer scale of the web and the variety you can find within it should be explanation enough as to why REST has become a popular paradigm. On top of that, it has the advantage of being a simple concept, and HTTP provides us with a ready-made implementation (REST, itself, is akin to a design pattern).

The four basic HTTP verbs (or methods) are GET, POST, PUT, and DELETE. The first two are pretty common among normal web applications and are used by browsers. Every time you open a web page, the browser is issuing a GET request, and when you submit data to a website, the information is typically sent as a POST.

To implement a REST API in Hubbub, all you have to do is decide what resources should be available and ensure that the application can handle all four HTTP methods for each of them. We'll only look at Hubbub posts in the following examples, but the same techniques can be used to expose other parts of the application, such as adding and removing friends.

As you know from browsing the web, you specify the location of a resource with a URL. Ideally, the URLs you use should have the following attributes:

- *Unique to a resource*—Each URL should only represent a single resource. For example, you shouldn't have a single URL that identifies two different posts. You can have multiple URLs per resource, but we think it helps avoid confusion if you don't.

- *Long-lived*—A URL should always point to the same resource, preferably until the end of time. That may sound like a bit much to ask for, and the HTTP specification acknowledges this with temporary and permanent redirects. Yet you should endeavor to ensure that your URLs *are* long-lived, or you might get a bad reputation for broken links—one of the banes of the web.

Bearing these points in mind, what should the URLs for our Hubbub posts look like? Simplicity is good, so why not use http://.../posts to represent all the posts in the system and http://.../posts/$id to represent a single post, where $id is the internal ID of that post?

Good URL design

We only highlight two recommendations for URLs here, but they aren't the only contributing factors to good URL design. Some would argue that URLs should also be short, easy to understand, and easy to remember. These aren't directly related to REST, but such principles can help users and developers. You can find out more by searching for "good URL design" on the web.

NOTE Our URLs include the location of the server (and possibly the servlet context). As long as the ID is unique within the application, each URL is guaranteed to be globally unique.

All this raises the question of what we should use for the post's ID. The obvious choice is the ID of the domain instance, but although this is the default behavior in Grails scaffolding, there are implications you need to be aware of.

CHOOSING RESOURCE IDS

We want long-lived URLs for our REST API. In a standard Grails application, the ID is generated by the database (it's the primary key). As long as your application runs against the same database for its entire life, that's not a problem. But what if your application becomes so popular you need to migrate the data to the latest and greatest database?

To do so, you would probably export your data as SQL statements (including the current ID of each record) and import all of it into the new database. This would certainly work for the existing records, but what would happen when your application created a new domain instance? If you're lucky, the auto-increment feature would automatically start generating IDs after the last record in the corresponding table, but that's not something you want to rely on.

Another downside to using the standard primary key in your URLs is that attackers can easily guess valid values. It also gives attackers clues as to the underlying implementation of your application. This may not be an issue for you, but if you're storing highly confidential information, you should consider an alternative source of IDs.

A couple of options to consider are using GUIDs or UUIDs for the domain class's primary key or using a different (but unique) field as the ID in the URL (such as a username or an email address). Hubbub isn't a high-risk application, so we'll use the standard primary key to keep things simple.

We've now decided on the format of the URLs we'll use for posts, so the next stage is to provide implementations for each HTTP method.

PROVIDING ACCESS TO THE RESOURCES

So far in this book, you have only seen one-to-one mappings between URLs and controller actions. We could continue with that approach and have our action do something different based on the HTTP method, like this:

```
def handlePosts = {
    if (request.method == "GET") {
        ...
    }
    else if (request.method == "POST") {
        ...
    }
}
```

This does the job, but those condition statements won't be easy to maintain, and they will also make refactoring difficult.

Let's try another way, using URL mappings:

```
class UrlMappings {
    def mappings = {
        ...
        "/posts"(controller: "postRest") {
            action = [ GET: "list", POST: "save" ]
        }
        "/posts/$id"(controller: "postRest") {
            action = [ GET: "show", PUT: "update", DELETE: "delete" ]
        }
    }
}
```

As you can see, we can set a URL mapping's `action` parameter to a map that associates HTTP methods with action names. In this case, a `GET` request on /posts is handled by the `list` action, whereas `PUT` on /posts/$id is dealt with by `update`. Note that we've mapped the URLs to the postRest controller rather than the existing post controller to keep things simple. You'll soon see that you don't have to use a separate controller for REST requests.

POST versus PUT

A common source of confusion in REST revolves around when you should use `POST` and when `PUT`. According to the specification (http://www.w3.org/Protocols/rfc2616/rfc2616-sec9.html), `PUT` is used for creating and updating resources *at a given URL*.

In most cases with Grails, the ID of a new resource isn't known before it's created, so `PUT` doesn't have a URL to work against. Instead, you perform a `POST` to the parent URL, say /posts, which creates a subordinate resource, such as /posts/10.

In the case of an existing resource, you know the ID, so you can use `PUT` to update it.

The mapping isn't much good without a controller to back it, so let's rectify that now. The one big decision we have to make is what form our post data should take. This is the "representational state" bit of REST. You could technically choose any form you like, even binary, but XML is probably the most common format in use today. Partly for that reason, we'll use XML here—it also helps that Grails provides a dedicated syntax to make life easy for us.

Our GET handlers (the list and show actions) are straightforward:

```
package com.grailsinaction

import grails.converters.XML

class PostRestController {
    def list = { render Post.list() as XML }
    def show = {
        Post post = Post.get(params.id)
        render post as XML
    }
}
```

It doesn't get much simpler than that. Both actions generate XML responses using some magic that we'll look at in the next subsection. For now, try out the show action by running the application and pointing your browser at http://localhost:8080 /hubbub/posts/1. You should see a page containing some XML that looks a little like the fragment shown earlier in figure 11.1.

How are those XML responses generated? To understand that, you need to learn a little about Grails converters.

11.1.2 Serializing and deserializing domain instances

The XML class is an example of a Grails converter. The sole purpose of these converters is to convert or serialize domain instances into a particular format, such as XML. Although Grails only provides two converters by default (XML and JSON), you can add your own by extending the AbstractConverter class and implementing the required methods (see the API documentation for more information).

Under the hood, Grails overrides the asType() Groovy method for domain classes (via the core converters plugin) so that you can do as XML and as JSON. You can also use the as keyword with your own converters. But this is only part of the story: as XML won't generate an XML string for you; it will create an instance of the XML class. To generate the corresponding text, you must use either the render(Writer) or render (HttpServletResponse) method on the converter instance, as demonstrated by this code fragment:

```
def xml = obj as XML
xml.render(response)
```

It's the latter of these two methods that's used when you call render post as XML from your controller.

The converters plugin not only overrides the asType() method but also adds an extra render(Converter) method to the controllers that delegates the response-writing to the converter. In addition to writing the response, the converter also sets the appropriate content type for it.

With almost no effort, we've implemented the GET method for our posts so that an XML representation is returned. The next step is to create new posts via the HTTP POST method. To do this, we can make use of a dynamic property added to the request by the converters plugin, as demonstrated by the save action shown in listing 11.1.

Listing 11.1   Handling a POST request containing XML

```
package com.grailsinaction

class PostRestController {
    ...
    def save = {
        def xml = request.XML          ← ➊ Extracts XML
        def post = new Post()               from request
        post.content = xml.content.text()        ➋ Initializes post
        post.user = User.get(xml.user.@id.text())   from XML data

        def markup
        if (post.save()) {
            markup = {
                status("OK")
            }
        }
        else {
            markup = {
                status("FAIL")
            }
        }
        render contentType: "text/xml; charset=utf-8",   ➌ Sends back XML
            markup                                            response
    }
    ...
}
```

We start by retrieving the XML from the request ➊. The object returned by the XML property is a GPathResult, which is the usual result you get from parsing XML with Groovy's XmlSlurper. We then use that result to populate a new Post instance ➋ with the data provided in the request. We assume that the root element contains child content and user elements like the XML generated by post as XML:

```
<post>
  <content>...</content>
  <user id="..."/>
</post>
```

We then finish off by saving the new post and sending back an XML response ➌ indicating whether the post was successfully created.

To be a truly good citizen, we'd normally include some information in the XML about the reasons for any failure, but we avoid that here to keep the code simple. Ideally, we'd also set the status of the response to an HTTP error code, such as 400. We'll look more closely at status codes at the end of section 11.3.

XML content types

When sending XML content over HTTP, you can choose from several different MIME types: `text/xml`, `application/xml`, or `application/...+xml`. The last of these is a pattern for specific XML languages, such as `application/xhtml+xml` for XHTML.

If your content conforms to a specific XML language with an associated MIME type, it's best to use that. Otherwise, for general XML, RFC-3023 recommends that you use `text/xml` if a casual user can read *and understand* the content, or `application/xml` if not. This is because tools that don't understand XML will display `text/xml` as plain text.

One final thing: if you choose to set the response content type to `text/xml`, add the `charset` parameter as we've done in the example. Otherwise, well-behaved software clients will assume an encoding of US-ASCII.

We now have a properly functioning REST API for Hubbub posts, but you shouldn't take that on trust alone. Why don't you try it out? Testing the GET handling is easy because you can point your web browser at the relevant URL and see what response you get back. The other HTTP methods are more problematic because web browsers only use POST when submitting forms (no XML here!) and most don't support PUT or DELETE.

What you need is a dedicated REST client that will allow you to send any type of HTTP request with any content you want. If you use the Firefox web browser, your best option is to install the Poster plugin. Other options include a Java client that uses a Swing user interface (http://code.google.com/p/rest-client/) or if you like the command line, you can't get much better than the flexible curl utility (http://curl.haxx.se/).

To test the REST API, you can send the following XML content in a POST request to the /posts URL of Hubbub:

```
<post>
  <content>I'm posting this via REST!</content>
  <user id="1"/>
</post>
```

Make sure that the user ID you specify is valid—"1" should be fine when running against HSQLDB or MySQL, but it's unlikely to work with a default PostgreSQL configuration. Figure 11.2 shows the results of sending this request via the Poster Firefox plugin.

Manual testing using a client like Poster is great for experimentation, but in the long run you know you need automated tests. That may sound difficult, but it's not much harder than testing standard controllers.

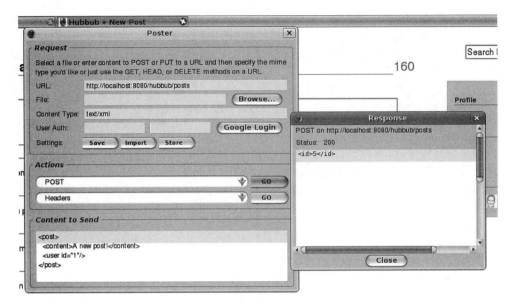

Figure 11.2   Sending a test POST request to Hubbub using the Poster plugin for Firefox. The request should create a new post for the specified user, and the ID of the new post should be returned in the response.

11.1.3 Testing the API

Because we're using controllers to implement REST, we can unit-test them in the same way we tested controllers in chapter 7. By extending ControllerUnitTestCase, our own test gets all the goodies we need, including an extra feature that hasn't been discussed before.

Listing 11.2 contains a unit test for the postRest controller that you saw in the previous subsection. It makes sure that both the show and save actions work as expected, although it isn't as thorough as it could be.

Listing 11.2   Unit-testing a REST controller

```
package com.grailsinaction

import grails.test.ControllerUnitTestCase

class PostRestControllerUnitTests extends ControllerUnitTestCase {
    protected void setUp() {
        super.setUp()
        mockDomain(Post, [
                new Post(content: "First"),
                new Post(content: "Second"),
                new Post(content: "Third") ])
    }

    void testShow() {
        this.controller.params.id = 2
        this.controller.show()
```

```
        def responseContent = this.controller.response.contentAsString
        def xml = new XmlSlurper().parseText(
            responseContent)                                    Parses response
        assertEquals "Second", xml.content.text()        ❶    as XML
    }

    void testSave() {
        mockDomain(User, [ new User(userId: "peter") ]

        setXmlRequestContent {                    ❷  Sets request
            post {                                    content to
                content("A new message")              XML
                user(id: 1)
            }
        }
        this.controller.save()
                                                  ❸  Checks XML
        assertEquals "<status>OK</status>",          response content
                this.controller.response.contentAsString
    }
}
```

You're already familiar with much of the setup for the test, so let's focus on what's new. When testing the show action, we set the id parameter, call the action directly, and then parse the response content using XmlSlurper ❶. Why parse it? XML is tricky to deal with because neither whitespace nor the order of element attributes is significant. You could have one XML document with nice indenting over multiple lines and another compressed into a single line, both semantically equivalent! As soon as you start doing string comparisons with XML, you leave yourself open to major problems. Parsing the XML string first makes your test robust in the face of changes to the XML formatting.

In order to test the save action, we have to somehow provide XML content for it to process. This is easily done with the setXmlRequestContent() method ❷. The particular variant we use in this example generates the XML using markup builder syntax. You can also set the content with a string using setXmlRequestContent(String). Once any variant of this method is called, the action can access the XML content via both the request's input stream and its dynamic XML property.

Finally, we check that the action succeeded by looking at the content of the response ❸. It's not worth parsing XML that contains a single element, because it's unlikely to have different formatting. We use a simple string comparison instead.

That's it! Unit-testing a REST controller is that simple. We'll demonstrate a few more features of the unit-test framework in the next section, but you've already learned the bulk of what you need to know. We also recommend performing functional tests on your REST API to make sure everything is working properly, but how you do that depends on the testing framework you use. At the time of writing, the Functional Test plugin doesn't support sending XML requests, but that feature is on the roadmap and may be available by the time you read this. Check out the plugin's home page.

With confirmation that our REST API is working as expected, is there anything else to do? One weakness of the approach we took is that we've limited ourselves to XML requests and responses. What about JSON? Your initial thought may be to create a whole new set of controller actions, but then you would need separate URLs for XML and JSON—not RESTful! There's another way: content negotiation.

11.2   *Negotiating the representation*

Imagine a traveler wandering through a market in a remote part of the world. He sees something he wants to buy, but in order to do that he needs to communicate with the trader. The first step involves agreeing on a language that both sides understand— even if it's just improvised sign language. This is analogous to how a client and server must agree on a format for data interchange in REST.

Grails provides a facility called "content negotiation" that manages different formats and handles the negotiation with the client. The client can specify its preferred content format a variety of ways, and, on the server side, Grails makes it easy to render different content based on that format. Figure 11.3 illustrates how this works at a high level.

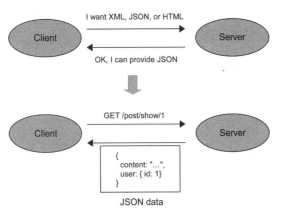

Figure 11.3   **The process of content negotiation in action. The client lets the server know what types of content it would like to receive, and the server returns the content as one of those formats.**

How does content negotiation affect your REST API? As far as the application is concerned, you only have to consider two aspects: dealing with the content of incoming requests and rendering the appropriate content to the response. For requests, you don't want to write code to handle each type of content, so it may come as some relief to hear that Grails unifies access to the request data through the standard params object.

> **NOTE**   Content negotiation assumes symmetry. This means that Grails expects the content type of the request to match the content type of the response, except in the cases of GET and DELETE.

11.2.1 *REST and the params property*

You already know that the `params` object contains both URL parameters and `POST` data (from HTML forms). What you may not realize is that when content negotiation is active, Grails can add both XML and JSON data from the request. Of course, it helps to know how the structured data in the request is mapped to the `params` object, so we'll take a quick look at how an arbitrary XML document becomes parameter data.

Let's say our request contains this XML:

```
<post>
    <content>A new post.</content>
    <tags>
        <tag>Music</tag>
        <tag>US</tag>
    </tags>
    <user id="10">
        <userId>dilbert</userId>
        <password>hjdj23r0fn</password>
    </user>
</post>
```

Note that this XML is simply for illustration—it won't work with Hubbub.

Assuming that the client and server have negotiated a content type of XML (you'll see how that happens in subsection 11.2.3), Grails adds an entry to the `params` object with a key of `post` (named after the root element) and the following map as its value:

```
[ content: "A new post.",
  tags: "Music US",
  "user.id": "10",
  user: [ userId: "dilbert", password: "hjdj23r0fn" ],
  "user.userId": "dilbert",
  "user.password": "hjdj23r0fn"
]
```

Each element in the XML that has an `id` attribute corresponds to a nested map. All other elements map to strings (even the contents of the `tags` element). This map of data can readily be bound to either domain or command objects, as you have seen done with normal parameter data:

```
Post post = new Post(params["post"])
...
```

The preceding line should be pretty familiar from previous controller code, and it will work regardless of whether the data is passed in as XML, JSON, or HTML form data.

Grails won't automatically parse the content of requests, so you have to explicitly enable this feature. You have two options: use either the `resource` or `parseRequest` parameter in your URL mapping.

The `resource` parameter replaces the `controller` and `action` parameters to make a RESTful mapping:

```
class UrlMappings {
    "/posts/$id?"(resource: "postRest")
```

```
    . . .
}
```

This mapping will apply the default REST behavior to the postRest controller so that GET maps to the show action, POST to save, PUT to update, and DELETE to delete. It also causes Grails to automatically parse the content of matching requests.

The parseRequest parameter, on the other hand, *only* affects the parsing of requests. Like resource, it's a per-mapping setting:

```
class UrlMappings {
    "/items/$id?"(controller: "item", parseRequest: true) {
        action = [ GET: "list", POST: "save" ]
    }
    . . .
}
```

With one simple parameter, your action can access the XML content via params or request.XML.

TIP   The resource parameter is problematic. You may remember from before that PUT expects an id in the URL, but POST doesn't. Implementing that behavior correctly with resource would require more work than not using it in the first place! If you want a correctly behaving REST API, we recommend that you avoid the resource parameter.

Before we move on, there are some important points to make about mapping XML to entries in the params object. First, object relationships only work if the id attribute is given. That means, for example, that you can't create a post *and* its associated user at the same time, but you can create a new post linked to an existing user. Second, one-to-many relationships aren't supported at all.

Finally, the default scaffolded views don't add a prefix to the names of their input fields, so they won't work with the previous fragment of controller code (post = new Post(params["post"])). The scaffolded edit page would contain something like this in the HTML:

```
<input type="text" name="content" id="content" value="..." />
```

But it needs to be this:

```
<input type="text" name="post.content" id="post.content" value="..." />
```

Note how the input field name is prefixed by post., which results in the value being available via params["post"].content.

If you can live with these limitations, using the params object for REST-style requests works quite well. We'll discuss other options in section 11.3, but for now let's move away from handling request content and look at the response instead.

11.2.2 *Handling multiple response formats*

Let's consider the `show` action we created for the postRest controller. In its current incarnation, it will always render an XML response; but what if the client wants the post data in JSON form instead?

Your first impulse is probably to check the requested format in a condition, which is possible because Grails adds a dynamic `format` property to the request object:

```
def show = {
    Post post = Post.get(params.id)
    if (request.format == "xml") {
        render post as XML
    }
    else if (request.format == "json") {
        render post as JSON
    }
    else { ... }
}
```

Although this works, we've come to expect better of Grails. Listing 11.3 demonstrates a much cleaner and more readable approach using the special `withFormat` block. You can try this out with a browser by appending a `format` parameter to the URL and setting its value to one of the supported formats, such as `xml` or `json` (say http://.../post/1?format=json). You'll see in the next subsection why this URL parameter works, when we look into how Grails determines the format for a request.

> **Listing 11.3 Using `withFormat` to generate format-specific responses**

```
package com.grailsinaction

class PostRestController {
    def show = {
        Post post = Post.get(params.id)

        withFormat {                        ←── ❶ Handles different formats
            html {
                [ post: post ]             ←──  Returns model for HTML view
            }
            xml {                           ── ❷ Returns model for XML view
                [ post: post ]             ←──┘
            }
            json {
                render post as JSON
            }
        }
    }
}
```

The syntax of the `withFormat` block ❶ is straightforward. For each format you want to support, you add an extra block with the name of that format. In this example, we respond to requests for HTML, XML, and JSON. If the action has no entry for the request's format, Grails picks the first one (`html`, in this case).

You should treat each format block as a separate controller action. That means if you want to render the appropriate view (show.gsp, in this case), you return a map as we've done for the HTML and XML ❷ formats. You can also use the render() method directly if you choose (as we've done with JSON). The main requirement you need to be aware of is that the withFormat block must be the last bit of code in the controller action.

> **Unit-testing withFormat**
>
> If you want to unit-test an action that uses withFormat, all you have to do is set the format on the request like so:
>
>   this.controller.request.format = "xml"
>
> You don't even have to mock the withFormat method, because it's already done for you by ControllerUnitTestCase.

Something in that last paragraph may have jarred. In effect, we said that show.gsp is used for both the HTML and XML responses, but how can that be? We're unlikely to want to return the same content for both, and we want to make sure that the appropriate content type is set on the response. Don't worry: this is easily resolved with another nice Grails convention. You can create GSP files with the naming convention <action>.<format>.gsp, which means that you can have different views for each format.

For our example, we'd have views/postRest/show.xml.gsp, looking something like this:

```
<%@ page contentType="text/xml; charset=utf-8" %>
<post>
  <content>${post.content}</content>
  <user id="5"/>
</post>
```

This is a standard GSP that generates XML rather than HTML. The most important aspect of the preceding code is the @page directive, which ensures that the content type of the response is set to XML. Without that line, the response type would be text/html, which would be not only incorrect, but a particularly bad idea with clients that treat HTML and XML content differently.

> **Format order**
>
> The order in which you declare your withFormat handlers is important because if the format has a value of all or no value at all, Grails triggers the first handler. Several old web browsers send an Accept header that Grails interprets as requesting the all format, so we recommend that you always put the html handler first (unless your action doesn't support HTML). We look at the Accept header in the next section.

Although we've used a format-specific view in conjunction with the `withFormat` block, such views will work equally well without one. In fact, if we dispense with the JSON handler in listing 11.3, we can get rid of the `withFormat` block too, because the model for the XML view is the same as the one for HTML:

```
def show = {
    Post post = Post.get(params.id)
    [ post: post ]
}
```

This means you only need to use the `withFormat` block if you do different things in the action for each of the formats.

We've covered a fair bit about content negotiation already, but an important piece is missing: how does Grails decide what the format for a given request is?

11.2.3 *How the response format is decided*

Several factors influence the format that Grails settles on for a request. Here they are, in order of precedence:

1 The URL file extension
2 The `format` URL parameter
3 The request content type (via the HTTP `Content-Type` header)
4 The HTTP `Accept` header

We'll look at them in turn.

THE URL FILE EXTENSION

The first of these factors is pretty self-explanatory. Given a URL like http://localhost:8080/hubbub/post/1.xml, Grails will set the format to `xml`—the bit after the last period (`.`). This means both 1.xml and 1.tmp.xml correspond to a format of `xml`. But if you use this approach to serve a single resource in multiple forms, you'll have multiple URLs representing a single resource—not good practice for URLs, as we said before.

Another thing to bear in mind is that the extension is only treated as a format if it's recognized by Grails. There's no need to panic: if you take a look at the Config.groovy file for your project, you'll see a `grails.mime.types` property with a map as its value. Grails recognizes any format that appears as a key in that map.

This is the default setting:

```
grails.mime.types = [ html: ['text/html','application/xhtml+xml'],
                xml: ['text/xml', 'application/xml'],
                text: 'text/plain',
                js:  'text/javascript',
                rss: 'application/rss+xml',
                atom: 'application/atom+xml',
                css: 'text/css',
                csv: 'text/csv',
                all: '*/*',
                json: ['application/json','text/json'],
```

```
form: 'application/x-www-form-urlencoded',
multipartForm: 'multipart/form-data' ]
```

By default, Grails recognizes most of the important content types used on the web. It's trivial to add your own by inserting extra map entries.

WARNING   By default, Grails strips the extension from the URL if it matches a known format. This means that you can't match URLs with patterns like /post/$filename.xml in your URL mappings. You can either use the pattern without the extension, /post/$filename, and generate the correct content based on the request format, or you can disable this behavior by setting the `grails.mime.file.extensions` option in your configuration to `false`.

THE FORMAT URL PARAMETER

The `format` URL parameter acts in a similar fashion to the file extension, but it has no impact on the name of the resource because it's a query parameter: http://local-host:8080/hubbub/post/1?format=xml. This is probably the simplest and most reliable way for the client to request a particular format.

THE REQUEST CONTENT TYPE

The last two items in the list are different because they deal with MIME types rather than simple format names. This is why the `grails.mime.types` configuration option is a map rather than a list or set: Grails needs to know how to go from a MIME type to the name of the corresponding format.

The `Content-Type` header is straightforward, but it's limited in that most GET requests have no content type associated with them, nor should they. In practice, this option only makes sense for POSTs and PUTs. Even then, you need to watch out: browsers post data with a content type of `application/x-www-form-urlencoded`, yet they generally want the response back as HTML. This is one example where the symmetry inherent in Grails' content negotiation isn't ideal.

THE HTTP ACCEPT HEADER

The `Accept` header is a different kettle of fish: it contains a list of preferred content types that the client can handle, along with some q (or `quality`) ratings that rank them in order of preference.

Consider, for example, this value for the `Accept` header:

```
application/xhtml+xml,application/xml,text/html;q=0.9;text/xml;q=0.8
```

This states that the client prefers both XHTML and XML (via `application/xml`) over HTML, which, in turn, it prefers over the `text/xml` MIME type. The q rating has a value of 0 to 1, with higher values corresponding to greater preference. If a particular MIME type has no q rating (as with XHTML in the example), Grails assigns it a value of 1.

We could go into more detail about the `Accept` header and its interpretation, but we don't think it will help at this stage. You can find a bit more information in the Grails reference guide if you need it. The problem is that Grails has a rather complex (partially heuristic) algorithm for determining the request format from the `Accept` header. This is designed so that you end up with a request format of `html` for most of the popular web browsers, even though they all have quite different `Accept` headers. Unfortunately, that complexity means that `Accept` headers from other types of clients may not work as well.

That description may be a bit too abstract to grasp at first, but put simply it means that relying on the `Accept` header for content negotiation can be fraught with difficulties. We recommend you use the `format` query parameter wherever possible: it's simple and consistent in its behavior.

While we're on the topic of the `Accept` header, remember that special `all` format we mentioned earlier? That exists because many older browsers send an `Accept` header with the value `*/*`, which means "I accept all types of content." This MIME type corresponds to the `all` format, as you can see by looking at the `grails.mime.types` map in the configuration.

Those are the basics (and not so basics) of Grails REST support. You now have the full set of tools at your disposal, so you can quickly implement a REST interface for any Grails application. The question is, how do you best take advantage of those tools?

11.3 REST in practice

Implementing a simple REST interface for your Grails application is straightforward using the various features we've shown you so far. The trouble is, there are some problems with the built-in support. In this section, we introduce some best practices and the reasons behind them.

11.3.1 Keeping the API stable

Let's start with one of the neatest features: the converters. In one line of code, you can serialize a network of domain instances to XML, JSON, or some custom format. So what happens when you change a domain class, by removing a field, for example? The serialized version of the domain class also changes—the field you removed no longer appears in the XML (or whatever format you're converting to).

This is a problem, because REST interfaces are typically public APIs, which means that they should be stable and maintain backward compatibility. If you generate XML responses (for example) using the standard converter, your public API becomes dependent on internal implementation details—a bad thing indeed! Ideally, you should decouple your REST interface from the implementation.

On the other side of the conversion coin, we have the issue of getting data from XML or JSON requests. As you saw earlier, Grails will automatically parse HTML form data, XML, and JSON from requests and populate the `params` map with the data. This is fine as long as all the data ends up there, but that isn't the case for XML. The parser ignores all attributes except `id`, and it only creates nested maps for elements with an `id` attribute. Take this fragment of arbitrary XML as an example:

```
<item category="general">
   <name>New message</name>
   <owner>
```

```
        <id>glen</id>
        <firstName>Glen</firstName>
        <lastName>Smith</lastName>
    </owner>
</item>
```

The `category` attribute on the root element won't appear in the `params` object, nor will any of the structured information inside the `owner` element, which has no `id` attribute. That's a lot of significant information to lose.

What's the alternative? For a truly stable API, you must define the request and response messages supported by each URL and build your implementation around them. That effectively rules out converters, but for XML you could do a lot worse than using `XmlSlurper` to parse request messages and `render()` (with markup builder syntax) or GSP to generate the response messages.

> ### What about JSON requests and responses?
>
> Typically, REST interfaces use XML as the prime resource representation, so REST recommendations and techniques are mainly focused on that format. The same considerations apply to JSON as well, but the techniques less so. For example, the structure of JSON matches the nested maps approach of the `params` object quite nicely, so you might be better off letting Grails automatically parse JSON requests and retrieving the required information from the `params` map.
>
> On the response front, the JSON syntax doesn't sit well with GSP syntax, so having a view like show.json.gsp is less appealing than using the `render()` method with JSON markup.

Developers writing clients for your application generally appreciate a definition of the API, which should include the URLs and the structure of the messages. You could provide this with some online human-readable documentation, but there are now two standards that allow you to formalize the definition of a REST API: Web Application Description Language (WADL) and Web Service Definition Language (WSDL) 2.0.

We don't have much experience with either, but the advantage of using WADL or WSDL 2.0 is tool support. It's also easier to precisely define the behavior of your API when using a dedicated language. Neither is particularly easy to read, though, so it's a good idea to have some human-readable documentation as well.

NOTE You can find a primer for WSDL 2.0 at http://www.w3.org/TR/2007/ REC-wsdl20-primer-20070626/ and the specification for WADL at https://wadl.dev.java.net/wadl20061109.pdf.

Now that you know the best approach to keeping your REST API stable, let's take a look at it in action, using Hubbub as an example.

11.3.2 *Applying the theory*

You've seen the theory, so now let's apply some of this reasoning to Hubbub. We'll start with the URL mappings you saw earlier:

```
class UrlMappings {
    def mappings = {
        "/posts"(controller: "postRest") {
            action = [ GET: "list", POST: "save" ]
        }
        "/posts/$id"(controller: "postRest") {
            action = [ GET: "show", PUT: "update", DELETE: "delete" ]
        }
    }
}
```

Now we need to consider what form the XML messages will take for each of these mappings. To keep things simple, we'll only look at GET and POST for the /posts URL and GET for /posts/$id, but the example source code for Hubbub includes the complete implementation.

The GET method on /posts/$id should return an XML response looking like this:

```
<post>
    <content>Message content goes here</content>
    <created>2008-01-05</created>
    <user>
        <username>glen</username>
        <fullName>Glen Smith</fullName>
    </user>
</post>
```

This is superficially similar to the XML generated by render post as XML, but it doesn't include any domain instance IDs. We return the username (corresponding to the userId field of the User class) instead, which also uniquely identifies the user in the system.

The problem with domain instance IDs is that they're opaque, which makes debugging problems in the API difficult. Imagine that you're trying to debug Hubbub by looking at the XML content passing between the client and the application. Which would you prefer to see: an integer ID or the username? Also, using domain instance IDs leaks an implementation detail into your API.

The GET for /posts returns a root element, <posts>, containing multiple child <post> elements. For POST we use something even simpler:

```
<post>
    <content>New content goes here</content>
</post>
```

This will create a new Hubbub post for the logged-in user. We discuss how users log in via REST at the end of this section.

Now that we've defined the messages, we can move on to the server-side implementation. Listing 11.4 contains the latest code for our postRest controller, which implements the API we've just defined.

Listing 11.4   Manually parsing XML requests in a REST controller

```
package com.grailsinaction

class PostRestController {
   def authenticateService
   def postService

   def list = {                                    ❶ Uses XML view
      [ posts: Post.list() ]       ◁──────
   }

   def show = {
      def post = Post.get(params.id)
      if (post) {
         return [ post: post ]
      }
      else {                                        ❷ Generates 404 if ID
         response.sendError(404)    ◁──┘               doesn't exist
      }
   }

   def save = {
      def user = authenticateService.userDomain()   ❸ Gets XML content
      def newContent = request.XML.content.text()  ◁──  from request
      def post = postService.createPost(user.id, newContent)

      if (post && !post.hasErrors()) {              ❹ Generates 201 for
         response.status = 201    ◁──┘                new resource
         render ""
      }
      else {                                        ❺ Generates error
         response.status = 403    ◁──┘                response
         render contentType: "text/xml", encoding: "utf-8", {
            errors {
               post?.errors?.fieldErrors?.each { err ->
                  field(err.field)
                  message(g.message(error: err))
               }
            }
         }
      }
   }
}
```

We're limiting ourselves to supporting only XML in listing 11.4 to keep the code short. The list action has a simple implementation because we delegate the XML generation to the view ❶.

The same goes for the show action, and this is its GSP (grails-app/views/postRest /show.xml.gsp):

```
<%@ page contentType="text/xml; charset=utf-8" %>
<post>
 <content>${post.content}</content>
 <created>
  <g:formatDate date="${post.created}" format="yyyy-MM-dd"/>
```

```
  </created>
  <user>
    <userId>${post.user.userId}</userId>
    <fullName>${post.user.profile.fullName</fullName>
  </user>
</post>
```

The `show` action is slightly more interesting than `list` because it will also send a 404 error ❷ if there's no post with the requested ID. Using the HTTP status codes like this is good practice, and you'll read more about them at the end of this subsection. Normally, you don't have to mess with the status code, because the default 200 code is fine for actions that complete successfully.

> ## On sendError()
>
> The `sendError(int code)` method on the response is the standard way for Java web applications to report errors via HTTP status codes. There are some limitations to it, though. First, you can't provide any content for the response. Second, the response content type will be `text/html`.
>
> You have two options to get around these limitations: set the response status manually and generate the content for the response as you normally would, or add a status code mapping to your URL mappings:
>
> ```
> "500"(controller: "errors", action: "serverError")
> ```

The `save` action is a little more involved, although the code should be familiar to you by now. We first get hold of the currently logged-in user so that we can associate the new post with that user, and then we extract the content for the new post from the request's XML ❸. After that, we delegate the creation of the post to the relevant service and check that it was, in fact, created.

According to the HTTP specification, successful creation of a new resource should result in a 201 status code, so that's what we do ❹. We should also provide a value for the `Location` HTTP header field, but problems with reverse URL mappings make that difficult without hard-coding the URL. On the other hand, if the new post can't be created for any reason, we create an XML response that contains the details of why it failed ❺. We also use an HTTP status code of 403 to indicate that the request failed and that resubmitting the request won't help.

USING HTTP STATUS CODES

Identifying the appropriate status code to use for any given response can be tricky, so we've listed some of the most common ones in table 11.1, along with recommendations on when to use each of them. For a full list with descriptions, see http://www.w3.org/Protocols/rfc2616/rfc2616-sec10.html.

Used wisely, status codes enrich a REST API and help to provide clients with tremendously useful feedback that's easy to access. Combined with suitable content for the responses, you have a system that can handle pretty much any situation.

Table 11.1   Common HTTP status codes and when to use them

Code	Short name	Description
200	OK	The request completed normally.
201	Created	A new resource was created. The `Location` header should contain the "most specific" URI of the new resource, and the response content should include a list of possible URIs.
301	Redirected Permanently	The resource has moved to a different URI permanently.
302	Found	This indicates a temporary redirect. The `redirect()` method works by returning this status code.
400	Bad Request	The content of the request is incorrect or malformed. For example, use this code when the wrong XML message is used for a particular URL or when the message contains invalid XML.
401	Unauthorized	The client isn't authorized to access the resource. This code is only valid if one of the standard HTTP authentication methods is used (Basic, for example).
403	Forbidden	The request isn't allowed. This is a multipurpose status code that covers validation errors and any other client-side errors that can't be matched to another status code.
404	Not Found	The resource was not found—everyone knows this one!
500	Internal Server Error	This usually indicates an error in the server code. Servlet containers typically return 500 if there's an uncaught exception.

Status codes are also related to how we might authenticate software clients via REST. If you take another look at table 11.1, you might see a clue: the code 401.

AUTHENTICATING SOFTWARE CLIENTS

We have a strong access-control system in place for Hubbub, but in order for it to work, clients must first authenticate. Human users can do this via the home page, which contains the login form, but software clients don't tend to work against HTML pages. They could access the login URL directly, but then they'd have to manage the relevant cookies.

A simpler solution is provided by HTTP: Basic authentication. Clients can provide the identity and credentials via HTTP headers in each request. If the credentials are valid, access is granted; otherwise the server returns a status code of 401.

There are two main problems with this approach. First, you have the overhead of passing the credentials in every request. The application also has to verify those credentials each time. This isn't usually a significant problem. Second, the credentials are passed in plain text, so anybody can discover them by intercepting the traffic between the client and the server.

In Hubbub's case, neither is an issue, because we don't store any particularly confidential information. For systems that do, you should use Basic authentication in combination with HTTPS.

That concludes our coverage of REST. The basic principles are quite simple, and Grails offers a good selection of features to support your endeavor, from implementation to testing. Add in a suitable security plugin, and everything is covered.

As you have seen, REST is a powerful and flexible architecture pattern that can work well for many applications. That doesn't mean it's suitable for all situations, though. Consider a trivial example: an application that simply echoes back whatever is sent to it. In this case, there are no resources, just the "echo" operation, so REST is the wrong pattern to use.

A more appropriate solution would be an operation-oriented approach, and we'll look at several such implementations in the next section that work with services rather than controllers.

11.4 *Operation-oriented remoting*

Grails' REST support is inherently controller-based because it works with resources and representations of their content. Another remoting model in wide use is based instead on services and methods. This model is often easier for object-oriented programmers to understand and use because they call methods on objects in day-to-day life. It's an approach they know well.

Java comes with its own remoting protocol that you may already be familiar with: Remote Method Invocation (RMI). This allows you to call methods on Java objects that are located in a different JVM or even on a different machine.

We'll start by showing you how to make your Grails services available using RMI. Then, we'll introduce the other protocols that you can use and discuss the pros and cons of each (including RMI). Finally, we'll take a look at the big daddy of remote service invocation: Web Services. Although we aren't fans of the technology, it's used widely enough to deserve a discussion. But first, simple remote object invocations.

11.4.1 *The Remoting plugin*

An easy way to give software clients access to your application is to allow Remote Procedure Calls (RPCs) on your Grails service. The traditional way of doing this in Java applications is RMI, and we'll show you how easy it is to RMI-enable your application by doing it for Hubbub's post service.

Let's get started by installing the Remoting plugin:

```
grails install-plugin remoting
```

The next step involves a bit more work. Grails services usually don't implement interfaces, but without at least one interface, services can't be exported via RMI or any of the other protocols. The interface is the API definition, and the Grails service is the implementation. That means we need to create an interface for our post service.

Where should the interface go? The best location is under the src directory, which is where all the code that isn't Grails-specific goes. Should we use Java or Groovy? Interfaces are simple beasts, so there's little benefit to writing them in Groovy. Write it in Java, and you can copy it directly into either a Java or Groovy project.

We're only going to make the createPost() method available to remote clients, so the interface is pretty simple:

```
package com.grailsinaction;

public interface RemotePostService extends java.rmi.Remote {
   long createPost(String userId, String content)
                 throws java.rmi.RemoteException;
}
```

This definition goes into the src/java/com/grailsinaction/RemotePostService.java file. We've called it RemotePostService rather than PostService to avoid a name clash with the service implementation. Unfortunately, RMI forces us to extend the Remote interface and declare all methods to throw RemoteException; otherwise the code would be simpler and cleaner.

Now that we have our interface, we need to modify the service implementation to use it. The signature of the current service method looks like this:

```
Post createPost(long userId, String content)
```

That doesn't match the signature in the interface, so we either have to change the current implementation or add an extra method. Because we have code that depends on the existing method, we'll add a new one. You can see the result in listing 11.5, which also shows you how to activate RMI for the service.

Listing 11.5 RMI-enabling the Hubbub post service

```
import com.manning.graina.hubbub.RemotePostService

class PostService implements RemotePostService {       ❶ Exports service via RMI
   static expose = [ "rmi" ]                       ◀──┘
                                                          Implements method
   long createPost(String username, String content) {  ◀──┘ from interface
      def user = User.findByUserId(username)
      if (!user) throw new RuntimeException("'$username' not found.")

      def post = createPost(user.id, content)
      if (!post) throw new RuntimeException("Creation failed.")
      return post.id
   }

   Post createPost(long userId, String content) {
      ...
   }
}
```

Enabling RMI for a service is straightforward: add a static expose property, and set its value to a list containing "rmi" ❶. You can also add other protocols to the list, as you'll see shortly.

We deliberately avoided some complications by only using basic types in the method signature, which is why the interface method returns a `long` rather than an instance of `Post`. That doesn't mean to say you can't pass types like `Post` between the client and server (you most definitely can), but there's a bit more work involved.

First, you need to make sure that the type is available on the client. A good approach is to package all interfaces and types that are shared between the client and server into a separate JAR file, which you then include as a dependency in both. In the case of Hubbub, we might call it hubbub-client.jar, for example. Second, the types should be in packages, because only classes in the default package can access other classes in it. Third, domain classes don't always travel well over the wire, and clients definitely don't need to see the constraints, mappings, and other internal information. For that and other reasons, people tend to copy the necessary data from the domain objects into what are known as Data Transfer Objects (DTOs)—simple classes that contain only data fields. That's all there is to it.

A client is useful for testing the service, so we've included a simple one with the book's sample source code. You can find it in the rmi-client directory under this chapter's folder. It includes a simple Ant build file that allows you to run the client:

```
ant -Dmessage='This is a new Hubbub post via RMI.' run
```

If you're feeling particularly adventurous, consider creating a second Grails application that uses the Remoting plugin to access the Hubbub post service via RMI. You can find out more about turning a Grails application into a remoting client from the plugin's documentation: http://grails.org/Remoting+Plugin.

Now that you know how to export a Grails service via a remote protocol, let's take a look at the available protocols and how they stack up against each other.

11.4.2 *Comparing the remoting protocols*

Along with RMI, the Remoting plugin provides support for three other protocols, which you can enable by adding these entries to the `expose` property: `httpinvoker`, `hessian`, and `burlap`. All of the protocols can happily work side by side, so you can put any combination of them in the `expose` list, or even all four. Which of them should you use, and why?

RMI

RMI is the original remoting protocol but not necessarily the best. RMI has existed since JDK 1.1, so it has been around for quite a while. If your clients will only ever be written in Java, RMI is worth contemplating, particularly as it doesn't depend on anything beyond the JDK itself.

The major downside to RMI, other than it being Java-only, is that it's invasive. Any interface you expose via RMI must extend `java.rmi.Remote`, and all its methods must be declared to throw `java.rmi.RemoteException`. These days, developers rightly expect that implementation details like this should not leak into a public API.

It also doesn't help that RMI requires a separate registry server and doesn't work over HTTP. That makes it a poor candidate in environments with firewalls. Fortunately, there's an alternative that eliminates such problems and is even easier to use.

HTTP INVOKER

Spring comes with a custom protocol that it calls "HTTP invoker." In essence, it's RMI over HTTP using standard Java serialization. That means it works well with firewalls, and you don't need a separate registry because the URL defines the location of the remote service.

Those are big advantages over RMI, but our favorite improvement is that it's non-invasive. Your classes and interfaces don't need to extend or implement anything specific to HTTP invoker. For these reasons, we strongly recommend you use this protocol instead of RMI.

It would be remiss of us not to mention the downsides of the protocol. Like RMI, it only works with Java, but there's an additional constraint: your client will have to use Spring. Whether this is a deal-breaker depends on your requirements, but we like to see it as a good reason to use Spring in all your applications!

HESSIAN AND BURLAP

The remaining two protocols come from the same company, Caucho. In fact, Burlap is an XML-based version of Hessian (a binary protocol). The major advantage of these protocols over the other two is that you can use them from non-Java clients. They also use HTTP as their transport, so you should have few problems with firewalls.

On the downside, you might run into problems with complex object graphs because the protocols don't use standard Java serialization. You might also find that Hessian is a bit slower than HTTP invoker, but probably not enough to worry about.

We only recommend Hessian if non-Java clients need access to your application. As for Burlap, we don't see much point in it. The only advantage it has over Hessian is that you can read the messages passed between client and server because they're XML, so it may be worth switching to for debugging purposes.

As you have seen, both REST and remoting are nice and simple approaches to interapplication communication; but because they're simple, they lack some heavy-duty features such as secure and reliable messaging, control over routing of messages, and plenty of others. If the simple solutions don't meet your requirements, you probably need to enter the world of Web Services.

11.4.3 *Web Services via SOAP*

If you have been working in the Java field for any length of time, you'll almost certainly have heard of Web Services. Many of the big names in software have put a lot of effort into developing and promoting the technology. Certainly, the promise of Web Services is alluring: secure and reliable messaging over the internet with complete interoperability between different systems. In practice, the associated complexity has caused problems on the interoperability front in the past. Efforts since then, such as the Web Services Interoperability Organization (WS-I), have improved the situation somewhat.

What are web services? Fundamentally, they're services that interact with clients via SOAP, usually over HTTP. Some people use the term "web service" to describe a REST interface too, but the family of technologies that come under the "Web Services" umbrella are all SOAP-based.

SOAP itself was originally a Remote Procedure Call (RPC) mechanism using XML to describe the methods, their arguments, and the return data. Nowadays it's often better to view it as a message-passing system where you send an XML message to the web service and get another one back. Figure 11.4 shows the simple request-response nature of most SOAP interactions and highlights the basic structure of a SOAP request. As you can see, the model of a SOAP request isn't all that different from an HTTP request.

The world of Web Services is large and deserves a book to itself. We can't do it credit in a short section here, but we'll show you a quick example using one of the available Grails plugins and follow up with a discussion of when to use Web Services (if ever).

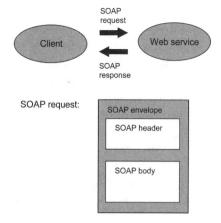

Figure 11.4 How a client interacts with a web service using the request-response model. Beneath that is the basic structure of a SOAP request—note the similarity to HTTP.

WEB SERVICE PLUGINS

At the time of writing, there are two main plugins for Web Services, each using a different Java library: xfire and axis2. Xfire is based on the XFire library, which has now been superceded by CXF. It's likely that the plugin will start using CXF in the not too distant future. In the following example, we'll use axis2, which is based on the Apache Axis 2 library.

To get started, we install the axis2 plugin in the usual way:

```
grails install-plugin axis2
```

Next, we export the post service as a web service by adding the string `axis2` to the expose list:

```
class PostService {
    static expose = [ "rmi", "axis2" ]
    ...
}
```

That's it! Don't believe us? Run the application, and point your browser at the URL: http://localhost:8080/hubbub/services/post?wsdl. All being well, you should see some rather horrific XML.

The name for the XML language is the Web Service Definition Language (WSDL), and it's used to describe the interface for a web service, such as the permitted operations and the content of the SOAP messages. You should be able to pass this WSDL to your favorite Web Services library or toolkit, which will generate the classes you need to create a client application.

This example barely scratches the surface of SOAP and Web Services, so it doesn't provide a particularly useful yardstick for either the complexity of the technology or its benefits. Should you go down this road?

TO SOAP, OR NOT TO SOAP

Although it appeared trivially easy to create a web service based on SOAP, if you want to get serious about Web Services, you need to start with the request and response messages rather than the service implementation, like with REST. That means dealing with WSDL and, by extension, XML namespaces—you might even need to dust off your XML Schema skills. As you saw, WSDL isn't the most succinct XML language ever devised, nor is it easily comprehended by mere mortals. That said, there are tools to help with developing and using WSDL.

This complexity makes Web Services flexible and powerful, and many features have been built on top of SOAP and WSDL: attachments, for including binary data with a message; WS-Addressing, for determining where messages should go; WSS, for access control to web services and encrypting messages; and others. In fact, the range of extensions to the basic platform is truly bewildering.

We think this comes at the cost of developer productivity, because web services can be difficult to understand and debug. Certainly, tools can make life easier for you; but if we've learned anything from our years in software development, it's that you eventually have to understand what's happening under the hood. That's not to say we think you should never touch Web Services—far from it. We recommend that you understand all the options available so that you can choose the appropriate solution for any given situation. Unnecessary complexity is a productivity killer, but a solution that doesn't meet your requirements is also bad news.

Although REST has become popular in recent years, we hope we've demonstrated that it isn't the only option when it comes to interapplication communication. When you control both the client and server, remoting can be far simpler and quicker to implement, whereas web services often form the basis of service-oriented architecture (SOA) solutions. The key as always is to use the right tool for the job.

11.5 *Summary and best practices*

Giving software clients access to your application requires a different approach from the usual HTML-based user interfaces. Whereas real users require data presented in a manner that's easy to read and understand, software clients only care about the data. You could rely on clients screen-scraping your application (parsing the raw HTML) to interact with it, but that's unreliable and inconvenient. As you've seen, it's relatively easy to provide an interface to your application that makes life easy for software clients, so why not do it?

We've mainly focused in this chapter on implementing the REST architectural pattern, which is ideally suited to web applications and supported by Grails out of the box. By leveraging the HTTP protocol, you can easily create a secure and reliable API for your application.

Despite the heavy focus on REST, you should be aware of the other options available to you—the operation-oriented mechanisms can be a more appropriate fit for your API. Also, Java developers tend to find remoting technologies based on services easier to understand and work with, because they're based on the familiar concepts of interfaces and methods.

Here are a few guidelines to ensure that your API becomes a favorite of developers:

- *Use the easiest solution for your needs.* Developers often find themselves caught up in the latest buzz surrounding some technology and feel obliged to use it because it's the current or next big thing. Remember, you're trying to develop a useful API as quickly as possible, not promote a particular piece of technology.

  Go for the simplest solution that matches your requirements. If you control both the client and the server, that might be remoting—even though it's seriously uncool. If you have complex requirements, Web Services may be the only answer. For many situations, though, REST is both powerful and simple enough to be the right solution.

- *Put some thought into your URLs.* Good URLs are long-lived, consistent, and easy to understand. Although poor URLs are unlikely to have an impact on your API feature-wise, they can make life harder for those using it. If you do that, users will not bother using it. You can find plenty of articles online about good URL design.

- *Take a message-centric approach with REST.* If you develop a REST interface to your application that you expect to be used for years, it's critical to decouple the API from the implementation. That means you should start by designing both the URLs and the messages that go in the relevant requests and responses.

  Once you have designed those messages, document them so that users know how you use your API. Also consider using either WADL or WSDL 2.0 for a formal specification.

- *Use the appropriate HTTP methods.* Map the various HTTP methods to actions that conform to the expectations and requirements of the methods. For example, don't map GET to an action that adds, removes, or modifies data on the server. Doing so breaks the contract defined by HTTP.

- *Make use of HTTP status codes.* It's easy to return a status code of 200 for all requests and use the content of the response to determine whether a request was successful or not. Easy, but bad practice. You would be giving up a flexible and well-defined mechanism for error reporting—one that can be understood by any HTTP client (such as a browser) and not just those written specifically for your API.

- *Apply access control.* You usually don't want human users to have free access to all the data in the system, and the same goes for software clients. Remember, anyone can access your application via HTTP, not just well-behaved clients. Make sure that your REST interface has appropriate access control in place.

From interapplication communication, we move on to internal communication systems that enable you to coordinate either different parts of an application or multiple internal applications or subsystems.

Understanding messaging and scheduling

12

In the last chapter, we spent some time investigating remoting options for Grails applications and looked at generating and consuming interapplication messages. In this chapter, we'll keep you in that enterprise headspace, but we'll look at sending intra-application messages. In particular, we'll examine how different components in an application can communicate *internally* while different events in the application's lifecycle unfold. One of the most popular ways of doing that is via messaging queues, an architecture sometimes referred to as *message-oriented middleware* (MOM).

If you've been around enterprise circles for a while, you've probably used or heard of MOM architectures. You might be thinking it's some kind of heavyweight old-school technology that just won't die. Nothing could be further from the truth. In fact, with the birth of service-oriented architecture's (SOA's) Enterprise Service Bus (ESB), and the rise of massive Web 2.0 social networking sites, we're experiencing an explosion of interest in messaging architectures.

You might be wondering why these styles of architecture have had such a resurgence in recent years. From Twitter to Digg to LinkedIn, if you look behind any of today's big Web 2.0 applications, you'll find that they're backed by an extensive messaging infrastructure. These messaging architectures are so prevalent at high-volume sites for three reasons:

- They lead to loosely coupled architectures, which means you can replace parts of your infrastructure without any client downtime.
- They have high scalability—you can add more components to process work on your queue.
- They offer a reliable transport that ensures your messages and transactions don't get lost in the system.

In this chapter, we'll add a messaging system to Hubbub so we can create a link between Hubbub and Jabber, a popular instant messaging (IM) system. By the time we're done, you'll be able to post messages to your Hubbub account via your IM client, and we'll also bridge the other way so you can be notified of your friends' Hubbub posts in your IM client. Along the way, you'll learn the ins and outs of all the common messaging scenarios and get some ideas on how to apply them to your current projects.

But messaging isn't the only asynchronous game in town. In many situations, a lightweight scheduling solution is all you need. Kicking off a daily backup? Sending out daily digest emails? Regenerating your full text index? Every developer needs to deal with these kinds of scheduled events occasionally, and Grails offers a robust and easily configurable scheduler based on the popular Quartz framework. We'll look at the different ways you can schedule jobs—how to write daily-digest type jobs, how to turn them off and on while your application is running, and how scheduling works in clustered environments.

We'll get into the details of scheduling a little later. For now, let's sink our teeth into some messaging.

12.1 A hitchhiker's guide to messaging

Messaging has been around for ages, but its predominant use has been in large enterprise scenarios, so you may never have been exposed to how this style of architecture works. In this section, we'll discuss the basics of how messaging works and get you sending and receiving Java Message Service (JMS) messages. Buckle up!

12.1.1   *Learning to think in async: what are good messaging candidates?*

Often, parts of your application are time- and resource-intensive and don't need to be done immediately. One example is generating a PDF flight itinerary and emailing it to the user. When the user books the flight, you tell them you're emailing the PDF to them, but the work doesn't have to be done that instant. Generating the PDF is likely to be CPU-intensive, and you don't want to hold up all users' web experience while the server is bogged down generating one user's PDF. Realistically, the PDF can be generated and emailed anytime in the next minute or so. It needs to be done soonish, and it needs to be done reliably.

This is a classic example of a candidate for messaging, and this "do it soon" approach is known as *asynchronous processing*. Here's how it might work behind the scenes. When the user requests a flight itinerary, a message is placed on an itinerary message queue. That can be done immediately, and you can report to the user that the PDF is in the mail. Another process, perhaps even on a different server (inside a firewall, with access to a mail server), retrieves the itinerary request off the queue, generates the PDF, and emails it to the user. Figure 12.1 shows the PDF request flowing through the queue to the target process.

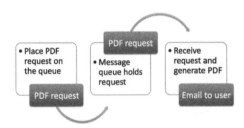

Figure 12.1   A PDF request flows through a message queue to a target process.

One of the cool parts of this asynchronous approach is that the messaging server persists the messages on the queue, which means that the messages will remain until a client is available to service them. If generating PDFs is a bottleneck, you can have many clients listening on the queue to partition the work of generating and mailing PDFs, and the messaging server will preserve the transactional semantics, making sure requests are removed from the queue once they've been serviced.

Now that you understand where asynchronous systems can make sense, it's time to get acquainted with some of the implementation terminology you need to know. Let's implement our first queue-based feature for Hubbub.

12.1.2   *Messaging terminology: of producers, consumers, topics, and queues*

Before you implement messaging, you need to understand some of the basic JMS terminology. All of the plugin documentation and sample articles will assume you know what topics, queues, and producers are, so we'll first cover that and give you a feel for which situations lend themselves to which messaging techniques.

First, there are two types of actors in the JMS market:

- *Producers* produce and place messages on the queue.
- *Consumers* pull entries off the queue.

In our PDF example, the web application (the producer) posts new PDF requests to the queue, and the PDF-emailing application (the consumer) pulls them off.

How do consumers and producers communicate? JMS offers two main communication models:

- *Queues*—Queues operate on a FIFO (first in, first out) principle, where each message that a producer places on a queue is processed by one (and only one) consumer. This is sometimes known as *point-to-point* messaging, and it's demonstrated in figure 12.2.

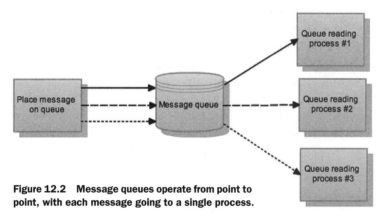

Figure 12.2   Message queues operate from point to point, with each message going to a single process.

- *Topics*—Topics use a *broadcast* model where all listeners on the topic get a copy of the message. The producer places one message on the queue, but that message is duplicated and shuffled off to many consumers simultaneously. This design is shown in figure 12.3.

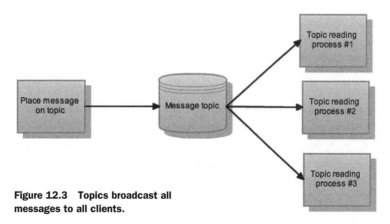

Figure 12.3   Topics broadcast all messages to all clients.

One example that may work well with a topic-style architecture is a network-monitoring application. For example, when a device in the system experiences an outage, a monitoring application can broadcast on a topic to notify other system components to use an alternative device. In this scenario, all listeners on the topic process the incoming message. In our PDF example, you only want your PDF-generation messages processed once, so you should use a queue.

12.1.3 Installing and configuring the JMS plugin

With the theory out of the way, let's take a look at how to implement a basic messaging system for Hubbub. The first step is installing the JMS plugin:

```
grails install-plugin jms
```

Next, you need to make some decisions about choosing a messaging provider. There are currently a few dominant ones in the industry—some are open source (ActiveMQ, Open MQ, JBoss Messaging) and some are commercial (IBM's WebSphere MQ). It's a requirement of the Java EE specification that an application server ship with a JMS container, so the decision may have been made for you (Open MQ ships with Glassfish, for example, and it's a great JMS server).

But if you're planning to deploy to a servlet container (like Tomcat or Jetty), then you're free to choose any provider you like.

Only small differences in configuration exist between the vendors, so we'll use ActiveMQ, a popular open source messaging server, in this chapter.

NOTE   If you get a message saying "Compilation error: java.lang.NoClassDef-FoundError: javax/jms/MessageListener" when installing the JMS plugin or when running the first time after installing, it means you need a J2EE JAR file in the lib directory of your Grails application. This JAR file defines the JMS interfaces and supporting classes. If you're using Open MQ, you can use jms.jar. If you're using ActiveMQ, use activemq-all-5.1.0.jar.

INSTALLING ACTIVEMQ

ActiveMQ is open source, free, and popular—it's currently the messaging stack used by LinkedIn, for instance (http://hurvitz.org/blog/2008/06/linkedin-architecture). It's the messaging provider we'll be using in this chapter.

To install it, download a copy of ActiveMQ from http://activemq.apache.org/ and unzip it into your preferred installation location. No configuration is required, so start /activemq/bin/activemq from a new command prompt. Once the startup process is complete, you can access the ActiveMQ console via the browser at http://localhost:8161/admin/. Figure 12.4 shows the interface in action.

The ActiveMQ console lets you browse your queues and topics to make sure your messages are getting through—we'll explore that later. Now that the messaging server is running, it's time to configure Hubbub to point to it.

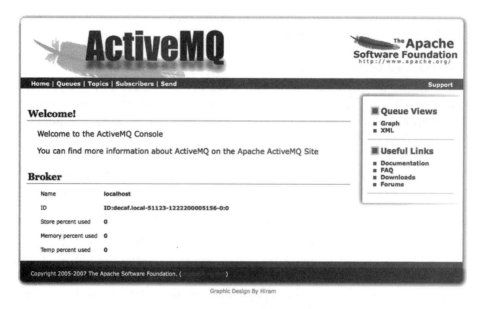

Figure 12.4   The ActiveMQ console is available via a browser interface.

CONFIGURING YOUR PROVIDER

After installing the JMS plugin and starting your messaging server, you may need to do two further things to set it up:

- Configure your messaging service in /grails-app/conf/spring /resources.groovy.
- Add your JMS provider's JAR file(s) to your project's /lib directory.

Let's tackle the message-service configuration first. Each JMS provider supplies a connection factory class that is responsible for establishing connections to your JMS provider. For ActiveMQ, the connection factory needs the hostname and port of the messaging server, so let's update resources.groovy to give the plugin the information it needs. Listing 12.1 shows the required changes.

Listing 12.1   Updating resources.groovy to connect to ActiveMQ

```
import org.apache.activemq.ActiveMQConnectionFactory          ◁── Imports
                                                                   broker factory
beans = {

    connectionFactory(ActiveMQConnectionFactory) {            ◁── Defines broker
        brokerURL = "tcp://localhost:61616"        ◁──            connection
    }
                                            Configures broker
}                                               endpoint
```

Next up, you need to copy the ActiveMQ JAR files into the application's lib directory. For the current version of ActiveMQ, there's just one JAR file, activemq-all-5.1.0.jar. This provides the ActiveMQConnectionFactory class.

We're now configured and ready to go. It's time to harness the power of the Grails JMS plugin to send some JMS messages.

12.2   Using the Grails JMS plugin

The Grails JMS plugin gives you a simple way to both send to and receive from JMS topics and queues. Like most Grails plugins, it uses a sensible Convention over Configuration approach to make sure you spend your time sending messages, not configuring queues (although there are overrides for all the conventions if you want to set up your own queue names).

In this section, we'll cover the basics of getting messages onto a queue and reading them off. We'll also beef up Hubbub with an instant messaging gateway.

12.2.1   Our killer Hubbub feature: IM integration with Jabber

Let's consider what messaging features we should implement for Hubbub. One that would be cool is instant messaging (IM) integration, so for Hubbub we'll write a simple IM gateway to bridge to the popular IM networks. For this example, we'll write a messaging gateway for Jabber, a popular open source IM system that can gateway to other clients (AIM, Yahoo! IM, and so on).

If a Hubbub user registers their IM account, we can let them post from their favorite IM client; and if they're online, we can even send them back posts from users on their timeline to keep them up to date in real time. When the user adds a new post, we'll put it on a messaging queue (to be broadcast to any followers that are IM active). Similarly, if the user sends an IM message to the Hubbub bot, we'll put it on an incoming queue to be posted on the Hubbub website. We'll use the IM transport to read and send.

Figure 12.5 shows our basic architecture with messages flowing between Hubbub and the gateway through the queue.

But before we can implement our gateway, we need to look at what's involved in putting outgoing messages on a JMS queue.

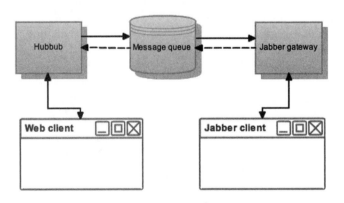

Figure 12.5   Our Jabber gateway architecture

12.2.2 Sending JMS messages

The JMS plugin works by empowering all your service and controller classes with new JMS-related methods. Which method you invoke depends on whether you're sending your message to a queue or a topic. Table 12.1 lists the methods for each destination type.

Table 12.1 Method names for each destination type

Destination	Method
Queue	sendJMSMessage()
	sendQueueJMSMessage()
Topic	sendPubSubJMSMessage()
	sendTopicJMSMessage()

There are two methods each for queues and topics, but they're aliases to one another, so feel free to use whichever makes more sense to you. For our examples, we'll use sendQueueJMSMessage() for queues and sendTopicJMSMessage() for topics because they make things explicit (which is a good thing for other developers).

Whether you're dealing with queues or topics, the method parameters are the same. The first parameter is the destination name (that is, the name of the queue or topic in your messaging server), and the second parameter is the payload of the message. ActiveMQ doesn't require that you precreate queue names, but your provider may differ.

In listing 12.2, we add a `JabberService` class that handles sending our messages. We'll place a `Map` holding all of our relevant message data on the queue.

Listing 12.2 Implementing a Jabber service

```
class JabberService {

    void sendMessage(post, jabberIds) {

        log.debug "Sending jabber message for ${post.user.userId}..."
        sendQueueJMSMessage("jabberOutQ",
            [ userId: post.user.userId         Places Map on
              content: post.content,           the queue
              to: jabberIds.join(",") ] )

    }

}
```

All the infrastructure is in place, but nothing is available yet to read off the queue. Let's write a test harness to generate some traffic. Listing 12.3 shows a basic test case to exercise the service.

> **Listing 12.3   Exercising our Jabber service with an integration test**

```
class JabberServiceTests extends GroovyTestCase {

  def jabberService

  void testWriteToQueue() {

    def post = [user: [userId: 'chuck_norris'],
      content: 'is backstroking across the atlantic']
    def jabberIds = ["glen@grailsinaction.com",
      "peter@grailsinaction.com" ]
    jabberService.sendMessage(post, jabberIds)

  }

}
```

Make sure you've started up ActiveMQ, and then give the test case a run with `grails test-app JabberService`. This test will show that you can put elements on a queue.

After the test is finished, point your browser to the ActiveMQ console at http://localhost:8161/admin. In figure 12.6, we have selected the Queues menu to see our new jabberOutQ queue.

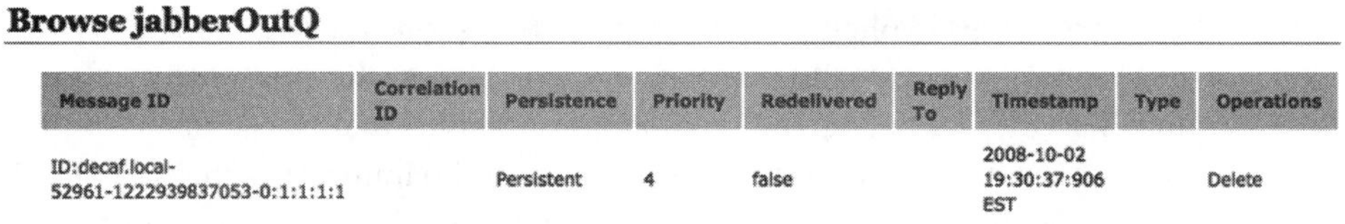

Browse jabberOutQ

Message ID	Correlation ID	Persistence	Priority	Redelivered	Reply To	Timestamp	Type	Operations
ID:decaf.local-52961-1222939837053-0:1:1:1:1		Persistent	4	false		2008-10-02 19:30:37:906 EST		Delete

Figure 12.6   Browsing the Jabber queue using ActiveMQ's web interface

You can click individual messages to see that everything has arrived safely. Figure 12.7 shows what you'll see when you inspect the contents of an individual message.

All our message details look in order, and our `Map` of data is persisted on the queue awaiting a listener to retrieve it. But before we look at how to read messages, let's take a detour into what types of payload you can put on a queue.

You've just seen map messages being put on a JMS queue, and you might be wondering what sorts of things are queueable. You can send several basic JMS data types to a destination, and they're listed in table 12.2.

Table 12.2   The basic data types for JMS messages

Type	Example
String	"Message from ${user.name}"
Map	[name: "glen", age: "36", job: "stunt programmer"]
byte[]	image.getBytes()
Object	Any object that implements `Serializable`

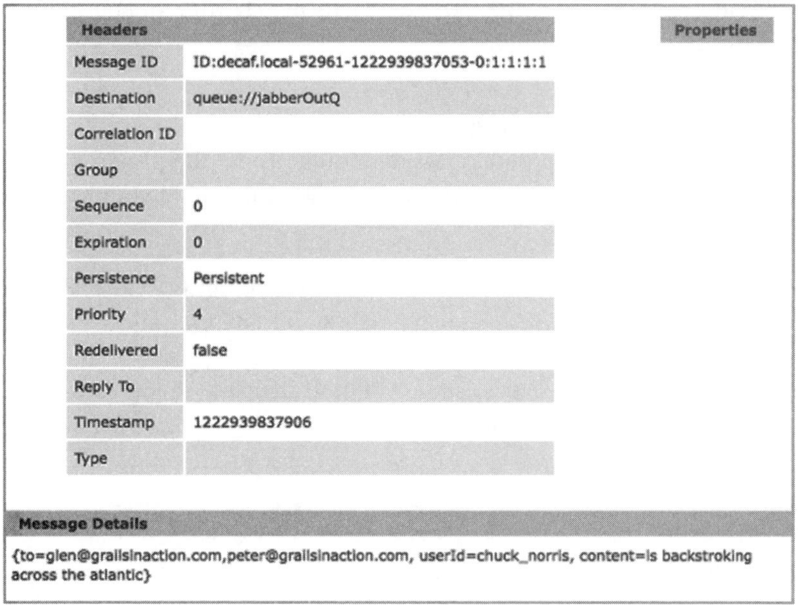

Figure 12.7 Inspecting a message on the queue

Although some people prefer to use XML payloads in the string data type, we've found the Map style message to be the most flexible. Using a Map means you can easily add new properties to objects you're sending to a destination without having to worry about breaking any parsing code elsewhere in the system.

How does type conversion work?

If you've worked with JMS before, you know that JMS supports its own type system (TextMessage, MapMessage, BytesMessage, and so on). The JMS plugin does the conversion of payload data to the appropriate type for you, leaving you to get on with building your application.

Behind the scenes, the JMS plugin uses the standard Spring JMS Template class. By default, this class delegates all type conversion to Spring's SimpleMessage-Converter, which handles marshaling the basic types listed in table 12.2.

We've done the hard work of getting everything on our queue, so it's time to implement the queue-reading side of things so we can get our work done.

12.2.3 Reading the queue

By taking advantage of a convention-based model, the JMS plugin makes the reading process straightforward. For the basic implementation, you need to do three things:

- Add an entry to your service class to expose it as a queue or topic listener.
- Provide an onMessage() method to handle incoming messages.

- Override conventions (when required) to match your queue names and the quantity of listener threads.

Let's cover each of those steps to get you up and running.

IMPLEMENTING YOUR FIRST ONMESSAGE()

First, only services can be exposed as JMS endpoints. To let the plugin know that a service is a JMS endpoint, you need to include the following line in your class definition:

```
static expose = ['jms']
```

The expose property is used by a number of remoting plugins (XFire, Remoting, Jabber), and you can happily mix and match SOAP and JMS endpoints in the same service class.

Next, we need to add an onMessage() method that the plugin can call when new messages arrive. That gives us a complete messaging class. Listing 12.4 implements the new feature.

Listing 12.4   Handling an incoming message in the service

```
class JabberService {

    static expose = ['jms']                    ❶ Names queue
    static destination = "jabberInQ"    ◄─┘       to listen on
                                                        ❷ Specifies number of
    static listenerCount = 5                  ◄─┘          listening threads

    void onMessage(msg) {
        log.debug "Got Incoming Jabber Response from: ${msg.jabberId}"
        try {
            def profile = Profile.findByJabberAddress(msg.jabberId)
            if (profile) {
                profile.user.addToPosts(new Post(content: msg.content))
            }
        } catch (t) {                                           ◄─┐
            log.error "Error adding post for ${msg.jabberId}", t │
        }                                                        │
    }                                              Catches error │
                                                    conditions ❸ ┘

    void sendMessage(post, jabberIds) {

        log.debug "Sending jabber message for ${post.user.userId}..."
        def msg = [userId: post.user.userId,
            content: post.content, to: jabberIds.join(",")]
        sendQueueJMSMessage("jabberOutQ", msg)

    }

}
```

Notice that we've specified the destination property of the queue ❶. Following convention, the JMS plugin takes the queue name from the service, so our JabberService defaults to a queue name of "Jabber". In this example, we want our incoming and outgoing queue names to follow a different standard, so we overwrite the destination property to tell the plugin what name we want.

In addition to customizing the queue name, we've also customized the number of threads that will be listening on the queue ❷. The default is 1, but we increased that to 5 because we're expecting a lot of messages on the queue.

Finally, we're particular about handling exception cases ❸. Some messaging servers get upset if clients don't behave well when reading from open connections, so we make sure that we terminate nicely when experiencing stray or malformed messages.

PULLING OUT THE STOPS: IMPLEMENTING A JABBER GATEWAY APPLICATION

Now that our messaging interface is up and running in the web-facing portions of Hubbub, it's time to write an application to interface with the Jabber protocol. To make things simple, we'll write our gateway application as a Grails application and use the JMS and Jabber plugins to interface with the rest of the internet.

You can install the Jabber plugin using the normal Grails plugin installation mechanism:

```
grails install-plugin jabber
```

The Jabber plugin works much like the JMS plugin you're already familiar with. The Jabber plugin identifies any service class marked with an expose = ['jabber'] property and automatically adds a sendJabberMessage() method. If the service offers an onJabberMessage() closure, the plugin will call it when any Jabber message arrives on the configured queue.

After installing the JMS and Jabber plugins, the whole application is implemented in a single service class as shown in listing 12.5.

Listing 12.5 A gateway service that reads and writes Hubbub messages to Jabber

```
class GatewayService {
                                          ❶ Marks service as JMS
                                            and Jabber-aware
    static expose = ['jabber', 'jms']                          ❷ Sets JMS
                                                                 queue name
    static destination = "jabberOutQ"    ❸ Receives incoming
                                           JMS messages
    void onMessage(msg) {

        log.debug "Incoming Queue Request from:
            ${msg.userId} to: ${msg.to} content: ${msg.content}"

        def addrs = msg.content.split(",")
        addrs.each {addr ->
            log.debug "Sending to: ${addr}"          ❹ Sends message to
            sendJabberMessage(addr, msg.content)       Jabber queue
        }

    }
                                          ❺ Receives incoming
                                            Jabber messages
    void onJabberMessage(jabber) {

        log.debug "Incoming Jabber Message Received
            from ${jabber.from()} with body ${jabber.body}"
        def msg = [jabberId: jabber.from, content: jabber.body]    ❻ Sends message
        sendQueueJMSMessage ("jabberInQ", msg)                       to JMS queue

    }

}
```

NOTE   The complete source for the application is included with the source code
for this chapter under the name jabber-gateway.

Our `GatewayService` starts with the configuration for receiving both JMS and Jabber
messages ❶ and for setting up the name of the JMS queue (`destination`) it will be
listening on ❷. It then implements `onMessage()` for JMS messages ❸ and takes
incoming JMS messages and sends them to a Jabber destination that it pulls from the
message ❹.

Finally, the service implements `onJabberMessage()` ❺, which receives Jabber messages and places them on the message queue for Hubbub to process and add to users'
timelines ❻.

With those 20 or so lines of code, we've implemented a two-way gateway from Jabber to JMS! As you can see, harnessing the power of plugins can lead to massive reduc-
tions in the code you'll need to maintain.

When to topic, when to queue?

We've now had a good look at sending and receiving JMS messages via a queue.
Using a queue made a lot of sense in this case, because we only wanted our messages to be processed once.

Topics, on the other hand, are ideal for broadcast scenarios—where you want all listeners to be updated about a particular event. Imagine writing a network-monitoring
system to keep track of when your services go up or down. The node responsible for
probing servers might want to let everything else in the system know when a server
crashes. Topics are ideal for this kind of broadcast scenario.

That covers the basics of messaging. It's now time to explore another, more lightweight, alternative for our asynchronous needs: Grails scheduling.

12.3   Grails scheduling

We've looked at messaging architectures and seen some easy ways to take advantage of
their asynchronous approach to making systems simpler, more scalable, and more
flexible. But quite a lot of infrastructure is involved in getting such a reliable and performant architecture.

Sometimes, you want a simple asynchronous solution to run some function at a
scheduled time (for example, a daily report, an index update, or a daily backup). For
those scenarios, Grails offers a fantastic, easy-to-use scheduling capability, and it's time
to explore it in some depth.

12.3.1   Writing a daily digest job

Grails' support for scheduling operations is handled by the Quartz plugin. Quartz is a
popular Java library with robust and powerful scheduling capabilities, and the Quartz
plugin gives you a simple Grails-style way to access all that power. Let's use it to send a

daily digest email to each Hubbub user, outlining all the activity on their followers' timelines for the past day.

We'll start by installing the plugin:

```
grails install-plugin quartz
```

With the plugin installed, you'll notice that two new commands are available:

```
grails create-job
grails install-quartz-config
```

The first is used to create new job templates (much like `grails create-service`), and the second installs a custom Quartz configuration file (which is only needed for advanced use cases like clustering; we'll talk more about it later).

To create our daily digest email, we need to create a new job that will run each night:

```
grails create-job DailyDigest
```

This newly created job class is located in grails-app/jobs/DailyDigestJob.groovy.

The simplest way to use jobs is to specify a `timeout` value in milliseconds. Every time an interval of `timeout` passes, the plugin invokes your job. Listing 12.6 shows the shell for our daily digest job.

Listing 12.6 A basic daily digest job (using `timeout` style)

```
class DailyDigestJob {

    def timeout = 24 * 60 * 60 * 1000        ◁── Runs job once per day
    def startDelay = 60 * 1000               ◁── Delays first run for one minute

    def execute() {
        log.debug "Starting the Daily Digest job."
        // ... do the daily digest
        log.debug "Finished the Daily Digest job."
    }

}
```

Notice that we've also added a `startDelay` field, which is the initial wait period before the plugin invokes your job. This is if handy you have tight timeouts (a few seconds) but you want to make sure the rest of your Grails application has finished bootstrapping before the first job fires.

At this stage, you might be tempted to implement your business logic in the job class. This is supported, but it's almost never a good idea. Because jobs support the same injection-based conventions as other artifact classes, it's much better to call an injected service rather than implement the process inline. Using an injection-based approach makes things much more testable, and it also fosters code reuse. Our newly created job is refactored in listing 12.7 to tidy things up.

Listing 12.7 A basic daily digest job

```
class DailyDigestJob {

   def timeout = 24 * 60 * 60 * 1000
   def startDelay = 60 * 1000

   def dailyDigestService

   def execute() {
      log.debug "Starting the Daily Digest job."
      dailyDigestService.sendDailyDigests()     ⟵─┐ Encapsulates logic
      log.debug "Finished the Daily Digest job."    in service class
   }

}
```

By defining our `dailyDigestService` field, the Quartz plugin will make sure everything is nicely wired together before any jobs are started.

Now that our daily digest is up and running, it's time to rethink our scheduling mechanism. So far, we've been using simple Quartz scheduling, which is fine for jobs that need to fire every so many seconds. But we'd prefer our daily digest to be sent out at the same time each day: perhaps 1 A.M., when things are quiet on the servers. To get that kind of calendar-based flexibility, we'll need to get acquainted with the cron scheduler.

12.3.2 *Fine-grained scheduling with cron*

If you have any kind of UNIX background, you're probably familiar with the cron service. Cron is a UNIX facility that allows you to schedule jobs to run on certain days at certain times, or on a particular day of the week or month, with all kinds of flexibility. With that flexibility comes a rather arcane syntax that only a hardcore command-line fiend could love. Figure 12.8 shows the basic components of a cron expression.

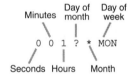

Figure 12.8 The basic components of a cron expression

As shown in figure 12.8, each field of the cron expression refers to a different time period. This example tells cron to run the job at 1 A.M. every Monday.

Cron expressions give you incredible scheduling power, but the syntax is certainly something to wrestle with. All fields in a cron expression can take numbers, wildcards (*), ranges (5-15), sets (5,10,15), or increments (10/15). There are some special cases for the month and day-of-week fields where you can use special literals. For months, you can use expressions like JAN-MAR; and for the days of the week, you can use expressions like MON-FRI.

It's much easier to understand cron expressions when you see a few in action. Table 12.3 lists some common expressions.

Table 12.3   A series of basic cron expressions

Expression	Description
0 0,45 1 ? * MON-FRI	Every weekday at 1 A.M. and 1:45 A.M.
0 0/15 1 ? * MON	Every 15 minutes from 1 A.M. to 1:45 A.M. on a Monday
0 0 10-12 1 * ?	10 A.M., 11 A.M., and 12 P.M. on the first of the month
0 0 0 1 1 ?	Midnight on New Year's Eve

TIP   The Quartz website has a comprehensive reference to cron expressions and more examples. Check out the tutorials section of the website for a comprehensive walkthrough: http://www.opensymphony.com/quartz/wikidocs/CronTriggers%20Tutorial.html.

With that little bit of dangerous knowledge under our belt, let's re-implement our daily digest service so that it runs at 1 A.M. each weekday. Listing 12.8 shows the new version of our job.

Listing 12.8   A basic daily digest job with custom cron settings

```
class DailyDigestJob {

    def cronExpression = "0 0 1 ? * MON-FRI"        ◁── Supplies cron-style
                                                         expression to Quartz job
    def dailyDigestService

    def execute() {
        log.debug "Starting the Daily Digest job."
        dailyDigestService.sendDailyDigests()
        log.debug "Finished the Daily Digest job."
    }

}
```

That covers the basic scheduling operations available in Grails. It's time now to explore some of the more advanced options for putting the scheduler to work.

12.4   Advanced scheduling

We've covered a lot of the common scenarios for Grails scheduling, and you're probably full of ideas for adding these kinds of jobs to your next Grails application. But there's still plenty to explore. In this section, we'll create, trigger, and control jobs programmatically, and we'll add an administrative UI so we can control them directly from our application. We'll also look at sharing data between job runs, or sharing jobs in a cluster. By the time we're finished, you'll know the fine points (and gotchas) of all these scenarios.

Let's start by getting acquainted with how the scheduling plugin handles stateful and re-entrant jobs.

12.4.1 *Dealing with re-entrance and stateful jobs*

By default, the Quartz plugin creates a new instance of your job class and calls it each time your job runs. But there may be situations when you don't want two instances of your job to fire at the same time.

Imagine you have an SMS notifier for Hubbub. A timer job fires every 10 seconds to see if there are any unsent SMS messages; if there are, it shuffles them off to an SMS web service that sends them. But what happens if the SMS service takes 60 seconds to time out? Your job might fire again, and again, and again within the same minute, resulting in multiple (annoying) message sends. You could work around this by keeping a `processed` field on the message itself, or use a JMS queue for the sending; but assuming you've ruled those out, you'll want a way to make sure your job is never run concurrently.

The Quartz plugin protects against concurrency via the `concurrent` property. Listing 12.9 demonstrates this feature.

Listing 12.9   Using the `concurrent` property to stop re-entrance

```
class SmsSenderJob {

    def timeout = 10000 // execute job every 10 seconds
    def concurrent = false

    def execute() {
        log.error "Sending SMS Job at ${new Date()}"
        Thread.sleep(20000)                          ◁─┐  Simulates web
        log.error "Finished SMS Job at ${new Date()}"    service delay
    }
}
```

If you run this application, you'll see that even though the timeout is specified to run every 10 seconds, the simulated delay means it runs only when the job isn't already running. Here's the output of this sample SMS job:

```
[22642] task.SmsSenderJob Sending SMS Job at Tue Oct 14 13:40:38 EST 2008
[42643] task.SmsSenderJob Finished SMS Job at Tue Oct 14 13:40:58 EST 2008
[42646] task.SmsSenderJob Sending SMS Job at Tue Oct 14 13:40:58 EST 2008
[62649] task.SmsSenderJob Finished SMS Job at Tue Oct 14 13:41:18 EST 2008
[62653] task.SmsSenderJob Sending SMS Job at Tue Oct 14 13:41:18 EST 2008
[82654] task.SmsSenderJob Finished SMS Job at Tue Oct 14 13:41:38 EST 2008
```

It's important to understand that if a job is scheduled to run, but another instance is already running, the new job is skipped rather than batched up to run later.

Another consequence of marking a job as not concurrent is that the plugin creates the job as a Quartz `StatefulJob`. That means a shared state area, called a `jobDataMap`, is available for you to share information with subsequent jobs. In our SMS gateway example, we might use a counter to keep track of the number of failed sends, and raise a warning when a large number of jobs have timed out. Listing 12.10 shows how we might implement this.

Listing 12.10 A stateful job gets a persistent context to work with

```
class SmsSenderWithTimeoutJob {
   def timeout = 10000 // execute job every 10 seconds
   def concurrent = false
                               ❶
   def execute(context) {       ◁─┘
      log.debug "Sending SMS Job at ${new Date()}"

      def failCounter = context.jobDetail.jobDataMap['failCounter'] ?: 0
      log.debug "Failed Counter is ${failCounter}"
      try {
         // invoke service class to send SMS here
         failCounter = 0
      } catch (te) {
         log.error "Failed invoking SMS Service"
         failCounter++
         if (failCounter == 5) {
            log.fatal "SMS has not left the building."
         }
      }
      context.jobDetail.jobDataMap['failCounter'] = failCounter      ◁─❷
      log.debug "Finished SMS Job at ${new Date()}"
   }
}
```

In this example, you'll notice that we changed our execute() method to take a Quartz jobContext argument ❶.

The second thing to note is that you can store any kind of Serializable object in the context ❷: numbers, dates, strings, collections, and so on. Try it out to see the counter value being passed into subsequent executions.

12.4.2 Pausing and resuming stateful jobs programmatically

So far, we've explored stateful jobs and looked at how we can handle re-entrance. But what if we want to take control of scheduling programmatically?

The Quartz scheduler lets you pause and resume individual jobs, groups of jobs, or the entire scheduler. In order for your job to be easily controllable, you need to place it in a group. Listing 12.11 shows our first crack at a pausable job.

Listing 12.11 The group property makes it easy to control jobs programmatically

```
class ControllableJob {

   def timeout = 5000 // execute job once in 5 seconds
   def concurrent = false

   def group = "myServices"                      ◁┐  Sets group property
                                                    to control job
   def execute() {                                  programmatically
      println "Controllable Job running..."
   }
}
```

Notice that we've specified a `group` attribute on the job. Later, we'll use the scheduler to gain access to this job via its `group` name.

For now, though, we need a way of getting a handle to the scheduler itself. It will come as no surprise that this can be done via the standard Grails injection pattern. In listing 12.12, we create a controller to tinker with our jobs programmatically.

Listing 12.12   A controller for pausing and resuming jobs programmatically

```
class JobAdminController {            ❶ Obtains handle to Quartz
                                         scheduler object
    def quartzScheduler

    def index = { redirect(action:'show') }

    def show = {

        def status = ""
                                      ❷ Determines which operation
        switch(params.operation) {       the user selected
            case 'pause':
                quartzScheduler.pauseJob("ControllableJob", "myServices")
                status = "Paused Single Job"
                break
            case 'resume':
                quartzScheduler.resumeJob("ControllableJob", "myServices")
                status = "Resumed Single Job"
                break
            case 'pauseGroup':
                quartzScheduler.pauseJobGroup("myServices")
                status = "Paused Job Group"
                break
            case 'resumeGroup':
                quartzScheduler.resumeJobGroup("myServices")
                status = "Resumed Job Group"
                break
            case 'pauseAll':
                quartzScheduler.pauseAll()
                status = "Paused All Jobs"
                break
            case 'resumeAll':
                quartzScheduler.resumeAll()
                status = "Resumed All Jobs"
                break
        }

        return [ status: status ]

    }
}
```

Our `JobAdminController` introduces a few important aspects of job control. First, we define the `quartzScheduler` property to inject the scheduler ❶. The `switch` statement demonstrates the different ways you can pause and resume jobs—by name, by group, or globally ❷.

In listing 12.13, we add a basic UI so we can drive the scheduler.

Listing 12.13 A basic web UI for interacting with our jobs

```html
<html>
   <head>
      <title>Job Admin</title>
      <style>
         div#status {
            margin: 1em;
            padding: 1em;
            border: 1px solid blue;
            background: lightblue;
         }
         body {
            font-family: "Trebuchet MS",Helvetica;
         }
      </style>
   </head>

   <body>
      <h1>Job Admin</h1>

      <g:if test="${status}">
         <div id="status">
            ${status}
         </div>
      </g:if>

      <g:form action="show">
         <fieldset>
            <legend>Job Admin Operations</legend>
            <label for="operation">Select an operation:</label>
            <g:select id="operation" name="operation"
                  from="${ [
                  'pause', 'resume',
                  'pauseGroup', 'resumeGroup',
                  'pauseAll', 'resumeAll'
                  ] }" />
            <g:submitButton name="go" value="Go"/>
         </fieldset>
      </g:form>

   </body>
</html>
```

Open http://localhost:8080/quartz/jobAdmin/show to see this admin UI in action, as shown in figure 12.9.

Figure 12.9 Pausing a job via our new admin UI

Looking at the Grails output to the command line, log messages show that `ControllableJob` (and our other jobs) can be started and stopped via the admin UI. This kind of control comes in handy for the administrative section of your applications, where you want the ability to pause scheduled jobs when dealing with emergency situations (like your SMS service provider going down).

We've now looked at handling stateful and re-entrant jobs. But what happens to our scheduled jobs and their `jobDataMaps` when the application server gets restarted? And what happens when we want to run our jobs in a cluster? For these sorts of cases, you need to learn a little about how Quartz handles persistence.

12.4.3 *Persistence and clustering*

The default storage mechanism for Quartz is the `RAMJobStore` class, and as you can probably guess from the name, it's fast, but it isn't persistent. If you restart your server, all of your jobs will terminate, and any persistent data in your `jobDataMaps` will be lost. If you'd like your stateful jobs to be persistent, you need to swap out that `RAMJobStore` for something permanent, like a `JDBCJobStore`.

To do that, you need to create a Quartz plugin config file:

```
grails install-quartz-config
```

The preceding command will write a new file in /grails-app/conf/QuartzConfig.groovy that lets you enable JDBC storage. It looks like this:

```
quartz {
    autoStartup = true
    jdbcStore = false
}
```

When `jdbcStore` is set to `true`, your job state will be persisted in the database. But before that can happen, you need to create the required tables.

The SQL to create the tables is found in /plugins/quartz-{version}/src/templates /sql/tables/ inside the Quartz plugin. SQL scripts are available for all the common databases, so use your favorite database admin tool to import the scripts and create the tables.

Once your database has the required tables, you can modify QuartzConfig.groovy to turn on Quartz persistence:

```
quartz {
    autoStartup = true
    jdbcStore = true
}
```

Job persistence is now enabled, but one final change is required before we can rerun an update of listing 12.10 and see if the job state of our counter job survives a restart of the application.

By default, all Quartz jobs are marked as volatile, which means their state won't be persisted to the database. Let's set that right now by marking one of our jobs as non-volatile, as shown in listing 12.14.

Listing 12.14   Marking jobs as nonvolatile

```
class SmsSenderWithTimeoutJob {
    def timeout = 10000 // execute job every 10 seconds
    def concurrent = false
    def volatility = false
    def execute(context) { ... }
}
```

We're in business. Let's restart our application and see our job write its counters out.

A special note for HSQLDB users

HSQLDB persistence is broken in Quartz 1.6. It may be fixed by the time you read this, but if not, you'll need to create a /src/java/quartz.properties file to customize the Quartz query strings. Place the following line in that file, and you're in business:

```
org.quartz.jobStore.selectWithLockSQL=
   SELECT * FROM {0}LOCKS WHERE LOCK_NAME = ?
```

If you want to see persistence in action on HSQLDB, you'll need to change your data source `url` property to a persistent version, such as:

```
jdbc:hsqldb:file:devDB;shutdown=true.
```

And with our exploration of persistent jobs complete, we've finished our tour of Grails messaging and scheduling features. Let's wrap things up with some best practices to take away.

12.5   Summary and best practices

We covered a lot of asynchronous territory in this chapter. We started by introducing you to the nature of asynchronous technologies and the sorts of applications they're well suited to. We then took you on a tour of basic messaging terminology and jumped in the deep end with the JMS plugin.

After applying our JMS plugin skills to build a Jabber gateway for Hubbub, we moved on to explore the lightweight asynchronous options of Grails scheduling. We looked at using cron-style expressions to implement a daily digest email and then discussed programmatic uses of scheduling.

It's time to review some best practices:

- *Know your application server.* Your application server probably already ships with a JMS provider, and it's time to try using it. If you're running on a servlet container, Open MQ and ActiveMQ are the best options.
- *Choose queues or topics.* Use queues when you want a message to be processed by one listener, and use topics for broadcast scenarios.
- *Favor maps.* Favor map-style messages on queues and topics—they give you greater flexibility to evolve your API over time.

- *Override convention when needed.* Don't be afraid to override default settings (such as destination names) if it makes your system easier to maintain. It's nice to know what a destination is used for by looking at its name (such as `sms-IncomingQueue` and `smsOutgoingQueue`).

- *Know your throughput.* Set the number of queue listeners to match your expected throughput. Don't guess—do some basic profiling to see what your system is capable of under load.

- *Use your console.* The ActiveMQ admin console gives you good insight into what's happening on your queues—take advantage of it. For other servers, Hermes is a good open source queue-browser alternative that works with any JMS container.

- *Separate business logic.* Don't put business logic in Quartz job classes. Make use of service injection to wrap your logic in service classes that are more testable and more reusable.

- *Favor cron.* Cron-style expressions are concise and expressive and give you more consistency than straight `timeout` values.

- *Expose jobs programmatically.* Always give your jobs a `group` attribute so you can get easy programmatic access to them later on.

- *Be cluster-aware.* If you're running in a cluster, you can take advantage of Quartz database persistence to share state and partition the work between nodes.

In the next chapter, we'll move into some of the more advanced use cases for GORM. We'll explore caching, performance optimizations, and integrating legacy databases.

Part 4

Advanced Grails

In part 4, we'll introduce you to some of the most advanced features that Grails has to offer. You'll learn about performance tuning, legacy integration, database transactions, custom build processes, and even how to develop and publish your own plugins.

Chapter 13 will take you on into GORM—the Grails object relational mapping implementation. You'll learn a lot about less-frequently used modeling options that can be real time-savers. You'll also explore caching, performance profiling, and some comprehensive legacy-integration examples.

Chapter 14 takes you into the heart of Spring integration in Grails. You'll learn all the different ways of defining and interacting with Spring-managed beans in your application. We'll then tour transactions—how they work and what they're useful for.

Build infrastructure is an important part of professional software development, and chapter 15 takes you deep inside the Grails build system. You'll start by learning how to add your own Grails commands. We'll then teach you how to integrate your Grails build with both Ant and Maven, the two most commonly used build tools in the Java space. Then, we'll give you strategies for handling data migration as your application grows, demonstrating how third-party plugins can help.

Finally, we'll conclude with a detailed look at how you can develop your own Grails plugins. You'll learn about the plugin lifecycle and how you can augment Grails with new features. You'll also learn how to publish your new plugin to the Grails plugin repository for others to share.

By the end of part 4, you'll have taken your Grails skills to a whole new level. You'll be ready to write the next uber-scalable, world-changing Web 2.0 social networking application. Remember us when you hit the big time.

13

Advanced GORM kung fu

In chapter 3, you had your first exposure to Grails' domain classes. Life was simple: we saved, we validated, and we used dynamic finds. You can go a long way with that knowledge—probably all the way to your first few publicly hosted Grails applications. But then you'll hit the wall. As users flock to your stunning new social networking applications, you'll wonder how you can tune your queries to run more efficiently. You'll start to think about query-caching options. You'll want to refactor your domain classes. And you'll want to monitor where all your cycles are going. In short, you'll want to take off the safety harness and get into some serious GORM kung fu. When you hit the performance and scalability wall, this is the chapter for you.

If you're currently working in enterprise Java, you probably already have some legacy databases (perhaps with existing Hibernate mappings). We'll explore the ins and outs of integrating Grails applications with your existing tables, JNDI data sources, and other things your enterprise might have lying around. But it's no good understanding the high-level stuff if you don't have some idea how the underlying engine works, so we'll take a peek underneath to see how Grails interacts with Hibernate and how you can tune it to make it all faster.

13.1 Domain model kung fu

In chapter 3, we explored the common domain model relationships: 1:1, 1:m, and m:n. But as you develop your Grails applications, you'll probably come across situations that don't fit into those three standard relationships. In this section, we're going to explore some of the less common domain modeling options, and we'll start with inheritance.

13.1.1 Exploring inheritance options

Relational databases aren't designed for object-oriented data, and inheritance relationships don't map comfortably to a relational design. With that acknowledgment out of the way, what *can* GORM do about domain classes that use inheritance? GORM provides two basic options for handling inheritance: table-per-hierarchy and table-per-subclass approaches.

By default, GORM uses one table per hierarchy, which means that your base class and its subclasses are stored in the same table.

An example will make this clearer. Let's modify Hubbub to support a special starred post that will always appear with a star and the reason it was starred. All of a user's followers will notice these starred posts, marked with a special icon.

We could implement `StarPost` by hacking our existing `Post` object:

```
boolean starred
String reasonStarred
```

But if we did this, `starred` would be `false` for nearly every post, and `reasonStarred` would be `null`, which means that our constraints would have to be relaxed.

Let's do the proper OO thing, and subclass our `Post` domain class, as shown in listing 13.1.

Listing 13.1 A StarPost class inheriting from Post

```
package com.grailsinaction

class StarPost extends Post {          ⟵┘ Inherits Post's
                                            features
    String reason

    static constraints = {             ⟵┘ Augments Post's
        reason(maxSize: 50)                 constraints
    }

}
```

Our `StarPost` is now implemented, and it inherits everything from the base `Post` class. That means we also have to make modifications to our `Tag` class to explicitly mention the new relationship:

```
static belongsTo = [ User, Post, StarPost ]
```

With our `Tag` class updated and our `StarPost` ready to roll, it's time to create an integration test to make sure that all the relationships work as we expect. Listing 13.2 shows an integration test for our new `StarPost`.

Listing 13.2   An integration test for our `StarPost`

```
package com.grailsinaction

import grails.test.*

class StarPostIntegrationTests extends GrailsUnitTestCase {

    void testInheritQuery() {

        def u = new User(userId: 'glen', password: 'password').save()
        u.addToPosts(new Post(content: "First Post"))
        u.addToPosts(new Post(content: "Second Post"))
        u.addToPosts(new StarPost(content: "Third Post",
                       reason: "I shine on 3"))

        assertEquals 3, Post.countByUser(u)
        assertEquals 1, StarPost.countByUser(u)

    }
}
```

❶ Counts Posts (including StarPosts)

❷ Counts StarPosts only

When we have domain classes in a hierarchical relationship like this, we can take advantage of polymorphic queries. We can now retrieve all of a user's posts ❶, or just their starred posts ❷, by taking advantage of the polymorphic query mechanisms that GORM dynamic finders give us for free.

We said that GORM uses one table per hierarchy by default. One of the disadvantages of this approach is that you can't have a nullable constraint in any of your subclasses (because base classes do inserts in the same table as your subclasses). But this is a small limitation compared to the power of polymorphic queries.

What if you want to use one table per subclass? You can, but it requires a little GORM DSL magic. Add the following mapping to your root class (`Post` in our case):

```
static mapping = {
   tablePerHierarchy false
}
```

If you do use one table per subclass, GORM will use outer joins to load instances, so performance can suffer if the class hierarchy is large. But you will be able to use nullable constraints on your domain class fields, so there's a trade off.

13.1.2 *Embedding domain classes*

Sometimes you want the convenience of a domain object, but you don't want the overhead of a separate table. This is particularly likely in legacy scenarios when you have a 1:1 mapping logically, but all the object properties are implemented as separate columns in one big table. For these situations, GORM lets you use *embedding*. Embedding lets you model one table as two or more related objects.

Let's take the example of our `Profile` object. Each user has one `Profile` object containing their email address and other personal data. But suppose we decide we don't want the overhead of managing a separate `Profile` table—we just want to embed the profile information directly in the `User` table. Listing 13.3 demonstrates how we could rework those classes to make that happen.

> **Listing 13.3 Embedded relationships stored in a single table**

```
class User {

    String userId
    String password
    Date signupDate = new Date()
    Profile profile
    static embedded = ['profile' ]          Stores Profile in same
    // ...                                   row as User
}
class Profile {          Declares embedded Profile
                         object in same source file
    byte[] photo

    String fullName
    // ...

}
```

As you can see, embedding is done with the `embedded` construct. For this to work, you have to define the `Profile` class in the same Groovy file as the `User` class (User.groovy)—otherwise, you'll end up with an empty `Profile` table in your database.

Embedding gives you a chance to keep your OO semantics without taking up unnecessary table space in your database.

13.1.3 *Using maps for quick and dirty (or cheap and cheerful) tables*

Although having a custom domain class manage your data is a logical approach, in some situations you don't want the overhead of writing a custom class.

Let's imagine that Hubbub supports custom plugins. Users can add these custom widgets to their Hubbub home page, and they configure them with various properties. We could create a domain class called `PluginProperty` with strings for the property name and value, but it's a little contrived. All we want is a map to store our key/value pairs.

For these cases, GORM lets us declare things as maps. Listing 13.4 shows an example of storing map-style properties.

Listing 13.4 Using maps for quick and dirty property storage

```
class User {

    String userId
    String password              Stores Maps as varchar(255)
    Map pluginProperties    ◁⎯  for key and value
    // ... other stuff here

}
```

Behind the scenes, Grails stores `pluginProperties` as a `Map` of key/value pairs of type `varchar(255)`, so you're constrained to only storing strings.

Here's how you might test it:

```
user = new User(userId: 'glen', password: 'notlong',
        pluginProperties: ['colour':'green']).save()

user.pluginProperties = [ one: "1", two: "2" ]
```

Storing free-form string data in maps can quickly become a maintenance nightmare, so you should use this capability with caution. Still, it's convenient for quick and dirty tables like `pluginProperties`.

13.1.4 Exploring domain model events

GORM handles a lot of the drudgery of getting data into and out of the database. But sometimes you need to integrate with GORM's lifecycle to add your own features. For example, imagine implementing an audit capability that logs any changes to the domain model each time an object is modified. GORM events provide a mechanism to do just that, giving you a way to hook into GORM just before and after an object is saved or loaded.

GORM exposes seven main events:

- `beforeInsert`
- `beforeUpdate`
- `beforeDelete`
- `afterInsert`
- `afterUpdate`
- `afterDelete`
- `onLoad`

If you want to catch any of these, define a closure with the corresponding name, like this:

```
def beforeDelete = {
    log.warn "${id} is toast by ${jsec.principal}"
}
```

None of the closures take any arguments or return any values, so if you need some state, it will need to be on the domain class itself or retrievable via the current thread. (In the preceding example, we retrieve the JSecurity user from the current thread.)

GORM makes one more allowance around events, to handle the common case of timestamping. One of the most common uses of events is to timestamp the creation or modification of a domain class. For example, you might catch `beforeUpdate` and set the modification time (or catch `beforeInsert` and set the creation time). For these situations, GORM offers a convenience convention: if you name two `Date` fields on your object `dateCreated` and `lastUpdated`, GORM will automatically set these fields to the current time:

```
class User {
    Date dateCreated
    Date lastUpdated
    String userId
    // ...
}
```

This is a special case, but it's one of the most common uses of events (along with audit logging), so it's handy having it as a built-in feature. We took advantage of this in our `Post` object when we created it in chapter 3, and it's been a real timesaver.

Now that we've taken you through some of the corner cases of domain modeling, it's time to explore a few tricks and tips to improve your query performance.

13.2 *Caching kung fu: moving from 2 users to 2^10*

In previous chapters, we've issued complex queries without much concern for how hard the underlying database might be working to catch up. That's fine if your site gets only a few hundred hits a day; but when you're aiming your sights higher, you need to explore caching and performance tuning.

In this section, we'll look at how GORM handles caching and see how you can determine which parts of your application would benefit from caching and when to tune the knobs. It all starts with understanding GORM's use of Hibernate second-level caching.

13.2.1 *Hibernate settings: should you use the second-level cache?*

Whenever you interact with the object model in Hibernate, an internal first-level cache is always in play—the session. For the cases where you change multiple properties on a given object during a request (such as changing the user's last login time and IP address), Hibernate can batch updates and execute a single SQL `UPDATE`.

Sometimes, the first-level cache is not enough. Take the scenario of the 1:m relationship (for example, each user having many posts). Every request in which you do a `user.posts.each { }` will result in a requery of the database. If your posts change infrequently (or not at all), that's a lot of wasted querying.

NOTE Calling `user.posts.each` twice in the same request will not requery the database because the collection is cached in the session.

For these scenarios, you can enable the *second-level cache*. When the second-level cache is enabled for a domain class, Hibernate first searches in this cache before looking in the database. Hibernate will also handle evicting objects from the cache when posts are added, edited, or deleted.

The only time you need to be careful about having a second-level cache in play is when you're working with clustered application servers. In that scenario, you need to ensure that none of the servers is working with stale data by configuring your caching provider to be cluster-aware.

As a rule of thumb, you definitely want a second-level cache in play to make things more performant. But how do you configure and tune it? Before we start tuning, let's configure the basic cache settings.

13.2.2 Cache configuration

Now that you know what a second-level cache does, it's time to learn how to configure it for use in your Grails application. The first thing you need to get familiar with is DataSource.groovy. You saw this file before when we configured our database connection parameters, but it also includes a `hibernate` section that we haven't explored yet. Check it out:

```
hibernate {
    cache.use_second_level_cache=true
    cache.use_query_cache=true
    cache.provider_class='com.opensymphony.oscache.
➥     hibernate.OSCacheProvider'
}
```

Our Hibernate second-level cache is enabled, as is some kind of query cache (which we'll get to later). A cache provider class is also specified—this tells Hibernate which underlying caching library to use (there are several). Grails uses OSCache by default, but we'll switch to Ehcache because it's a better caching library:

```
cache.provider_class='org.hibernate.cache.EhCacheProvider'
```

NOTE Most Hibernate users will be familiar with Ehcache as a common underlying caching provider, so why does Grails use OSCache by default? It's because OSCache plays more nicely when it's reloaded by Grails in a development environment. If you're used to using Ehcache, feel free to switch your caching provider to Ehcache when you're ready to go to production.

Each caching provider has its own configuration mechanism. Ehcache uses a single XML file (ehcache.xml) that needs to be in the root of the classpath; place it in either the /src/java or the /grails-app/conf directory. Listing 13.5 shows you a sample ehcache.xml file to get you started.

Listing 13.5   A sample ehcache.xml configuration file

```
<ehcache xmlns:xsi="http://www.w3.org/2001/XMLSchema-instance"
    xsi:noNamespaceSchemaLocation="ehcache.xsd">

    <defaultCache
        maxElementsInMemory="1000"
        eternal="false"
        timeToIdleSeconds="3600"              Expires objects in cache after
        timeToLiveSeconds="3600"          ◁┘ 1 hour (3600 seconds)
```

```
        overflowToDisk="false"
        diskPersistent="false"
        diskExpiryThreadIntervalSeconds="120"
        memoryStoreEvictionPolicy="LRU"
    />

</ehcache>
```

A full discussion of Ehcache is beyond the scope of this book, but these default settings will cache objects for 1 hour (3,600 seconds), after which they'll be timed out and refreshed from the database when next queried.

Ehcache supports many configuration options including a distributed cache, the ability to persist the cache to disk to survive restarts, and various eviction policies for quiet or stale elements. The online documentation (http://ehcache.sourceforge.net/) is excellent, so check it out to learn more.

13.2.3 *Caching individual domain classes*

To enable caching for individual domain classes, a little more work is required. You need to add a mapping block to each domain class that you wish to cache, like this:

```
static mapping = {
    cache true
}
```

Or, if you need more control over your caching options, you can pass in a map:

```
static mapping = {
    cache: "read-write"
}
```

The cache setting refers to how Hibernate handles concurrent access to the underlying cache (see table 13.1). Remember that Hibernate writes to that cache too, every time you update, create, or delete a domain class instance. If you're querying reference data, and you know there won't be any updates to the data (if it contains a list of time zones, for example), you can safely set the cache setting to read-only for better performance.

Table 13.1   All the standard Hibernate caching strategies are supported by Grails; these are the common ones you'll use.

Cache option	Description
true	The same as read-write caching
read-only	Only useful for static reference data; otherwise concurrency problems are inevitable
read-write	The default setting; implements concurrency on the cache

For Hubbub, our main caching requirements relate to a user's posts. In those cases, we'll want to employ caching strategies when we walk the object graph from User to Post. For this scenario, we'll need to add some modifications to our User class:

```
static mapping = {
   cache: true
   posts cache:true
}
```

TIP   Remember that you have to enable caching in two places. First, you need to turn caching on globally in DataSource.groovy (this is `true` by default). Second, you have to enable caching for your individual domain classes.

But that's only half of the story. Now that our `Post` object is cached, we may want to tune the timing of that particular cache. We need to revisit our ehcache.xml file and add a new cache element with a `name` that matches the name of the domain class:

```
<cache
      name="com.grailsinaction.Post"          ◁┐  Sets up cache for
      maxElementsInMemory="10000"              │   Post object
      eternal="false"
      timeToIdleSeconds="300"
      timeToLiveSeconds="600"
      overflowToDisk="false"
   />
<cache                                             ┐  Sets up cache for
      name="com.grailsinaction.User"          ◁─┘  User object
      maxElementsInMemory="10000"
      eternal="false"
      timeToIdleSeconds="300"
      timeToLiveSeconds="600"
      overflowToDisk="false"
   />
```

NOTE   If you put your domain classes in packages, you need to put your package name in the `name` field too, as we did in the preceding example (`com.grailsinaction.Post`).

In the preceding settings, we set the idle time to 300 seconds (so that if no one accesses an instance in the cache in 300 seconds, it will be evicted) and a maximum time to live of 600 seconds (whether the object is active or not, it will always be discarded after 600 seconds). Those are fairly aggressive settings, but it's a good starting point for our profiling exercise.

TIP   There's no one-size-fits-all answer for caching strategy. The strategy you select is dependent on how objects are used in your system. If you're in a low-write, high-read environment (like we are for a user's posts in Hubbub), it makes sense to embrace caching at some level. When we cover performance profiling in the next section, you'll learn about tools you can use to evaluate your caching needs.

Now that we've tuned all the settings on our cache, let's look at profiling to see if we can find any bottlenecks in our application performance.

13.2.4 *Enough talk, let's profile*

If you're into a first-principles approach, your profiling journey may start with inspecting some of the SQL queries that your application generates. You can modify your DataSource.groovy file to print GORM queries to the console:

```
development {
   dataSource {
      logSql = "true"
   }
}
```

That will give you some insight into query generation, but it won't tell you how long your database took to satisfy the query. For that, you'll need to do some query profiling, and the easiest way to do that in Grails is via P6Spy.

P6Spy is a small JDBC driver that wraps your real driver to provide a basic stopwatch. It then logs how many milliseconds the database took to satisfy your query. There's even a Grails plugin for P6Spy, so let's install it:

```
grails install-plugin p6spy
```

When the plugin is installed, it modifies your DataSource.groovy file to add a conveniently commented version of P6Spy as a potential database driver. Let's update our development dataSource class to use the new P6Spy version:

```
development {
   dataSource {
      dbCreate = "update"
      driverClassName =                          Changes driver
        "com.p6spy.engine.spy.P6SpyDriver"   ⟵┘ class only
      url = "jdbc:hsqldb:mem:devDB"
   }
}
```

Notice that we don't change the URL—P6Spy will proxy using the username, password, and URL of our database. But we have to tell it the real driver to use, and for that we need to modify the P6Spy config file: spy.properties. The plugin creates a template file for us in the grails-app/conf directory. Have a look at it now. Notice the realdriver setting, which tells P6Spy which database it's proxying:

```
realdriver=org.hsqldb.jdbcDriver
```

It has defaulted to our sample HSQLDB database, so we're in business.

With our database profiling in place, let's run Hubbub and see what profiling data we can collect. You'll notice that you now have a spy.log file in the root directory of your project. Inside, you'll find the output and timing of every query that went to your database. Here's a single-line extract from spy.log:

```
13:40:23|0|1|statement||create table account_account
➥ (user_followers_id bigint, user_id bigint, user_following_id bigint)
```

This is good, but we want something more readable. Enter SQL Profiler: a small Swing application that processes P6Spy log files and shows which queries take the longest. You can download it from http://sourceforge.net/projects/sqlprofiler.

SQL Profiler listens on a socket for log data from P6Spy, so you have to reconfigure p6spy.properties to tell it where to log. You can find the customized p6spy.properties file in the Hubbub source code.

Once you have the logging configured, start SQL Profiler before you run `grails run-app`, and watch the logs flow as you interact with your application. Figure 13.1 shows the stream of SQL queries being processed by the profiler. Click the Pause button at the top of the window to see the results of the analysis.

SQL Profiler's top pane shows the queries and how many milliseconds they took to run. Using HSQLDB as an in-memory database can mask performance issues, but using a real database (like PostgreSQL or MySQL) will generate values that are closer to what you'll see in production. Clicking an entry in the top window populates the bottom pane with the full SQL of the query, so you can see which joins are used.

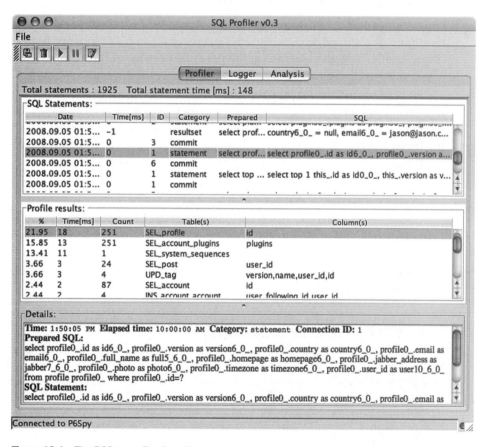

Figure 13.1 The P6Spy profiler in action

To get profiling data, use the Play and Pause buttons to profile just a few queries. Click Play, interact with a particular screen in your application, click Pause, and view the results in the middle pane. The middle pane tells you which queries took the longest time. The rightmost column tells you which table columns are used in the query (which is useful for identifying which columns would benefit from index creation).

To simulate how your database might perform under a real load, consider exploring a load-generation tool such as Apache JMeter (http://jakarta.apache.org/jmeter/). JMeter offers ways of simulating hundreds (or thousands) of users accessing your application concurrently, and it can be a great way to identify how your app performs under pressure.

P6Spy can give you basic database profiling information, and it's great for working out which queries in your application could most benefit from caching or tuning. But once you have some insight into where the bottlenecks are, you'll want to add some indexes. Let's explore how that's done in Grails.

13.2.5 *Improving performance with indexed fields*

Once your profiling efforts give you some insight into which retrievals are taking the most time, you should add indexes to your database to make lookups more efficient. Grails handles custom indexing via the versatile `mapping` closure (you saw this closure when configuring caching).

Suppose our reporting process does a lookup on the `User` table and creates some reports around `dateCreated`—the date the user signed up for our service. Given the popularity of our website, it makes sense to index on the `dateCreated` field. Creating the index involves giving the index a name (in our case, `date_created_idx` to keep the DBAs happy) and then attaching it to the domain class field we wish to index on:

```
static mapping = {
    dateCreated index:'date_created_idx'
}
```

Using indexing and profiling with P6Spy can be a great way to identify which queries in your application might benefit from caching.

It's now time to explore what facilities Grails offers to accelerate query performance through caching.

What if I need distributed caching?

Second-level caches are great, but traditionally they haven't had the best support for clustering, making them significantly less useful in high-availability settings. Replication technologies were typically chatty and not very performant, but great progress has been made in this area. Commercial-strength distributed caches like the open source Terracotta platform now have excellent Grails support through plugins. Ehcache now has distributed cache options, too. If you're running in a cluster, be sure to check them out.

13.2.6 *What about query caching?*

So far, we've talked a lot about second-level caching and how that can improve performance when navigating the object graph. But what about when you just want to cache queries?

Options are available for this, but it's not likely they'll be helpful. GORM will only cache query results if none of the tables included in the query have changed since your last query. If GORM has changed any of the items in any of the tables, the cached results will be discarded, and you'll hit the database directly. In fact, you'll also incur the overhead of the cache check.

But if you still want to make use of query caching, you have a few options. The first is to use a cache argument to dynamic finders, like this:

```
def entries = Post.findAllByUser(user, [cache: true])
```

This works great if the query that you need to execute can be expressed in a dynamic finder. Unfortunately, that's often not the case, so you're left with two options: criteria queries and HQL.

Criteria queries are the neatest solution and the one we recommend. Imagine you want to cache a user's recent posts; specify the cacheable(true) setting, and you're ready to go:

```
def entries = Post.createCriteria().list {
    eq('user', user)
    cacheable(true)
}
```

But remember, if either the Posts or Users table changes (not just for this user, but for anyone), this query will be evicted from the cache.

Criteria queries make this straightforward. But if you're already using HQL, you can use Hibernate directly:

```
def recentPosts = {
    def posts = Post.withSession { session ->
        session.createQuery(
            "select p from $Post.name p where p.user.id=:userid")
            .setCacheable(true)
            .setString("userid", params.userid)
            .list()
    }

    [posts : posts ]
}
```

As you can see, this technique is more powerful but less elegant than dynamic finders or criteria queries, which we prefer for all caching queries (where practical).

By default, all queries are cached in a single cache called org.hibernate.cache .StandardQueryCache. You can define a cache with this name in your ehcache.xml file if you want to control how long the cache should live. If you don't, it will use your defaultCache settings. Alternatively, you can use different *cache regions* for each of your cached queries.

To use cache regions, define a cache element in ehcache.xml with the name of the cache (such as `hourlyCache`). With this cache region defined, pass its name into your criteria:

```
def entries = Post.createCriteria().list {
    eq('user', user)
    cacheable(true)
    cacheRegion('hourlyCache')
}
```

Alternatively, if you're using HQL to perform your query, chain a call to `setCache-Region('hourlyCache')` to get the same effect.

That's a lot of query performance-enhancement options. But before we finish this section, there's one server-level query performance enhancement we haven't explored yet. JNDI data sources, provided by most servers, give you an efficient way to manage database connections. It's time to explore this and other benefits they offer.

13.2.7 *JNDI? That's so old school...*

If you've always lumped Java Naming and Directory Interface (JNDI) into the category of "old-school J2EE stuff that's long past," it's time to have a second look. There are some compelling reasons to use JNDI data sources in your next Grails project—particularly for the production data source:

- You don't need to hardcode usernames, passwords, database names, or even types, making for a source-control-friendly check-in for your project even on public sites like GitHub, SourceForge, and Google Code.
- It offers efficient pooling of resources by your server, including adding connections to the pool when needed and reconnecting dead instances.
- Each developer can easily use their preferred DBMS without custom configuration and library files.

But JNDI has some drawbacks, too:

- The JNDI naming format can differ from container to container.
- Configuration for Jetty is problematic and requires a custom jetty-env.xml file in your /WEB-INF/ directory.

There's almost no good reason to not use a JNDI data source for your production data source, and we encourage you to make this your first change after doing `grails create-app`. We've deployed small apps to production accidentally using an embedded HSQLDB, and we don't want you to suffer the same pain.

Listing 13.6 shows an example of how JNDI data sources are configured for the Glassfish application server in DataSource.groovy. This configuration varies from server to server, so check the documentation.

Listing 13.6   Configuring JNDI data sources for use in Glassfish

```
// environment specific settings
environments {

   // ...

   production {
      dataSource {
         dbCreate = "update"              Configures JNDI name
         jndiName = "jdbc/hubbub"     ◁───┘ in application server
      }
   }
}
```

Once you've updated your DataSource.groovy file, you'll need to define the JNDI data source itself in your application server. Usually, your server admin console lets you create JNDI data sources and configure the database username, password, connection pools size, and so on.

That completes our survey of query and data source tricks and tips. It's time now to look at legacy concerns. Integrating with legacy databases is an important part of enterprise development, so we're going to spend the second half of this chapter exploring the common issues you're likely to encounter when integrating your new Grails applications with historical data.

13.3   Legacy integration kung fu: dealing with multiple data sources

The Grails data source mechanism makes it easy to configure a single data source, but what if your application needs more than one? Take the example where you need to access a reference data table of countries and their codes in another team's database.

The best way to handle this is via Burt Beckwith's Datasources plugin, which lets you map different domain classes to different databases. You can still use dynamic finders, and Grails routes the query to the appropriate data source based on your configuration.

The first step is installing the plugin:

```
grails install-plugin datasources
```

Next, you need to specify which domain classes map to which data sources. The plugin uses a special file called /grails-app/conf/Datasources.groovy (note the plural) to define the alternative data sources and indicate which domain classes map to which data sources.

Listing 13.7 shows a sample definition of Datasources.groovy that loads two reference table classes from a separate PostgreSQL database. Most of the settings will be familiar, because you've seen them specified in the standard DataSource.groovy file.

Listing 13.7   Configuring multiple data sources in /grails-app/conf/Datasources.groovy

```
datasources = {

    datasource(name: 'countries') {
        domainClasses([com.grailsinaction.CountryCodes,
                com.grailsinaction.RegionCodes])
        readOnly(true)
        driverClassName('org.postgresql.Driver')
        url('jdbc:postgresql://localhost/reference_db')
        username('glen')
        password('password')
        dbCreate('update')
        logSql(true)
        dialect(org.hibernate.dialect.PostgreSQLDialect)
        hibernate {
            cache {
                use_second_level_cache(false)
                use_query_cache(false)
            }
        }
    }

}
```

Specifies which domain classes use data source

Marks data source as read-only

You can configure as many data sources as you like in this file and make appropriate entries in the `domainClasses` component to list each class. Once your definition is in place, you can then access your domain objects with the usual dynamic finders, such as `CountryCodes.findByCode('au')`. Save and update operations work as well.

The plugin is still under development, but it shows great promise as an easy way of integrating multiple data sources into one Grails application. Consult the online documentation for the plugin at http://grails.org/plugin/datasources for more information on the available configuration options.

Now that you know how to handle multiple data sources, the next legacy integration challenge is dealing with databases that have horrible table structures.

13.4   *Dealing with difficult legacy databases*

It would be nice if we could start with a clean data model each time, but life is rarely that simple. You'll often have an existing database that your DBA won't modify. Like all decent frameworks, Grails is comfortable playing nicely with your existing environment.

In this section, we'll examine two techniques for migrating an existing database application to Grails. First, we'll look at how you can reuse your existing Hibernate mappings and Java domain objects, and build a Grails UI in front. After that, we'll look at the situation where you have an existing legacy database but no existing Hibernate mappings. In that case, you can skip the Hibernate step entirely and use the GORM legacy mapping DSL to map your Grails domain objects directly to your existing database schema.

But first, we'll introduce you to a poorly constructed legacy database. This is a real data model found in a real enterprise (with the names changed to protect the innocent). This model has all the nasty surprises you'd expect: string-based natural keys, auto-incrementing keys not based on sequences, many-to-many tables with link attributes, several data types used for table keys (including char), and more. The basic layout of the data model is shown in figure 13.2.

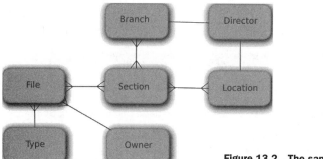

Figure 13.2   The sample legacy database

Let's step through the process of writing a simple one-page UI that lets us browse the data model. If you have Hibernate mappings for the database, it would be nice to reuse them. Let's explore that option first.

13.4.1 Recycling Hibernate mappings

If you're coming to GORM after using a lot of Hibernate, you'll be familiar with Hibernate annotations and mapping files. You probably have .hbm.xml files and matching domain classes. There's no need to throw them away.

Lurking quietly in the grails-app/conf/hibernate directory is a space for you to place your existing mapping files. Drop your domain classes in /src/java/ (or possibly as a JAR file in your /lib directory), and you're in business. If you name your Hibernate configuration file /grails-app/conf/hibernate/hibernate.cfg.xml, there's nothing more to do.

Listing 13.8 shows a sample hibernate.cfg.xml file for the legacy database in figure 13.2.

Listing 13.8   Reusing existing Hibernate XML mapping files

```
<?xml version='1.0' encoding='UTF-8'?>
<!DOCTYPE hibernate-configuration PUBLIC
      "-//Hibernate/Hibernate Configuration DTD 3.0//EN"
      "http://hibernate.sourceforge.net/hibernate-configuration-3.0.dtd">
<hibernate-configuration>
   <session-factory>
      <mapping resource="org.hbm.xml"/>
   </session-factory>
</hibernate-configuration>
```

Notice that there's no data-source configuration like you typically see in hibernate.cfg.xml—this is already configured in the data-source definitions in DataSource.groovy. But we do need to reference our existing org.hbm.xml file, which contains our Hibernate domain class mapping definitions for the sample database. We can use annotations to specify these mappings, but because this is a legacy setup, let's assume we're lost in a world of pointy XML.

Our org.hbm.xml file is a standard Hibernate mapping file. It specifies the mapping from a series of bizarrely named underlying tables to a set of standard Java classes. Listing 13.9 shows an extract of our mapping file to give you a feel for it.

Listing 13.9 An extract from a legacy Hibernate mapping file

```xml
<?xml version="1.0" encoding="UTF-8"?>
<!DOCTYPE hibernate-mapping PUBLIC "-//Hibernate/Hibernate Mapping DTD//EN"
    "http://hibernate.sourceforge.net/hibernate-mapping-3.0.dtd">

<hibernate-mapping auto-import="true" default-lazy="false"
            package="com.grailsinaction.legacy.db">
  <class name="Branch"
      table="BK_BRANCH" mutable="false">
    <cache usage="read-write"/>
    <id name="name" column="BRANCH_NM">
       <generator class="assigned"/>
    </id>

    <set name="sections" table="BK_BRANCH_TO_SECTION"
        cascade="save-update">
        <key column="BRANCH_NM"/>
        <many-to-many class="Section" column="SECTION_ID"/>
    </set>

    <set name="files" table="BK_BRANCH_TO_FILE"
        cascade="save-update">
        <key column="BRANCH_NM"/>
        <many-to-many class="File" column="FILE_ID" />
    </set>

    <one-to-one name="manager" class="Manager" cascade="save-update"/>

  </class>
```

The syntax is ugly, but it does a lot of heavy lifting. The full set of mapping files for this domain is included in the book's source code.

PIMP MY DATA MODEL: ADDING AN AJAX INTERFACE

Suppose we've got our legacy model running by importing our existing Hibernate mappings, and we have access to our Java DTOs too. Let's write some controller logic so we have a basic UI for browsing our domain model.

We don't have scaffolding options because the standard scaffolds make some assumptions about the existence of ID fields, which we don't have. We could customize the scaffolding templates, but that sounds like a lot of work for what we want. Let's create a quick Ajax-based controller to browse the database.

Here's our browser controller:

```
import com.grailsinaction.legacy.db.*

class BrowserController {

    def index = { redirect(action: 'list') }

    def list = {
        // Pass through to Ajax browser form
    }
}
```

There's no rocket science here—we're exposing a `list` endpoint to pass through to our Ajax form. In listing 13.10, we create our list.gsp with our Ajax-populated drop-down list.

Listing 13.10 Implementing a list.gsp with Ajax

```
<html>
<head>
    <title>Legacy DB Browser</title>
    <g:javascript library="prototype"/> </head> <body>
</head>
<body>
    <fieldset>
        <legend>Browse Branches</legend>
        <g:form action="showDetails">
            <label for="id">Branch:</label>
            <g:select name="id"
                from="${com.grailsinaction.legacy.db.          Populates drop-
                       Branch.list()}"                          down box with list
                optionKey="name" optionValue="name"/>           of branch objects
            <g:submitToRemote value="Show Details"              Performs Ajax submit
                update="details"                                of selected branch
                url="[action: 'showDetails']"/>
        </g:form>
    </fieldset>
    <div id="details"></div>       Holds DIV for content
</body>                            returned via Ajax
</html>
```

Not much exciting stuff is happening there. We have a combo box full of available branch names and a Show Details button that submits the request to the controller and replaces a DIV with the returned value. Figure 13.3 shows the UI so far.

Figure 13.3   The Branch browser combo box launches an Ajax submit.

Let's implement our controller logic to handle the submit and return some well-formed HTML. Using markup builder is the simplest way to generate the HTML, so let's implement some code to return the manager for the selected branch. Listing 13.11 shows the initial backend code.

Listing 13.11   Implementing the Ajax backend to show branch details

```
def showDetails = {
    def branch = Branch.findByName(params.id)          ◁┐ Queries legacy
                                                          │ database to
    def writer = new StringWriter()                       │ find branch
    def html = new groovy.xml.MarkupBuilder(writer)

    // Could do all this directly in a render() call
    // but it's harder to debug
    html.div {                  ◁┐ Uses markup builder to
        div(id: 'manager') {      │ render branch as HTML
            fieldset {
                legend('Manager Details')
                dl {
                    dt('Name:')
                    dd(branch.manager.name)
                    dt('Rating:')
                    dd(branch.manager.managementRating)
                }
            }
        }
    }

    render(writer.toString())

}
```

One thing to notice in listing 13.11 is that we're using a dynamic finder, `Branch.find-ByName()`, on our legacy DTO class. Grails has decorated our DTO with a proxy that implements the persistence and querying logic that Grails needs, so we get all this for free on our legacy classes.

With our markup builder in place to navigate our data model, let's take the UI for a spin in figure 13.4.

Fantastic! We have our Ajax interface in action, but we haven't exercised all the potential relationships that could be navigated via the model. Let's fix that right now

Figure 13.4   Our basic manager details are in place.

with a much more complete markup builder example. Listing 13.12 shows code that navigates the entire legacy model.

Listing 13.12 A more complete `showDetails` that navigates all relationships

```
def showDetails = {
    def branch = Branch.findByName(params.id)

    def writer = new StringWriter()
    def html = new groovy.xml.MarkupBuilder(writer)

    // Could do all this directly in a render() call
    // but it's harder to debug
    html.div {
        div(id: 'manager') {
            fieldset {
                legend('Manager Details')
                dl {
                    dt('Name:')
                    dd(branch.manager.name)
                    dt('Rating:')
                    dd(branch.manager.managementRating)
                }
            }
        }

        div(id: 'sections') {
            branch.sections.each { section ->
                fieldset {
                    legend('Section: ' + section.name)
                    dl {
                        dt('Start Date:')
                        dd(section.start)

                        dt('Files:')
                        dd(section.files.size())

                        section.files.each { sectToFile ->
                            dl(style:
                                'padding: 1em; border: 1px dotted black') {
                                dt('File Name: ')
                                dd(sectToFile.file.name)
                                dt('Type:')
                                dd(sectToFile.file.resourceType.name)
                                dt('Created:')
                                dd(sectToFile.start)
                                dt('Owner:')
                                dd(sectToFile.file.owner.name)
                            }
                        }
                        dt('Locations:')
                        dd(section.locations.size())
                        ul {
                            section.locations.each { sectToLoc ->
                                li(sectToLoc.location.name)
                            }
                        }
```

```
            }
          }
        }
      }
    }
  }
  render(writer.toString())
}
```

That's a much bigger builder, but this time we've got a full navigation graph to make sure everything is working correctly. Check out the updated UI in figure 13.5.

We know that our legacy relationships are all in order, but we don't want to settle for read-only access to our data. It's time to explore our options for saving new objects to our legacy database, and it's also time to investigate how we can retrofit some validation constraints in the process.

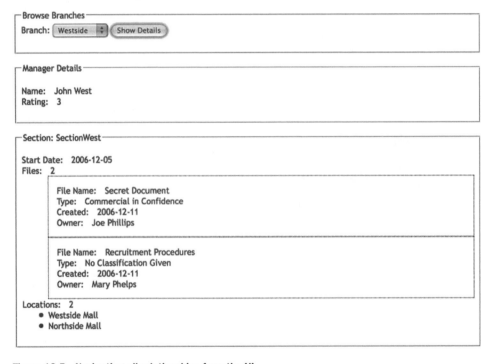

Figure 13.5   Navigating all relationships from the UI

Scaffolding on legacy Hibernate domain classes (POJOs)

You may be wondering whether the UI scaffolding features we covered in chapter 4 apply to these Java classes that we've pulled in via Hibernate legacy mappings. Amazingly, this does work! You can set up your scaffolding from your Grails controller with the full name of the Java DTO class:

```
def scaffold = com.grailsinaction.legacy.db.User
```

> ### Scaffolding on legacy Hibernate domain classes (POJOs) *(continued)*
>
> Grails will have a go at scaffolding it. Be warned, though, that this almost never works without some tweaking. Grails scaffolding code makes assumptions about your domain classes (including that they'll have an ID field called `id`). You can work around that by generating the template code for the scaffold controller and view (`grails generate-all`) and then editing by hand. It'll still save you lots of time.

ADDING CONSTRAINTS TO LEGACY POJO CLASSES

Now that we have our legacy classes mapped, it's time to look at some options for adding constraints. Even though our legacy classes are POJOs, Grails still gives us a convention-based facility for specifying legacy mappings.

You can't add `constraints` closures to Java classes (at least not in JDK6), but Grails lets you place Groovy constraint scripts alongside your Java classes following the convention of *DomainClassName*Constraints.groovy. Here's a sample BranchConstraints .groovy file:

```
package com.grailsinaction.legacy.db

def constraints = {
   name(size: 4..30)
}
```

Note that these classes are placed alongside your Java POJOs in /src/java (and not in /src/groovy, as you might expect). Also note that the `constraints` closure isn't static as in GORM classes.

Let's write a test case to confirm that our constraint is working as anticipated. Listing 13.13 shows a sample test.

Listing 13.13   Testing validation of legacy classes

```
import com.grailsinaction.legacy.db.*
import grails.test.*

class BranchTests extends GrailsUnitTestCase {

   void testBranchConstraints() {

      def branch = new Branch(name: 'a')       Fails validation
      assertFalse(branch.validate())           with short name
      branch.name = 'aaaa'                      Passes validation with
      assertTrue(branch.validate())            valid-length name

   }
}
```

If you run `grails test-app`, you'll find this test passes, telling us that our constraint is working fine.

With our exploration of constraints complete, we're now on top of all the options for Hibernate-based legacy integration. But what if you don't have legacy Hibernate mappings? It's time to look at what the GORM DSL offers for doing legacy mappings without all that XML.

13.4.2 *Using GORM DSL to access existing database table structures*

All this work around integrating legacy Hibernate mappings is fantastic if you have legacy Hibernate mappings to work with. But you might need to develop a snazzy UI for a legacy database that powers an old PHP application. For these situations, GORM offers a DSL for working with legacy databases.

By adding a `mapping` section to your domain classes (which you've already seen in section 13.2), you can change the name of the tables or columns, specify join tables, use custom key-generation strategies, and more. Behind the scenes, the GORM DSL configures the Hibernate mapping dynamically, so you can get to work with your domain classes and not get caught up in XML.

In this section, we'll redevelop our legacy database example from the previous section using the GORM DSL. First, we'll create a set of domain class objects in /grails-app/domains, because we're now going to be dealing with first-class Grails domain classes. We'll keep the same package names, because we can reuse the controller code we've already developed to browse the new object model. Figure 13.6 shows the reworked domain classes, this time rewritten in Groovy.

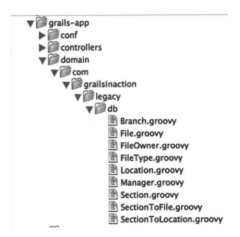

Figure 13.6 Our new domain structure

With our domain model in place, it's time to get acquainted with some of the mapping options available for hooking up legacy tables.

THE BASICS: CHANGING TABLE AND FIELD NAMES

DBAs have a long history of creating bizarre naming standards, so the first thing we need to learn is mapping to custom field and table names. You can map to fields named whatever you like by taking advantage of the `mapping` block.

Let's tackle something simple first, like the `FileOwner` object, which doesn't have any relationships. Listing 13.14 shows the reworked domain class.

Listing 13.14 A domain class with a legacy mapping block

```
package com.grailsinaction.legacy.db

class FileOwner {                    ❶ Uses int-based key
    int id
    String name
    String description

    static mapping = {       ❷ Declares custom          ❸ Turns off
        table 'BK_FILE_OWNER'      table name               Hibernate's
        version false                                       version field

        id column: 'FILE_OWNER_ID', generator: 'increment'   ◁
        name column: 'OWNER_NM'                        Specifies custom
        description column: 'OWNER_DESC'               column name and
    }                                                  generator for
}                                                   ❹ primary key
```

Our mapping closure introduces a few new constructs that you haven't seen before. We can change the name of the backing table ❷; and by specifying property names in the block, we can remap them to their corresponding database columns.

Another thing to note is version false ❸. Hibernate uses the version column to track object versions for optimistic locking. This isn't implemented in our legacy tables, so we turned the feature off.

We have also defined an int-based id field (the default type is long) to make sure everything matches up to our int-based id field in the database ❶. Alternatively, you can specify the type on the mapping itself (id column: 'FILE_OWNER_ID', type: 'integer'), which is convenient for some tricky timestamp formats or char fields (such as DB2's yes_no character field to handle Booleans).

The id field uses one of the built-in Hibernate generators for generating key values. In this case, we're using the increment strategy ❹, which uses the next incrementing number, but you're free to use any of the generators (which include sequences, hilo, or even assigned natural keys, which we'll cover shortly).

That gets us through the basics of mapping custom field and table names, but what about the more thorny issue of navigating relationships? It's time to dig a little deeper.

ADDING ONE-TO-MANY RELATIONSHIPS

One of the most common relationship types is the one-to-many (or many-to-one) relationship. Our File object has several many-to-one relationships mapped.

Listing 13.15 demonstrates mapping this complex class using mapping DSL entries.

Listing 13.15 Mapping a complex relationship using the mapping DSL

```
package com.grailsinaction.legacy.db

class File {

    int id
    FileType resourceType
```

```
String name
short securityRating
FileOwner owner
Date start = new Date()
Date end = new Date()                        Models many-to-many
String description                           relationships using
                                             linking object
static hasMany = [sections: SectionToFile]  ◁

static mapping = {
   table 'BK_FILE'
   version false

   id column: 'FILE_ID', generator: 'increment'   Applies custom
   name column: 'FILE_NM'                          column names
   start column: 'START_DT', type: 'date'       ◁ and types
   end column: 'END_DT', type: 'date'
   description column: 'FILE_DESC'
   securityRating column: 'SECURITY_RATING_VAL'
   owner column: 'FILE_OWNER_ID'
   resourceType column: 'FILE_TYPE_CD'
   sections column: 'SECTION_ID', joinTable: 'BK_FILE_SECTION_MAP'  ◁
}                                           Specifies custom join table
                                            name for many-to-many
}
```

`FileType` and `FileOwner` are the many-to-one relationships in this class. All that's required is a mapping from the field name to the database column for the foreign key. Once your mapping is in place, you're free to navigate the object graph like a standard Grails relationship.

MANY-TO-MANY: HANDLING JOIN TABLES

In our sample application, we need to model explicit join objects from `SectionToFile`. That's because there are custom attributes on the join itself (in our case, start and end dates for the file's ownership lifetime). Often, there are no attributes on the join, and you have a classic many-to-many with a join table containing only the two IDs for each object in the relationship.

We have pure join tables with no other attributes when linking sections to locations. The join table, BK_LOCATION_SECTION_MAP, has IDs for each side and no other attributes. Mapping this in the GORM DSL requires specifying a `hasMany` block and then adding an appropriate `joinTable` mapping. Listing 13.16 shows a mapping via a join table.

> **Listing 13.16   Mapping relationships that use join tables**

```
package com.grailsinaction.legacy.db

class Section {

   int id
   String name
   Date start = new Date()
   Date end = new Date()

   static hasMany = [files: SectionToFile,
```

```
              locations: Location,
              branches: BranchToSection ]

   static belongsTo = [ Branch ]

   static mapping = {
      table 'BK_SECTION'
      version false

      id column: 'SECTION_ID', generator: 'increment', type:'integer'
      name column: 'SECTION_NM'
      start column: 'START_DT', type: 'date'
      end column: 'END_DT', type: 'date'
      locations column:'SECTION_ID',          | Maps section to
         joinTable:'BK_LOCATION_SECTION_MAP'   | branch via a join table
   }
}
```

Take special note of our `locations` attribute. It uses the `joinTable` attribute to specify the name of the many-to-many link table, and it also specifies the column (`SECTION_ID`) of this side of the relationship.

CORNER CASE: HANDLING NATURAL AND COMPOSITE KEYS

We still have some key-related territory to cover. Not all tables have the luxury of a surrogate primary key; many depend on either a natural key or a collection of fields that form a composite key. GORM DSL has support for both, in varying degrees.

In our example application, we have a `SectionToFile` join object that models attributes of the join between `Section` and `File`. Being a join table, it has neither a natural nor a surrogate key, but we can model the composite of both fields as our key. This is shown in listing 13.17. Note that Hibernate requires these linking objects to implement `Serializable`.

Listing 13.17 Handling existing link tables in many-to-many relationships

```
package com.grailsinaction.legacy.db
                                                 | Implements Serializable
class SectionToFile implements Serializable {  <─┘ (as required)

   Section section
   File file
   Date start
   Date end

   static mapping = {
      table 'BK_FILE_SECTION_MAP'
      version false

      id composite:['file', 'section']
      start column: 'START_DT', type: 'date'
      end column: 'END_DT', type: 'date'
      file column: 'FILE_ID'
      section column: 'SECTION_ID'
   }

}
```

One thing that you lose with composite IDs is the ability to do `get()`s based on the composite ID. You need to use query by example to get back to your original object.

More tricky is the case of natural keys. In our `Branch` class, the `name` property forms the primary key for the table. Convincing GORM that this is a good thing involves a little sleight of hand, as shown in listing 13.18.

Listing 13.18   Handling natural keys with some GORM workarounds

```
package com.grailsinaction.legacy.db

class Branch {

    String id

    static transients = ['name']

    void setName(String name) {          Changes
        id = name                        underlying id
    }

    String getName() {          Returns
        return id               underlying id
    }

    static hasMany = [sections:Section]

    static mapping = {
        table 'BK_BRANCH'
        version false

        id generator:'assigned', column: "BRANCH_NM", type:'string'
        sections column:'SECTION_ID',
                joinTable:'BK_BRANCH_TO_SECTION',
                type:'integer'

    }
}
```

GORM depends on having an `id` field, and it's insistent that it appear in your mapping. In listing 13.18, we have a `name` field rather than `id`, so we rely on getters and setters to map our internal `id` field to a more public `name` field. It's not pretty, but it does the job.

You have to be careful when saving objects mapped in this way, because Grails views a non-`null` id as indicating a persistent instance. You need to use the `branch.save(insert: true)` option when using this approach.

That rounds out our exploration of legacy data sources. We took you through a worst-case database, so you should feel confident that you can tackle any structure that a DBA can throw at you.

> **When to use GORM DSL, and when to use Hibernate mappings**
>
> Now that you've had a good look at both GORM DSL and Hibernate mappings for the same nasty database, you may be wondering what the best option is. Obviously, if you have existing Hibernate mappings, it makes sense to reuse them. But what if you have a brand-new web application that needs to integrate with a crazy legacy database? As with most things, the answer is "it depends."
>
> If your database makes extensive use of natural (non-integer) keys or join tables with attributes, using Hibernate mappings is usually cleaner. That said, if your team isn't invested in Hibernate mappings, there's almost always a GORM DSL solution (but it may require some compromises in your object model—you may end up introducing join objects with composite keys to map the relationship).
>
> If your legacy database is fairly modern with lots of surrogate keys and not too much special sauce, GORM DSL is definitely the way to go. You'll end up with a clean set of object classes, and you can live your life without the tedious pointy XML of Hibernate mappings.

13.5 Summary and best practices

We've introduced a lot of advanced GORM functionality in this chapter. Some of the less-common relationship types (including inheritance) can prove to be real timesavers (and code neateners), but you have to remember the pros and cons of each choice.

We've also taken you through the details of query and second-level caching, and we covered cache tuning in some detail.

We looked at some performance-measurement options for the data tier and explored a profiling tool to help you work out what to tune. Finally, we undertook a detailed range of options for getting Grails working with legacy databases (including reuse of existing Hibernate mapping files and the GORM legacy mapping DSL).

Before we move on to exploring Spring and transactions in chapter 14, let's review a few key best practices from this chapter:

- *Understand inheritance.* When evaluating your inheritance options, understand the potential performance cost of using a one-table-per-class strategy, and weigh that against the relaxed validation constraints required when using the one-table-per-hierarchy approach.
- *Use JNDI data sources.* Use JNDI for production data sources (and change your database setting for production to JNDI straight after running `create app`).
- *Don't guess, profile.* P6Spy will give you good insight into your query timings. Combined with a load tool like JMeter, you can get pretty good simulations of how your app will perform if you get Slashdotted.
- *Don't be overzealous with query caching, but do use second-level caches.* Sometimes you will be better off rolling your own caching mechanism for high-churn data (such as for summary tables that update regularly but are backed by an

expensive query). Always enable second-level caching (although there are always caveats to this, particularly when running in clusters).

- *Reuse Hibernate mappings.* If you have existing Hibernate mappings for your legacy database, use them. GORM DSL requires compromises that aren't worth it if you've already done the hard work of writing real Hibernate mappings.

- *Favor GORM DSL for well-designed database and Hibernate mappings for evil ones.* For brand-new development on well-designed legacy databases, favor GORM DSL. There's less to maintain, and it means your team doesn't need to learn Hibernate. When working with legacy databases that have bizarre schemas, favor raw Hibernate mappings (particularly if you have existing Hibernate mapping files). Hibernate mappings have much more power than straight GORM DSL, and you'll end up with a much cleaner solution.

In the next chapter, we'll dive deep into the heart of Grails with a thorough exploration of Spring and transactions.

Spring and transactions

After plumbing the depths of GORM and Hibernate, it's time to move back up the abstraction hierarchy and look at the application infrastructure. GORM is wonderful as a database abstraction layer, and you can work some magic with controllers and GSPs, but just as a vertebrate needs a backbone to hold all its appendages together, so too does an application.

Fortunately, Grails is built around a tried and tested framework that will help you grow your application: Spring. We've mentioned it in passing a few times, and it tends to remain invisible if your application remains fairly simple. The trouble is, if it stays invisible, you'll miss out on powerful tools in your armory. We can't have that, so this chapter will explain some of the basics of the framework and how Grails allows you to interact with it directly.

After that, we'll look at a feature that will come in handy after all the talk of databases in the previous chapter: transactions. Although not part of the core

Spring framework, Spring's transaction support is instrumental in building reliable, data-oriented applications. It's an important topic that deserves, and receives, thorough treatment.

Let's find out what Spring can do for you.

NOTE   If you're already a Spring aficionado, we suggest you skim the next section and give the introduction on services a brief once over.

14.1 Spring and Grails

Some time ago, a new paradigm emerged in application design called Inversion of Control (IoC). The principle is simple: instead of an object managing its own dependencies, the code creating that object manages them. The application delegates the responsibility for creating and initializing its objects to a third party—an IoC container. Figure 14.1 illustrates the difference between the two approaches.

When you look at figure 14.1, it seems obvious that the traditional approach is simpler to understand, so why bother with IoC? There are several significant advantages to using IoC, but the critical point is that the complexity of dependency management is taken out of the class, leaving the important logic. The code for dealing with creating or finding the appropriate dependencies can be the nastiest stuff in a class, so why not make it somebody else's problem? Your classes become simpler and easier to manage, and, as a side effect, they become much easier to test.

The most common form of IoC nowadays is known as *Dependency Injection*, which is the pattern implemented by Spring. It's beyond the scope of this book to provide a detailed description of Dependency Injection, but you can find out more on Wikipedia: http://en.wikipedia.org/wiki/Dependency_injection.

As a Dependency Injection implementation, Spring manages the lifecycle of an application's objects, which is just a fancy way of saying it creates, initializes, and destroys them. These managed objects are called "Spring beans," and they're regular

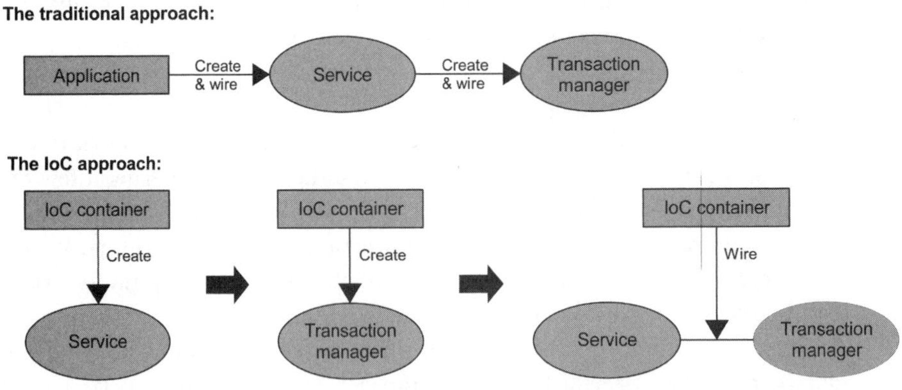

The traditional approach:

The IoC approach:

Figure 14.1   Inversion of Control compared to the traditional approach of dependency management: all objects are created by the IoC container rather than by the object themselves.

Java objects—they don't even have to comply with the JavaBeans specification, which makes the name slightly confusing.

Note that Spring is rarely used to manage *all* the objects in an application. Developers commonly use it to manage the singletons in their applications. For example, this class could be a Spring bean without any changes:

```
class MyService {
    TransactionManager transactionManager

    void doTransaction() {
        ...
    }
}
```

See how there's no reference to Spring in this class? Whether it's a Spring bean depends entirely on whether it's managed by the Spring framework.

Because a Spring bean is a Plain Old Java Object (POJO), the framework needs some way of knowing how to connect, or *wire*, different beans together and what values to initialize their properties to. This is achieved through a *bean descriptor* that contains the required *bean definitions*—the information necessary to initialize each object. Every bean managed by Spring must have an associated bean definition.

So how does one go about creating one of these bean descriptors? Traditionally, you would create an XML file that followed a particular schema, but Grails simplifies the whole business through convention and a nice DSL. We'll look at both the XML and DSL forms in section 14.1.2 (both have their uses), but we'll start by looking at Grails' entry-level Spring beans: services.

14.1.1 A conventional approach

In a typical Grails application, you start with some of your domain classes and then progress to writing the controllers and views. As you progress, the temptation is to put more and more logic into the controllers, making them heavy and giving them responsibility for more than the UI. You then find that you need to reuse some of that functionality (for example, from a web service gateway) and discover that controllers can't easily be called from other parts of your application.

For a variety of reasons, best practice dictates that business logic—the stuff unrelated to the UI—should go into Grails services. What this best practice is doing is following the principle of Separation of Concerns (SoC), where a "concern" is a self-contained area of functionality or, perhaps more accurately, responsibility. For example, the UI is one concern, database access is another, and access control might be a third. By limiting a single class to only one concern, the application code is easier both to understand and modify. Typically controllers stick to UI-related matters, and services host the business logic of the application.

In practice, this means that the real work of the application should be implemented in services. As a general rule of thumb, controllers should not access the database directly except in the case of trivial queries that have little reuse value. Unfortunately,

> ## More on SoC
> You shouldn't stop thinking about Separation of Concerns once you split your code between controllers and services. Applications themselves are often collections of concerns, so you should apply the principle throughout your code. In Hubbub, for example, managing individual posts could be treated as one concern, searching as another, and managing friends and followers as a third. Also, packages are an ideal way of grouping classes by concern.

hard-and-fast rules are difficult to come by, but the overall effect we're after is illustrated in figure 14.2.

You've already seen services in action in chapter 5, and you've seen how they can be injected into controllers and other Grails artifacts. How does all that magic happen? Under the hood, Grails creates Spring beans for services such that the name of the bean is the class name with a lowercase first letter. So `PostService` becomes a bean named `postService`.

TIP   Because closures behave a lot like methods, you may be tempted to use them in services instead of methods. This isn't a good idea because transactions and other features that depend on method interception won't work properly. The problem is that neither Spring nor Java know anything about closures, so they're treated as fields. Only methods get special treatment.

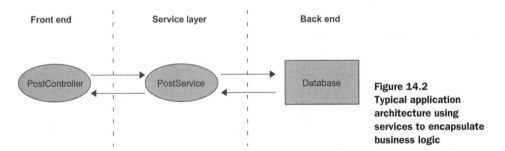

Figure 14.2 Typical application architecture using services to encapsulate business logic

Bean names are an important part of Spring, because they're used for wiring objects together. In typical Spring applications, the interdependencies between beans defined in bean descriptors, but Grails uses a special feature of Spring to magically inject a bean with its dependencies.

DEPENDENCY MANAGEMENT BY MAGIC

Let's take another look at the post controller and service from chapter 5. The two classes look something like this:

```
class PostService {
    boolean transactional = true

    Post createPost(String userId, String content) {
        ...
```

```
      }
   }

class PostController {
   def postService

   def scaffold = true
   ...
}
```

You should now see that the controller has a property with the same name as the Spring bean resulting from `PostService`. That's the key to automatic Dependency Injection.

Spring has a feature called "autowiring" that takes the rigmarole out of manually declaring dependencies, and it works like this: if one Spring bean has a property with the same name as another bean, Spring automatically wires the second bean into that property. Hence the `postService` property in the post controller is initialized with the actual post service. All of this magically happens before any bean is used, so your service methods and controller actions can happily assume that the relevant properties have already been initialized.

Autowiring by type

Experienced Spring developers will know that you can also autowire beans by type. All the beans managed by Grails are autowired by name, and you can't change that, but when we discuss user-defined bean descriptors, you'll see that you can autowire your own beans by type.

While we're on types, did you notice that `postService` is declared as a dynamically typed property? That's partly because class-reloading currently fails if you declare the property with the static type of the service. It's a class-loading problem that may take some time to fix, so at the moment it's best to use `def` for injected services.

Hold on a second. If the autowiring only works for Spring beans, how come the controller is injected with the post service? Simple: controllers are also Spring beans. That said, we strongly recommend that you don't attempt to wire controllers into other beans. There are no guarantees that the bean names and types will stay the same in the future, and controllers can't easily be reused by other code.

Any named bean can be injected in this way. Grails defines many beans itself, and you can see a select list of them in table 14.1. Some of these can be useful when the usual Grails mechanisms can't help.

The `grailsApplication` bean is useful for getting information about the application, such as its configuration, the Spring application context (covered next), and the loaded artifacts. If you need direct access to Hibernate, inject the `sessionFactory` bean into your classes. Want to parse GSP pages yourself? Consider using the `groovy-PagesTemplateEngine` bean. And last but not least, the `messageSource` bean allows you to manually look up the appropriate text for a given message code.

Table 14.1   Some useful Spring beans in Grails

Bean name	Type	Provided by
grailsApplication	DefaultGrailsApplication	Grails core
sessionFactory	org.hibernate.SessionFactory	Hibernate plugin
groovyPagesTemplateEngine	GroovyPagesTemplateEngine	Controllers plugin
messageSource	ReloadableResourceBundleMessageSource	I18n plugin

That's only a taste of what's available; almost every plugin adds its own beans to the mix. The main obstacle to using them is knowing that they exist in the first place! Some documentation (both for Grails and plugins) may mention them, but often the only way to find out is to ask on the Grails mailing lists or look at the plugin descriptors. You'll find out more about the latter in chapter 16. Fortunately, you rarely need to access the Spring beans directly, and the relevant documentation will surely improve.

Dependency Injection works well and makes life easy, but sometimes you want to get hold of beans from within objects that aren't managed by Spring. What then?

THE SPRING APPLICATION CONTEXT

We'll move out of the realm of convention here to look at another way of fetching Spring beans. Let's say you have a servlet that you want to add to your application, and it needs access to the services. The only way to get a reference to a service is via Spring, but how do you access Spring from an unmanaged object?

The answer to this conundrum is Spring's application context, the singleton object that manages the beans and the loading of resources. It's, in essence, the core of the Spring IoC container. It provides several helpful features, but the one we're interested in right now is the getBean() method:

```
PostService postService = applicationContext.getBean("postService")
```

That's pretty straightforward, but we've skirted the issue of how you get a reference to the application context in the first place. You have a couple of choices here. You can get the application context from the servlet context by issuing this magic incantation:

```
import org.springframework.context.ApplicationContext
import org.springframework.web.context.support.WebApplicationContextUtils

ApplicationContext appCtx =
    WebApplicationContextUtils.getWebApplicationContext(servletContext)
```

Talk about a mouthful! Verbosity aside, this is a useful approach if you have ready access to the servlet context, as you would in a servlet. The alternative is to use the Grails application instance, like so:

```
import org.codehaus.groovy.grails.commons.ApplicationHolder

def grailsApp = ApplicationHolder.application
def appCtx = grailsApp.getMainContext()
```

This is the preferred method if you need to get hold of the application context but the servlet context isn't available. For more information on this marvelous object, check out both the Spring reference guide and the API documentation.

The conventional approach that we looked at in this section is easy to use and quite powerful. But at some stage, convention invariably becomes a limiting factor when creating and configuring Spring beans. In the next subsection, we'll look at a more powerful and flexible technique for that job.

14.1.2 Creating and defining your own beans

We mentioned earlier how Grails defines quite a few Spring beans itself, and you now know that your services are Spring beans too. But what if you have classes that don't fit the mold of services? They may be provided by a Java library in a JAR file, for example. You need some way of informing Spring about them.

As you would expect, Grails has the answer. In fact, it has two of them. You can add Spring bean definitions to the grails-app/conf/spring/resources.xml file, the grails-app/conf/spring/resources.groovy file, or both. They work in similar ways, but the format for defining the beans in the two files is quite different: one is XML-based and the other uses a Groovy domain-specific language (DSL).

> **Load order**
>
> Both resources files are loaded after all the core Grails and plugin beans have been defined. This means that you can refer to Grails and plugin beans from your resources files, but plugins can't see the beans you define.
>
> More importantly, you can override beans that have already been defined by a plugin. For example, if you define a bean named `messageSource`, it will be used instead of the bean defined by the i18n plugin.

That leaves us in a bit of a quandary. Which method is better depends on whether you're more comfortable working with XML or the DSL. Consider this: the Spring DSL allows you to use variables, conditions, loops, and all manner of Groovy goodness. XML is just XML.

We'll only be looking at the Spring DSL in detail here, but if you would like to find out more about Spring XML bean descriptors, take a look at the Spring reference guide: http://static.springframework.org/spring/docs/2.5.x/reference/. It will give you a good grounding in the features available in Spring and how to use them.

INTRODUCING THE SPRING DSL

We'll admit that we don't like working with XML much. Fortunately, we don't have to in order to define Spring beans. Like most Groovy-based DSLs, the Spring DSL uses method and closure notation to describe the bean configuration. In essence, any call to a nonexistent (or missing) method is treated as the start of a new bean definition.

Listing 14.1 contains an example resources.groovy file that we will deconstruct so that you can see how it works. This particular example sets up Hibernate statistics collection via JMX (Java Management Extensions).

Listing 14.1 Example bean definitions in resources.groovy

```
import org.springframework.jmx.support.MBeanServerFactoryBean
import org.springframework.jmx.export.MBeanExporter
import org.hibernate.jmx.StatisticsService

beans = {
    hibernateStats(StatisticsService) {          ❶ Starts new bean
        statisticsEnabled = true                        definition
        sessionFactory = ref("sessionFactory")   ❷ References a
    }                                                   named bean
    mbeanServer(MBeanServerFactoryBean) {
        locateExistingServerIfPossible = true
    }
    exporter(MBeanExporter) {                 ❸ Provides alternative
        server = mbeanServer                       bean reference
        beans = ["org.hibernate:name=statistics": hibernateStats]
    }
}
```

Because resources.groovy is a plain Groovy script, you can pretty much put anything you like in there. But to define Spring beans, you must declare a beans script variable and assign a closure to it. If any of your bean definitions fall outside of that closure, they won't be picked up by Grails and will likely cause an exception.

What does a bean definition look like in this DSL? It consists of the bean name followed by the bean class in parentheses ❶; the method name becomes the bean name, and the argument maps to the bean class. In an XML file, the bean class would be a string, but because this is Groovy, you can use class literals. That means you can use imports to keep the definitions tidy.

If you want to configure properties of the bean, you must follow the declaration with a closure block as we've done for all three bean definitions in the example. Inside this block, you can set properties using the simple <property name> = <value> notation. In contrast to the XML form, in which everything is a string, the value in the DSL should be of the appropriate type for the corresponding property. In listing 14.1, we set both Boolean and map properties. This syntax means that initializing collections and maps is far more succinct than with the XML format.

Using bean references is the manual approach to wiring beans together. They're specified in the same way as normal properties, but you have two options for what goes on the right side of the assignment. First, you can set the property to the name of the bean definition without quotes ❸, but this only works if the target bean was defined earlier in the same file. The second option is to use the ref() method ❷, which takes the name of a bean as a string. Of these two options, we prefer the second because it will always work regardless of where the target bean is defined or of the order of the bean definitions in the resources.groovy file.

That was easy. We may not have shown many techniques in this example, but you'll find that they suffice for a large percentage of cases. To get some insight into the more specialized features, we'll compare the DSL to the XML format. This will allow you to learn the intricacies of Spring from another source and then apply that knowledge to the DSL.

COMPARING SPRING'S XML AND DSL FORMATS

The Spring DSL supports almost all of the features you'll find in the Spring XML descriptor format. In table 14.2, you'll see the equivalent DSL syntax for various XML forms. If you don't understand what a particular form is or what it does, check out the online Spring reference manual, which covers all of these variations and more.

Table 14.2 Comparing the Spring XML descriptor format to Spring DSL

Feature	XML	Spring DSL

Bean attributes	```<bean id="ex" class="o.e.Ex"```
	`    scope="prototype"`
	`    autowire="byType"`
	`    init-method="init"`
	`    destroy-method="finish"/>`
		`ex(o.e.Ex) { b ->`
		`    b.scope = "prototype"`
		`    b.autowire = "byType"`
		`    b.initMethod = "init"`
		`    b.destroyMethod = "finish"`
		`}`

Lists	`<bean id="ex" class="o.e.Ex">`
	`    <property name="items">`
	`        <list>`
	`            <value>1</value>`
	`            <value>2</value>`
	`            <value>3</value>`
	`        </list>`
	`    </property>`
	`</bean>`
		`ex(o.e.Ex) {`
		`    items = [1, 2, 3]`
		`}`

Static factory methods	`<bean id="ex" class="o.e.Ex"`
	`    factory-method="create"/>`
		`ex(o.e.Ex) { b ->`
		`    b.factoryMethod = "create"`
		`}`

Instance factory methods	`<bean id="ex"`
	`    factory-bean="myFactory"`
	`    factory-method="create"/>`
		`ex(myFactory: "create")`

As you can see from the table, some features are much more concise in the Spring DSL. That, along with being able to use real types for property and constructor argument values, would be enough to sway even the most ardent of XML fans. But as we mentioned earlier, you can use Groovy's flow control in the DSL as well.

Consider this example, where `serviceName` and `isTransactional` are variables set elsewhere:

```
def beanNames = [ "transactionInterceptor" ]

"${serviceName}Manager"(org.example.ServiceManager) {
   service = serviceName
   if (isTransactional) {
      interceptors = beanNames.collect { ref(it) }
   }
}
```

This demonstrates how you can create a bean whose name isn't resolved until runtime and how you can use conditions to affect the configuration. We also throw in a gratuitous `collect()` for good measure. The ability to mesh regular Groovy code with bean definitions opens up a whole world of opportunities.

A recent addition to the Spring DSL is support for namespaces. These were originally introduced as XML namespaces to simplify configuration, but you can now experience their benefits from Groovy.

NAMESPACES IN THE SPRING DSL

In order to show you how to use namespaces, we'll use a simple example based on Spring's aspect-oriented programming (AOP) support. We won't go into detail about what AOP is, but suffice it to say that the following example will time every method call on the `sessionFactory` bean:

```
beans = {
   xmlns aop: "http://www.springframework.org/schema/aop"

   aop.config {
      aspect id: "profiling", ref: "profileInterceptor" {
         around method: "profile", pointcut: "bean(sessionFactory)"
      }
   }

   profileInterceptor(com.manning.gria.ProfilingInterceptor)
}
```

First, you have to declare the namespace and assign it a prefix (`aop`, in this case), which you do with the built-in `xmlns()` method. You can declare additional namespaces by adding extra named arguments to the method, like so:

```
xmlns aop: "...", context: "...", ...
```

Once you've declared a namespace, you can use a property with the same name as the namespace prefix to access the custom features, as we do for `aop.config` in the preceding example. Note that the `aspect()` and `around()` methods aren't prefixed because they're nested within a method that is. You could also use this syntax:

```
aop {
   config {
      aspect ...
   }
}
```

There isn't any more to using Spring namespaces than that. Any documentation for specific namespaces will refer to the XML format, but now you know how to translate from XML to Spring DSL. You're good to go! For even more information on the

Spring DSL, we recommend the Grails user guide, which gives significant coverage of this topic and is well worth a look.

We're almost done with our discussion of Spring, but one item from table 14.2 deserves some discussion. One of the bean attributes listed is `scope`, and this is directly supported by Grails services.

BEAN SCOPES

All Spring beans are by default singletons, which means that there's only one instance of each bean of that type in an application. That makes any state stored in the bean, such as a simple field, effectively equivalent to a global variable—not a good idea in a multithreaded environment!

Stateless singletons are ideal, but if you want to store state in a bean, you can make your life easier by controlling the visibility of the shared data. Say your bean is inherently tied to the HTTP request processing. You would be pretty safe if the bean's state were only shared within a single request, particularly as a request is typically a single thread. Each request would have its own copy of the data, so it could safely update the information without affecting any other requests.

This concept of visibility is known as the "scope," and you can change it for a service by declaring a static field:

```
class MyRequestService {
    static scope = "request"
    ...
}
```

The `singleton` and `request` scopes aren't the only ones available to you either. Here is a quick rundown of all of them:

- `singleton`—Only one instance of the bean exists for the entire application (the default).
- `prototype`—A new instance is created each time a bean is retrieved from the application context.
- `request`—There is one instance per HTTP request.
- `session`—There is one instance per HTTP session.
- `flow`—There is one instance per flow or subflow—see chapter 9 for more info.
- `conversation`—There is one instance per conversation—see chapter 9 for more info.

As you saw in table 14.2, you can also set the scope within your bean definitions.

Now that you know how to define extra beans for your application, the full power of Spring is open to you. If you discover a cool library that comes with dedicated Spring integration, you'll know how to make use of it from Grails. We can only touch on the features of Spring here, so for serious development it's well worth looking into documentation and books that are dedicated to the subject.

With the fundamentals under our belt, we can now boldly face one of those extra Spring features that Grails relies quite heavily upon but that can cause a little confusion: transactions.

14.2   Using transactions with GORM

In some fields, transactions are a big deal. Microsoft created Microsoft Transaction Server (MTS) and then COM+ to make developing transaction-based applications easier than they used to be. EJBs and their servers were also designed with transactions in mind. So what are they? Let's start with a definition:

DEFINITION   A *transaction* is a unit of work in which everything is done or none of it is. It isn't possible for only part of a transaction to complete.

It's all or nothing. As a practical example, consider a transaction that updates several database tables. If any of those updates fail, none of the changes are committed to the database. Only if all updates are successful does the transaction complete. Transactions are therefore a way of ensuring data integrity.

So why the fuss? The classic example is banking software. Imagine a bank customer wants to transfer funds from one account to another. At a superficial level, this consists of two steps: removing the funds from one account and depositing them in the other. What if the first step succeeds but the second one fails for some reason? Without transactional behavior, the customer would lose their money! That's a big problem.

Without further ado, let's look at how we can use transactions within a Grails application.

14.2.1   Easy transactions with services

In order to investigate the properties of transactions, we'll have to add some transactional behavior to Hubbub. It's not naturally a transaction-oriented application, but we have just the ticket.

Let's say that users can reply to others' posts by including the string @<user ID> in their own message. We'd like to keep track of these replies and whom they're directed to, so let's introduce a new domain class:

```
class Reply {
    Post post
    User inReplyTo
}
```

Next up, we want to make sure that every time a user posts a reply, a `Reply` instance is created. In addition, if Hubbub doesn't recognize the user ID specified in the message, it shouldn't commit that message to the database. Being a sensible person, you would check the user ID before saving the post, but we're not going to do that. Instead, we'll first save the message and *then* check the user ID, just so that we can effectively demonstrate how transactions work.

NOTE   In order to see the correct behavior, you should use a database that supports transactions, such as PostgreSQL, H2, or MySQL with the InnoDB engine. Nontransactional databases, such as MySQL with MyISAM tables, won't work as expected.

Where shall we add the code for all this? It's time to dust off our old friend `PostSer-vice`. The beefed up implementation, in which we create replies, is shown in listing 14.2.

Listing 14.2   The reply-aware post service

```
package com.grailsinaction

class PostService {
    Post createPost(String userId, String content) {
        def user = User.findByUserId(userId)
        def post
        if (user) {
            post = new Post(content: content)
            user.addToPosts(post)

            if (!user.save()) {
                throw new PostException(
                    message: "Invalid or empty post", post: post)
            }

            def m = content =~ /@(\w+)/        ⟵── Finds "@..." in post
            if (m) {
                def targetUser =               │ Checks that target
                    User.findByUserId(m[0][1]) │ user exists

                if (targetUser) {
                    new Reply(post: post, inReplyTo: targetUser).save()
                }
                else {
                    throw new PostException(
                        message: "Reply-to user not found", post: post)
                }
            }
        }
        throw new PostException(message: "Invalid User Id")
    }
}
```

As you can see, the post service now saves the new post, looks for a reply-to user ID, and then checks that the user exists. If it does, a new `Reply` is saved; otherwise an exception is thrown. With the service now ready for prime time, what do we need to do to make it transactional? Nothing!

By default, all public methods in a service are transactional. If you were to post a message containing @dilbert (assuming dilbert isn't a user in Hubbub), not only would you see an exception trace in the browser, but you should also discover that the post hasn't been saved. Why not try it out and see for yourself? Try these two posts:

- @glen hi there mate!
- @dilbert do you really exist?

The first appears in your list of posts, but the second doesn't—just as we'd hoped for. This raises an interesting question: how does Grails know that the transaction should

> **Under the hood**
>
> Transactional services are implemented using Spring's AOP mechanism: each one is wrapped by a proxy created using Spring's `TransactionProxyFactoryBean`. When you have a reference to a service, it's in fact a reference to that proxy.
>
> Transactions themselves are controlled by a `transactionManager` bean that is an instance of Spring's `HibernateTransactionManager` by default. You can override this in one of the resources.* files if you need a special transaction manager or custom settings.

be rolled back (not committed)? The method throws an exception, so Grails (or more accurately, Spring) infers that the transaction failed.

Before going any further, we should get rid of that stack trace. And while we're at it, some way of seeing the saved replies would be useful. Modify the add action in the post controller so that it looks like this:

```
def add = {
    def content = params.postContent
    if (content) {
        def post = null
        try {
            post = postService.createPost(session.user.id, content)
        }
        catch (e) {
        }

        if (post) {
            flash.message = "Added new post"
        }
        else {
            flash.message = "Failed to add new post"
        }
    }
    redirect(action: "list")
}
```

The key change is that we catch the exception. We don't need to do anything with it because we treat a thrown exception and a `null` return value in the same way. In a real system, the error reporting should be more informative, but this will suffice for the purposes of demonstration. You should also add a dynamically scaffolded controller for the `Reply` domain class:

```
class ReplyController {
    def scaffold = true
}
```

That will allow us to check whether the replies are being saved or not. With that done, let's move on.

A common problem that people have with transactions in Grails is related to the exception handling. To see what we mean, change this line

```
throw new PostException(message: "Reply-to user not found", ...)
```

in the post service to read as follows:

```
throw new Exception("Reply-to user not found")
```

All we've done is change the exception type, but when you try to post the @dilbert message now, the new post appears in the list! Why did that happen?

Testing transactions

Integration tests run inside a transaction by default, which is then rolled back after each test finishes. This ensures that data changes don't affect other tests, but it means you can't check whether transactions are rolled back or not. If you want to test transactional behavior, you need to add a static `transactional` property to your test:

```
static transactional = false
```

The alternative is to use functional tests for this job.

The default behavior for Spring mimics that of EJB containers: transactions are only rolled back automatically for runtime exceptions and errors. It expects you to handle checked exceptions yourself. Because Java forces you to deal with checked exceptions (or declare them on the method), that isn't much of a problem. Groovy, on the other hand, lets you treat checked exceptions as if they were runtime exceptions, so it's not immediately obvious why transactions aren't rolling back. That can lead to lots of wasted time if you're not aware of this issue.

What if you don't want your service to have transactional behavior? Then set the static `transactional` property to `false`:

```
class PostService {
    static transactional = false
    ...
}
```

Make sure that you revert the previous change (the service method should throw a `PostException`), and then start the application and try to post the @dilbert message again. Notice any difference? The message appears in the list now! So even though dilbert isn't a recognized user ID (and a runtime exception is thrown), the post is saved to the database. We no longer have transactional behavior.

Interestingly, if you remove the `try...catch` block from the post controller, you'll find that the post is no longer saved. What's going on there? To understand that, you have to learn how transactions and the underlying Hibernate session relate to each other.

14.2.2 *Transactions, the session, and me*

The way Hibernate works can be quite confusing for newcomers. When you add transactions on top of that, it's time to reach for the aspirin. Part of the trouble is that the Hibernate session appears to exhibit some transactional behavior, as you just saw. If you step through your application code in a debugger, you'll notice that calls to save() don't appear to commit anything to the database. So is it transactional or not?

The Hibernate session is effectively a cache that sits in front of the database, which is why it's also known as the *first-level cache*. When you save a domain instance, all you're doing is updating this in-memory cache. The data isn't committed to the database until the cache and database are synchronized, a process known as "flushing" in Hibernate. You can see all this in figure 14.3.

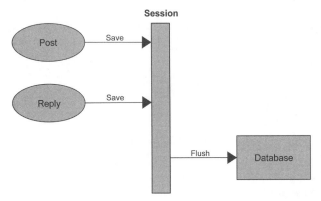

Figure 14.3 The Hibernate session is an in-memory cache that stores data changes locally and then persists them to the database when it's flushed.

Remember that example from the end of the last subsection: when we stopped catching the runtime exception thrown by the service, the exception propagated out and stopped the active session from flushing. If you put the try...catch block back in place, the action returns normally, allowing Grails to flush the session and commit the new post to the database. As you can probably gather from this, Grails opens a session for you before your controller action is called and flushes it if and when the action returns normally.

You can even manually trigger a flush if you wish. The easy way to do that is to pass the flush: true named argument to either the save() or delete() domain methods.

Under the hood

Grails uses a custom version of a Spring web interceptor to ensure that a session is open before an action executes. The Spring class is OpenSessionInViewInterceptor, but Grails modifies it slightly to change the flush mode of the session to manual after an action returns but before the view is rendered. This allows views to access lazy-loaded collections and relationships, but it prevents them from making any changes that will automatically be committed to the database.

All changes made in the session up to that point will then be committed to the database. For a quick example, make sure that the post controller's add action is *not* catching the exception, and then use the flush argument when saving the user in the post service:

```
...
post = new Post(content: content)
user.addToPosts(post)
user.save(flush: true)
```

Now if you try to post a message in reply to dilbert, that message will be saved to the database—just load the post list page to see the evidence.

The main thing to be aware of is that making changes to the database is a two-stage process: you first update your domain objects (or save new ones) and then flush the session. The next question is, how do transactions fit into this model?

When is a Hibernate session created?

It's all very well knowing how the Hibernate session works, but that's not much good if you don't know when they're created and how long they remain open. So here is a quick rundown of the most common scenarios:

- A session is opened before a controller action is called and it's flushed when the action returns. It isn't closed until either the view is rendered or the response is committed (say via a redirect or error).
- If a session isn't already open, a transaction will open a new one and keep it open for the life of the transaction.
- Queries and methods like get() will automatically create a session if one doesn't exist. The session is closed as soon as the method returns.

Let's make PostService transactional again, but leave the flush: true in there. What happens when you try to post a reply to dilbert now? You get the stack trace as before, but when you reload the post list, you won't see that message. Even when you catch the exception in the controller, the post is still not persisted to the database. This is starting to look a little too much like black magic. Shouldn't Grails have saved the post to the database because we have an explicit flush? No, and if you go back to the definition of a transaction, you'll understand why.

Any changes made within a transaction must happen in their entirety or not at all. Even an explicit flush must not commit the changes made up to that point. Grails manages this feat by starting a *database* transaction at the beginning of an *application* transaction (for example, on entry to a transactional service method). When Grails flushes the session, the changes are added to the database transaction, but they're not committed. Once the application transaction has finished, Grails flushes the session automatically and commits the database transaction, persisting the changes made up to that point. Without a transaction, the Hibernate session operates in autocommit mode, which is why changes are always persisted to the database immediately on a flush.

WARNING When a transaction flushes the session, it will commit *all* the changes associated with that session, including ones made before the start of the transaction. If you choose to use transactions, we recommend that you only ever change or save domain objects within them.

One question that might be bugging you is what happens when you have transactions within a transaction. Let's say that our post service (in transaction mode) calls *another* transactional service method. Does the second method start its own transaction? Does it have any impact on the original transaction? The answer is that nested transactions join their parent, so there's only ever one transaction in progress (the parent). The Hibernate session is only flushed when the parent transaction finishes, and if the parent transaction fails, all child transactions are rolled back too.

So far, you've only seen transactions in the context of services. But what if a service is overkill, or you need finer-grained control over when a transaction starts and finishes?

14.2.3 *Fine-grained transactions*

When might you want a bit more control over what goes into a transaction? One possibility is that you may want to update the database from a controller directly, because that particular change only happens in the one place. Or perhaps you want to execute multiple transactions within a single service method.

Let's say we want to move the post creation code back into the controller, but we still want it to run in a transaction. This isn't recommended practice, but we'll do it for demonstration. All we have to do is use the `withTransaction()` static method that's available on all domain classes. You can see the resulting code in listing 14.3. For the sake of brevity, we've removed some of the variable checks.

Listing 14.3   Using `withTransaction()` for fine-grained transactions

```
import org.springframework.transaction.TransactionStatus

class PostController {
   ...
   def add = {
      Post.withTransaction { TransactionStatus status ->      ❶ Starts
         def user = User.get(session.user.id)                      transaction
         user.addToPosts(content: params.postContent)
         user.save()

         def m = content =~ /@(\w+)/
         if (m) {
            def targetUser = User.findByUserId(m[0][1])
            if (targetUser) {
               new Reply(post: post, inReplyTo: targetUser).save()
            }
            else {                          ❷ Rolls back
               status.setRollbackOnly()          changes
            }
         }
```

```
        }
            ...
    }
        ...
}
```

Although we still recommend that you use a transactional service instead, this neatly demonstrates how you can quickly add a transaction to a block of code. The key is the withTransaction() method ❶, which accepts a closure as an argument. Everything inside that closure is run within a transaction. An additional benefit of this approach is that you're given access to the Spring TransactionStatus instance, which allows you to manually roll back the transaction without throwing an exception ❷.

One thing that might puzzle you is why we call withTransaction() on the Post domain class rather than User. In fact, it doesn't matter which domain class is used—it has no effect on the transaction block at all. You could even use Tag, which isn't even used within the transaction block. Not surprisingly, users are often a little confused by this. Think of the domain class as something that the method can attach to—a surrogate host, if you like.

So when should you use transaction blocks rather than transactional services? That's difficult to say and depends on the situation. Transactional services are the recommended approach, plus they're less verbose than transaction blocks and form nice reusable components. The transaction block is good for one-off transactions and in cases where you don't already have an open session and can't readily get hold of a service. The BootStrap class and integration tests are typical places where you might want to use transaction blocks over services.

Transactions are hugely important to many applications, and you've seen that Grails makes them easy to use. They can appear to exhibit odd behavior sometimes, particularly when combined with the Hibernate session, but now that you know what is going on under the hood, you'll be able to tackle any problems that arise.

14.3 *Summary and best practices*

As you've seen, Spring is a fundamental part of Grails, and although you can happily develop simple applications without ever being aware of its existence, you need to take advantage of it as your application grows. Fortunately, this is easily done with services and the automatic Dependency Injection that Grails provides.

When you start using Java libraries and integrating your application with other Java systems, you'll often find that services don't help. For the integration to work well, you have to define your own beans using the resources.xml and resources.groovy files, so that they can be easily slotted into the various Grails artifacts. If you do a lot of this integration, we recommend you become more familiar with Spring itself, either through the online documentation or a book. The framework contains far more than the classes related to the core IoC container.

Grails transaction support is one example of other features Spring brings to the table, and you've seen how easy they are to use. If you write an application that performs updates to a database, you ought to make yourself familiar with transactions and the effects they have on reliably saving and modifying domain objects.

So what recommendations do we make for your projects?

- *Put your business logic into services.*   Not only does this conform to the principle of the Separation of Concerns, resulting in code that's easier to understand, maintain, and test, but you can also easily reuse the functionality from web service gateways, remoting interfaces, and the like.

- *Make important singleton objects Spring beans.*   Lifecycle management and Dependency Injection mean that any singleton objects benefit hugely from becoming Spring beans. Use the resources.* files to define beans for classes under the src directory or in JAR files.

- *Prefer Spring DSL.*   Whether you're a fan of XML or not, the advantages of defining Spring beans in code are massive, with support for conditions, loops, and environment-specific definitions.

- *Update the database within a transaction.*   Making changes to the database outside of a transaction means that you have to be aware of how the Hibernate session operates, and you can easily end up with inconsistent data. Transactions are so easy to set up, why not use them?

   Note that there's an overhead associated with transactions, so if you need to perform a high volume of updates, you may need to come up with a different solution. This is pretty specialized, though, so it's unlikely to affect you.

With your application structured along these guidelines, you'll find that further development, testing, and maintenance become easier than you have a right to expect.

15

Beyond compile, test, and run

In this chapter

- Packaging your application
- Extending the Grails command set
- Building Grails projects using other tools

So far in this book, we've treated the Grails application in isolation. You've seen how to write an application, test it, and then run it, but that's all. What happens when you want to make your application available for use by customers or the general public? What if you want to distribute the application so that others can install it? Maybe this application is one cog in a larger project—what then?

These questions relate to the larger picture of application development. Figure 15.1 highlights the key stages of the development cycle that we'll cover in this chapter.

In essence, the story doesn't end when the code is "finished": the application must still be made available to users, and there may be several steps involved in the release process. You're undoubtedly used to builds that automate the compilation

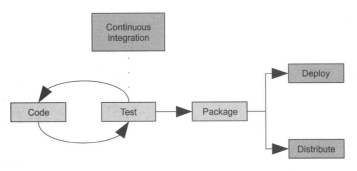

Figure 15.1 The typical development cycle for Grails applications. The code, test, and package steps are implemented by the Grails build system; the others must be implemented manually or by a plugin.

and testing of an application (when was the last time you invoked the Java compiler directly?), but you can often automate the release process as well, using the same build tool. This automation is important in reducing the likelihood of errors and improving reproducibility. Sadly, humans are prone to making mistakes, particularly when tired.

You may not be aware of it, but Grails comes with its own build system that covers the spectrum of compile, test, run, and package. Every time you run one of the Grails commands, you're initiating that build. Nor is the build system set in stone: we'll show you how you can extend it to support a hypothetical release process.

> **Continuous integration**
>
> Many projects, and almost all open source ones, use a technique called continuous integration (CI). The basic idea is that a server continuously checks out the latest source code for your project, builds it, and then runs the tests. If there are any failures, it sends notifications so that the team gets quick feedback when the build is broken.
>
> There are several CI products available, but none of them have direct support for Grails applications. Instead, you have to use a shell script, batch file, Ant build, or something similar to execute the relevant Grails commands and scripts. Which you use depends on the product you work with, but creating an Ant build for CI is quite common. One product we recommend is Hudson (https://hudson.dev.java.net/), which has a plugin for building Grails projects.

Then there are the situations in which the Grails build system isn't the preferred option, or not even an option at all. Maybe your company enforces a particular build tool, such as Maven, or maybe your Grails application is one cog in a larger project that requires a single multiproject build. Whatever the reason, you can find yourself wondering how to build a Grails application using a different build tool. To help out, we'll discuss the options available. In particular, you'll find that building a Grails application with either Apache Ant or Apache Maven isn't only possible, but quite straightforward.

But first, let's look at the Grails build system: at what help it provides in packaging your application, how it works, and what you can do to extend and customize it.

15.1 The Grails build system

In a typical project, you manage the phases in the development cycle (shown in figure 15.1) with a build tool, such as Ant or Maven. Grails could have used one of these and relied on the user to install the required build tool, but that would go against the Grails philosophy of providing everything you need out of the box (except Java!). Instead, it comes with its own build system that you interact with via the command line.

This isn't just a build tool, though. You don't have to manually set up a build file so that the tool knows how to compile your project or run the tests—everything is done for you. That's why we call it a build *system* rather than a build *tool*. But Grails needs to implement the commands somehow, and for that it uses a dedicated build tool that you may not be familiar with: Gant. We'll talk more about it in section 15.1.2.

Looking at the development cycle in figure 15.1, you'll notice that the Grails build system provides nothing for the distribution and deployment stages, so you'll have to get your hands dirty and learn how to extend it. Don't worry, we'll turn you into an expert later in this section.

But first, let's take a look the packaging phase of the development cycle, which hasn't had much exposure yet in this book.

15.1.1 Packaging an application

Before we can either distribute or deploy a Grails application, we must first package it into a form that works for both cases. As you probably know, the standard package format for a web application in the Java world is the WAR file (short for web archive), which is a JAR file that conforms to a well-defined directory and file structure. A WAR file can be dropped into any standards-compliant servlet container, such as Apache Tomcat or Jetty, and the application will just work.

Because application deployment is such a fundamental part of the development cycle, Grails comes with a dedicated command for packaging your application:

```
grails war
```

This one command will take all your application's classes, dependencies, and resources, and place them in the correct location within the final WAR file.

Why not try it out? Let's say we want to deploy Hubbub to a Tomcat instance that we've installed. Running the `war` command creates a hubbub-0.1.war file in the root of the project directory that you can copy to the Tomcat webapps folder. Start Tomcat and point your browser at the application's URL, which will typically be http://localhost:8080/hubbub-0.1/.

> **WARNING** Grails also has a `package` command that you'll see if you run `grails help`. But this command doesn't create a WAR file, nor does it do anything else that's useful to the end user. It will probably be deprecated and removed sometime in the future.

Do we want that version number in the URL? It kind of ruins the look and is a pain for anyone typing the address manually. There are a couple of ways to remove the version, but the easiest is to change the name of the generated WAR file:

```
grails war hubbub.war
```

You don't have to limit yourself to changing the filename either. What about generating the WAR file directly in the Tomcat webapps directory? Pass the full path and filename to the command like so (where `$TOMCAT_HOME` is an environment variable containing the location of the root Tomcat directory):

```
grails war $TOMCAT_HOME/webapps/hubbub.war
```

By default, the WAR file will be created for the production environment, but you can specify an alternative if you wish. For example, to package the application with the development settings, run this command:

```
grails dev war
```

The other core environments are `test` and `prod` (for "production").

> **Under the hood**
>
> You might wonder how an application packaged as a WAR file knows what environment to run in. Normally this information is provided at runtime via commands, such as `test-app` and `run-app`. But in a servlet container, this isn't possible. Instead, Grails inserts the environment into the application.properties file, which is then packaged in the WAR file. The deployed application reads the configured environment from there.

We haven't quite reached the end of the packaging story yet, although what we've covered is more than sufficient in the majority of cases. If you need more control over the process, though, Grails offers several configuration options that allow you to influence the WAR file generation. As an example, suppose that your application requires a different version of a library from the one packaged with Grails, such as the latest and greatest version of Hibernate. Ideally you could put the version you require in your application's lib directory and all would be well, but the generated WAR file would contain both versions of the Hibernate JAR file, which almost certainly would cause problems. How can we keep the Grails version out of the WAR file?

Before the WAR file is generated, all the files that go into it are first copied to a temporary directory called the staging area. We can remove the offending JAR from the staging directory before it's zipped up into the WAR file—there's a hook that allows us to do that. Create the file grails-app/conf/BuildConfig.groovy and add these lines to it:

```
grails.war.resources = { String stagingDir ->
   delete(file: "${stagingDir}/WEB-INF/lib/hibernate3-3.2.6.jar")
}
```

The closure specified will be called just before the WAR file is created, and, as you can see, Grails passes it the location of the staging directory. The delegate is an instance of Groovy's AntBuilder, which you'll see more of later, but for now take it on trust that the line in the closure uses the Ant `delete` task to remove the Hibernate JAR from the staging area.

The BuildConfig.groovy file has the same syntax as the Config.groovy file that you're already used to, but whereas the latter contains configuration information for the running application, BuildConfig.groovy is concerned with the build. Because affecting the WAR file generation isn't a function of the application but of the build, you can see why the `grails.war.resources` setting goes where it does.

The other configuration options that you can use (all of which go into BuildConfig.groovy) are listed in table 15.1, but because they're pretty specialized, we won't dwell on them. Just be aware of their existence—you never know when they might come in handy.

Table 15.1 Influencing WAR file generation

Config option	Type	Description
`grails.war.destFile`	String	Specifies the path to the generated WAR file, including its name. This is overridden by any explicit argument to the `grails war` command.
`grails.war.copyToWebApp`	Closure	All Ant filesets defined in this closure are copied to the root of the staging directory. This is ideal for controlling which files under web-app are included in the WAR file. The closure delegate is an Ant-Builder, and it's passed the `grails war` argument if one is used.
`grails.war.dependencies`	Closure or list	If set to a closure, this defines the Ant filesets that are copied to the WEB-INF/lib directory. Its delegate is an AntBuilder, and it has no arguments. If set to a list, the list includes Ant file patterns defining which JARs are copied from Grails' lib directory.
`grails.war.resources`	Closure	This is a one- or two-argument closure in which you can do any last-minute processing before the WAR file is generated. The first argument is the location of the staging directory, and the optional second argument is the `grails war` command argument. The closure's delegate is an AntBuilder.

With your WAR file in hand, you can now start thinking about the distribution and deployment stages of the development cycle. Which you choose will depend on your situation, but don't worry—we'll cover both. The question is, how do we proceed? We seem to have reached the end of the line as far as Grails commands go.

15.1.2 *Going it alone: how to create a dist command*

Look high and low, and you won't find any Grails commands that take you beyond the packaging stage. As far as the build system is concerned, you're on your own once the WAR file is ready. To be fair, once you enter the realm of distribution and deployment, users' requirements vary considerably, so it would be difficult for Grails to provide anything meaningful in this arena.

Undoubtedly some people would say that dropping a WAR file into a servlet container is hardly rocket science, yet anyone experienced in builds and deployment knows that human error can creep in even here. Nor are all deployments so simple. The same goes for building and publishing distributions. In both cases, automation aids reproducibility and makes life much easier for the person involved. If that person is you, all the better!

The ideal solution would be to extend the Grails build system to include commands for these processes. Let's do that.

ENTER STAGE LEFT: GANT

Each Grails command is implemented as a Groovy script. This isn't any ordinary script, though: it uses a syntax that can be interpreted by a special build tool called Gant.

If you take a look in the $GRAILS_HOME/scripts directory, you'll find lots of these scripts, many of which have familiar names (corresponding to the core Grails commands). You can also provide your own scripts in several locations (where $HOME is your home directory and <app> is the directory containing your application):

- $HOME/.grails/scripts
- <app>/scripts
- plugins

Any scripts in your home directory become always-on Grails commands. You can use them from any project or none at all. In contrast, scripts in the application directory are only available when you run Grails in that application's directory. In the next chapter on plugin development, you'll also see how you can extend the Grails command set via plugins.

What is Gant? Back in the day, Ant was pretty much the definitive build tool for Java projects. Times have changed, and there are now new kids on the block challenging Ant's dominance. Some of these are based on Groovy, and one such is Gant. According to its author, it's principally a means of scripting Ant tasks, but it has some of the trappings of a full-blown build tool, such as targets and dependencies.

Because Grails uses Gant for its build system, you have to learn how to write Gant scripts in order to provide extra commands. Rather than describe these scripts in all their gory detail (well, not so gory really), we'll kill two birds with one stone and show you how to create a script that builds a distribution package for Hubbub. At the end of this process, we'll have a brand new command (grails dist) to play with.

Let's start by looking at what we want this command to do. Not everyone has a servlet container lying around, so it would be nice to include Jetty in the distribution, along with some scripts for running Hubbub inside it. We'll also add the project documentation for the sake of completeness. All of these should be packaged inside a zip file that can be put on a website or emailed. Here's what the contents of the final zip file will look like:

```
+-- bin
|   |
|   +-- startHubbub
|   +-- startHubbub.bat
|
+-- lib
|   |
|   +-- jetty-6.1.12.jar
|
+-- docs
|   |
|   +-- ...
|
+-- hubbub.war
```

With a clear scope of work, we're now ready to write a script that does the necessary business. It could be argued that the distribution we described is quite generic and could apply to any Grails application, but for the purposes of this example, we'll create the script in the project.

Of distributions and data sources

The biggest problem with distributing a Grails application is the data source configuration. The database connection settings are compiled into the DataSource class, so the end user can't change them!

One approach is to specify a JNDI name in the data source configuration. The user can then associate database connection settings with that name.

Alternatively, you can declare a set of external properties files in Config.groovy that Grails will load configuration information from:

```
grails.config.locations = ["file:.../custom.properties"]
```

See the Grails user guide for more information on this setting.

The name of the file will be Dist.groovy. Why? Because Grails infers the name of the corresponding command from the name of the script, so the Dist.groovy file becomes the `grails dist` command. More generally, the command name is formed by lowercasing the initial letter of each "word" and separating them with hyphens. For example, CreateDomainClass.groovy becomes `create-domain-class`. If in doubt, create the script and run `grails help` to see what Grails thinks is the corresponding command name.

It's not just the command that the script name affects: you can also use it to determine whether the script is available as a command at all, or whether it can be run from outside of a project. Prefix the name with an underscore (_), and Grails will treat it as an *internal* script—no command will be available to run the script. Use the underscore as a suffix instead, and the script can be run from outside of a Grails project, like the create-app command. The underscore doesn't form part of the command name.

As soon as you save the Dist.groovy file, you can run the dist command, even if you leave the file empty! It won't do anything, but we'll soon fix that. Listing 15.1 contains the code for our new script.

Listing 15.1   The dist script

```
includeTargets << grailsScript("_GrailsWar")        ❶ Loads Grails scripts
includeTargets << grailsScript("_GrailsDocs")

target(createDist: "Creates Hubbub distribution") {
    depends(docs, war)                              ❷ Specifies target's
                                                       dependencies
    zipFile = "${basedir}/hubbub.zip"

    createZip()        ❸ Calls target
}                         explicitly
target(createZip: "Packages the required files into a zip") {
    def warFile = new File(warName)    ❹ Calls Ant's zip task

    ant.zip(destfile: zipFile) {
        zipfileset(dir: "${basedir}/src/templates/bin", prefix: "bin")
        zipfileset(dir: "${grailsHome}/lib", prefix: "lib") {
            include(name: "jetty*.jar")
        }
        zipfileset(dir: "${basedir}/docs", prefix: "docs")
        fileset(file: warFile)
    }
}                                      ❺ Specifies default
setDefaultTarget("createDist")            target for script
```

We want to make sure that both the documentation and the WAR file are generated before we try to create a distribution that includes them. It doesn't make sense to do it ourselves, because there are commands that do both of these things. Commands imply the existence of corresponding scripts, so we can use those. We include the targets from the scripts we're interested in ❶, and those targets immediately become available to us.

The includeTargets << syntax is generic Gant, but the grailsScript() method is unique to Grails scripts and should only be used to include the core scripts provided by Grails itself. You can include targets from your own scripts (or those provided by plugins), but you'll need to specify a file on the right side like so:

```
includeTargets << new File("${basedir}/scripts/Other.groovy")
```

Note that you have to give the path to the script file itself—the .groovy extension must be included. The extension should *not* be used with grailsScript().

A Gant target (similar in concept to an Ant target) is defined using target(), and its general form is

```
target(<name> : <description>) {
    ...
}
```

where <name> is a string representing the name of the target and <description> is a brief summary of what the target does (which also happens to be displayed by grails help). The target implementation goes inside the curly braces, as you can probably guess. In this case, the target is called createDist.

Inside the body of the target, we can declare what other targets should be run before this one by using depends() ❷. Note that you don't have to put quotes around the names of the targets inside depends(), but you can do so if you wish. In our script, this one line will ensure that the docs and WAR file are generated before we create the zip file.

With the dependencies declared, we then initialize a script variable, zipFile, with the location and name of the distribution zip file. This is a contrived example because we could easily hard-code the path in the createZip target, but it's important to see how you can pass information from one target to another. Anyway, this approach means that another script or target could call createZip and specify a different file path.

> ### Script and local variables
> As well as local variables, class fields, and method arguments, Groovy scripts have another type of variable that we call a *script variable*. These are created whenever a variable is initialized but not declared anywhere. So where
>
> ```
> def var = "Test"
> ```
>
> creates a local variable,
>
> ```
> var = "Test"
> ```
>
> creates a script variable if var hasn't been declared anywhere else. The most significant aspect of script variables is that they're global. Whereas a local variable follows the regular scope rules, a script variable is available everywhere in a script once it's created, no matter what scope it was created in.
>
> One final thing: not only are script variables global within a script, but in Gant they're also available to all included scripts too. This also works in the other direction: script variables created in an included script are available to the one including it. This is one way of passing data between targets, but be aware that this global namespace can easily become polluted with variables, increasing the chances of name clashes.

We're nearly done with the script—there are just a few more items to cover. Not only can you declare target dependencies via depends(), but you can also call targets directly as if they were methods ❸. One of the great advantages of this technique is that it allows you to control exactly when the specified target is executed. On the other hand, depends() ensures that a target is only ever executed once during a build, even if more than one target depends on it.

Inside our second target, we get the location of the generated WAR file from the warName script variable, and use Ant's zip task to generate our distribution zip file **❹**. The name and path of the zip file come from the zipFile script variable, which we set in the main target. Where does the location of the WAR file come from? The warName variable is set by the war target in the _GrailsWar script. You'll also notice the ant property: this is an implicit variable provided by Gant, and it's an instance of Groovy's AntBuilder. Any Ant task can be executed by invoking a method of the same name on the builder—for example, ant.echo() runs Ant's echo task. Each named argument maps to an attribute of the task, and nested elements can be added within a closure. For example, the equivalent of **❹** in Ant's XML format is as follows:

```
<zip destfile="${zipFile}">
    <zipfileset dir="${basedir}/src/templates/bin" prefix="bin"/>
    <zipfileset dir="${grailsHome}/lib" prefix="lib">
        <include name="jetty*.jar"/>
    </zipfileset>
    <zipfileset dir="${basedir}/docs" prefix="docs"/>
    <fileset file="${warName}"/>
</zip>
```

In fact, the mapping between the XML and Groovy code follows a common pattern for XML, where elements map to method calls, attributes map to named arguments, and nested elements map to closures.

At the end of the script **❺**, we set the default target—the one called by Grails when executing the corresponding command. In this case, when we call the grails dist command, Grails invokes the createDist target. The setDefaultTarget() method must come *after* the named target, or it will throw an error.

Phew! That's a lot of detail to take in at once. The key features to remember are targets, dependencies, includes, and the AntBuilder. With a little practice, you'll get the hang of it, and there are plenty of open source plugins that you can mine for ideas. As for AntBuilder, now that you know how to map Ant's XML syntax to Groovy, the best source of information is the Ant reference manual at http://ant.apache.org /manual/.

What about existing targets, though? How do you know which of the Grails scripts you should include and what targets to call? This depends on the state of the Grails user guide, but to get you started, we list some of the more useful scripts in table 15.2, along with their main targets.

As you get more experienced with writing scripts, there's no better way of finding out what scripts and targets are available than going to the source: the Grails scripts themselves! If you've installed Grails locally, you can find them in $GRAILS_HOME /scripts, unpackaged and unencrypted.

One script that deserves special mention is _GrailsEvents, which provides the build system's event mechanism.

Table 15.2 Some useful Grails scripts and their targets

Script	Targets	Description
_GrailsSettings	N/A	Sets up useful variables and does some other essential stuff, but has no targets. If you don't include any other scripts, include this one—almost all other Grails scripts do.
_GrailsArgParsing	parseArguments	Parses any command-line arguments passed to the script—these arguments are accessible using the `argsMap` variable.
_GrailsClean	cleanAll, clean	Does what it says on the tin. `cleanAll` removes test reports, whereas `clean` doesn't.
_GrailsCompile	compile	Compiles the application source files.
_GrailsTest	compileTests, testApp	Compiles and runs the tests.
_GrailsRun	runApp, runWar	Runs the application.
_GrailsWar	war	Generates the application's WAR file.

BUILD SYSTEM EVENTS

Grails provides an event mechanism for scripts that allows them to trigger and act upon named events. For example, Grails' compilation step fires an event before all the source files are compiled, and another one afterwards. Every target also fires start and end events as illustrated in figure 15.2.

To manually fire events, your script must first include the _GrailsEvents script (either directly or indirectly via some other script) and then call the event() method:

```
event("DistCreated", [zipFile])
```

The first argument is the name of the event, and the second argument is a list of parameters that will be passed to any event listeners. Because this is effectively the sole definition of the particular event, you should document somewhere what it means and what parameters it passes. That makes it easier for application writers and plugin authors to hook into your scripts.

Events aren't much use if code can't listen to and act upon them, so let's take a look at how to implement an event listener. First, you need a file called _Events.groovy in the scripts directory. You then define event handlers by creating an appropriately named script variable and setting its value to a closure:

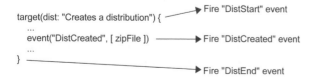

Figure 15.2 Targets in Grails automatically fire start and end events, and the `event()` method allows you to fire them manually.

```
eventDistCreated = { String zip ->
   println "Created distribution zip ${zip}"
}
```

The name of the script variable is the event name prefixed by "event". Unfortunately, events like this tend to be poorly documented, so you usually have to search through the scripts themselves to find out how many parameters are passed for a given event and what they are. Hopefully this situation will improve in future, but to aid you in the meantime, we've listed a few of the more useful ones in table 15.3. Note that although arguments are passed to event() as a list, the event handler closure receives them as separate arguments.

Table 15.3   Some useful script events

Script name	Arguments	Description
StatusUpdate	Status message (string)	Notifies a listener of the current build status; mainly used for logging purposes.
CompileStart, CompileEnd	A string	Fired before/after the application source has been compiled. The argument indicates what is being compiled; for example, source for the main application source, and tests for the test cases.
CreateWarStart, CreateWarEnd	Two arguments: the name of the WAR file (including path) and the location of the staging directory (both strings)	Fired before/after the WAR file for the application has been created.
CleanStart, CleanEnd	None	Fired before/after the project has been cleaned.

Scripts may not be the most exciting part of Grails, but they're real workhorses and can make life a lot easier for users. If you have experience with Ant, you should have no problems getting to grips with them, and we're sure you'll enjoy the freedom of using a real programming language—witness how much easier it is to implement conditions and loops in Gant scripts compared to Ant.

If you aren't familiar with Ant or don't see the point of scripts, that's OK. Grails provides a pretty comprehensive collection of commands already, so there may be no reason for you to write any extra ones. But before you push them out of mind, maybe we can change your mind with another example: automatic deployment of a Grails application to Tomcat.

15.1.3 Deployment

Creating a distribution for Hubbub allowed us to look at Gant scripts without many distractions: we didn't have to think beyond what we wanted to include in the zip file.

Now it's time to look at the deployment phase of the development cycle, the last remaining box in figure 15.1. Deploying a web application directly to a servlet container or Java application server is far more common than distributing one, so stay with us!

Automating deployment is a good idea because it reduces both the likelihood of error and the stress level of the person doing the deployment. Unfortunately, this isn't an area that lends itself to the "one size fits all" paradigm, so any script we use as an example will have only limited application (unless you customize it). Still, a script that automates deployment to Tomcat will be helpful to many people while also serving as a useful example, so that's what we'll look at now.

AUTO-DEPLOYMENT IN TOMCAT 5.5

When you download Apache Tomcat, you aren't just getting a servlet container. It comes with a prepackaged web application called Tomcat Manager that handles remote deployment of user applications to the container. All we have to do is learn how to access the web application and then use its API.

First things first: how do we enable the manager? Although the manager web application is installed and ready for use in the standard Tomcat distribution, no user has the required rights to access it. Therefore, you must start by configuring a Tomcat user that *is* allowed to use it.

Edit the <tomcat>/conf/tomcat-users.xml file (where <tomcat> is the location of the Tomcat installation) and add the following line:

```
<tomcat-users>
  ...
  <user username="overlord" password="Kr@kat04" roles="manager"/>
</tomcat>
```

In general, you should opt for a nonstandard username and as strong a password as possible, because the manager application gives the user a great deal of power. Any Tomcat user assigned the manager role is authorized to access the manager application.

You can try the configuration out by starting the Tomcat server (usually by running either the startup.sh script or the startup.bat Windows batch file) and pointing your browser at http://localhost:8080/manager/html. After entering the username and password you just created, you should see something like the web page shown in figure 15.3.

Feel free to play with this web application, but it isn't what we're interested in right now. Remember, we want to automate deployment from a script, so an interactive UI isn't much use to us. Fortunately, we can send GET and POST requests to specific manager URLs in order to deploy, undeploy, start, or stop an application. You can even do this from the browser. For example, if you point it at this URL, http://localhost:8080/manager/deploy?war=file:/tmp/hubbub.war, the manager will attempt to deploy the WAR file located at /tmp/hubbub.war.

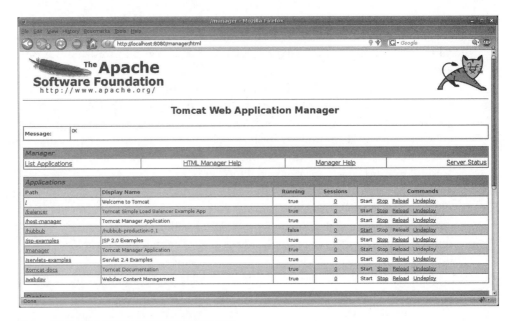

Figure 15.3   The Tomcat Manager application

Now that we know how to use the manager application, it's time to put that knowledge into action and write a Tomcat deployment script for Hubbub.

DEPLOY IT, BABY!

What does this deployment script need to do? As before, with our `Dist` script, we have to make sure that there's a WAR file to deploy. Once we have that, we need to send a `GET` request to the Tomcat manager application, passing the location of the WAR file in the URL. Easy! The script code is shown in listing 15.2.

Listing 15.2   The tomcat-deploy script

```
scriptEnv = "production"                                    Sets default
includeTargets << grailsScript("_GrailsWar")    ❶ environment

target(deploy: "Deploys Hubbub's WAR to Tomcat") {
  depends(war)

  def username = buildConfig.tomcat.mgr.username      ❷ Reads data from config
  def password = buildConfig.tomcat.mgr.password

  Authenticator.setDefault([                            Authenticates user with
    getPasswordAuthentication: {->                      Tomcat Manager
      new PasswordAuthentication(username, password)
    }
  ] as Authenticator)

  def url =
    "http://localhost:8080/manager/deploy?war="    Builds deploy URL
  url += warName
  url += "&path=/hubbub&update=true"
```

```
    def response = new URL(url).text
    if (response.startsWith("OK")) {
        println "Application deployed successfully!"
        return 0         ◁─────┐
    }
    else {                      ❸ Returns exit code
        println "Application failed to deploy: $response"
        return 1
    }
}

setDefaultTarget("deploy")
```

All this script does is generate the WAR file (which it delegates to the war target), send a GET request to the Tomcat Manager, and read the response. There are a few new features that the script introduces, the first of which is the scriptEnv variable ❶.

When you run a Grails command, you don't normally give the environment explicitly—Grails uses a sensible default. So grails run-app defaults to the development environment, and grails war defaults to production. With custom scripts like this, Grails doesn't know what the default should be, so it uses development. We don't want this for our deployment script, though. Just like grails war, we want production to be the default environment, and that's exactly what the line at ❶ does for us.

There are two important things to know about the scriptEnv variable. The first is that you should set its value to the long name of the environment, not the short name used on the command line, so production instead of prod. Second, you *must* initialize it before including the targets from the _GrailsSettings script. Note that _GrailsSettings is automatically included via almost all the Grails scripts— _GrailsProxy is the only notable exception.

Next up is the buildConfig script variable ❷. You saw earlier that along with the Config.groovy file, users can put configuration information in a BuildConfig.groovy file. The data from both are available to scripts via the config and buildConfig variables respectively. To access a property called tomcat.mgr.username, we use the syntax buildConfig.tomcat.mgr.username. How do you decide which configuration file the data should go into? As a general rule of thumb, any configuration option required by a script should go into BuildConfig.groovy, so our deployment script uses buildConfig.

The other new feature is the return statement ❸. If a target returns an integer value, Gant treats it as an exit code for the build. This is important because tools, particularly continuous integration servers (which we'll discuss shortly), often use the exit code to determine whether the build succeeded. A 0 value indicates that everything worked OK, whereas a non-0 value indicates an error of some sort. Typically you would use 1 if there were any problems executing the target (as we do in the deployment script), because it acts as a generic error value. It's only worth using other values if you need or want to distinguish between different problems.

One more thing: that text property on the URL is added by Groovy. It opens a connection to the URL, reads the response, and returns the content of the response as a string.

A final word of advice

What goes into the WAR file is important, which is why we recommend that any WAR file you plan to deploy to production (or even to staging) is generated from a fresh checkout of the project. You should preferably check out a particular label or version that has been tested. Generating WAR files from developer working copies is almost guaranteed to cause problems due to local modifications, extra files, and so on.

What are you waiting for? Try out your new `tomcat-deploy` command and discover how a little effort on the script front has saved you the burden of manual deployment.

Congratulations, you're now officially a script master! We've shown you how easy it is to write a couple of scripts that do something useful, and we're sure that the ideas will start flowing freely now. If you're productive in this area, you could even package the scripts as a plugin—something that we look at in the next chapter.

Although we've spent a lot of time on the Grails build system, we've only looked at it from the perspective of the Grails command line. For many users, the command line is all they need, but as we said at the beginning of the chapter, sometimes you have to use a different tool to build your Grails applications. Setting up such tools to successfully build a Grails project is no walk in the park, though, and how would you deal with plugins that hook into the build process? What we need is some way to reuse the existing build system from other build tools.

15.2 Build integration—not for the hobbyist

The existing Grails build system is flexible and extensible, but sometimes it isn't appropriate for your needs. What if your company has standardized on Maven for its projects, or your Grails application is part of a larger project that uses Ant for its build? Telling the people in charge of a build that they have to do something different for your application will go down like a ton of bricks. Be prepared for a lot of shouting!

This issue is well recognized by the Grails development team, so there are already mechanisms to smoothly integrate the Grails build system into both Ant and Maven builds, the two most popular build tools in the Java world. Let's start with Ant, which is still phenomenally popular.

15.2.1 Ant

This is the forefather of build tools for the Java platform. Although showing its age compared to some of its younger rivals, it's robust, flexible, and widely used. Perhaps the greatest compliment to it is that several other build tools allow you to run Ant tasks directly. With that kind of background, surely it's easy to build Grails projects using it? Thankfully, yes.

Imagine that we have a simple Ant build file that has targets for compiling the application classes, compiling the tests, running the tests, and building the WAR file. Normally, these targets would contain the relevant Ant tasks, such as `javac` and `junit`, but a Grails application isn't a simple beast to build, and it's far preferable to delegate as much work as possible to the Grails build system. Another point to bear in mind is that some plugins hook into the Grails build system in order to provide certain features, so if you manage the entire build yourself in Ant, those features won't work.

Grails comes with a dedicated Ant task that bootstraps the Grails build system and allows you to execute any Grails script you want. Listing 15.3 shows you how to set up the task and then use it.

Listing 15.3   An Ant build for a Grails application

```
<project name="my-app" basedir=".">
   <property environment="env"/>
   <property name="grailsHome" value="env.GRAILS_HOME"/>          Stores location of Grails

   <taskdef name="grails"                        ◁——❶ Defines Grails Ant task
      classname="grails.ant.GrailsTask"
      classpath="${grailsHome}/dist/grails-bootstrap-1.1.jar"/>

   <target name="compile">
      <grails home="${grailsHome}" script="Compile"/>    ◁——❷ Calls the task
   </target>

   <target name="test">
      <grails home="${grailsHome}"           Executes script
         script="TestApp" args="-unit"/>     with argument
   </target>
</project>
```

The first trick is to make sure that the grails-bootstrap JAR is on the classpath when defining the task ❶. In the example build file, we explicitly set the classpath in the task definition, specifying the location of the JAR relative to a Grails installation. You could also include the JAR on Ant's own classpath, but that's a less common approach. The important point is that the `grails.ant.GrailsTask` class is contained in the bootstrap JAR.

Once the task is defined, we can start using it. To compile the application's classes, we invoke the `Compile` Gant script ❷. The application references plenty of Grails classes, so the compilation needs to know where it can find them. In this case, we pass the location of the Grails installation to the Ant task via the `home` attribute. The required `script` attribute contains the name of the script to run, and the `args` attribute contains a space-delimited list of arguments to pass to the script. `Compile` doesn't make use of arguments, but the `TestApp` script can accept several, and we demonstrate one of them in listing 15.3 (-unit, telling Grails to run just the unit tests).

This approach works well and is pretty simple, but there's a drawback: it relies on Grails being installed locally. You may think this isn't a problem; after all, it has worked well for us so far. But consider this: how many software builds have you come across that require anything other than the build tool to be installed? Probably not many (if any). Certainly most Java web application frameworks can be used without such a requirement. Your team members are unlikely to take kindly to installing yet another piece of software. Fortunately, you can use Grails without installing a distribution, but it does require more configuration.

NO GRAILS?

When you have a Grails distribution installed, all the JARs in its lib and dist directories are added to the classpaths for compilation and testing, which makes life pretty easy for you. But what happens when you don't have a Grails distribution? Those JARs have to find their way onto a classpath somehow, and it's your job to get them there.

In the specific case of the Ant task, we can use some nested elements designed specifically for the job. But we first have to look at the question of the *task's* dependencies. You only need the grails-bootstrap JAR on the task definition's classpath, but running the task requires a few more libraries, such as Groovy and Gant. In the previous example, the task got the libraries from the Grails distribution (via that home attribute we specified), but we can also pass their locations to the task either by using the `classpathref` attribute,

```
<grails script="..." classpathref="grails.classpath">
```

or by using a nested `classpath` element:

```
<grails scripts="...">
   <classpath>
      <pathelement location="..."/>
      ...
   </classpath>
</grails>
```

Both should be familiar from some of the core Ant tasks.

That's the easy bit. The hard bit is determining what JARs should be added to the classpath and where to store them. You could put the grails-bootstrap JAR plus all the JARs from the Grails lib directory into your *application's* lib directory. All you would have to do then is set the classpath to include all the JARs in that directory. The downside is that you end up including quite a few libraries that are completely unnecessary. Is there no other option?

> **Grails and Ivy**
> When you create a project using Grails, you'll find a ready-made Ant build file and some Ivy files in the project's root directory. You can use this build straight away, and it's particularly useful for continuous integration.

All the Grails JAR files, including grails-bootstrap, have corresponding Maven Project Object Model (POM) definitions. These include a description of the artifact's dependencies. Manually parsing POMs isn't much fun, but you can use Apache Ivy (http://ant.apache.org/ivy/) or the Maven Ant tasks (http://maven.apache.org/ant-tasks/index.html) to fetch the required dependencies for you.

Let's say you've decided to use the Maven Ant tasks and have loaded them into the `artifact` namespace in the build file. This fragment will download the dependencies

required by the Grails Ant task and create a path from them with the ID `grails`
`.classpath`:

```
<project ...>
    ...
    <target name="dependencies">
        <artifact:dependencies pathId="grails.classpath">
            <dependency groupId="org.grails" artifactId="grails-bootstrap"
                version="1.1" scope="runtime"/>
            <dependency groupId="org.grails" artifactId="grails-scripts"
                version="1.1" scope="runtime"/>
        </artifact:dependencies>
    </target>
    ...
    <target name="compile" depends="dependencies">
        <grails script="Compile" classpathref="grails.classpath"/>
    </target>
    ...
</project>
```

For a full explanation of how to use the Maven Ant tasks, see the website. The most
important pieces of information contained in the preceding fragment are the two
dependencies: you need both grails-bootstrap and grails-scripts (plus their dependencies) in order to run any of the Grails scripts via the Ant task.

COMPILE, TEST, RUN ...

The classpath required to use the Ant task is different from the ones needed for compiling, testing, and running the application. After all, the build system only needs
grails-bootstrap and grails-scripts, but the application itself more often than not needs
GORM, the controllers and views support, the testing support, and other Grails components. As we mentioned earlier, Grails normally picks up the required libraries
from its installation directory, but an alternative approach is necessary when it hasn't
been installed at all.

Although the Grails distribution bundles all its dependencies into the lib directory,
the build system internally maintains three different classpaths: one for compiling the
application classes, another for compiling and running the tests, and a third for running the application. These are rarely the same, but how do you know which JARs
should be in which classpath? It's fairly obvious for libraries that you use directly from
your own code, but the Grails artifacts are a different kettle of fish.

As with the classpath for the Ant task itself, one option is to put all the Grails libraries into your application's lib directory. You can then use something like this:

```
<project ...>
    <path id="grails.classpath">
        <fileset dir="${basedir}/lib" includes="*.jar"/>
    </path>
    ...
    <target name="compile">
        <grails script="Compile" classpathref="grails.classpath">
            <compile-classpath>
                <path refid="grails.classpath"/>
```

```
        </compile-classpath>
        <test-classpath>
            <path refid="grails.classpath"/>
        </test-classpath>
        <runtime-classpath>
            <path refid="grails.classpath"/>
        </runtime-classpath>
      </grails>
    </target>
    ...
</project>
```

Each of the `*-classpath` elements behaves like a `classpath` element, so you can embed filesets as well as path references and path elements. As before, there's a fair bit of redundancy with this approach, and you would be better off using the Maven Ant tasks or Ivy.

That leads us to a build tool that makes dependency management one of its foundations: Maven.

15.2.2 *Maven*

Love it or loathe it, Maven is widely used and here to stay. Its core principles of build conventions and dependency management can simplify many builds and help with consistency across multiple projects. Manually integrating a Grails application into a Maven build would be an exercise in masochism, though, because both are opinionated but with different opinions! Fortunately, easy integration is provided via a Maven plugin and an archetype.

The simplest way to start with Maven and Grails is to create a new project using the Grails archetype:

```
mvn archetype:generate -DarchetypeGroupId=org.grails \
    -DarchetypeArtifactId=grails-maven-archetype \
    -DarchetypeVersion=1.0 \
    -DarchetypeRepository=http://snapshots.repository.codehaus.org \
    -DgroupId=example -DartifactId=my-app
```

This will create a new application called `my-app` with a group ID of `example`. Note that you don't need to install Grails for this to work. All you need is Maven 2.0.9 (or greater).

Let's take a look at what the command has created for us:

```
my-app
  |
  +--- pom.xml
  |
  +--- src - main - webapp - WEB-INF - web.xml
```

The pom.xml file is the Maven project descriptor (the POM), which includes everything you need to build a Grails application with Maven. It contains a standard set of Grails dependencies and the configuration for the Grails Maven plugin. The web.xml file is empty and is only there to ensure that the Maven WAR plugin doesn't generate an error when packaging the application. Leave it well alone.

One thing you'll notice immediately is that it doesn't look much like a Grails application. That's easily rectified with this command:

```
mvn initialize
```

Maven will download all the required Grails artifacts (and their dependencies) and then create the standard project structure that you're familiar with. You're now good to go.

Under the hood

Although the Grails Maven plugin hooks into the standard build cycle, it uses smoke and mirrors to make the integration look tighter than it is. None of the standard Maven plugins are used to build the Grails application. Instead, each phase delegates to the corresponding Grails script, so `compile` delegates to the `Compile` script, `test` delegates to the `TestApp` script, and `package` delegates to `War`. In effect, the integration relies on the standard plugins not doing anything because the project structure doesn't match the convention.

Another point to make is that the Grails script dependencies are still taken into account, so not only does `mvn package` invoke all the previous phases (such as `compile`), but the `War` script also invokes the Grails compilation. In other words, the Grails `compile` target is invoked more than once. It's not ideal, but it does work.

The Grails Maven plugin hooks into the standard Maven build cycle, so you can invoke the phases you're used to, such as `compile`, `test`, and `package`. Also, you declare the application's dependencies in the POM rather than dropping the relevant JARs into the lib directory, as you would with any regular Maven project. The plugin ensures that the libraries are added to the appropriate classpaths, so you don't have to worry about all those classpath references we looked at in the section on Ant. Everything is taken care of for you.

In addition to the standard build phases, the plugin also adds quite a few goals for you to use, such as `run-app` and `install-templates`. In fact, there are equivalent goals for most of the Grails commands—you can find a complete list in the Grails user guide. To run one, use this syntax:

```
mvn org.grails:grails-maven-plugin:1.0:run-app
```

That works, but we can't imagine that you want to type out such a long command on a regular basis. The reason for the verbosity is to avoid conflicts between plugins that provide goals with identical names. Fortunately, you can cut out lots of typing by adding this fragment to your $HOME/.m2/settings.xml file:

```
<settings>
   ...
   <pluginGroups>
```

```
        <pluginGroup>org.grails</pluginGroup>
    </pluginGroups>
</settings>
```

This little piece of XML turns that monster of a command into this:

```
mvn grails:run-app
```

Far easier on the eyes and the fingers we think you'll agree.

You now know how to create a new Maven-enabled Grails project, but what if you have an existing one that you want to convert to Maven? Simple:

```
mvn grails:create-pom
```

This command will create a POM and some other files for the project so that you can immediately start building it with Maven.

One final point: the nature of the Maven integration means that some Maven plugins won't work with Grails projects, such as the Jetty plugin. Anything that relies on the standard Maven project structure is unlikely to work unless you can configure it for the Grails project structure. Despite that, the Maven integration should be quite sufficient for most projects, and it has the added benefit of being easy to set up.

If you need to integrate with something other than Ant or Maven, the techniques we've discussed won't help much. Instead, you need to work with the Grails bootstrap classes directly. That's a topic beyond the scope of this book, but it's useful to know it's possible. Hopefully other build tools will feature direct support for Grails projects in the future.

We've talked a lot about both build tools and the Grails build system, but there's at least one other significant aspect of application deployment that we haven't considered yet. Making it easy to deploy new versions of an application is great, but what about the database schema? As your application grows, the schema is likely to change, and it's important to manage those changes.

15.3   *Coping with a changing data model*

Most Grails applications are built upon a data model backed by a database. In an ideal world, your first attempt at designing that model would be perfect, and you'd never have to change it. But as we all know, this ideal is a long, long way from reality. Data models constantly evolve and require changes to the database schema. This often happens *after* real data has started accumulating in the database.

Managing these changes is an important part of both development and deployment of an application. How can you improve the schema and incorporate new features without messing up the existing data? We'll start by looking at whether we can develop an approach based on the dbCreate data source setting, and then follow that up with a look at a plugin dedicated to solving the problem.

15.3.1 *Schema migration with Hibernate*

While developing the Hubbub sample application, you were taking advantage of a Hibernate feature called "automatic schema export." This feature uses your domain model to create the relevant tables in the backing database. Figure 15.4 illustrates where it fits into the application startup process.

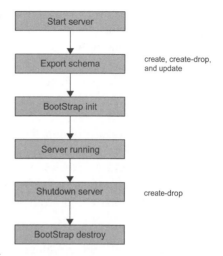

Figure 15.4 **Where Hibernate's schema export fits into application startup and shutdown. The strings on the right highlight which dbCreate settings are active for each phase.**

You control the behavior of the automatic schema export via the dbCreate data source setting, which you saw in chapter 1 (section 1.4.1). During development, you typically set this to either create or create-drop. These values ensure that your database remains free of old tables and columns, but at the cost of losing all the data every time you run the application. If you need some reference or test data, you should create it in the application's BootStrap.

Once the data model starts settling down, this habit of losing the data can become irritating at best, particularly if you're building up a good set of data while you manually test your application. At that point, you should switch to update as the dbCreate setting. This will preserve your data while keeping the database schema in sync with your data model.

The update setting is fine for development, but there are some serious problems with it that mean you shouldn't use it in production systems. First, it can't perform some migrations. The classic example is a column rename: Hibernate will create the new column but it won't migrate the data to the new column, nor will it remove the old column. That leads us to the second problem, which is that old tables and columns are left in the database gathering dust and causing confusion. Finally, Hibernate doesn't keep track of schema changes, which means that it's nearly impossible to roll back to an old version.

The traditional solution for such controlled data migration is to use manually crafted SQL scripts that both update the schema and migrate the data. You can certainly go down this road, but to do so you must remove the dbCreate setting entirely. This prevents Hibernate from doing anything to the database schema.

If you decide to use SQL scripts for this job, you may be interested in the following Grails command:

```
grails schema-export initial-schema.sql
```

This generates a SQL Data Definition Language (DDL) script that you can use to recreate the application's database schema in a fresh database. Rather than relying on

Hibernate's automatic schema export, you can execute the SQL script against an empty database so that it will work with your application. If you don't pass an argument to the command, it creates the file ddl.sql.

Writing and maintaining SQL scripts sounds like a lot of hard work, though—something that we're not used to with Grails. Let's look at a plugin that promises to make life easier when it comes to migrating data.

15.3.2 *Intelligent migration with Autobase*

The Autobase plugin tries to solve two problems: migrations that Hibernate can't manage by itself and migrations that have already been applied to a database. Both problems have already been tackled by a Java library called LiquiBase, and it's this library that the plugin is based on.

The first step on your path to intelligent data migration is to install the plugin:

```
grails install-plugin autobase
```

On installation, the plugin will create a new directory, migrations, in the root of your project. This is where the information about schema and data changes is stored.

What happens next? Let's say we want to rename the userId field in Hubbub's User domain class to username. If the dbCreate setting is update, we can make the change and restart the application. Hibernate creates the new username column as expected, but the old column is left containing all the old user IDs. This is obviously a problem.

Instead of using update, we should remove the dbCreate setting altogether. This means we have to take responsibility for *all* changes to the database, but at least we're in control—that's important. Once that's done, we need to define some migrations that Autobase can apply. Creating a new migration script is as simple as running this command,

```
grails create-migration RenameUserId
```

which will create the migrations/<login>/RenameUserId.groovy file, where <login> is your login name.

The newly created file is pretty bare, so let's add a migration to rename the user_id column. Note how we refer to the name of the database column, not the name of the domain class field.

```
changeSet(id:'RenameUserId', author:'peter') {
    renameColumn(tableName:"account",
            oldColumnName:"user_id",
            newColumnName:"username")
}
```

We've defined a single changeset here that performs the column rename using what LiquiBase calls a "structural migration"; in other words, something that modifies the structure of a table or database view. Figure 15.5 illustrates the effect we're after.

Where do the `changeSet()` and `rename-Column()` methods come from? The above DSL is markup builder syntax that maps to the equivalent LiquiBase XML changelog format. That makes it easy to use the existing LiquiBase documentation, which refers to the XML format, because you already know how to convert between the two forms. You can find out what other refactorings are available here: http://www.liquibase.org/manual/home.

Figure 15.5 The effect of renaming the account table's `user_id` column to `username` without affecting the data

Now when you start Hubbub, Autobase will automatically apply this migration. It's even clever enough to ignore changesets that have already been applied to the database.

Under the hood

LiquiBase records the last changeset that was applied to a database in its own table. Whenever it performs a data migration, LiquiBase only executes the changesets that come after that last recorded one.

Changesets are applied in the order that they're defined in a migration script. There's no guarantee, by default, as to what order migration scripts are applied, though. You can change this by editing migrations/changelog.groovy and replacing the `includeAll()` method with an `include()` for each individual script in the order you want them to run. The latter method takes the path of a single script as its argument.

That's just one migration, but you'll undoubtedly want to add more in your own applications. You can either add `changeSet` blocks to the existing migration file or create a new one. Which you do comes down to personal preference, but it's easier to manage a few files containing multiple changesets than lots of files with a single changeset each.

What should you put in a changeset? This is a good question, but there's no easy answer. One strategy is to create a new changeset each time you need to make a change to the database schema. If the change is large, you should break it down into multiple changesets. For example, adding a new relationship may involve creating an extra column or two and adding a foreign key constraint, all of which could go in a single changeset.

Although there's plenty of room for discretion in choosing what goes into a changeset, the one thing you should not do is define one that leaves the database in a "broken" state. For example, removing a column without removing foreign keys that depend on it.

Refactorings like renaming columns aren't the only changes you can make. Autobase comes with a command that allows you to do some powerful stuff:

```
grails create-groovy-migration UpdateData
```

This command creates the usual migration script that you would expect, but it also creates a plain Groovy script in migrations/<login>/.scripts. The code in the script has access to some important objects, such as a `groovy.sql.Sql` instance (see the generated script for information on others), which you can use to manipulate the data in the database directly.

That's all there is to it! Just remember that once you remove the `dbCreate` setting, you have to create a migration for every change to the domain model that also requires a change to the database schema.

WARNING   Autobase can't currently create the database schema from scratch, so it won't work with a fresh, empty database. Hopefully this problem will be resolved in the near future. In the meantime, consider running the `schema-export` command before you apply any migrations. You can then run the generated SQL against a fresh database before running the application (with Autobase) against it.

Controlled data migration using a tool like Autobase may seem inconvenient at first, compared to Hibernate's automatic schema export, but in the long run it saves a lot of grief. You know what migrations are applied, and it's easy to associate them with feature requests and bug reports. You can also easily roll back to previous database states. These features ensure that when the crunch comes and the pressure is on, you have the information and tools to deploy new versions of an application against an existing database.

15.4   *Summary and best practices*

As you've seen in this chapter, software development involves more than writing code. You have to be able to run the tests, run and package the application, and probably deploy it too. Grails provides a comprehensive build system that takes the burden of creating a system off your shoulders, while also allowing you to both hook into and extend it. Yet it doesn't provide support for the full development cycle, so you may have to write your own Grails scripts.

Then you have the situations where you can't use the Grails build system directly, but must use an alternative build tool. You've seen that Grails provides Ant and Maven integration out of the box, so you won't have any worries there. In fact, it raises the question of whether you should use one of these tools out of choice rather than necessity.

Here are some pointers to help you out with all this build and development cycle stuff:

- *Write scripts for any repetitive task that you can.*   Automation is important in reducing errors and improving reproducibility. On top of that, a little investment of time early on can pay big dividends later. When crunch time comes, you'll be glad you just have to type in a single command for any task.

- *Use continuous integration.*   This is almost mandatory for any team bigger than one to catch those bugs that appear when changes from different people are merged together. Even for sole developers, continuous integration is useful for running your full suite of tests, in case you forget to run them locally or they take too long.
- *Use the build tool you're comfortable with.*   At the end of the day, you should use the build tool that meets all your requirements and that you're most comfortable with. If you're happy with the Grails build system, use it if you can—it saves you a fair bit of effort. Consider the other build tools if your application is just one part of a larger project.
- *Start using controlled data migration.*   Although Hibernate's schema export feature is convenient, its usefulness is limited in the long run. Start using a tool like Autobase as soon as the data model has settled down or just after the first deployment at the latest.

Whatever option you eventually choose, you can rest assured that Grails will support that decision and allow you to use your chosen build tool with a minimum of fuss.

Plugin development

16

In this chapter

- How plugins work
- Writing your own plugins
- Managing plugin repositories

We looked at build integration and project management in the previous chapter, so now we'll look at a way to modularize and extend your application by developing your own plugins. We introduced you to the Grails plugin system back in chapter 8, and you saw then how useful plugins can be. They're a fundamental and powerful part of the Grails infrastructure, and even if you never need to write your own plugins, understanding how the system works will set you in good stead for the future.

When might you need or want to create your own plugin? We don't want to limit your thinking on this, but here are three common uses:

- Integrating an existing library or tool into Grails
- Providing a specific feature
- Modularizing an application

You've already seen many examples of the first use, such as Searchable (which integrates Compass), Spring Security, and others. The Authentication and Functional

Test plugins are examples of the second use, providing access control and functional testing respectively. The difference between those two uses is more technical than practical, so it's not necessarily worth distinguishing between them.

The last common use we listed relates to breaking an application into modules. This doesn't make sense for a small application like Hubbub, but large applications can easily become difficult to maintain and understand if they remain monolithic. Breaking the application's functionality into individual plugins helps counter those problems, and you can then reuse those plugins in other applications. This approach works particularly well if you maintain a separation of concerns. For example, imagine you have a business application that handles invoicing, payroll, business tax, and so on. Each of these "features" could be implemented using plugins, which you could then install into a single project to create the application. The plugins could even be developed by separate teams.

Now that you know why you might want to develop a plugin, it's time to jump into the deep end and look at how to do it. In this chapter, we'll use the example of writing a security plugin for our Hubbub application. This may seem like a stupid idea, because we already have the Spring Security plugin in place, but bear with us. It's a useful way of demonstrating all the important features we want to discuss.

16.1 Creating your first plugin

You always have to start somewhere, and developing a Grails plugin is no different. In this section, we'll create a project for our security plugin and lay the first bricks. In this case, that means adding some artifacts, much as we do when creating a new Grails application.

16.1.1 Are you sure it's not an application?

So how do we go about creating a plugin project? That's easy—we start with a magic incantation:

```
grails create-plugin security
```

This will create a directory named security and populate it with the skeleton of a plugin project, as shown in figure 16.1. It's no coincidence that the project looks a lot like a Grails application. You can run it like one using the regular run-app command—useful for testing.

The most visible difference between a plugin and an application is the presence of a plugin descriptor, the SecurityGrailsPlugin.groovy file (highlighted in figure 16.1). The descriptor not only contains information about the plugin, such as the author and a description of what it does, but it also contains the code that allows you to hook into Grails and modify the behavior of applications at runtime.

The name of the plugin descriptor class is important, because it determines the official plugin name. Rather than store the name in a field of the class, Grails infers it by chopping off the "GrailsPlugin" suffix, converting uppercase letters to lowercase,

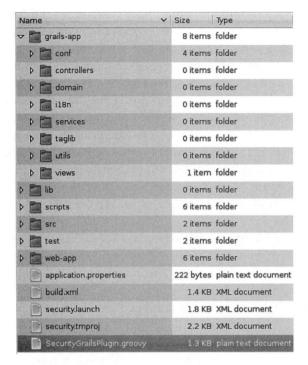

Name	Size	Type
▽ 📁 grails-app	8 items	folder
▷ 📁 conf	4 items	folder
▷ 📁 controllers	0 items	folder
▷ 📁 domain	0 items	folder
▷ 📁 i18n	0 items	folder
▷ 📁 services	0 items	folder
▷ 📁 taglib	0 items	folder
▷ 📁 utils	0 items	folder
▷ 📁 views	1 item	folder
▷ 📁 lib	0 items	folder
▷ 📁 scripts	6 items	folder
▷ 📁 src	2 items	folder
▷ 📁 test	2 items	folder
▷ 📁 web-app	6 items	folder
📄 application.properties	222 bytes	plain text document
📄 build.xml	1.4 KB	XML document
📄 security.launch	1.8 KB	XML document
📄 security.tmproj	2.2 KB	XML document
📄 SecurityGrailsPlugin.groovy	1.3 KB	plain text document

Figure 16.1 The directory structure of a plugin project. Note how it's almost identical to the structure of a Grails application. The plugin descriptor is highlighted.

and separating words with a hyphen. For example, `SecurityGrailsPlugin` becomes `security` and `MyTagsGrailsPlugin` becomes `my-tags`.

Now let's take a look at the descriptor we just created. Listing 16.1 contains a slightly condensed version of its initial contents.

Listing 16.1 Initial plugin descriptor

```
class SecurityGrailsPlugin {
    def version = 0.1                              ❶ Declares plugin version,
    def grailsVersion = "1.1 > *"                     dependencies
    def dependsOn = [:]

    def pluginExcludes = [                         ❷ Excludes files from
      "grails-app/views/error.gsp"                    packaged plugin
    ]

    def author = "Your name"
    def authorEmail = ""
    def title = "Plugin summary/headline"          ❸ Declares information
    def description = '''\                             about plugin
Brief description of the plugin.
'''

    def documentation =                            ❹ Specifies location
        "http://grails.org/Security+Plugin"           of plugin docs
```

```
    def doWithSpring = { ... }
    def doWithApplicationContext = { ctx -> ... }
    def doWithWebDescriptor = { xml -> ... }
    def doWithDynamicMethods = { ctx -> ... }
    def onChange = { event -> ... }
    def onConfigChange = { event -> ... }
}
```

❺ Declares plugin hooks

We start with the version and dependency information for the plugin ❶. The version field contains the plugin's current version. Although the initial value is a number, you can also use a string. That means "0.1-SNAPSHOT" and "merlin" are also valid versions. That said, Grails expects plugins to use a major.minor.patch numbering convention, where each part is an integer and the final patch number is optional. For example, both 1.0.4 and 2.1 follow the convention. Appending a "-SNAPSHOT" suffix is common when releasing a development version, such as when you want to solicit feedback on changes to a plugin.

The grailsVersion field indicates which versions of Grails the plugin works with. This can either be a single version or a range of the form:

```
lowerBound > upperBound
```

You should read this as "any version from lowerBound up to upperBound, inclusive." You can also use the wildcard (*) for either bound. This means "any version up to and including 1.1":

```
* > 1.1
```

This one means "any version from 1.0 upwards":

```
1.0 > *
```

These ranges also work in the dependsOn field, which is a map of plugin names to versions (or version ranges). For example, if a plugin depends on the Quartz and Remoting plugins, it might include this line:

```
def dependsOn = [ quartz: "0.4", remoting: "0.3 > *" ]
```

Note that there is no equivalent range syntax using the < symbol.

Next we have the pluginExcludes field ❷. Grails packages the files that make up a plugin into a zip file. You may not want some of those files packaged, particularly if they're only used for testing, and you can exclude them by adding their paths to the pluginExcludes field. We'll look further at packaging a plugin in section 16.2.

The plugin information specified in ❸ is mainly for the benefit of end users. The list-plugins command will display the plugin name and its title, and plugin-info will display all the fields.

As for the documentation field ❹, that's a URL pointing to whatever documentation the plugin has. Most plugins in the central Grails repository have one or more pages on the Grails web site.

After the documentation field, things get more interesting. Those doWith* and on* closures ❺ are the hooks that allow our plugin to influence the runtime behavior of the application. These are key to providing smooth integration with Grails, such as that provided by GORM. Table 16.1 briefly describes what each of the hooks allows you to do and lists the arguments Grails passes to the associated closure. The first three are shown in the order in which Grails invokes them on application startup.

Table 16.1   The hooks that allow a plugin to integrate closely with a Grails application

Property	Arguments	Description
doWithSpring	none	This closure allows you to define and configure Spring beans.
doWithDynamicMethods	applicationContext	This closure allows you to add dynamic properties and methods to classes and artifacts. Its sole argument is the fully configured Spring application context.
doWithApplicationContext	applicationContext	This closure allows you to work with the fully configured Spring application context. You can only manipulate bean instances, not bean definitions.
doWithWebDescriptor	webXml	This closure allows you to modify the application's web descriptor. It is passed a GPathResult object (created by XmlSlurper) that you can use to insert elements, such as servlet and filter definitions.
onChange	event	This closure allows you to react to changes to any artifacts that the plugin is watching.
onConfigChange	event	This closure allows you to react to changes to the application's Config.groovy file.
onShutdown	event	This closure allows you to react when the application shuts down. The Spring application context is still available at this point

Note that all of the hooks are closures; if you try to use a method instead, it won't be executed. We'll come back to these hooks in the next section, but they're only part of the story. We'll first look at how to provide ready-made domain models and web pages.

16.1.2   *Controllers, views, and other artifacts*

The easiest way to enhance an application is to provide ready-made artifacts with your plugin, such as domain classes and controllers. Consider our security plugin: we want to assign roles to users and store that information, so some domain classes might come in handy. Also, logging into an application is pretty standard stuff, so why don't we provide our own controller and views to handle that? Finally, we could do with some tags that show parts of a web page only if the user has a particular role or is logged in. For example, a Remove Post button for Hubbub should only be visible to administrators.

> ### Holy artifacts, Batman!
> You'll see the term "artifact" used throughout the rest of this chapter, but what does it mean? Some types of classes are given special treatment by Grails, such as domain classes, controllers, and tag libraries. These are collectively known as "artifacts" and reside under the grails-app directory of a project.

Most Grails artifacts that you've seen so far can be included in a plugin, and we'll start by looking at the domain classes our security plugin might provide.

DOMAIN CLASSES

Because we want to assign users to roles, it makes sense that we need one domain class to represent our users and another for the roles.

Our Role class is going to be simple, consisting of just a name:

```
class Role {
    String name

    static constraints = {
        name(blank: false, unique: true)
    }
}
```

The given constraints ensure that every role has a unique name. The other required domain class poses a problem: Hubbub already has a User class, but it contains fields that are inappropriate for plain access control, such as signupDate and followers. These are specific to Hubbub, so they shouldn't be included in the plugin's domain class.

This situation cries out for domain class inheritance: we can factor out the userId and password fields into a new class and modify the existing User class to extend it. The new class, which we'll call Account, can happily be incorporated into the plugin, whereas User remains in the application. The new arrangement looks like this:

```
// In plugin
class Account {
    String userId
    String password

    static hasMany = [ roles: Role ]

    static constraints = {
        // Same constraints for userId and password as before
        ...
```

```
    }
}

// In application
class User extends Account {
    ...
}
```

We now have Account.groovy and Role.groovy files under security/grails-app/domain and User.groovy under hubbub/grails-app/domain. This now means that Hubbub won't compile unless our security plugin is installed.

Domain classes provided by a plugin materially affect the domain model of any project that the plugin is installed into. The user has no way of disabling, modifying, or removing them without editing the plugin files directly, so be careful what domain classes you package with your plugin.

In our case, the plugin depends on the Account and Role domain classes, so it makes sense to provide them as is. An alternative approach is to copy the behavior of the various create-* and generate-* commands and provide scripts to create the domain model. You saw this technique used by the Spring Security plugin with its generate-manager command. We'll explain how to implement it in section 16.3.5.

The next step is to provide users with a means to log into the application.

CONTROLLERS

All we want to do is accept a username and password and check those against the values stored in the database. If the login is successful, we'll place the relevant User instance in the session; otherwise we'll redirect back to the login page. That means we need a login page, an action for performing the login, and an action for logging out. Because we support roles, we'll also include an action that users will be redirected to if they don't have permission to access a particular page—an "access denied" page. Here's the outline of our LoginController:

```
package com.grailsinaction.security

class LoginController {
    def index = {}
    def signIn = { ... }
    def signOut = { ... }
    def unauthorized = { ... }
}
```

The implementations of these actions are immaterial to the discussion, but you can see them in the chapter's example source code.

The key point is that we can place this controller under the plugin's grails-app /controllers directory and its associated views under grails-app/views/login. Once the plugin is installed in an application, the controller and views behave as if they were part of the application. In the case of Hubbub, for example, you could point your browser at http://localhost:8080/hubbub/login/index, and it would show the login page provided by the plugin. You don't have to do any configuration whatsoever.

Once the plugin is installed, you can override the controller and views in your application. For example, if you don't like the look of the standard login page, you can place your own index.gsp file under the application's grails-app/views/login directory. Alternatively, you can change the login behavior completely by providing your own `LoginController` implementation. The one thing you can't do is override just the controller and use the plugin's views with it. Only plugin controllers have access to the plugin's views.

> ### Under the hood
>
> To make overriding the controller easy, we put it in a package. So long as the overriding controller has the same name as the one provided by the plugin, it all works smoothly.
>
> But beware: all artifacts in both the application and installed plugins are compiled to the same directory, so classes with the same name and package will conflict.

TAG LIBRARIES

Tag libraries work much like controllers and are common in the plugin world. We strongly recommend that any plugin tag libraries you provide use a namespace that's likely to be unique for the plugin. For example, we use a namespace of hsec for our security plugin (an unoriginal combination of "h" from "Hubbub" and "sec" from "security"). There's no guarantee that some other plugin won't use the same namespace, but a careful choice will help minimize the risk.

Why would a plugin provide tags? Custom tags provide an easy way to access a plugin's functionality from GSP views. This may not be useful for all plugins, but our security plugin, for example, provides tags that display or hide their contents based on whether the user is logged in.

VIEWS

We quickly mentioned views in conjunction with controllers, and they work like any other views. The one complication is when a tag refers to another resource in the plugin. When you execute the `run-app` command from within the plugin project, the path to the plugin's resources (such as JavaScript and CSS files) is different compared to when the plugin is installed in an application. In the latter case, the path includes the plugin name to avoid name clashes between plugins.

Making sure that the appropriate path is used requires a little bit of magic. Imagine that our plugin provides a JavaScript file, and we include it from one of the views. You should construct the path to the JavaScript file using the dynamic `plugin-ContextPath` property:

```
<g:resource dir="${pluginContextPath}/js" file="security.js" />
```

The generated link will look like /myapp/js/security.js when running the plugin directly, or /myapp/plugins/security-0.1/js/security.js if it's installed in an application.

If your views refer to templates, you need to use a different technique. The render tag accepts a `plugin` attribute that does what we need:

```
<g:render template="roleList" plugin="security"/>
```

This will render the security plugin's `roleList` template, regardless of whether the tag is used in an application or a plugin view.

You can see in figure 16.2 where the artifacts are stored in the plugin—they're in exactly the same places as they would be in an application. Grails does all the work required to make those artifacts available to the applications that the plugin is installed into.

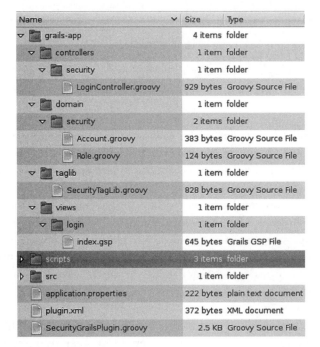

Figure 16.2 **The artifacts provided by the security plugin**

We have a domain model and sign in and out functionality now, but no mechanism for controlling access to an application's pages. You'll see how to add that in section 16.3, but now would be a good time to practice publishing our plugin.

16.2 *Publishing your plugin*

A plugin in isolation is a sad thing. Without an application to host it, it has no meaning. You saw how to resolve this unhappy state of affairs back in chapter 8, which explained how you could install a plugin into an application either from a zip file or from the central Grails plugin repository. You'll now see how that zip is created and how the plugin is added to the central repository.

The first step to publishing a plugin is to make sure that it works properly. It's time to get our testing tools out again.

16.2.1 Testing plugins

A plugin has an almost identical structure to an application, which means that the unit and integration testing you're already familiar with applies to plugins as well. Both types of testing are useful for checking that the artifacts work correctly, and you write the tests exactly the same as you would for an application, putting them in the plugin's test/unit and test/integration directories. What neither unit nor integration tests do is make it easy to test the hooks in the plugin descriptor.

That means functional testing is critical to ensuring that a plugin works as expected once it's installed in an application. It's the only type of testing in which the plugin is exercised in something close to its final environment. Grails provides two approaches: running the functional tests as if the plugin were an application, or creating separate projects and testing those with the plugin installed.

TESTING THE PLUGIN AS AN APPLICATION

With the first approach, you install a functional testing plugin directly into the project, and then create your tests as usual. The question is, what do you test? In the case of the security plugin, we need some pages that we can configure for access control and then test. The plugin doesn't have any likely candidates, though, so we have to add some test controllers and views, and maybe some domain classes as well. The trick is to make sure that those extra artifacts don't get packaged with the plugin.

Imagine that we've added `Post` and `User` domain classes to the plugin. We can exclude them from the "official" plugin package by using the `pluginExcludes` property of the plugin descriptor:

```
pluginExcludes = [
    "grails-app/domain/Post.groovy",
    "grails-app/domain/User.groovy"
]
```

This simple technique will ensure that users won't unexpectedly find their application creating Post and User tables when they install our plugin.

Testing the plugin as an application is fine as long as that list of excludes stays short, but thorough testing is likely to see the list balloon in size. It's also difficult to test different configuration settings, because you can only use one setting value per project. That's where the second approach we mentioned comes in.

USING MULTIPLE TEST APPLICATIONS

Creating test applications for the plugin allows you to create a thorough suite of tests. For example, you could have each application use different configuration settings for the plugin. The problem is that the whole package and install process is too clunky to be useful. Every time you want to test a change to the plugin, you have to package it up and install it in an application. Fortunately, there's another way: you can configure an application to load a plugin from its (the plugin's) project directory. Simply add a line like this to the application's BuildConfig:

```
grails.plugin.location.security = "/path/to/plugin/dir"
```

Any changes you make to the plugin's source files will be seen by the application the next time you start it. Note that if you use this setting, don't install the plugin as well.

Figure 16.3 illustrates the typical setup with an application containing two installed plugins and referencing the project directory of our security plugin.

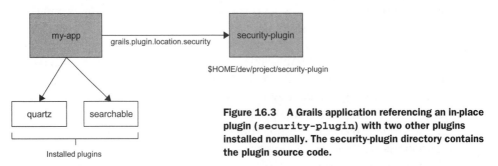

Figure 16.3   **A Grails application referencing an in-place plugin (security-plugin) with two other plugins installed normally. The security-plugin directory contains the plugin source code.**

You can now set up as many test projects as you need to test all the features of your plugin. We like to keep them in a test/projects directory alongside test/unit, with each project containing this setting in its BuildConfig.groovy file:

```
grails.plugin.location.security = "../../.."
```

Anyone can then check out the plugin source and run the functional tests inside each test project.

Once you have some solid tests behind you, you can start thinking about packaging and releasing the plugin.

16.2.2   *Releasing the plugin into the wild*

In order to make a plugin available for public use, you must first package it into a zip file that can be used by the install-plugin command. You can then publish the plugin to either the central Grails plugin repository or a custom repository, so that users can easily install it. We'll look at the publishing mechanism shortly, but let's look at the packaging first.

PACKAGING THE PLUGIN

Packaging is an essential part of software distribution, whether it involves creating an executable JAR file, a WAR file, or something else. In the case of a Grails plugin, the package is a simple zip file, and Grails comes with a dedicated command for creating it:

```
grails package-plugin
```

This command will create a zip file with the name grails-<name>-<version>.zip, where <name> and <version> are the name and version of the plugin.

You can put this file on a shared filesystem, on a web server, or distribute it as you deem fit. Users can then get hold of the zip file and install it:

```
grails install-plugin grails-security-0.1.zip
```

Under the hood

When you package a plugin, Grails creates a plugin.xml file that contains the meta-information (such as version, author, and so on) and a list of the artifacts and other resources provided by the plugin. This file is added to the zip and is later used by Grails when installing the plugin and running the application.

Why do we mention this? Because the plugin will break Grails (in sometimes mysterious ways) if the plugin.xml file is either corrupted or inconsistent with the resources packaged in the plugin. We don't expect that you'll ever have to worry about the file, but we also realize that sometimes stuff happens.

Don't worry, the `package-plugin` command will only include the files that are necessary to use the plugin. All the tests, configuration files, and anything declared in the descriptor's `pluginExcludes` field will be excluded. You can find out exactly which files are included and excluded by looking at the `pluginIncludes` and `plugin-Excludes` script variables in the `_GrailsDev.groovy` script.

Although this approach to installing plugins is functional, it isn't as user-friendly as this method:

```
grails install-plugin security
```

For this command to work, the security plugin must be published to the central Grails plugin repository.

PUBLISHING TO THE CENTRAL REPOSITORY

The central repository is implemented using Subversion (which is a version-control system), as are all plugin repositories. You can't do this without the appropriate privileges, but you can request permission by following the steps described here: http://www.grails.org/Creating+Plugins. Once you have developer privileges, you're one step away from sending your plugin into the public spotlight. From the root directory of the project, run this command:

```
grails release-plugin
```

This will add your plugin project to the central repository and then check out a copy of the source code to a different directory. For example, if your plugin source is in the .../dev/projects/grails-security directory, the fresh Subversion working copy will be in .../dev/projects/checkout/grails-security.

We recommend that you replace your old project directory with the newly checked out one. Once the plugin source has been added to the repository, the `release-`

Don't like Subversion?

Although the `release-plugin` command is geared toward Subversion, you can use other clients like Git and Bazaar as well. You just have to manually commit your changes to the Subversion repository before running the command.

`plugin` command expects to run from a Subversion working copy (see the sidebar for a qualification). Next time you run the command (such as when you have version 0.2 ready), it will update your working copy with any changes that have been committed to the repository by others, commit your own changes, and then release the new version.

PUBLISHING TO CUSTOM REPOSITORIES

The procedure we've described so far will release your plugin to the central plugin repository, but what if you want to publish it to a custom repository? For example, maybe your plugin is private to your company, so it should only be published to an internal repository. In that case, you need to take these steps:

1 Assign the repository URL to an alias.
2 Pass a `--repository=<alias>` argument to the `release-plugin` command.

The first step involves adding the appropriate lines to your plugin's BuildConfig.groovy file. For example, add these lines to configure a repository with the alias `internalRepository`:

```
grails.plugin.repos.discovery.internalRepository =
    "http://.../grails-plugins/trunk"
grails.plugin.repos.distribution.internalRepository =
    "https://.../grails-plugins/trunk"
```

Note that you'll need to configure URLs for both the `discovery` and `distribution` options. Once you have those lines in your BuildConfig.groovy file, run this command to publish your plugin internally:

```
grails release-plugin --repository=internalRepository
```

You can then check that everything went OK by attempting to install it in a project:

```
grails install-plugin --repository=internalRepository security
```

The `--repository` argument in this case is optional. If it's not there, Grails will search *all* configured repositories, including the central one.

Custom repositories can be used to keep your own plugins private or to manage customized versions of public plugins. They can even be used to control which versions of public plugins are installed by default by your team. If you choose to create a custom repository, you can find out how in the Grails user guide.

You now know how to publish the security plugin, but it isn't quite in a state for publication yet. We have a domain model and login and logout functionality, but we have no access control. To add that, we have to start using those plugin hooks we mentioned earlier.

16.3 *Integrating with Grails*

Packaging and running a Grails application involves a fair bit of work under the hood that you don't often see as an application developer. As a plugin developer, you need to become familiar with the basic processes if you want your plugins to integrate seamlessly with Grails.

In this section, you'll learn how to do the following:

- Add your own dynamic methods, like the core Grails plugins do
- Handle reloading of classes at runtime
- Configure your own Spring beans
- Add entries to the application's web descriptor
- Implement extra commands

All of these, except the last, are done through the special plugin descriptor hooks that we listed in table 16.1. Without further ado, let's start by working some dynamic magic.

16.3.1 *Enhancing artifacts with dynamic methods*

To control access to an application's functionality, there has to be a gatekeeper. Our security plugin should fulfill that role, but *how* it does that depends on what you want to secure. It could be access to particular domain classes or service methods, but for simplicity our security plugin will only control access to URLs. The ideal place to do this is in Grails filters because you can prevent access by returning `false` from a `before` interceptor.

This raises an important question: how will the developer tell the plugin which URLs require a logged-in user and which require the user to have specific roles? It would be nice to have something like this:

```
class SecurityFilters {
    def filters = {
        all(controller: "*", action: "*") {
            before = {
                authcRequired()
            }
        }

        posts(controller: "post", action: "*") {
            before = {
                roleRequired("user")
            }
        }
    }
}
```

The idea here is to only allow authenticated users (ones that have logged in) to access the pages of the application. In addition, only users with the "user" role should be allowed to access any of the pages served by the post controller. The preceding format is concise, wonderfully clutter-free, and informative. Can we implement this, and if so how?

One option would be to provide `authcRequired()` and `roleRequired()` methods on an abstract filters class. Any class extending it could then call those methods, like our `SecurityFilters` class we just saw. There are several problems with this approach, though. First, both Groovy and Java allow only single inheritance of classes, so you immediately force developers to extend your class, limiting their room to maneuver.

Second, there's now an explicit dependency on your plugin, which means that the filters class won't compile if the plugin is uninstalled. This is an *intrusive* technique.

Are there no other choices? Of course there are! Remember that filters classes are written in Groovy, so we can make use of that nonintrusive technique you've seen already: *dynamic method injection.* We can inject the authcRequired() and role-Required() methods into all filters classes without the developer changing a line of code.

Grails encourages this technique by providing a special hook for plugins where they can add any dynamic methods and properties to any classes they choose. All your plugin needs to do is implement the doWithDynamicMethods closure. You need to know *how* to add such methods, or your closure will be pretty useless.

Now would be a good time to read the section in chapter 2 on dynamic methods if you haven't done so already. It will give you some background as to what this dynamic business is all about and smooth the way. In the case of the doWithDynamicMethods closure, dynamic methods and properties are added via a technique called *metaclass programming.*

METACLASS PROGRAMMING

In Groovy, every class has an associated metaclass that determines the runtime behavior of that class. When a method is called from Groovy, it's the metaclass that performs the method dispatch. That's why you add dynamic methods to the metaclass rather than the real class, and it's also why you can extend the JDK classes. This side of things is normally invisible to you as a programmer, but it comes to the fore when you enter the world of metaclass programming.

That's enough of the background—let's try it out! The syntax is straightforward:

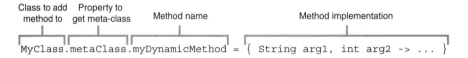

You start with the class that you want to add the method to. In this example, we're using a class literal, but it could equally be a variable referencing a class. You then get hold of the metaclass via the metaClass property and add the method definition using a closure.

Adding a property is similar because you do it via getter and setter methods:

```
MyClass.metaClass.getMyProp = {-> ... }
MyClass.metaClass.setMyProp = { String newValue -> ... }
```

Although you can provide a setter, you have to store the new value somewhere, preferably somewhere thread-safe. You can't add a field directly to the class, so this can be quite tricky. For this reason, dynamic properties are often read-only—only the getter is defined.

Note that the getter closure explicitly has zero arguments. The following will *not* work as a property:

```
MyClass.metaClass.getMyProp = { ... }
```

In this case, you'll end up with a `getMyProp()` method that takes a single optional argument.

By now you might be wondering how to access the object instance that your dynamic method is called on. Say you have a class that contains a collection of items, and you want to add a property that returns how many there are. Somehow, your method implementation needs to get hold of that list. As you would expect, this is already taken care of in Groovy: the closure has access to a `delegate` property that's a reference to the host object. The method implementation might look like this:

```
MyClass.metaClass.getTotal = {-> return delegate.items.size() }
```

In fact, all closures have a `delegate` property, but what it contains depends on the context.

Those are pretty much the basics. All that remains is to show you a couple of variations on the metaclass syntax that you might find useful:

```
MyClass.metaClass.static.myMethod = { ... }
MyClass.metaClass.myMethod << { ... }
```

The first of these allows you to add static methods to the class. In this case, the `delegate` in the closure is a reference to the class itself. The second form uses the left-shift operator (`<<`) rather than `=`. It does the same thing, but if the method already exists, Grails throws an exception. If you're planning to override an existing method, use `=`; otherwise, prefer `<<` so that the user is aware of naming conflicts when the application starts.

As you can see, the basics of metaclass programming are quite simple. That said, the method implementations can be tricky, particularly when it comes to name resolution. On the whole, anything that you expect to work will work, but if you do a lot of metaclass programming, you'll almost certainly come across some sticky issues. If that's the case, it's probably worth getting a book dedicated to Groovy that covers the ins and outs of Groovy's name resolution, particularly with regard to closures.

When you first start using metaclass programming, the temptation is to use it everywhere. It's novel, exciting, and as the saying goes, "when you have a hammer, everything looks like a nail." Some restraint is in order. As we mentioned in chapter 2, the dynamic features of Groovy can be awkward to debug, and they also make life difficult for IDEs. Remember, there are alternatives: static utility methods, Grails services, inheritance, and so on. But if you think the benefits of cleaner and easier to understand (and write) code outweigh the drawbacks, then go dynamic.

WARNING Be careful about modifying the standard JDK classes and other common classes, particularly if you plan to override existing methods or properties. The changes will be visible to all Groovy code in all threads, so a subtle change in behavior can have undesirable consequences in other parts of the code, and those bugs can be difficult to track down.

You now know how to implement dynamic methods, but what classes should you be adding them to? For our security plugin, we want to add them to all the filters in an application, but how do we do that? We don't know in advance what filters classes are in the application.

FINDING OUT ABOUT APPLICATION ARTIFACTS

Think about what happens when a plugin is installed in a Grails application. When you write it, you only know about the classes provided by the plugin itself, but as soon as you install it into an application, the plugin suddenly finds itself in an environment containing more classes than it's used to—classes that are provided by other installed plugins and classes that are part of the application. There must be some way to find out what's out there without resorting to querying the class loader, right? Thankfully there is.

The code you write in any of the hooks listed in table 16.1 has access to a property called `application`. This is the Grails application instance, and we can use it to find out what artifacts are available. Remember the GORM dynamic finders? The application instance has a similar set of dynamic methods and properties, but in this case they're based on the types of artifacts available rather than the fields in a domain class.

Say you wanted to get all the controllers in the application. It's easy:

```
application.controllerClasses
```

You could also retrieve all the services via `application.serviceClasses`. In fact, you can do something similar for all types of artifacts—table 16.2 lists the available methods and properties.

You'll see that we talk about *artifact descriptors* in table 16.2. Each artifact in the application has an associated descriptor that provides extra information about it, the key properties of which you can find in table 16.3.

Table 16.2 Querying the application about artifacts

Method template	Description
`<artifact>Classes`	Returns all the artifact descriptors in the application of type `<artifact>`. Note that the artifact type should start with a lowercase letter because it's a property.
`get<Artifact>Class(String artifactName)`	Returns the artifact descriptor of type `<Artifact>` for the artifact with a name of `artifactName`. For example, `getControllerClass("LoginController")` would return the artifact descriptor for `LoginController`. Note that `artifactName` must be a full class name, including the package if there is one.
`is<Artifact>Class(Class artifactClass)`	Returns `true` if the class is of type `<Artifact>`, otherwise `false`. For example, `isControllerClass(LoginController)` would return `true`.

Table 16.3   Artifact descriptor properties

Property	Type	Description	Example
clazz	Class	The class of the artifact	org.example.LoginController
metaClass	MetaClass	A shortcut to the artifact's metaclass; same as clazz.metaClass	N/A
name	String	The name of the artifact, minus any suffix or package	Login
shortName	String	The name of the artifact minus any package	LoginController
propertyName	String	The short name of the artifact in property form	loginController

Under the hood

The dynamic artifact methods are implemented by the DefaultGrailsApplication class using invokeMethod(). They map to physical methods like getArtefacts(), which means that you can access the same information from Java if you wish.

The artifact descriptors are instances of the GrailsClass interface. It's well worth becoming familiar with its methods for more advanced plugin work.

Back to the security plugin. We said that we wanted to add a couple of dynamic methods to filters, but filters are a special case. So first we'll show you how to add a has-Role() method to all the controllers in an application. In fact, we'll spice it up a little by only adding the method if the controller defines a static property called secure with a value of true. The result can be seen in listing 16.2.

Listing 16.2   Injecting a method into controllers

```
package com.grailsinaction.security

import org.codehaus.groovy.grails.commons.GrailsClassUtils as GCU        ◁─┐
...                                                                   Imports a
class SecurityGrailsPlugin {                                          useful utility class ❶
  ...
  def doWithDynamicMethods = {                                      Iterates over all
    application.controllerClasses.each { cClass ->         ◁─┘      controllers
      def isSecure = GCU.getStaticPropertyValue(
          cClass.clazz,                                    ❷ Gets value of
          "secure")                                          secure property
      if (isSecure) {
        cClass.metaClass.hasRole = { name ->      ◁─┐
          def u = session.user                      ❸ Adds method to
          if (u) {                                    controller
```

```
                u.merge()                                    ⊲┐ Reattaches to
                return u.roles.any { it.name == name }        │ Hibernate session
            }
            else {
                return false
            }
        }
    }
  }
  ...
}
...
}
```

GrailsClassUtils ❶ is a useful class for plugin authors, and we use it here to read the value of the static secure property ❷. Once we have that value, we check it and only add the hasRole() method ❸ to that particular controller if the value is true. This dynamic method will return true only if the user has the named role.

That was easy enough, so what about adding methods to filters? Unlike most other artifacts, the filter instance isn't of the same type as the *Filters class that you add the definitions to. For example, a post controller is an instance of PostController, but a security filter isn't an instance of SecurityFilters. Instead, all filters are instances of a FilterConfig class, so adding dynamic methods to them is this simple:

```
import org.codehaus.groovy.grails.plugins.web.filters.FilterConfig
...
FilterConfig.metaClass.authcRequired = {-> session.user != null }
```

The preceding line should go inside the doWithDynamicMethods closure—we've left out the rest of the class to avoid unnecessary clutter.

The security plugin can now block access to an application's pages in a user-friendly fashion (see the chapter 16 source code for the implementation). And with so few lines of code!

We're almost done here, but there is one more thing that we need to take care of. What happens when the developer changes a controller class while the application is running?

16.3.2 *Dealing with class reloading*

Grails' ability to reload changes to application files on the fly is a major benefit for users. Unfortunately for plugin writers, users expect plugins to play well with this feature and take advantage of it themselves. As one example, any dynamic methods on a controller will disappear when that controller is reloaded—it's up to the plugin to restore the methods that it originally added. This is where the onChange and onConfigChange closures come in.

Grails maintains lists of what it calls *watched resources*, which are filepath patterns similar to the ones you may have used with the Ant build tool. Whenever a file that matches one of the patterns is modified, Grails first reloads it (if it contains a Groovy class or script) and then notifies interested plugins by calling their onChange closures.

Core plugins and their names

Much of Grails' functionality is provided as plugins that are packaged in the framework's JAR files. We refer to these as *core plugins*. There is also a plugin named `core`, but if we ever refer to it we'll make that clear. Examples of core plugins are controllers, domainClass, i18n, and services.

Obviously the first step for your plugin is to register an interest in such changes. There are two approaches you can take: "observe" an existing plugin or specify a list of watched resources. Let's say you want Grails to notify you when any controllers are modified. Because the core controllers plugin already watches for changes to controllers, observing it will mean that your plugin will also be notified of those changes. In fact, your plugin will receive exactly the same notifications as the observed plugin, so be aware of what those might be—the controllers plugin also watches tag libraries, for example.

Observing a plugin is as simple as adding an `observe` property to the plugin descriptor, like so:

```
def observe = ["controllers"]
```

Each entry in the list is the name of a plugin you want to observe. If any of those plugins isn't installed in the current application, they're quietly ignored. Table 16.4 shows some of the more useful plugins and the resources that they watch.

Table 16.4   The files watched by some of the core plugins

Plugin name	Resources watched
controllers	Controllers and tag libraries
services	Services
filters	Filter classes
urlMappings	URL mappings
hibernate	Hibernate configuration files
i18n	I18n bundles (`messages.properties`, for example)

The other approach you can use is to specify a `watchedResources` property that contains one or more file patterns that match the files you're interested in. For example, to watch controllers, we could use this,

```
def watchedResources = "file:./grails-app/**/*Controller.groovy"
```

or this,

```
def watchedResources = ["file:./grails-app/**/*Controller.groovy"]
```

Before we move on to dealing with the change notifications themselves, let's take a quick look at the example file pattern.

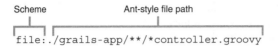

```
file:./grails-app/**/*controller.groovy
```

The scheme is optional and determines how to access the file. The second part is the filepath pattern, which follows Ant's conventions. A double-asterisk (`**`) wildcard matches any number of nested directories (or none at all), whereas a single asterisk (`*`) can be used to match a single directory level or any part of a file or directory name. For example, the preceding pattern would match ./grails-app/MyController.groovy and ./grails-app/org/example/MyOtherController.groovy, amongst others.

If you do use the `watchedResources` property, we recommend that you always use the `file:` scheme and start the filepaths with `./`. For more information on these filepaths, read the section on resources in the Spring reference manual.

Now that you know how to register for change notifications, how do you deal with them? Your `onChange` closure will be passed an event object with the following properties:

- `source`—The file or artifact that changed. If a class changed, the source will be the class instance (`java.lang.Class`); otherwise, it will be a Spring resource (`org.springframework.core.io.Resource`).
- `application`—The Grails application instance, which is useful for getting information about artifacts. This is redundant because the `onChange` closure has access to an `application` dynamic property.
- `ctx`—The Spring application context, from which you can access any beans you might need.
- `manager`—The plugin manager.
- `plugin`—The plugin descriptor instance.

Of these, `source` is the most useful. Armed with this information, you can do whatever is necessary to ensure that the plugin continues working as it should.

In listing 16.3, we return to the security plugin and make sure that we add the `has-Role()` dynamic method back to any controller that has changed, because the dynamic properties and methods are lost when a class is reloaded.

Listing 16.3   Responding to controller modifications

```
class SecurityPlugin {
    ...
    def observe = ["controllers"]      ◁——— Observes controllers plugin
    ...
    def onChange = { event ->
        if (application.isControllerClass(         ❶ Checks source is
            event.source)) {               ◁┘        a controller
```

```
event.source.metaClass.hasRole =
    { String name ->
    ...
    }                                    Adds method to
    }                                    controller again
    }
}
```

Here we're observing the controllers plugin, so we have to ignore changes to tag libraries. We do this by using the Grails application object to determine what type of artifact has been modified ❶. The `isControllerClass()` method is dynamic, so there are similar methods for all registered artifact types. For example, you could also use `isDomainClass()`.

This example is a simple one, but you're in good shape to deal with class and file reloading in the most common cases. One thing to be aware of is that the `onChange` closure is called when a new artifact is created, not just when artifacts are modified. This typically has no impact on your code, but you should be aware of it in case.

We've covered how to deal with changes to artifacts, but what about configuration changes? Fortunately, this is pretty easy. All you need to do is add an `onConfigChange` closure that takes an event as an argument. That's it—you don't even have to set up any watched resources or observe a particular plugin. The main difference is that the event's `source` property is the new configuration object, which you can use to access whatever settings you need in the normal way.

So when should you add reloading support to your plugin? You definitely should if you add dynamic methods or properties to artifacts; otherwise, those methods will disappear in a puff of smoke after a reload. Another common case is when your plugin reads values from an artifact, such as from a property. The developer may change that value, so your plugin should ensure that the new value takes effect. Other than that, there are no hard and fast rules. It comes down to whether changes to artifacts affect the behavior of the plugin.

We already have a functional security plugin that can control access to an application's pages, yet we've only used a fraction of the features that are available to a plugin. You don't need to implement everything just because you can, and in practice most plugins don't need or use all the integration points. That said, we need to go through the remaining features, so let's extend our plugin with some extra functionality.

16.3.3 *Leveraging Spring*

Remember how we configured Spring beans via the resources.* files back in chapte 14? You can do something similar with plugins too. Consider how the plugin stores passwords at the moment: it's hard-coded to hash the plain-text passwords using the SHA-1 algorithm. It would be nice if instead we could allow users to pick a hashing algorithm, but to do that we need to tackle both storing the password and comparing passwords during authentication.

In a typical Java application, an appropriate solution would be to create an interface that deals with storing and comparing passwords. Different implementations of that interface could use different hash algorithms. Here's an example of what it might look like:

```
public interface PasswordHandler {
   String encode(String plain)
   boolean passwordsMatch(String plain, String encoded)
}
```

The `encode()` method converts a plain-text password to its hashed form and `passwordsMatch()` compares a plain password to an encoded one.

All we need now is a way to set up a default password handler with a default hashing algorithm. That's where the `doWithSpring` closure comes in. You can define beans inside it using the Spring DSL, as demonstrated in listing 16.4.

Listing 16.4   Simple example of the Spring DSL

```
import security.HashPasswordHandler
import security.Sha1Hasher
...
def doWithSpring = {                            Configures default
   hashMachine(Sha1Hasher) {        ◁─┘         hashing algorithm
      salt = "jfhw4h942hvkb2jh"
   }

   passwordHandler(HashPasswordHandler) {
      hasher = ref("hashMachine")    ◁─────  Links the two beans
      iterationCount = 5
   }
}
```

In this example, we define the password-handler bean (`passwordHandler`) and configure it to use an SHA-1 hashing algorithm to encode passwords. So how does the user override the hashing algorithm with this example?

Under the hood

You can use the Spring DSL because the delegate for the `doWithSpring` closure is an instance of `grails.spring.BeanBuilder`. All the other hooks (like `doWithDynamicMethods`) are executed with a delegate of:

`org.codehaus.groovy.grails.plugins.DefaultGrailsPlugin`.

When Grails starts up, it processes all `doWithSpring` closures provided by the installed plugins and populates the application context with those bean definitions. Only once all the plugins have been processed does Grails then load the bean definitions from resources.xml and resources.groovy. To use a different hashing algorithm, all the user needs to do is define a bean named `hashMachine` in one of those files. For example, it could be defined in resources.groovy:

```
beans = {
    hashMachine(security.Md5Hasher)
}
```

As long as the bean that the user defines has the same name as the one in the `doWith-Spring` closure, the former will override the latter. Easy!

We're almost done here, but we still need to explain what the `doWith-ApplicationContext` closure is for. This is called by Grails after all the plugins have had a chance to add their bean definitions and the application context has been configured. The sole argument to the closure is the application context itself, fully initialized and ready for use. The closure isn't often implemented by plugins, but if you ever need to do some work with the application context or its beans (rather than the bean definitions), this is the hook you want.

The last of the plugin hooks takes us away from Spring and into the world of servlets and servlet filters, which are important aspects of a web application.

16.3.4 *Playing with servlets and filters*

Grails is heavily geared towards web application development, and although it's easy to write a Grails application without thinking about the traditional web descriptor, it should definitely not be forgotten. Remember, this is the only way you can configure servlets and servlet filters.

The security plugin we've been developing in this chapter has no need to configure servlets or servlet filters, so we'll borrow an existing Grails plugin to demonstrate. The JSecurity plugin provides access control for Grails applications, and it just so happens that it needs to set up a servlet filter. We could force the user to manually configure this filter, but the plugin would quickly lose friends if it tried that approach. It has to configure the filter itself.

Reading the XML, modifying it, and then writing it out again would be quite tedious, so you'll be glad to hear that you don't have to. Instead, you implement the `doWithWebDescriptor` closure and modify an in-memory representation of the web descriptor. How does it work? Grails starts by parsing a template web descriptor using `XmlSlurper`, the result of which is passed to the plugin's `doWithWebDescriptor` closure as an argument. With that, we can modify the web descriptor.

We know that the argument passed to the `doWithWebDescriptor` closure is the slurper result from parsing the template web descriptor. We also know how to use that object to extract information that we might need. But how do we modify the XML? We have to do that somehow if we're going to configure a servlet filter. The XML slurper provides the one facility for doing this, and listing 16.5 shows you exactly how to configure the JSecurity filter.

Listing 16.5   Configuring a servlet filter at runtime

```
def doWithWebDescriptor = { webXml ->                    ❶ Gets all <context-param>
    def contextParam = webXml.'context-param'   ⬅┘          elements

    contextParam[contextParam.size() - 1] + {    ⬅┐
        'filter' {                                    ❷ Appends new
            'filter-name'('securityContextFilter')       filter config
            'filter-class'('org.jsecurity.spring.SpringJSecurityFilter')
            'init-param' {
                'param-name'('securityManagerBeanName')
                'param-value'('jsecSecurityManager')
            }
        }
    }

    def filter = webXml.'filter-mapping'.find {          ❸ Finds specific
        it.'filter-name'.text() == 'charEncodingFilter'      filter mapping
    }

    filter + {
        'filter-mapping' {
            'filter-name'('securityContextFilter')
            'url-pattern'('/*')
        }
    }
}
```

The order of filter definitions doesn't matter, so the JSecurity one is added immediately after the last `context-param` element ❶ and ❷. See how the element name is in quotes ❶? This is because method and property names may not contain hyphens, so we take advantage of Groovy's freedom to use strings instead. The `contextParam` variable represents a list of elements, so we use the array access syntax to get hold of the last element. Why don't we use an index of -1? For some reason, this doesn't work with `XmlSlurper`, so we have to do it the old-fashioned way instead.

The key to modifying the XML is the next bit. Once we have an element that we want to insert content after, we can use the plus (+) operator with a closure ❷. The content of the closure is pretty self-explanatory if you're familiar with the web descriptor syntax for filter definitions. Each method name corresponds to the name of an element, and a new closure marks the start of nested elements. In practice, it's equivalent to this:

```
<filter>
    <filter-name>securityContextFilter</filter-name>
    <filter-class>org.jsecurity.spring.SpringJSecurityFilter</filter-class>
    <init-param>
        <param-name>securityManagerBeanName</param-name>
        <param-value>jsecSecurityManager</param-value>
    </init-param>
</filter>
```

Although `filter` is in quotes in the listing, the quotes aren't strictly necessary. They're mainly there so that all the elements look consistent.

We said that the order of the filter definitions doesn't matter, but it's a different kettle of fish when it comes to the filter *mappings*. The order in which they're defined is the order in which they're executed. For this reason, you need to be a bit more careful about where your mappings are inserted. In ❸ we look for the filter mapping for the `charEncodingFilter`, which is pretty much guaranteed to be there. Almost all filters should come after this one, and that's what the code in the listing does with the JSecurity filter mapping. The only time that this approach won't work is when the user has customized the template web descriptor and removed the `charEncodingFilter` mapping. In such cases, it's best to fall back to inserting your filter mapping at the front (index 0).

> **Where are the other filters?**
>
> Grails provides a few servlet filters itself. There is one for URL mappings and another that adds extra information to the request, among others. Try as you might, though, you won't find the definitions in the web descriptor passed to your closure. Anything added by a plugin isn't visible to plugins loaded later.
>
> This somewhat limits your ability to control where filters go in the filter chain, but all isn't lost. With judicious use of the `loadAfter` property, you can still make sure that your filter comes after some of the core ones. Unfortunately, there is currently no way to insert an element *before* another one.

Once you're comfortable with the syntax for the XML slurper, you've effectively mastered the `doWithWebDescriptor` closure. There isn't any more to it than that. You'll be able to add context parameters, set session timeouts, configure servlets—anything supported by the web descriptor.

We've now covered all the plugin descriptor integration points. There aren't many, but they're powerful, and hopefully you can envision some of the many possibilities they offer. The last integration point we'll look at is the scripts directory.

16.3.5 *Augmenting the available Grails commands*

So far we've looked at the ways in which a plugin can affect the runtime behavior of a Grails application, but what about at development time? You saw in the previous chapter that you can extend the Grails command set by writing scripts for your application, and you can do the same for your plugin. Grails packages those scripts with the plugin so that when it's installed, the corresponding commands become available to the application.

What kind of commands do plugins implement? Almost anything under the sun. There are commands for running tests, performing database migrations, creating application files from templates, performing special compilations, and more. Listing 16.6, for example, shows a script that creates the controllers and views for a user-management UI that works with our security plugin.

Listing 16.6   A script that creates a user-management UI for the security plugin

```
includeTargets << grailsScript("_GrailsEvents")

target(installMgmtUI: "Installs the user management UI") {
    depends(checkVersion)

    templateDir = "${securityPluginDir}/src/templates"

    ant.copy(todir: "${basedir}/grails-app/controllers") {
        fileset(dir: "${templateDir}/controllers", includes: "*.groovy")
    }

    ant.copy(todir: "${basedir}/grails-app/views") {
        fileset(dir: "${templateDir}/views", includes: "**/*.gsp")
    }
}

setDefaultTarget("installMgmtUI")
```

❶ Gets location of templates

There's no rocket science here. The script copies controller and view templates from the plugin to the application. One crucial aspect is how the location of the templates is derived ❶. Grails adds a variable named `<pluginName>PluginDir` to the script binding for every plugin that's installed in an application. It contains the absolute location of the unpacked plugin, so we could use `securityPluginDir` to locate the templates. You could even get the location of a different plugin if you wanted, although this is less common.

In addition to your own scripts, every plugin is created with three internal ones all ready and waiting to go: _Install.groovy, _Uninstall.groovy, and _Upgrade .groovy. The first is automatically called when the plugin is installed into an application; the second is called when the plugin is uninstalled; and the last is invoked when an application is upgraded from one version of Grails to another via the `grails upgrade` command. This last one is pretty redundant because it has nothing to do with upgrading the plugin. Scripts are an integral part of plugin development and can make life considerably easier for the users of a plugin. Because one of those users may be you, it's worth investing a bit of time in thinking up some script ideas and implementing them.

We've now introduced all the main features of plugins and shown how you can utilize them to extend and customize the Grails platform. It's been a tough ride, but you've made it. It's time to catch your breath while we do a quick recap.

16.4   *Summary and best practices*

Plugins are a complex topic because they can feasibly interact with almost every aspect of Grails. Yet they're such a fundamental part of the Grails platform that you need to understand them if you want to harness its full potential. Even the most trivial of applications will almost certainly use one or more plugins.

You've seen numerous plugins throughout the book, and these form only a fraction of the publicly available ones. The sheer variety demonstrates how flexible and powerful the plugin system is. The public plugins can also serve as a source of inspiration and ideas.

Whether you use plugins to modularize your application or package up self-contained features, they can dramatically simplify development for the plugins' users and promote reuse of code. This chapter has shown you how easy it is to get started in plugin development, but it has also given you the tools to take that development further.

You can also use existing plugins as learning material. For example, the JSecurity plugin has a significant plugin descriptor with implementations for many of the hooks. It also has a few scripts that you can look at. The GWT plugin has a good selection of scripts that use more advanced techniques than JSecurity's.

To finish off, here are some guidelines for designing and developing your own plugins:

- *Keep it simple.* Use only the minimum number of features and hooks that you need to implement your plugins. For example, if it doesn't make sense to add dynamic properties or methods, then don't.

  It's also important to realize that plugins don't have to be hulking, complex beasts. They can be very simple indeed, and the cost of building such plugins is quite low. Remember, a plugin is always an option for code that's self-contained or shared between projects, no matter how trivial.

- *Implement* onChange *when necessary.* If your plugin adds dynamic methods or properties, make sure that it also implements the onChange hook, so that those methods and properties are retained after a reload. Users get quite attached to the reloading feature, so plugins that break it become unpopular.

- *Use local plugin repositories for teams.* Local plugin repositories serve several purposes. First, they allow you to control which versions of plugins are installed by your team by default. Second, they allow you to customize public plugins for your own purposes. Last, they can be useful for modularizing applications.

- *Modularize large or complex applications.* The Separation of Concerns pattern is powerful, and plugins allow you to apply it to your Grails applications. You can either use the in-place plugin mechanism (via the `grails.plugin.location.*` configuration setting) or a local plugin repository to manage the modularization.

- *Write functional tests for your plugins.* For plugins to be reliable, you should write functional tests. The in-place plugin mechanism is particularly useful for this, allowing you to create multiple test projects that load the plugin from source.

index

MORE TITLES FROM MANNING

Groovy in Action

by Dierk König
    with Andrew Glover, Paul King,
    Guillaume Laforge
    and Jon Skeet

ISBN: 1-932394-84-2
696 pages
$49.99
January 2007

Spring in Action, Second Edition

by Craig Walls
    with Ryan Breidenbach

ISBN: 1-933988-13-4
768 pages
$49.99
August 2007

For ordering information go to www.manning.com

Struts 2 in Action

by Donald Brown, Chad Michael Davis,
and Scott Stanlick

ISBN: 1-933988-07-X
424 pages
$44.99
May 2008

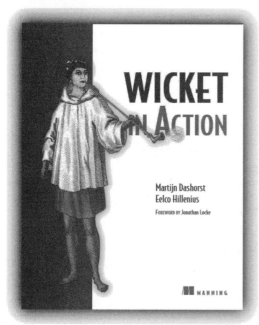

Wicket in Action

by Martijn Dashorst and Eelco Hillenius

ISBN: 1-932394-98-2
392 pages
$44.99
August 2008

For ordering information go to www.manning.com

MORE TITLES FROM MANNING

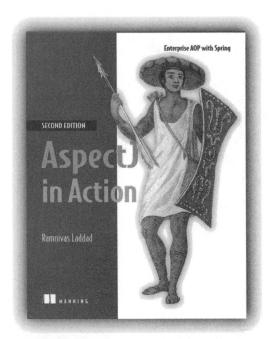
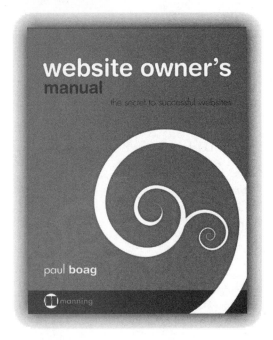